*i*

# Credit Management Handbook

**Second edition**

EDITED BY

**Herbert Edwards**

A Gower Handbook

Published by
Gower Publishing Company Limited,
Gower House,
Croft Road,
Aldershot,
Hants GU11 3HR,
England.

and

Gower Publishing Company,
Old Post Road,
Brookfield,
Vermont 05036,
U.S.A.

Reprinted 1986, 1988

British Library Cataloguing in Publication Data

Credit management handbook.—2nd ed.
  1. Credit management—Great Britain
  I. Edwards, H.
  658.8'8'0941    HG3729.G8

Library of Congress Cataloging in Publication data

Credit management handbook.
    Includes index.
  1. Credit-Management-addresses, essays, lectures.
  I. Edwards, Herbert.
  HG3751.C728   1985     658.8'8     84-21170

ISBN 0-566-02499-3

Typeset in Great Britain by
Guildford Graphics Limited, Guildford, Surrey
Printed in Great Britain by Redwood Burn Limited,
Trowbridge, Wiltshire

# Contents

Settlement rebates—Penalty interest—Cash competitions—Use of sales force—Field warehousing—Factoring—Collection agents—Credit insurance—The credit
armoury

## PART VII  EXPORT CREDIT AND FINANCE

## PART VIII   CONSUMER CREDIT

## PART IX   COMMERCIAL CREDIT LAW

## PART X EXTERNAL CREDIT AND FINANCE

# Illustrations

# Notes on Contributors

*Herbert Edwards* (Editor; Collection Practices; Budgets, Ratios and Reports; Sources of Credit Data) is Managing Director of Jardine Financial Risk Management Ltd in the City of London. He spent 26 years in credit and treasury work in industry, latterly with the ITT Group. He is a Fellow of the Institute of Credit Management and also of the Institute of Export, a faculty member of Management Centre Europe in Brussels and a member of FCIB Europe.

*W. V. (Bill) Adams* (Introduction; Export Credit and Collections) has now retired from full-time business after 30 years as Credit Manager (Home and Export) of Mullard Ltd. A Vice-President and past Chairman of Council of the Institute of Credit Management and a long-serving member of Council and Executive of the Institute of Export he is currently a freelance commercial credit consultant and a frequent lecturer on all aspects of credit management in industry.

*John Argenti* (Insolvency Signposts), best known for his work in the field of corporate planning, published a book called *Corporate Collapse* in 1976 in which he described how companies fail. The process he described there has become accepted very widely as a most accurate and useful account. He has now been able to quantify many of the features of that process.

*Peter Austin* (Leasing Finance), now retired, was for many years Leasing Manager at ICFC, where he worked for almost 30 years. He held departmental and management appointments in London and the provinces and was for a time seconded as an advisor to a Development Bank overseas. Mr Austin was a member of the Management Committee of the Equipment Leasing Association.

*M. A. Barry* (Legal Enforcement of Contractual Rights; Receiverships and Liquidations) is Principal Lecturer—Credit Management Training. A practising consultant in credit management, writing regularly on credit and legal topics.

*R. M. V. Bass* (The Nature of Credit and its History; Improving Liquidity through Credit Control; Structure, Responsibilities and Relationships), formerly Group Credit Manager of the GKN Group, is now National Credit Manager, Systime Computers Ltd. He is a Fellow of the Institute of Credit Management, and a member of the Institute of Export. A regular lecturer on credit management, he is the author of *Credit Management* (Business Books, 1979).

*Anthony J. Best* (Selection of Terms and Conditions of Sale), was until recently credit manager for Mobil Oil Co. Ltd, where he has presented financial and credit management training for his company and advanced all credit systems to achieve new standards of control and performance. A Fellow of the Institute of Credit Management where for many years, he served as a Council member with special responsibilities for seminars and the oil industry.

*A. F. Cook* (Credit Cards) joined Barclaycard in 1973 after retail banking in Martins & Management Services in Barclays. Since then he has worked in marketing, legal & customer relations, and from 1978 as Manager, Training.

*W. R. J. B. Cross* (Leasing Finance), a director of ICFC Leasing Ltd, is Manager, Leasing at ICFC, part of Investors in Industry (3i). From 1972 to 1977 he was a London-based partner of Josolyne Layton-Bennett & Co. (now part of Arthur Young McClelland Moores) where he specialised in investigations and insolvency work. After joining ICFC in 1977, he took on his present responsibilities in 1982. He is a member of the Economic and Industry Committee of the Equipment Leasing Association.

*R. G. Haskett* (The effective Use of Computers) is Data Processing Manager for Dytecna Ltd. He started his career in data processing as a systems analyst following extensive experience in statistics and cost accounting with Unigate. He has since specialised for over 20 years in a wide range of financial control systems. Mr Haskett has lectured on computer subjects and is a Member of the British Computer Society.

*H. B. Jackson* (Export Finance) has had over 50 years' experience in the export trade, starting in banking before moving into the City in foreign exchange and documentary credits. Mr Jackson was a chief executive of a bank subsidiary, providing export finance to exporters and has led export sales missions abroad for UK companies.

*A. S. Loveland* (Computer Aids and Innovations) has been Group Credit Control Manager for Carreras Rothmans Ltd with responsibility for both home and export business. He has also held positions in the company of Office Controller, Controller Export Distribution and Controller Distribution Planning, and has played a significant role in the design, development and operation of computer and other advanced office systems. He is a past member of the Council of the Institute of Credit Management.

*Pauline Malindine* (Telephone Cash Collection) is an independent telephone communication consultant with 14 years' experience in the disciplines associated with telephone training and consultancy. Her experience ranges from switchboard/receptionist training through to full consultancy advice on the implementation of telephone selling. She regularly runs training programmes on the discipline of telephone cash collection, both at public seminars and on an in-house basis, tailormade to suit specific company requirements.

*Owen G. Mayo* (Finance Houses). After retiring as Director of Group Management Board of Mercantile Credit Co. Ltd, he became an Advisor to BESO a charity organisation whose advisors go anywhere in the Commonwealth to give their expertise free; he has served many months in Singapore, Jamaica, etc. He is Fellow, one-time

Chairman, and Vice-President of the Institute of Credit Management and author of *Consumer Credit Control* (Gower, 1971).

*C. C. Mitten* (Home Trade Credit Insurance) is a Consultant to Trade Indemnity plc having spent 30 years as a specialist credit insurance broker. He is a past Chairman of the United Kingdom Credit Insurance Brokers' Committee of the British Brokers' Association.

*P. G. L. Mudge* (Retail Credit Management) is Credit Controller, Currys Group plc. He was elected Chairman of the Institute of Credit Management for 1983 and 1984. Also a member of Council of the Consumer Credit Trade Association and Chairman of the Retail Stores Committee of the CCTA. Mr Mudge became Credit Controller of Currys in 1972 after a varied career in the management of tea estates, consumer advisory services and Lloyds and Scottish Finance Ltd.

*P. J. Patrick* (Consumer Credit Law) is the Director of the Consumer Credit Trade Association. He is editor of the CCTA journal *Consumer Credit* and author of the Association's latest 110-page 'Short Guide' on the regulations made under the Consumer Credit Act. He is also a member of the Council of the Institute of Credit Management and, at the time of going to press, Chairman of its Education Committee.

*Roger Pilcher* (Factoring) started initially as Commercial Manager of International Factors before becoming Managing Director. He left to establish Credit Factoring International, a wholly-owned subsidiary of the National Westminster Bank. Mr Pilcher has been involved in the development of advanced systems in factoring both in the UK and internationally. He is a past Chairman of the Association of British Factors.

*Robert A. Rand* (Export Credit Insurance) is a director of Jardine Credit Insurance Ltd handling all forms of credit insurance and related activities. He previously worked for ECGD for 16 years, latterly as Regional Director of the Department's Cambridge office.

*Howard J. Tisshaw* (Automated Insolvency Risk Assessment) is Managing Director of Performance Analysis Services Ltd. Prior to starting with PAS he gained experience in auditing, management accounting and financial analysis before becoming a lecturer at The City University Business School where he developed particular reserach interests into the characteristics of failing companies. He is a Fellow of the Association of Certified Accountants and gained his Ph.D. by investigating the use of accounting information in decision making.

*M. H. Warmsley* (Foreign Exchange) is a Chief Dealer (Training) with Barclays Bank International Ltd. The original author, Mr Squirrel, sadly died in 1983.

*Bryan D. Watson* (Collection Agencies) is Managing Director of Inter-Credit International Ltd, a company specialising in debt collection, credit reporting and credit management seminars. He is an underwriting member of Lloyds, and Fellow of the Institute of Credit Management and has spent five years as Marketing Consultant to the Ontario Government.

*Ann Westoby* (Sales Ledger Administration) is Credit Manager of Avdel Ltd having responsibility for credit assessment, collections, and administration of the home and export ledgers. She is a Fellow of the Institute of Credit Management and was formerly a Council Member serving on the Seminar Committee.

*D. G. S. Williams* (Establishing Credit-worthiness; Credit Limits and Risk Categories) is the Treasurer of UK operations for a major international electronics company—Texas Instruments Inc., and was for several years its European Credit Manager. He has served both as a Council member of the Institute of Credit Management in the UK, and as a Director of FCIB, the international affiliate of the National Association of Credit Management of the USA, of which he is now an advisory councillor. He is a regular speaker on credit management topics both in the UK and Europe, and has contributed to several books on the subject.

# Foreword

**Sir Kenneth Cork GBE, DLitt, FCA, FICM**
**President of the Institute of Credit Management**

As a practising accountant of many years' experience and one who had been intimately connected with insolvency problems, I am glad to contribute a short Foreword to this revised edition of Herbert Edwards' excellent book. The first edition was published in 1976 and has clearly lived up to my expectation that it would prove a most useful tool for people in credit management—a field of work and a profession in which I have a particular interest, not least because I have been President of the Institute of Credit Management since 1965.

In the ever-changing world of contemporary commerce, it seems to me essential that management should realise the vital importance of employing experienced and skilled credit managers.

That this handbook is both practical and comprehensive even a cursory glance at its contents will demonstrate, and the ten parts cover a wide field ranging over all the most important aspects of credit management and control. There are also highly practical guides to topics such as consumer credit and commercial credit law which have become increasingly important in recent years.

I am well aware, of course, that good credit management is essentially an art rather than a science and that there is no substitute, ultimately, for practical experience. But it is surely the function of management to ensure that its credit managers are provided with the best possible instruments, not the least of which will be the aid offered by this handbook. I have no hesitation in saying that it will prove of inestimable benefit to everyone concerned with company financial management.

Finally, I also commend the book to students taking the examinations of the Institute of Credit Management and to their lecturers who will find that it covers some of the most important parts of the Institute's challenging syllabus.

# Introduction

**W. V. Adams**

The volatile business conditions of the last decade have created problems of cash flow and interest charges never before encountered in the industrial post-war economy. Over those ten years companies large and small have, in many cases for the first time, come to realise that the item trade debtors (or receivables, as our American friends call them) on the balance sheet represent a very substantial and expensive consumer of capital employed. They are also now beginning to accept that, in total, trade debtors represent an investment in the market-place on which the expected return is the profit to be earned once payment has completed the sale. At the same time, like all investments, those trade debtors are subject to the risks arising from the effect of the economic climate on that market-place generally.

In the same way this last decade has seen the business world come increasingly to appreciate that the total investment in trade debtors is only an aggregate of a whole series of smaller ones—the seller's resources invested in each account holder by way of unpaid balances.

There has regrettably been all too little statistical research into the importance of trade debtors in the asset structure of British companies. To some extent this gap in management knowledge was repaired by P. R. A. Kirkman, MSc, FCCA, ACIS of Exeter University who, in the early 1970s commenced a detailed research programme which shows that debtors in 1960 represented 26.6% of net assets of quoted companies; a figure which peaked at 39.9% in 1970 falling to 34.3% by 1973, reflecting the greater attention give to the management of this asset from 1970 onwards. Much of Mr Kirkman's research work has been published by the British Institute of Management in its *Management Guide No. 6* and the figures quoted therein confirm, if indeed confirmation is needed, that trade debtors form a very important part of a company's asset structure.

1984 saw the publication of an excellent small survey by Janusz Heath of Control Data. He found that 'good' companies, i.e. those achieving 55 DSO or less on monthly terms had consistently better management attitudes to all the elements of good credit control than in the companies with 75 DSO or more, often in the same industries. The effect of 20 DSO difference on corporate profitability is, of course, enormous.

At long last we now see an increasing growth in the number of companies wishing to protect their investments by proper management and expertise. The purpose of this book is to help management toward that objective.

Credit management is, unfortunately, still regarded in far too many companies, some of them household names, as being concerned solely with the collection of debts. A back-end operation coming into effect only when the product or service has been invoiced and is unpaid on due date. Very frequently in quite sizeable concerns the credit control department consists of a supervisor and three or four ledger clerks, with the supervisor responsible to an accounting manager, in turn responsible to the deputy/assistant chief accountant. The same supervisor is none the less honoured with the soubriquet 'credit manager', with nothing to manage but the volume of paper on the desk, with no voice, and frequently no interest in the job role effect on company profits and marketing strategy.

In terms of net income, a company's sales operation does no more than transfer finished stock into debtors, thereby bringing closer to reality the notional profit to be earned. That profit ceases to be notional only when the sales proceeds are in the bank. However, it is in the very process of transferring the investment from stock to debtor that additional risk is incurred to profit realisation by potential erosion arising either from account delinquency or by bad debt.

It is often said that if the bad debt write-off is nil or very low the credit policy of the company is too restrictive, but this is true only if it can be shown that business has been lost as a result. Bad debts should, of course, be kept to a minimum commensurate with the overall company sales objectives and forecasts. Sound accounting practice dictates that essential reserves are set aside from profit to provide for any such losses. What those reserves cannot do is to provide cover for the wasted sales effort needed to recoup the loss. The most serious risk to a company's profit on the sale is, however, by way of interest expense from non-payment to time. In essence, that is what credit management is all about and its objective can be said to be 'to have the highest possible debtors (sales) for the shortest possible time (collection/profit)'.

Although happily diminishing, there still remains a lack of understanding by management, particularly sales management, of the role of credit control in overall company well-being. There are still companies so completely sales-orientated that they will not allow the person responsible for accounts receivable to visit a customer lest the sales relationship be disturbed. There is an enormous educative job still to be done in this direction in terms of getting sales and marketing to understand that net income targets are achievable only if their individual sales outlets are sound investments for the company's funds and can and will pay to time. They must come to appreciate that these two essential requirements of a successful sales operation need expert judgment, assessment and control, and that it is the credit manager who can or should provide it.

Sound credit management falls midway between the ambitions of sales and those of treasury—it is not primarily a strict accounting function. The good credit manager is or should be very much more sales-orientated in outlook than accounting-orientated. He must, of course, understand the principles of accounting, otherwise he cannot do his job, as the credit sanction chapter of this book will show; but he must be forever conscious of his prime job role, 'How can I achieve this possible business as a sound investment for the company?'.

It cannot be refuted that there are many small and medium-sized concerns which do not need or cannot afford a full-time credit manager; it is important that within such organisations some senior executive (board or otherwise) is formally given and accepts the responsibility for the management of the asset created by the sales effort. Default in this respect is one of the prime causes of the illiquidity which is so prevalent in this very important element of the private sector.

Because the asset 'trade debtors' is the end-product of the purchase/production/sales chain of events and because it is the prime source of corporate revenue, this book should appeal to a much wider range of business executive than simply the person concerned directly with the sales ledger. It will certainly prove useful to them; but the buyer, production manager, sales manager, accountant and treasurer also have a vested interest in the successful outcome of their work, in terms of the sales volume generated and the profit earned. That success depends upon a proper application of credit control techniques. It is hoped that these people through this handbook can achieve a deeper insight into this aspect of their professional objective.

Industry as a whole embraces an enormous range of interrelated activity, much of which is possible only because of the trust extended by way of monetary credit. However, the 'technology' attendant upon this trust is different in each of the various elements of commercial life. The corner-shop retailer extending a monthly facility to local residents is involved in a credit control operation; but so long as he is aware of this and monitors his unpaid accounts with remedial action, he has little need, if any, of detailed techniques. The credit operation in a department store or finance house needs a vastly different application of basic principles from those in a large industrial group of companies. The small manufacturer with a hand-written sales ledger still perhaps needs help in maximising the information in that ledger as a tool of management, as does the computer-based concern with a data-bank available to it.

Happily, this book is an information source for everyone involved in the whole spectrum of monetary credit. The student will want to read it from cover to cover, learning and absorbing the wealth of information throughout the natural progressions of the complete work. The company concerned with changing or improving its credit operation, be it credit sanction, accounting system or collection practice, will find a great deal of expert information herein; whilst the established credit executive of the large corporation will be able to dip into its pages at random and profit from the exercise.

It was Shakespeare in his *Othello* who said 'He that filches from me my good name makes me poor indeed'. Delinquent creditors usually manage to filch their own good name and make themselves poor via the bankruptcy court. This book will help all those concerned with preventing this unfortunate event for their customers.

I felt complimented in being asked to write the introduction to the first edition and I am delighted now that a second edition enables me to repeat my words. There have in the past been a number of excellent books written about the art of credit management, but I cannot recall one that covers the topic in such wide range and depth. It deserves to be an essential reference work on every commercial bookshelf.

# PART I

# THE CREDIT MANAGEMENT FUNCTION

# 1

# The Nature of Credit
# and its History

**R. M. V. Bass, National Credit Manager, Systime Computers Ltd**

## INTRODUCTION

Modern definitions of credit and descriptions of the art of credit management invariably make use of the terminology of the business school and the accountant. 'Cash-flow', 'marketing tool', 'liquidity', 'risk-exposure'—all such terms are used to illustrate a basic truth which holds good in every period of human history: those with surplus assets—be they cash or goods—will use those assets to stimulate trade. The concept of deferred payment in return for immediate goods must always have existed in the earliest agricultural societies, as the incidence of a man's needs would seldom coincide with his ability to pay. For that he must await the next harvest.

The same principle applies today to the manufacturer who must buy components or raw material on credit, pending the sale of the finished article. Similarly, the holder of a credit card is enabled to obtain goods or services immediately on the basis that he has a regular income which ensures his ability to pay in the future. 'Buy now—pay later' is the abiding principle of credit; only the techniques change to match the demands—known or latent—of society.

The fundamental nature of credit therefore is that an element of trust exists between buyer and seller—the very word credit derives from the Latin *credere,* to trust. Without this trust the development of the modern industrial community would have been impossible.

Mass production and the consequent reduction of unit costs are only viable in an economy which allows continuous buying activity. The extent and variety of credit dealings throughout the ages reflect the varying needs of society for a commercial framework. It would be wrong to imagine that the use of credit in a complex and sophisticated form is only of recent origin. It does not belong solely—or even primarily—to the era of the limited liability company and international trade between nation-states, and to the age of supra-national banking and finance institutions. Traders in every period have used credit as fully as they needed. Whilst the instruments of credit—bills of exchange, cheques, bank deposits, credit cards—developed slowly over the centuries, the lack of what we have come to regard as essential tools was never an obstacle, granted the basic premise of a society sufficiently advanced to permit the establishment of trust between two parties. A brief examination of credit through the ages will help to illustrate and to explain the nature of credit before we look at the modern role of credit and credit management.

## CREDIT IN HISTORY

References to credit can be found at least 3000 years ago in the civilisations of Babylon, Assyria and Egypt and we are admonished in the Bible—'be not one of those who give pledges, who become sureties for debts' (Proverbs, 23:26). A credit manager seeking a personal guarantee from a customer is accustomed to find that this precept has been well learned and it is, of course, an integral part of banking doctrine. Medieval Europe is the first period rich in material for the credit historian. There is a mass of evidence pointing to the development of a complex system of credit trading from the twelfth century onward. Most of the commerce of Western Europe in those times hinged on the great trade fairs. The fairs of Champagne, each lasting for up to six weeks and moving from one town to another, were the most famous and successful. Merchants would journey regularly from fair to fair, buying and selling in many different currencies and establishing a network of credit arrangements. As a convenience, the merchants from Italy began to leave agents on permanent duty at the fairs. Through the use of the

'Cambium Contract'—a document which permitted the transfer of funds from one place to another (changing currency on route)—thriving businesses developed based entirely on credit and conducted from headquarters several days' or weeks' journey away. Typical of these traders was Symon di Gualterio, a Genoese merchant who, in March 1253 in Champagne, purchased English cloth from a Parman trader agreeing to pay in July, based on his receiving payment from the sale of spices at another fair in May.

More examples of credit trading are found in England, where from the thirteenth century, or earlier, dealings in wine, corn, leather, cloth, wool and all such basic commodities were based on credit. To quote one of the leading historians of the period: 'From the wool grower in the Cotswolds to the buyer of Dutch cloth in Poland or Spain there was one uninterrupted succession of credit sales' (Professor M. M. Postan, 'Credit in Mediaeval Trade', *Economic History Review,* 1928). Of particular interest is the existence of supplier credit in the wool trade. Flemish and later Italian merchants, who were generally wealthy men able to find cash quickly and easily, frequently gave advance payment to monasteries and other growers for wool to be delivered in the next season or even further ahead. In this way they foreshadowed the services of ECGD (Export Credits Guarantee Department).

Another example of credit techniques evolving to meet a need is the development of the bill of exchange in the Italian city-states of the fourteenth century, where the intricate debtor/creditor relationships demanded a simpler instrument than the Cambium Contract used by Symon di Gualterio. The principal contrast with the modern bill is that these medieval bills were rarely discounted or transferred by endorsement. To be of value credit had to be based on capital and this premise was upheld to the letter. Gold or silver coin had to be available to meet a bill and the idea that the volume of currency could be increased by the issue and transfer of paper money of greater nominal value than the original deposit did not take hold until the late seventeenth century.

This is not the place to describe the rapid and often frenzied growth of banking and public finance in Britain in the Hanoverian period. It was an essential stage in what is termed 'the industrial revolution', but like most new ideas these credit tools were frequently misused and misunderstood. The famous South Sea Bubble affair, besides laying bare the corruption of public life and the gullibility of the public, was a terrifying illustration of the abuse of this new power to create money. The result was the Bubble Act of 1720 which, *inter alia,* prohibited the raising of public capital, the issue of transferrable shares and the use of limited liability in business. Each partner in a business venture was made liable to his last guinea for all the debts of the business, and anyone investing in return for profit was regarded by the law as a partner and fully liable. Not until 1862 were the legal barriers to the use of limited liability companies removed. The use of trade credit became more and more widespread in the eighteenth and early nineteenth centuries. Facilitated by the mushroom growth of small 'county' banks who advanced money to local industrialists, credit played a significant role in the expansion of industry, but there is little evidence of any attempt at control.

This was largely due to the low cost of money—the normal commercial rate of interest in the mid eighteenth century was 3½% and rates above 5% were prohibited until 1832. The firm of Josiah Wedgwood supplied a London customer with pottery between 1808 and 1811 without once being paid.

Long credit—up to 12 months—was normal amongst merchants, but its costs did not always go unnoticed. As early as 1689 we find a Lancashire merchant named William Stout, complaining that 'it being now a year since I began trade. I find I have been too forward in trusting, too backward in calling'. This is echoed by a Scottish bookseller, James Lackington, whose comments deserve quoting at some length:

> It was some time in the year 1780 that I resolved from that period to give no person whatsoever any credit... I had observed that when credit was given, most bills were not paid within six months, some not within a twelvemonth and some not within two years... The losses sustained in interest of money in long credits and by those bills that were not paid at all; the inconvenience attending not having ready money to lay out in trade to the best advantage; together with the great loss of time in keeping accounts and collecting debts... [But] it was thought I might as well attempt to rebuild the Tower of Babel as to establish a large business without giving credit.

Whilst these observations derive from consumer rather than trade credit, they not only give a vivid picture of contemporary problems but unmistakable evidence that credit was accepted as a marketing tool. During the nineteenth century both the techniques and the instruments of credit changed. In 1800 only 3% of transactions were settled by cheques, against 70% by bills of exchange (27% was cash payment).

In 1875 these figures were reversed—the result of the demand of the business world for a simple means of transferring money between firms. This was made possible by the development of multi-branch joint-stock banking. Credit terms tended to shorten, not because money cost more (interest rates in mid-century were around 2½–3% p.a.), but principally because of the increasing availability of bank credit. In the last 100 years the tools of credit have continued to develop to meet the demands of a swiftly-changing society, but most of these new techniques have evolved in the field of consumer credit.

## GROWTH OF CONSUMER CREDIT

Unlike trade credit, consumer credit is of comparatively recent origin. Whilst the privileged few in every society have always enjoyed credit, the mass of the population possessed no buying power before the early nineteenth century and the question of credit did not arise.

An exception worth noting is the 'tally trade', developed in the eighteenth century. Itinerant traders, tallymen, mainly selling cloth and clothing covered small areas delivering goods against an agreement that small, regular payments would be made. These activities gradually died out in the face of the growing retail trade. For the ordinary working-man during the nineteenth century, the obliging local shopkeeper and the extortionate tommy shops, where workers were forced to buy from their employer goods on account of their wages, were the only source of credit available—apart from the traditional moneylenders and pawnbrokers. However, the steady rise in wages and living standards in the Victorian era, coupled with the advance of mass-production techniques, created a demand for consumer credit which continued to grow up to the present time. Hire purchase was introduced by the Singer Company in the mid-century to facilitate the sale of sewing machines. This and other forms of credit offered by finance companies gathered momentum as more and more household goods and consumer durables poured out of the factories, culminating in the age of the motor car. An adequate supply of personal finance, however, has only appeared since the end of the Second World War.

On the whole, the banks were slow in deciding to open their doors to the general public seeking short-time credit and, for many years, clung to the principle of no loans without security—in the form of tangible assets.

Not until the 1950s was it accepted that personal loans could be made against the security of a steady income—a principle recognised 200 years earlier by the tallymen. The last two decades have seen the floodgates of consumer credit flung wide open. Some of the principal sources are shown in Figure 1:1. Chapter 20 examines the management of consumer credit. A study of how credit has been used in different periods of history and how techniques have altered to meet changing conditions underlines the precept that credit depends upon the foundation stones of trust and capital. The extension of both trade credit and consumer credit demand that the borrower shall instil confidence and demonstrate his ultimate ability to pay. The need for both attributes remains, irrespective of the scale of transaction. The purchaser of a car on hire purchase must provide confidence through his previous credit record and evidence

| Banks | Finance companies | Retail shops |
|---|---|---|
| Overdraft | Hire purchase | Credit account |
| Personal loan | Credit sale | Credit sale |
| Credit card | Personal loan | Budget account |

*Other sources*
Mail order—instalment credit
Loans against life assurance policies
Second mortgage loans
Check and voucher trading
Moneylenders
Pawnbrokers

**Figure 1:1   Principal sources and forms of consumer credit**

of a regular income from which to meet his instalments. The government of a poor country seeking credit for its imports of capital equipment will not qualify for ECGD cover if it has a reputation for repudiating its debts and cannot export enough to finance its imports.

The judgement uttered by the *Morning Chronicle* following the great bank crisis of 1825 is equally applicable to trade credit as to consumer credit. It also illustrates why credit management is an art rather than a science:

> Credit, like the honour of a female, is of too delicate a nature to be treated with laxity—the slightest hint may inflict an injury which no subsequent effort can repair.

## THE CREDIT FUNCTION

The development of credit management has been stimulated by the need to find more effective ways of granting and controlling credit, as the nature of credit trading has become more complex. Credit terms now often stand alongside price and delivery as key factors in winning orders. The ever-increasing level of business failures, coupled with decreasing profit margins, has meant that no firm can afford to neglect credit control. Successful credit management requires the operation of tight financial controls coupled with a positive approach to the achievement of profitable sales.

## POSITIVE CREDIT MANAGEMENT

The most widely used form of trade credit today is unsecured open account credit, operating generally on net monthly or net 30-day terms. In many companies this is taken for granted, subject to weak and ineffective controls, and not contemplated as a possible instrument of sales growth. The cost of credit and its effects on profits and liquidity is examined in Chapter 2. Let us now examine some aspects of credit management in different business environments.

## Credit control and the trade cycle

The need to use credit more positively increases as a company's order-book dwindles. In boom times, when customers are queuing with orders and the factory is at full capacity, the credit manager's job is at its easiest. Slow-paying customers can be accelerated by the risk of losing their priority on the sales desk. New customers of doubtful standing and little capital can be asked for security.

This happy situation is usually short-lived as supply increases to meet demand and the credit manager has to adopt his more normal role of monitoring and controlling risks which the company cannot afford to turn away. In recent years the pendulum has swung even further in this direction. Excess capacity has been common and the most effective credit managers are those who succeed in turning 'high risk' business into profitable sales.

## Dealing with marginal customers

Flexibility of payment terms is a pre-requisite for the successful handling of marginal or high-risk customers.

For example, a new buyer wishing to order at £10 000 a month will need a credit limit of at least £20 000 if normal net monthly terms apply. If the information available to the credit manager indicates a maximum limit of, say, £10 000, it is clear that the business cannot be accommodated on ordinary terms. A possible solution is to offer a small discount in return for payment every two weeks. Under this arrangement a monthly turnover of £20 000 can be maintained without breaching the £10 000 credit limit. Whilst the discount reduces the rate of profit, the actual amount of profit will increase because of the higher sales volume. This is illustrated as follows, assuming a 1% discount:

> *Option A*  5% profit on £5000 a month on standard terms =
> £3000 p.a.
> *Option B*  4% profit on £10 000 a month on fortnightly terms =
> £4800 p.a.

The above principle can also be applied to instances where no credit at all is justified. If it is possible to agree cash-with-order or COD terms in return for a bigger discount, say 2%, the end result can be even more dramatic:

*Option A*  5% profit on zero sales = nil
*Option B*  3% profit on £10 000 a month COD = £3600 p.a.

There may be other circumstances where terms have to be lengthened rather than shortened in order to retain or win business. In such cases there are certain key questions the credit manager must examine before reaching agreement:

1  Will the increased credit risk be acceptable?
2  Are longer terms essential to retain or win business?
3  Will the business still be profitable?

Provided all these questions are answered in the affirmative, an extended credit arrangement may be made. It is worthwhile insisting that payments be covered by bills of exchange for the following reasons:

1  The supplier who holds a bill accepted for payment at the end of the following month is in a much better position than the supplier who relies on a cheque being sent.
2  A accepted bill is in itself a proof of debt. If it is dishonoured on presentation, the supplier can take legal action without having to provide any other evidence of debt.
3  The supplier takes the initiative in establishing the value of the bill—usually the net value of the month's transactions, instead of relying on the customer to remit the required amount.
4  The supplier may be able to discount bills before maturity if cash is needed.

Whether payment terms are set shorter or longer than normal, the basic principle remains the same. Adjust the terms to suit the merits of each case, looking always at the risk and the level of profit.

## Dealing with debtors in distress

From time to time many customers run into financial trouble, whether beyond their control or due to mismanagement. Whenever this happens, the credit manager should be alive to the situation and must judge how far his company should extend help—and when to stop. This is particularly important in a depressed market, since an unsympathetic or harsh attitude to a temporarily distressed but basically sound customer may not only turn away business in the short term but will probably have more serious results when business picks up.

Faced with a customer whose payments are arriving a little later each month but who is strong enough to survive, the credit manager has two principal options (apart from doing nothing or letting the sales director decide). He can continue to press, possibly cutting off deliveries and eventually obtaining payment when his threats or the need for more goods force the customer to surrender. This may be very successful in some cases but it cannot go on month after month and it will do nothing but harm to the supplier–customer relationship. The alternative is to contact the customer, preferably face-to-face, find out what his problems are and then decide what action to take. The final decision may still be to press for immediate payment, or it may be to agree a limited period of extended credit. This must include a detailed step-by-step plan for the ultimate return to normal terms. But whatever the decision is, it will be based on knowledge of the true position and it will stand up as a reasoned and justifiable action.

In some instances, personal contact with the customer will reveal weak credit control. Any assistance the credit manager can give, by helping the customer to install better systems and procedures will clearly be very beneficial. Not only will the customer's cash-flow be improved but the overall relationship will be strengthened. Such activities are often referred to as 'customer counselling' and are particularly relevant where the customer is a distributor.


## SUMMARY

The credit manager cannot hope to work successfully in any of these business situations unless he has the co-operation and respect of the sales and marketing team. In too many companies the credit manager has a negative image—the one who says 'No' to the fantastic order won from the competition, the one who wants to stop deliveries and to impose limits. All these 'negative' steps have to be taken from time to time. What matters is to establish sufficient confidence—not only with the sales director and manager but also with the salesmen in the field—that credit decisions, no matter how unpopular—are accepted as sensible and prudent. It is up to the credit manager first, to educate himself (and his department) and, second, to educate the sales team. Self-education means knowing something of the product and a lot about the customers. What are they doing with the product, how are their buying levels affected by changes in the industry and in the economy? It need hardly be said that the credit manager must have the latest financial facts about customers, but to be able to talk with his own sales people about them he must know far more than balance sheet details.

Education of the sales team means taking every opportunity to explain the financial impact of slow-paying and insolvent customers. The credit manager must ensure that every new salesman understands the credit function. He must also take pains to avoid running a department whose principal concern appears to be squeezing customers for money and complaining of bad faith. This is not easily achieved and will be referred to again in Chapter 3.

In this chapter the role of the credit manager has been viewed primarily as an aid to marketing. Chapter 2 will explore the financial constraints and obligations surrounding him. Chapter 3 will attempt to paint the balanced picture of how the credit manager fits into the management team.

Many companies have grasped the basic maxim that a sale is not complete until the money is in the bank. This truth is often to be found in the sales manual—although not usually on the front page. It is of equal importance that the front cover of the credit manual should acknowledge that the role of credit is to stimulate sales.

## FURTHER READING

David Alexander, *Retailing in England during the Industrial Revolution*. Athlone Press, 1970.

R. M. V. Bass, *Credit Management*. Business Books, 1979.

L. A. Clarkson, *The Pre-Industrial Economy in England 1500–1750*. B. T. Batsford Ltd, 1971.

Joseph and Frances Gies, *Merchants and Moneymen.* Arthur Barker Ltd, 1972.

P. Mathias, *The First Industrial Nation.* Methuen & Co. Ltd, 1969.

M. M. Postan, *Medieval Trade and Finance.* Cambridge University Press, 1973.

# 2

# Improving Liquidity through Credit Control

**R. M. V. Bass, National Credit Manager, Systime Computers Ltd**

## INTRODUCTION

In 1974 the British Institute of Management, having conducted a survey amongst its members, said that credit control was the most neglected area of financial management in the UK. It has not been neglected since then, in the sense that there has been a steady stream of seminars, conferences, books, articles and surveys devoted to credit control.

What is not clear is whether standards of credit management have improved proportionately to the attention given. The Institute of Credit Management has been very active in the last decade, yet its membership is still only a tiny percentage of the number of people engaged in credit control activity in the UK. The number of public companies alone exceeds 15 000! One of the most recent surveys, published by Control Data Business Advisors in November 1983, and based upon interviews in 57 medium-sized companies, recorded the fact that only two of the 57 managers were members of the Institute of Credit Management.

Regrettably there are still many firms who regard credit control merely as debt collection and who do not expect their credit controllers to participate in management. All too often credit control is the responsibility of a busy accountant with one or two clerical staff maintaining the ledger and making routine telephone calls.

The purpose of this chapter is to focus on the effect of good credit management (or the lack of it) on both profits and on liquidity.

## THE COST OF CREDIT

The cost of giving credit is easy to measure. Assume it costs 12% p.a. to borrow money. A sale of £100 unpaid for 12 months costs the vendor £12. If payment is received in 3 months, the cost reduces to £3. Payments to terms, within one month, therefore, costs 1% and each additional month's credit taken adds 1% to the vendor's costs. The only way this cost can be truly recognised and passed on is in the granting of discount for immediate payment and the charging of interest for delayed payment. Let us assume that three firms adopt these policies. Figure 2:1 shows that Firm A, whilst having no debtors to finance, has had to pay an equivalent amount for COD. Firm B bears the cost of one month's credit, whilst Firm C has offset the cost of two months' extended credit by charging interest. This is merely to demonstrate that all credit costs money. In practice the use of COD for a discount is not common, nor is the charging of interest on overdue accounts.

How many firms consciously include the cost of credit in their

|  | Firm A £ | | Firm B £ | | Firm C £ |
|---|---|---|---|---|---|
| Annual sales | 12 000 | | 12 000 | | 12 000 |
| Debtor level | Nil | | 1000 | | 3000 |
| Net profit excluding cost of credit | 600 | | 600 | | 600 |
| *Less:* Cost of 1% for COD | (120) | Cost of credit | (120) | Cost of credit | (360) |
|  | | | | Plus interest charge @ 1% per month | 240 |
| Net profit | £480 | | £480 | | £480 |

**Figure 2:1   The cost of credit**

price calculations? In periods of low interest rates and in a stable economy these costs may not be significant, especially if debtors are properly controlled. But a rate of 1% cannot be ignored and the added effect of an inflationary economy is savage. In mid 1975 a further 2% per month was needed to keep pace with inflation.

Debtors running at 90 days, therefore, were actually costing 9% to finance—a figure which no company can ignore but very few recognise. This is calculated as follows: a debt unpaid for 3 months costs 3% (with borrowing costs at 12% p.a.), plus 2% for each month to offset inflation @ 24% p.a., giving a total cost of 9%.

## THE EFFECT OF CREDIT ON LIQUIDITY

Liquidity may be defined as the ease and speed by which a company's assets can be turned into cash sufficient to meet its current liabilities. Stocks have to be turned into sales before they can generate cash and it is unprofitable to hold large cash balances. Debtors or accounts receivable are the prime factors in determing a firm's liquidity. The real value of any asset depends on how hard it is made to work to produce profits. In the case of debtors this means how frequently they are turned over.

The ability of a firm to meet its commitments regularly turns principally on the rate of its cash flow. Wages and salaries, rent and rates, factory expenses, raw material and components, hire-purchase repayments—all these have to be paid out of revenue. If the revenue is not arriving fast enough because debtors are too high, the result is what is commonly called a 'cash-flow problem'. In times of high inflation this problem is severely aggravated. Frequent price increases by suppliers who insist on prompt payment can wreck an otherwise acceptable cash-flow position. This is vividly illustrated in the automotive industry. The near-monopoly suppliers of raw material impose immediate price increases and demand settlement inside terms from customers who cannot recover the additional cost except after protracted negotiations with the vehicle manufacturers.

One of the principal objectives of credit management is to achieve the highest possible debtor figures for the shortest possible time. A debtor level of 3 months (on net monthly terms) means that debtors are only being turned over four times a year. Consequently, the revenue from sales of £120 000 p.a. is only £90 000 in the same period. If the sales curve is rising sharply through the year, even less revenue will go into the bank. This is illustrated by Figure 2:2.

| | Company A £ | Company B £ |
|---|---|---|
| Sales for year | 120 000 | 120 000 |
| Sales in 4th quarter | 30 000 | 50 000 |
| Debtors at year-end | | |
| (=3 months sales) | 30 000 | 50 000 |
| Income from sales during year | 90 000 | 70 000 |

**Figure 2:2   Effects of slow debtor turnover on liquidity**

Recognition of such a deteriorating liquid position usually comes from the bank statement. This may be too late for effective action. Every firm should produce a cash-flow forecast for at least 3 or possibly 12 months ahead. The credit manager has a crucial role to play here, since a cash-flow forecast is worthless if the debtor level is not accurately plotted and a realistic view of collections is not taken.

**MEASUREMENT OF DEBTORS**

It is appropriate to consider how debtors should be measured. Many different methods are in use, based either on the 'average day's sale' principle, or on the 'working-back' principle, or a combination of the two. Whatever method is used, the following features are essential:

1  Valid month-to-month comparisons must be possible.
2  Fluctuations in sales volume must not distort the trend.

One method is suggested here in Figure 2:3. From this type of measurement it is easy to produce a budget for debtors based on the monthly sales forecast which will require only simple amendments to reflect revised sales forecasts and the final sales invoiced.

Figure 2:3 assumes that terms of payment are net monthly or net 30 days. If varying terms are used, particularly when there is a substantial volume of exports, it may be worthwhile making

|  | £ |  |
|---|---|---|
| Total debtors at 30 June | 10 000 000 |  |
| *Less:* Current (June) sales | (5 500 000) | = 1.00 months |
| Overdue balance | 4 500 000 |  |
| Total first prior month's sales (May) | 5 000 000 |  |
| Overdue balance expressed as % of prior month's sales = | $\dfrac{4\ 500\ 000}{5\ 000\ 000}$ | = 0.90 months |
| = | 90% |  |
| Total debtors = 1.90 months | | |

**Figure 2:3  Measurement of debtors**

separate calculations. What might be judged an acceptable debtor level in the home market on monthly terms may be an impossibly low target for export receivables.

Another useful measurement by which credit performance can be judged is a periodic (usually monthly) aged analysis of debtor balances. Where a computer is used this should be produced whenever a new sales ledger is printed. The intention of this analysis is two-fold. First, it will reveal how much money is tied up on overdue accounts. A debtor level of say 2.50 months may appear reasonable, but it may hide the age analysis shown in Figure 2:4.

|  | % |
|---|---|
| Current | 40 |
| 1st overdue month | 26 |
| 2nd overdue month | 10 |
| 3rd overdue month | 4 |
| 4th overdue month | 4 |
| 5th overdue month | 4 |
| 6 months overdue and over | 12 |
|  | 100 |

**Figure 2:4  Aged analysis of debtor balance**

This is an unsatisfactory debtor position, indicating a lack of control on debts that remain unpaid beyond 3 months. The same debtor level—2.50 months—could also reflect the following ageing:

|                  | %  |
|------------------|----|
| Current          | 40 |
| 1st overdue month | 40 |
| 2nd overdue month | 20 |

The vital point is that measurement in terms of months' or days' sales should never be taken as the only standard of performance.

The second purpose of the age analysis is to identify those customers with particularly old or large balances who should be receiving priority attention from the credit department.

The level of overdues is often measured by expressing the total value overdue as a percentage of the total debtors. This method appears satisfactory but it only gives meaningful answers if monthly sales values are constant. A better yardstick is to relate the total overdue to the total outstanding at the end of the *previous* month. This removes the current month's sales from the calculation and gives a truer picture of credit control performance over a period of time.

## THE QUALITY OF DEBTORS

A firm's liquidity is largely determined by the quality of its debtors. Quality has two aspects—risk and age. Some industries have a history of high-risk receivables whilst others rarely incur bad debts. Every firm should decide what level of risk it is prepared to accept if it is to remain both competitive and profitable in its industry.

Suppliers to the building trade for example are certain to have a sales ledger with a considerably higher level of risk than manufacturers of equipment to the brewery business. The effect on profits of risks that go wrong, i.e. of bad debts, is examined later in this chapter. The effect on liquidity is less dramatic and part of the other aspect of debtor quality—age. All receivables should be capable of conversion into cash in as short a time as possible. This means tight control on overdue accounts since the older a debt becomes, the less certain are the prospects of collecting it. The following table, designed to show the real value of receivables, illustrates this:

|  | % |
|---|---|
| Current debts are worth | 100 |
| 30-day overdue debts are worth | 90 |
| 90-day overdue debts are worth | 80 |
| 180-day overdue debts are worth | 50 |
| Debts over 12 months' old are worth | 30 |

This deterioration in the value of the sales ledger takes no account of inflation but merely expresses a realistic view of the problems a credit manager must cope with. As far as the over 12 months' old debts are concerned, of the £70 not collectable out of a ledger figure of £100, it is not uncommon to find £35 or more written off because of lack of evidence to refute the customer's persistent denial that the goods were ever received. Debts due from large and valued customers may be 'safe' in the sense that the customers are staying in business.

To ignore them because of this may lead to greater losses than those resulting from insolvency.

## THE EFFECT OF CREDIT ON PROFITS

Extended credit is frequently used to promote sales—and rightly so. But unless the real cost of credit is recognised and included in the calculation of profit, the careless granting of long credit can easily have the opposite effect to that intended.

The expected additional profit generated by increased sales must be seen to outweigh the additional cost of financing longer credit, as illustrated in Figure 2:5. Selling on longer terms (column B) has increased turnover sufficiently to allow the higher profit to outweigh the increased cost of financing receivables. However, the result of a further lengthening of terms (column C), whilst increasing sales and profits, is not advantageous because the costs of debtor finance now outweigh the increased profit.

It is worth noting that if the cost of financing debtors rises to 12%, the bottom lines in columns A and B read the same—£3600. It drops to £2100 in column C. The higher the financing costs, the greater the effect on profit and the more doubtful the value of boosting sales by

| | A | B | C |
|---|---|---|---|
| Sales | £120 000 | £180 000 | £210 000 |
| Debtors | £20 000 | £45 000 | £70 000 |
| Credit period | 60 days | 90 days | 120 days |
| Net profit (5%) before cost of financing debtors | £6000 | £9000 | £10 500 |
| Cost of financing debtors (10%) | £2000 | £4500 | £7000 |
| | | | |
| Net profit after cost of financing debtors | £4000 | £4500 | £3500 |

**Figure 2:5   The effect of extended credit on profits**

long credit. A company which has to borrow money to finance an increasing debtor level can easily see its profits wiped out by interest charges.

This danger is present even without granting long credit. In times of dear or scarce money, it is normal to find companies looking for the cheapest form of finance—extended credit which is not agreed but just taken. Small firms tend to suffer particularly from this at the hands of their large customers, principally because small firms are generally unwilling or unable (through lack of management attention) to press their customers to the same extent that large companies can.

Small firms often fear that demanding payment may upset their customers and lose them business. Quite apart from this small firms are not able to devote much time or effort to chasing overdue accounts.

A study of the fortunes of small businesses in south Hampshire between 1981 and 1983 showed that cash-flow was a serious problem for over half of the 52 firms surveyed, evidenced by slow payers and bad debts. Of those suffering cash-flow problems 20% made no attempt to alleviate the situation.

There is no simple answer to small firms' credit control problems, but several points should be carefully considered:

1   How important to the customer is the product? The strength of a small firm often lies in the fact that it is providing a specialist product or service.

2   The owner is close enough to the problem to make a personal approach at a senior level to slow-paying customers.
3   How does the cost of financing extended credit and its effect of liquidity compare with the cost of employing an experienced credit controller?
4   Is factoring worth considering? (See Chapter 25 on this subject.)

Most small firms employ an accountant, full- or part-time, to look after the books and a clerk to operate the daily routine of ledger work. It is not surprising that credit control can be neglected and debtors arise. More companies fail in their early years from liquidity problems than lack of profits. More awareness of the effects of a high debtor level and the cost of reducing it could well help many firms to avoid cash problems.

The final point to be considered is the potential savings to be made by a reduction in debtors.

A company with sales of £12 million and debtors of £3 million has a level of 3.00 months (assuming an even sales distribution through the year) and an average day's sales value of £33 333. With finance costing 12% p.a. the cost of each additional day's credit is £4000 p.a. If debtors can be reduced to 2.5 months, the savings will be £60 000 in a year. The costs of achieving the reduction in debtors must be set against the saving but should be considerably below that figure.

A credit manager starved of resources and unable to control debtors properly should argue his case on this sort of basis. Similarly on a smaller scale the proprietor of a small firm suffering from the impositions of big customers can easily calculate how much can be spent on credit control before the costs begin to outweigh the benefits.

A reduction of two weeks on a turnover of £1 million will save £5000 and should be achieved for less than that. Apart from this, the bank overdraft facility will become available for other uses and pressure from creditors can be eased by the improvement in cash-flow.

## THE COST OF CREDIT—BAD DEBTS

It is frequently stated that a bad debt of £1000 is £1000 deducted from net profit. This is not necessarily true and it is important for the credit manager to know why not. The principle involves an understanding of basic cost accounting. The effect on profit of a bad debt is determined by the value of the debt after deducting the contribution to costs and profit contained in the sale.

This is illustrated in Figure 2:6. Two companies, X and Y, have the same sales volume (£1000) and the same net profit (£50 = 5%). Company X's variable costs (principally material) are £700 and its fixed costs (principally labour and plant running expenses) are £250. Company Y has an opposite mixture—variable costs £250 and fixed costs £700. These facts are given in column (a).

The second column (b) for each company shows the effect of a

|  | *Company X* | | | |
|---|---|---|---|---|
|  | *(a)* | *(b)* | *(c)* | *(d)* |
|  | £ | £ | £ | £ |
| Sales | 1000 | 1200 | 800 | 1000 |
| Variable costs | 700 | 840 | 560 | 700 |
| Fixed costs | 250 | 250 | 250 | 250 |
| Profit | 50 | 100 | (10) | 50 |
| Bad debts | — | (50) | — | (50) |
| Revised profit | 50 | 60 | (10) | — |
| % Profit on sales | 5% | 5% | (1.25)% | — |

|  | *Company Y* | | | |
|---|---|---|---|---|
|  | *(a)* | *(b)* | *(c)* | *(d)* |
|  | £ | £ | £ | £ |
| Sales | 1000 | 1200 | 800 | 1000 |
| Variable costs | 250 | 300 | 200 | 250 |
| Fixed costs | 700 | 700 | 700 | 700 |
| Profit | 50 | 200 | (100) | 50 |
| Bad debts | — | (50) | — | (50) |
| Revised profit | 50 | 150 | (100) | — |
| % Profit on sales | 5% | 12.5% | (12.5)% | — |

**Figure 2:6   Variable effects of bad debts on profit**

20% increase in sales by deliberate selling to marginal 'high-risk' customers, assuming a bad debt level of 25% on the new business. Company X because of its high variable costs gains nothing in terms of percentage profit on sales, since the loss in revenue cancels out the additional profit. Company Y on the other hand, with low variable costs, has considerably increased its profit margin. Whilst the actual value of bad debts is the same for each company (£50), the effects on profit are different.

The third column (c) for each company shows the situation where the factories are working 20% below capacity (i.e. sales of only £800) and the credit manager refuses to permit additional sales to high-risk customers. Company X has a smaller loss than Company Y due to its large reduction of variable costs.

The right-hand column (d) assumes that the credit manager has relented and brought the sales back to the normal level, at the same time incurring 25% bad debts on the additional sales. The result is that both companies achieve a break-even position, which means a substantial improvement for Company Y.

As another example, let us take a third company, Company Z. Company Z is operating below capacity and variable costs are 50% of sales. A new customer known to be shaky wants to place an order for £1000 per month on net monthly terms. Tight control of his account will limit the risk to £2000 maximum (this also assumes good liaison between sales, production and dispatch departments in adhering to the delivery schedule—in practice this needs careful control). Out of every £1000 received, therefore, £500 is a contribution to profits and fixed costs. When four monthly accounts have been paid £2000 will have gone into profit and if the customer then becomes insolvent (owing £2000) the bad debt will wipe out the contribution. For every additional month the customer continues to pay, the contribution is increased by £500—regardless of eventual insolvency.

These examples illustrate the fallacy of regarding all bad debts as 100% reductions against profit. In practice the alternatives are never as clear-cut. Distinctions between variable and fixed costs are often blurred and vary from firm to firm. The combination of high fixed costs with a below-capacity production needs to be positively identified before the credit manager starts to approve sales to previous high credit-risk accounts.

Many other factors will enter the decision area, such as the costs of reducing the labour force, the need to build-up a new market or a new product. These are usually outside the sphere of the credit manager but his contribution to profitability can increase if he understands his company's costing systems and he keeps himself aware of changing situations in the factory and the market-place.

Bad debts risks themselves vary enormously between different industries. Engineering firms producing goods to individual customer specifications clearly incur greater risks than distributors supplying components ex-stock. The failure of such a customer to buy a 'made to measure' product may leave the supplier with work-in-progress and raw material which has only scrap value.

On the other hand, the manufacturer of a complete and identifiable finished product may better be able to safeguard himself against a receiver by stipulating in his terms of sale that goods remain his property until paid for. This safeguard is of little value to a supplier of components which lose their identity in the buyer's product.

## BAD DEBT PROVISION

A responsibility the credit manager must not neglect concerns provisions against bad debts. No one else is able to make a proper assessment of the sales ledger and he must not shirk from identifying uncollectable accounts and recommending a reserve. The method used varies greatly from firm to firm. One approach is to reserve against a percentage of all debts aged beyond a certain date. Another is to examine every account for potential losses. The volume of accounts will probably determine which approach is used. Unless the percentage method is used, it is recommended that probable uncollectable items are identified and classified under headings such as:

1   Accounts already insolvent.
2   Accounts under legal action.
3   Accounts in outside hands for collection.
4   Invoices over, say, 12 months' old in dispute.
5   Accounts regarded as 'high-risk'.

Past experience should be a guide when considering disputed items or accounts with collection agents. The prevailing economic and industrial climate will affect the policy adopted towards 'high-risk' customers (including their identification). The overall financial policy of the company will probably determine how far the credit manager's recommendations are accepted.

Finally, a credit manager who sees the pareto principle operating (i.e. 20% of customers accounting for 80% of receivables), with the consequence that the failure of a major customer would have a serious effect on profits and liquidity, should think about credit insurance.

# 3

# Structure, Responsibilities and Relationships

**R. M. V. Bass, National Credit Manager, Systime Computers Ltd**

In the previous two chapters we have examined the nature of credit, defining it primarily as a marketing tool, and studied its effect on profits and cash-flow. It is clear that the extension and management of credit has a considerable impact on both solvency and profitability. Two conclusions should be drawn from this, which are of paramount importance to the successful use of credit in business.

1  Every company should have a credit policy.
2  Every company should ensure that its credit policy is operated by a properly qualified and experienced manager.

## CREDIT POLICY

There are two key questions which should be answered in a company's credit policy:

1  How much working capital does the company intend to employ on debtors?

This will be influenced by the nature of the market and the strength of the competition. The principal factor, however, is the total working capital available to finance both debtors and stocks.

This crucial question must be answered at board level. The amount of capital available to support receivables should be related to sales volume.

Thus a policy might state that investment in debtors should not exceed two months' sales. The credit manager has a yardstick to measure against and the level of receivables from month to month is immediately identified as above or below requirements.

2 Who is responsible for deciding credit limits and terms of payment?

A clear statement on these issues is very desirable. Whilst the utmost co-operation should be maintained between the marketing and credit departments, the ultimate decision should lie with the credit manager, since by training and by experience he is better equipped to make a proper judgment. The credit manager is responsible for obtaining payment within terms. He should determine the maximum exposure which should be permitted. Armed with this information, and taking advice from the sales department on the expected sales volume, he can then establish the most appropriate terms for achieving those sales within the limit.

Not all companies take this view, however. The most common alternative is for the sales director to have the final say in determining limits and terms. Wherever the responsibility lies it must be clearly identified and understood. A credit manager who is uncertain how far he should express his opinions and how vigorously he should press his case is not likely to operate efficiently.

It is not important to have a written policy, so long as the board and the management of the company are agreed on the policy and it is communicated to all areas of the company which may be affected. Providing the two key questions are answered and the answers are known to and accepted by all concerned—primarily the credit department and the marketing/sales department—the basis is laid for a successful operation.

## THE POSITION OF THE CREDIT MANAGER IN MANAGEMENT

The potential impact of credit management on sales, profits and cash-flow has been examined in Chapters 1 and 2. An attempt to enumerate the personal qualities necessary in any good manager runs a grave risk of specifying a kind of superman who exists only on paper. This is equally true of descriptions of good credit managers. Suffice it to say that he (or she) must have a fundamental grasp of and sympathy with both finance and marketing and the ability to make judgements and take risks.

For many years credit managers suffered the label of debt collectors and still do in some companies. This can only be changed by a more enlightened attitude by top management and by credit managers themselves proving their worth both to their colleagues in marketing and to their superiors. For a more detailed study of the place of the credit manager in business today, reference should be made to a paper entitled 'Credit Control or Credit Management', by D. G. S. Williams, published in *Credit Management,* the Institute of Credit Management magazine, May–June 1974. To quote from this, credit management should be 'an integral part of the total management structure of the company, offering a special combination of skills which together can make a positive contribution to the success of the business'.

The question of to whom the credit manager should be responsible will inevitably be determined by the attitude of top management to the job. In companies where he is regarded solely or primarily as a debt collector, he is usually found reporting to the chief accountant or the financial accountant. Other companies, seeing properly organised credit facilities as an essential part of marketing strategy have the credit manager responsible to the head of sales or marketing. Both of these reporting structures have serious drawbacks. A credit manager is *not* an accountant. He must have some basic knowledge of accounting and will obviously understand how his own company's accounting is operated. To place him under the control of an accountant whose training and experience is geared to the analysis and interpretation of figures and whose relationship with sales is probably limited to demands for forecasts will stifle and frustrate him.

Conversely, although the credit and sales departments must co-operate at all times, there can be serious obstacles to efficient operation if the credit manager is accountable to the sales department for the performance of his job.

There are two alternative reporting systems. The first is a direct line from credit manager to managing director. This is an uncommon practice in the UK—although more frequently found in the USA—

and can only be the final expression of the theory that credit is too important to be subservient to either sales or finance. But, regardless of theory, a credit manager can only achieve this status through being a top quality manager. The other reporting relationship is to the head of finance, be he finance director, controller or treasurer. This is perhaps the best alternative, since the ultimate responsibility of a credit manager is financial. Uncontrolled credit can play havoc with profits and liquidity and the credit manager must be close to the head of finance to ensure that credit decisions are in line with the overall management of working capital.

## FUNCTIONS OF THE CREDIT DEPARTMENT

All credit departments, regardless of size, should have two basic functions—assessment and collections. The efficiency of both operations depends upon a good information system.

Credit assessment and collection systems are examined in detail in Parts III and V of this book and the whole subject of information is examined later in this chapter. A major source of information is, of course, the sales ledger. Should maintenance of the sales ledger be part of the credit function?

There is a great division of opinion on this question. Advantages can be claimed for either side and for various compromise arrangements. These are worth some thought, since the answer can have a serious effect upon the successful operation of a credit department.

The principal benefit derived from separating the ledger and credit functions is that the latter can be staffed by specialists whose time and efforts are not diluted by ledger work. This is a positive advantage. In many firms ledger clerks are expected to do credit work and the result is very unsatisfactory. A good ledger clerk does not necessarily make a good credit clerk. Ledger work does not demand the ability to talk fluently and persuasively over the telephone, the art of good correspondence, or, above all, the capacity to make judgments as to the right course of action. In short, credit work calls for a higher level of skill and intelligence than is required for ledger work.

In addition there is the constant danger that the ledger routines will occupy the main part of the day, leaving credit to be fitted in if time permits. Computer deadlines for the input and reconciliation of cash and the production of monthly statistics impose disciplines which inevitably push the credit jobs to the bottom of the list. Good supervision and planning can prevent the expansion of ledger work but its occurrence is made even more likely when the staff are primarily ledger clerks, expected to undertake credit control as well.

Advocates of a joint operation can also put forward a strong case. A major argument is that credit clerks are totally dependent on the ledger being up-to-date, accurate and available for the performance of the collection function. Separation of jobs can result in considerable duplication of work—for instance, the marking up of payments by credit clerks before the ledger staff prepare their reconciliations. This can lead to overstaffing, particularly where the two functions are situated apart from each other. Separation of functions whereby the credit manager does not control the ledger staff is the worst arrangement, since the timing of statements, the availability of ledgers, and problems of deciding priorities in backlog situations are beyond his jurisdiction. Also, of course, the credit manager and his staff must have complete and absolute confidence in the ledgers, which is difficult if they are the responsibility of another manager. A further argument against separation is that a complete operation including both ledger and credit work produces greater job-satisfaction. This loses validity, however, if the staff are not competent in both disciplines.

A reasonable compromise between these two conflicting theories is to have both ledger and credit work performed by different people within the credit department and organised so as to produce the maximum co-operation and the minimum overlapping. These problems assume greater importance the greater the number of staff involved. The best solution for one firm may not be suitable for another. A credit manager intending to reorganise must always come back to the following fundamental points:

1   Proper credit control demands proper credit staff. Not all ledger clerks can be trained.
2   The condition and content of accounts receivable have such an immense impact on the credit manager's performance that he must be able to control the ledger.

In addition to the mainstream functions of credit assessment, collection and ledger maintenance, there are other responsibilities including, bad debt provisions, as covered in Chapter 2.

### Customer queries and debit notes

Even the most well-run ledger contains invoices under query and in many industries suppliers have to accept debit notes which if not attended to can grow into enormous problems costing a great deal to control, and often finishing up as 'write-offs'.

No credit manager likes to spend time on queries, and indeed avoidance of this responsibility is one argument against placing the sales ledger under his control. It is not to be avoided, however. Queries not dealt with result in messy accounts. Customers become increasingly irritated at receiving incorrect statements. A straightforward collection procedure becomes complicated. The debtor level rises higher than is explicable by the incidence of payments. At year-end provisions have to be increased and the auditors are unhappy.

Usually, most queries are solved outside the credit department and it is, therefore, difficult to control them. There are a number of actions the credit manager must take:

1  Maintain first-class records.
2  Operate a close liaison and reporting system with the sales department.
3  Ensure that credit staff are held responsible for following-up queries until they are cleared.

### Credit enquiries

Requests for information and opinions on customers feature in every credit manager's mail. These should always be answered promptly and accurately, whether the enquirer be another supplier, a credit agency or any other reputable organisation. Good communications and information sources are essential to credit management and a willingness to exchange information in confidence will pay dividends.

The credit manager should also provide a service to any department within his own company seeking information. The purchasing manager, for example, will often be looking for new or alternative sources of supply. No supplier should be engaged until the stability of his business has been checked. The sudden stoppage of materials essential for a production line can be as catastrophic as the failure of a major customer. The credit department should be an automatic referral point before commitment is made to a new supplier.

## Terms of business

An integral part of the credit function should be to give advice not only on payment terms, but also on other aspects of conditions of sale.

Payment terms are examined in detail in Part II. It is sufficient to note here that flexibility should be the credit manager's watchword. Just because in the past all home trade customers have been sold on net monthly terms, this is no reason to ignore the possibility of offering different terms. Seven- or fourteen-day terms may enable high-volume sales to be made to a suspect customer. Sixty days may be worth granting to keep valuable business. Even cash discounts are worth negotiating on occasion.

The scope for negotiating special terms is, of course, far wider in the export market. The credit manager must be acquainted with the techniques of exporting not only on terms of payment, but also with regard to foreign exchange contracts, banking procedures, consignment stock arrangements, ECGD and many other subjects. Only too frequently an export sales manager wins a contract but has to turn to the credit manager for advice.

Other aspects of conditions of sale on which the credit manager should become familiar and, therefore, able to offer guidance—on both home and export business—are the reservation of property and the charging of interest. These topics are covered in later chapters.

## ORGANISATION

The size and structure of the credit department will be largely determined by the size and nature of the business, and the amount of money made available.

Let us assume a situation where a credit manager is appointed in a well-established firm which has not had a credit policy and where the accounts receivable have been looked after by an accountant who has seen his primary job as the maintenance of a tidy and balanced ledger. Two key questions must be answered:

1   Is the credit manager to be responsible for the sales ledger?

This has already been examined. There must be a clear understanding at the outset, so that the credit manager can decide on his recruiting policy and on the immediate training needs.

2   Is the credit function to be centralised or local?

There are several arguments in favour of decentralisation—assuming, of course, that the company already has a sales/administrative operation on a branch basis. Credit problems are always best solved by direct contact with the customer and a local credit man has a distinct advantage over 'the man in head office', both in being physically closer to his customers and in being familiar with local conditions. For the same reasons the branch credit controller can develop a better relationship with the sales department.

On the other side, there are strong benefits from centralisation. Economy of size heads the list. Duplication of personnel and equipment is avoided and most expenses are lower—except perhaps travel. Control over both credit granting and collections is easier to maintain and the problem of ensuring up-to-date information at branches is overcome. Records are easier to maintain when kept in a central office than if scattered over a number of branches.

Ultimately, the deciding factor will probably be the size and nature of the business. The greater costs of decentralisation can only be justified if the company is selling direct to a very large number of customers whose sheer volume and complexity (i.e. frequent disputes) make it difficult for a central credit department to operate effectively.

Once these two questions are settled the credit manager can plan his organisation and staffing. The number of staff needed and their deployment will be dictated principally by the volume of active customers and by the spread of business between those customers.

The examples which follow illustrate this. In all cases it is assumed that ledger work is part of the function.

*1   Firm A.* Turnover £5 000 000. Number of active accounts, 500; business fairly evenly spread.

One or two clerks should be able to cope. Most of the collection work will be by telephone, with the credit manager making three or four customer visits per month.

*2   Firm B.* Turnover £10 000 000. Number of active accounts, 3000; 70% of sales made to 10% of customers.

Three or four clerks needed to look after the smaller accounts. Ledger work a big feature; some collections by phone, but most customers covered by a letter cycle. One or two staff under a supervisor should be given responsibility for the top 10% of customers. All collection work to be done by telephone and personal visit.

*3   Firm C.* Turnover £10 000 000. Number of active accounts, 10 000; business fairly evenly spread.

At least ten clerks needed, mainly involved in ledger work and a collection letter cycle. There should be two supervisors whose primary function is to identify problems and to do telephone follow-up on the largest accounts.

These examples are intended as a guide to some of the different ways a credit manager may have to organise his forces. He must, above all, be flexible in his approach and be able to identify special needs. In the case of Firm B above, it would be much easier merely to divide all the accounts equally between, say five clerks. What is then lost is the identity of 70% of the business, the ability to monitor performance and to exercise separate controls over that sector.

Staff directly involved in ledger work and collection activity may be classed as 'mainstream', and their work is usually based on a monthly routine. Staff outside the monthly cycle may be termed 'service', engaged in such activities as maintenance of customer records, control of debit notes, control over work-flow to and from computer, typing and filing. The first of these jobs—maintenance of customer records—should include responsibility for status information files and may also include control over the issuing of account numbers and the updating of name and address records.

In all but the smallest companies, it is worth producing an organisation chart showing areas of responsibility and lines of authority. The bigger the firm the more necessary this is, otherwise uncertainties and misunderstandings will develop and take root. Since a good organisation chart will show job titles as well as personal names, an essential corollary is a job specification file.

Every position in the credit department should be described and the qualities and qualifications required for it examined. A credit manager who does this is forced to think clearly and critically about his organisation. His staff will work better if they have a proper understanding of their responsibilities and authority. Delegation within the credit department is vital but often difficult to practise. In a large department, one or two levels of supervision are necessary and the manager must ensure that these different levels have sufficient authority to be effective. A number of functions can be readily delegated, being of a routine nature. These will include controls on the sales ledger, updating of status files, operating a collection-letter cycle, following up disputed items with the sales department. Certain functions should be delegated with great care and only when the manager is satisfied that the individuals involved are ready. These include decisions on credit limits, the handling of special accounts, and relationships with sales management.

## COMMUNICATION AND INFORMATION

Good credit management is not a mystique. It is a function highly dependent upon accurate information provided through clear lines of communication.

Information of all kinds constantly pours into the credit department. It is important that it should be handled efficiently and for the credit manager to be able to rely on finding the latest facts in the right place without delay. Good filing is easy to establish but its absence can be catastrophic. Three basic headings are necessary to make an initial classification of incoming data:

*1    Status files.* These will contain information on customers from all sources and must be regularly updated. See Part III for a detailed study of this subject.

*2 Correspondence files.* Generally filed under customer's name, these illustrate the supplier–customer relationship, including details of overdue follow-up.

*3 Account history files.* At the simplest level this will be no more than the sales ledger records over a period of time. The more sophisticated a department becomes—usually involving computer facilities—the more these files grow. Monthly age-listings, lists of credit limit deviations, analyses of payments by age of items paid, annual summaries of age listings (showing a year-at-a-glance picture of payment behaviour)—the average computer produces yards and yards of paper every month. The most difficult problem is what to keep and where to store it. Managers able to use microfilm techniques are fortunate. The others must strive to keep what is current or likely to be referred to as accessible as possible.

Computerised sales ledger systems can be classified under one of two headings—batch processing or realtime on-line. With a batch processing system, historical data can be stored in the memory of the computer and printed at whatever frequency is required. Whilst this is a major improvement over a manual system, there are still drawbacks. Firstly, the open item format of the ledger means that information and notes on the status of outstanding items which used to be permanently recorded (or scribbled!) on ledger cards have to be transcribed each month on to the new ledger print-out or else kept on separate record cards. Secondly, information on payment behaviour will normally be updated and printed monthly, whereas it may be required at any time.

These difficulties are overcome with a realtime on-line system. Data on payment history and sales volume is updated automatically by the application of cash or invoices to the ledger, and the credit manager can interrogate and call up on the screen whatever information he needs that is contained in the file. Such systems also have the facility to take notes, say, resulting from a telephone call which will then be shown on the screen the next time that customer's account is called up.

Another set of files often neglected and consequently difficult to use is that of customer payment or remittance advices. These are generally filed in bundles or boxes a month at a time. Referral is so much easier if each customer—or major customer at least—has his own file kept in date order.

Information into the credit department must, therefore, be properly classified and stored if it is to be of value. Equal if not greater importance should be devoted to the flow of information out of the department. The relationship with sales and marketing will be examined separately, after we have looked at the lines of communication with senior management and another important department. Whatever position the credit manager occupies in the company hierarchy and regardless of to whom he reports, he should ensure that information about the credit scene is produced regularly and in a digestible and meaningful way. Some companies have elaborate reporting requirements which become a monthly ritual, a meaningless chore to those delegated to fill in the forms, and a stream of statistics of no real value to management. The credit manager faced with this problem should have as a long-term objective the education of his superiors into a more constructive approach. Short-term he should, whenever possible, take the opportunity to highligh the areas he sees as important. The information management *should* be demanding on a regular basis includes the following:

1   Debtor level, measured in such a way as to allow month-to-month and budget-to-actual performance.
2   Debtor ageing, with some comparative figures to identify trends.
3   Cash collection, actual against budget.
4   Major problem accounts.
5   Major problem areas (i.e. products, markets, divisions).
6   Analysis of debtors into appropriate groupings (e.g. divisions).

Pure statistics never make easy reading and are often open to misinterpretation. A few lines of narrative can make a world of difference to an otherwise uninteresting report. The credit manager is safeguarding a major asset of the the company—frequently the biggest asset on the balance sheet. Any major problem or trend likely to affect the true value of that asset must be identified and highlighted.

A department with which a special relationship needs to be

developed is the dispatch or shipping department. Effective credit control involves the monitoring of deliveries. Whilst the first stage in this procedure must be liaison with sales, the ultimate control lies with the shipping manager and his staff. Reliable dispatch records are essential, not only to determine the value of shipments made earlier in the month but also to satisfy customers requests for proof of delivery and short-delivery queries. There must be a direct personal link between credit and dispatch.

## THE SALES–CREDIT RELATIONSHIP

Possibly the greatest threat to effective credit management is a lack of understanding with the sales department. It is only too easy for the credit manager to be seen as a negative figure whose aim in life is to restrict sales, impose limits and stop deliveries. The long-term answer to this problem is education by the credit manager both of his own staff and of the sales department.

Within the credit department, whilst priority has to be given to teaching the techniques of collection and the operation of controls over risks, the manager must train his people to look for ways of granting credit—with security if need be—rather than taking the easy way out of shutting the door automatically on every doubtful name. Very often one finds that sales staff who have been made aware of the need for credit control tend to over-react. The only alternative to net monthly is seen to be pro-forma. Letter of credit is essential for all new overseas buyers. In these situations the credit man who can suggest a middle way and possibly save the sale is fulfilling his proper function—using credit to make profitable sales.

Relationships with sales must be developed at all levels. From the sales director and sales managers through sales representatives to sales office clerks—the credit team should have a regular day-to-day contact, seeking information, explaining decisions, taking part in marketing conferences, helping in the training of salesmen, becoming involved and accepted as part of the company team.

One way to maintain and improve the credit/sales relationship which can be done in any company, big or small, is to hold regular meetings at which the previous month's debtor figures and collection results are discussed, and problems and queries are highlighted.

The main headings in defining the relationship can be summarised as follows:

What does the credit department expect from the sales department?

1 Early advice of problems that may affect payment.
2 Fast information and answers to solve queries.
3 Early notification of new prospects.
4 Advance notice of new products and marketing strategies.
5 No commitment without consultation.

As an illustration, a sales director decides to sell a particular product through a small number of major distributors rather than direct to consumers. Early discussion with the credit manager will avoid problems resulting from the need to approve high lines of credit for immediate use.

What does the sales department expect from the credit department?

1 Swift and reasoned decisions.
2 Early warning of potential problems.
3 Full information about special credit arrangements.
4 Immediate advice on queries.
5 Flexible procedures.

*Illustration:* a credit department wants to adopt a tougher approach with a persistently slow customer. Discussion with the sales manager reveals that next month he hopes to sign an important contract. It may now be possible to produce a total package including special credit arrangements.


## TRAINING AND RECRUITMENT

The ability to promote from within is the best measure of good training. Senior credit staff of managerial and supervisory level tend by definition to be specialists. Their replacement is never easy since there is a dearth of both experienced creditmen and good credit jobs in the UK.

In this setting the credit manager must pay serious attention to training, not only at senior level, but throughout the department. Facilities for training in credit in the UK, whilst still far from adequate, have improved considerably in recent years. Training can be external or internal or preferably a combination of both.

**External**

*(a)* A good foundation is the Dun & Bradstreet correspondence course in credit and financial analysis. This provides a solid theoretical basis, and is particularly useful for young office workers, introducing them into the financial environment and moving forward into the techniques and tools of credit management. Anyone thinking about a career in credit but not yet committeed would benefit from this course.

*(b)* The next stage of training is the credit seminar. The Institute of Credit Management holds several one- or two-day seminars both in London and in provincial centres and several commercial firms are also active in this field. The subjects normally covered include credit assessment, operating the sales ledger, collection techniques, legal proceedings and export credit. The quality of these seminars varies considerably and the credit manager should study the list of speakers before making a choice. Whilst academics are often good speakers, they may not get their message across as clearly as practising credit managers. Learning by participation should be a strong feature of seminars, and here the credit manager can outperform the academic by drawing on his own experience and providing concrete real-life situations as the basis for discussion.

*(c)* Membership of the Institute of Credit Management is essential for anyone intent on a career in credit. Managers should stimulate interest and encourage participation by their staff. Attendance at the local branch meetings is particularly valuable as the circle of acquaintances in the profession is widened.

Over the last two years there has been a rapid growth in the tuition organised by the Institute of Credit Management. Courses are held in the majority of UK colleges for english, accountancy and business law to the standards required for the Intermediate examinations. Evening classes for students in the specialised credit management subjects were arranged by the Institute in 1984 in a total of 16 centres. Tuition is also available by correspondence course through the Rapid Results College, 27–37 St. Georges Road, London SW19 4DS.

**Internal**

*(a)* The kind of training common to all jobs in all firms is 'on-the-job' training. This can be valuable providing it is regarded as part of the overall training programme and not as the sum total of it. A number of credit functions can only be learned by experience. A period of on-the-job training is invaluable in the field of credit assessment and balance-sheet analysis, for example, since these skills are not acquired overnight. The development of sound credit judgment takes time and needs the pressures and conflicts of real situations. A prerequisite for successful experience training is that the credit manager or another senior person should be available to give advice and to criticise and evaluate at regular intervals.

The worst kind of on-the-job training is where the new recruit is sat down next to Nellie and left to learn her methods—mistakes and all.

*(b)* In a department of any size, the credit manager can do a great deal to improve the level of knowledge and performance by arranging internal training sessions on selected subjects. Obvious choices for these seminars are 'How to Make the Best Use of the Telephone as a Collection Tool', 'How to Assess Credit Information and to Interpret Balance Sheets', 'How to Improve Liaison with the Sales Department'.

Every credit department from time to time needs to recruit from outside. If good training programmes have been carried out there will be less need to look outside, but most departments can benefit from new blood occasionally. A problem frequently encountered is whether to recruit an experienced creditman from outside and teach him the company's systems or to take someone already in the company and turn him into a creditman. Whilst no hard and fast rules can be applied, generally speaking the larger the company the more worthwhile it is looking for a likely prospect in another department. Credit people have relationships with a very wide range of functions in the company and a person who is at once familiar with the other employees and with the firm's policies and procedures and also flexible enough to be taught about credit may well be a better choice than the experienced creditman who has to settle into a totally new environment.

A manager is often defined as a person who achieves results through other people. A credit manager can achieve nothing unless he ensures that his team is thoroughly trained and equipped.

# PART II
# CREDIT TERMS

# 4

# Selection of Terms and Conditions of Sale

**Anthony J. Best, former Credit Manager, Mobil Oil Co. Ltd**

## CREDIT TERMS

Within the total profession of credit management it is hard to imagine anything which can be more important than the credit terms which are to be allowed to the buyer by the seller. At first glance it might be considered that the matter of credit terms is a simple one, that either one allows credit or one does not, and if facilities are to be provided, the seller will really have no choice but to offer those which are customary to his particular trade. The fact is that the credit terms decided upon and advised to customers necessarily must be the culmination of careful thought and evaluation, and a great deal will rest on the decision the seller has taken.

There are two reasons why this should be so. The first is that the credit terms decided upon will embody all the major factors and reasons why the seller is in business at all. They will take into account the potential profit expected, the character and limitations of the seller's finances, and the competitive situation. The second is that the terms will establish, in a few brief words, the most important consideration which exists in any sale—the moment when payment is to be in the seller's hands.

To ensure that the seller obtains maximum benefit from the credit terms, it will be necessary for him to insist on their strict observance.

The credit manager's role in the selection and establishment of credit terms clearly must be a key one. No one within a company knows, or should know, as much about credit as he does, and although the terms offered, of course, are a matter of total company policy, those who decide will be wise to take careful note of their credit manager's evaluation of the factors involved, and his recommendations. For this reason the credit manager must be expert in recognising the different considerations and viewpoints which will have a bearing on the selection of terms.

It may be argued that in the case of some businesses, decisions as to credit terms are not in fact given the careful treatment here implied. This may be true, but it is probably just as true to recognise that some managers in less efficient businesses also do not involve themselves in all the important decisions with which they should become involved, if they are to obtain the best marketing results. The fact is that to a small extent, most businesses have at least some room for a degree of error. Some will thrive despite shortcomings in management because strong marketing factors are working in their favour. Whatever the true position about this point may be, one thing is certain: businesses will only operate with maximum success when they are run by professionals who know what they are doing, and who consciously evaluate and act on all the factors which have an influence on the selection of credit terms.

## THE FACTORS INVOLVED

It is worth underlining at this point that the matter of credit terms and the decision as to which to grant, must rest with the seller alone. He is the one with something to sell; he must therefore be the one to decide under what conditions he will part with his merchandise, or whatever it is that he is in business to sell. The principal of all the conditions is of course payment. The buyer is, therefore, not the one to decide the seller's credit terms. It is true that his viewpoint will be important and it may well influence the seller a great deal, but in the end it is the seller who must decide on the facilities he will offer.

Many factors are involved in the selection of credit terms. Their number and relative importance will vary according to the character and type of trade concerned, and traditional factors particularly, will have a major influence on the decision as to which terms to allow. Apart from traditional factors, however, there are others of overriding importance which are likely to be present for most sellers, and they are:

1 The seller's place in the market, and the credit terms on which he is buying from his own suppliers.
2 The availability of the capital he needs to finance his own credit sales, and whether this is to be borrowed and, if so, at what cost; also, the availability of capital to finance the payment of his other overheads.
3 The existence of a buyer's or seller's market.
4 The volumes of sales planned and how these will be spread over his range of customers.
5 The profit margins to be obtained; whether these are to be evenly spread according to type and size of sale, and if major supply positions will involve lower profit margins and possibly special arrangements for settlements including variations to standard terms.
6 The competitive factors. Restricted facilities may be indicated but where competition is offering more advantageous credit terms, it may be justifiable to match them provided that profit margins and safety in exposure are satisfactory. Where practical however, it is better to avoid extending terms.
7 The character of the market.
 (a) The period the buyer will have the goods. For example, if the buyer will resell them at once, payment should be obtained promptly. If the buyer will resell the goods over a period, it is likely that the credit facilities to be allowed will also need to be extended. The same principle applies to sales to consumers.
 (b) The condition of customer finances and the degree of credit risk which credit sales will involve. It must always be remembered that the seller is not only concerned with the monthly total of sales to the customer, but much more with the maximum total exposure which could be outstanding at any one time, and therefore be at risk.
 (c) Seasonal and incentive factors. Seasonally, sales may be greater at certain times in the year than at other times. Incentives to boost sales may include increased credit

facilities. The effect of these on the exposure level, the risk and the cost, will need to be taken into consideration.

8   The existence of any form of cover for the exposure such as a legal charge, guarantee, retention of title or, in the case of a group of companies, a 'letter of comfort' from the parent company.

Each business, whether large or small, has its own special circumstances and conditions which will add to this list. These might include, for example, the degree of complexity or time which is involved in the production of the goods or machinery, or indeed, services for sale; the existence of monopoly factors; the marketing policy of the seller, possibly involving quality considerations; the repetitive character of the sales; their utility or luxury purpose; the degree of sensitivity of the seller's hold on the market; and so on. All these factors and others have a bearing on the nature of the credit terms which will be ideal, and whether they should be liberal or restrictive in character.

The credit terms decided upon, however, must not only be the right ones based on all the factors present, they must also be simple to understand and capable of enforcement. Weekly credit terms, for example, would be meaningless unless the seller and buyer both know and agree on what day the week starts and finishes, and on what day in the week which follows, payment is to be provided. Another example, this time of impractical terms, is: 'payment 15 days after receipt of invoice'. The date of receipt of invoice can only be guessed at by the seller and it would certainly be difficult to prove.

The seller must also consider another problem about credit terms. If he consistently fails to enforce them, and over a considerable period permits payment to arrive late, there is a danger that by this precedent he has established terms which he cannot reasonably change back at a later stage to the original facility he planned, without re-opening marketing negotiations.

## CONDITIONS OF SALE

Conditions of sale are also the prerogative of the seller subject to the protections afforded to the buyer by Act of Parliament. The conditions of sale include credit terms and an interpretation of their meaning where this could be in doubt. Also included are any other conditions relative to payment, resale, guarantees of quality or performance where appropriate, the provisions for the return or replacement of the goods involved, returnable packages, etc.

Parliamentary legislation, of course, has an overriding effect over all trading activities in the form of the Sale of Goods Act, the laws of contract, restrictive trade practices, the Consumer Credit Act, and other legislative areas designed to ensure fair trading, particularly for the benefit of the buyer.

Every sale, in fact, has in it all the ingredients of a contract in the eyes of the law. There is an offer to sell on the part of the seller, and an acceptance by the buyer. Both parties enjoy a consideration and they act voluntarily in the sale, or series of sales, when some form of package deal has been negotiated. Whether on a cash, payment in advance, or credit basis, the contract is there. It may not be in writing, it may not even rely on the spoken word, the sale contract being established only visually without a word being exchanged; but, whatever the circumstances of a normal sale, the offer and acceptance, and the consideration on both sides, is inherent in the transaction.

The point in drawing attention to the contract aspect of sales is of course that credit terms are a part of that contract, and every contract to sell must be free from duress or onerous condition. Near-monopoly conditions which could lead a seller to impose onerous credit terms are, therefore, vulnerable to legal pressure. Similarly, it may be construed that a long-term contract to sell a quantity of goods may not be breached by a single example of slow payment and it may be that the seller must establish a breach of contract by proving the intention of the buyer permanently to delay settlement thereby being in breach.

The seller's conditions of sale for long-term marketing agreements are best established by means of a written contract embracing all the commitments, arrangements and benefits to both sides. For other sales, the conditions are usually confirmed on the seller's delivery note, invoice or statement of account. Where additional establishment of the conditions is desirable this can be done verbally or in a letter acknowledging the order, and laying down the payment terms. In some real businesses, special conditions of sale are notified to customers by means of notices on prominent display. These can prove to be quite adequate, dependent upon the circumstances.

## TYPES OF CREDIT TERMS

Cash sales clearly offer ideal advantage to the seller, for he makes and completes his sale in an instant. The attractions of allowing credit facilities, therefore, are that the seller is able to make sales which would otherwise not be available to him; or that, by offering credit, he builds into the transaction a continuing supply position with his customer by which he obtains a brand of customer loyalty. With these considerations in mind, added to the limiting factors discussed earlier, the seller is ready to decide on the terms he will offer. As a broad principle, however, it is important that he will offer the shortest credit facilities necessary to enable him to secure the sale, and to give him good prospects of continuing his supply position with his customer.

Apart from the great mass of transactions which take place on a cash basis in retail shops and garages, most of the sales between traders, firms and companies are carried out on the basis of 'open account' credit terms. That is to say, credit accounts are maintained by suppliers for those customers who can be expected to reorder frequently. In addition to open account credit, a number of major transactions are handled on the basis of promissory notes, bills of exchange, letters of credit and sight drafts. These are types of documentary instruments of credit which, along with the more usual instruments such as cheques, National Giro and direct debits, are used extensively in the payment of open account credit terms.

## SELECTION OF CREDIT TERMS

The normal range of terms allowed in conjunction with open account credit is as follows, but it should be explained at this point that the term 'cash' usually means cash or cheques. Special intentions in this regard are additionally advised by the seller:

*Payment geared to delivery:*

| | |
|---|---|
| CWO | Cash with order. |
| CIA | Cash in advance. |
| CBS | Cash before shipment (alternatively, pro-forma terms have CBS conditions confirmed by pro-forma invoice). |

| | |
|---|---|
| COD | Cash on delivery. |
| Net | Payment due on delivery. |
| CND | Cash next delivery. |

*Payment geared to time:*

| | |
|---|---|
| Net 7 | Payment seven days after delivery (Net 10 therefore requires payment ten days after delivery, and so on). |
| Weekly credit | Payment of all supplies Monday to Sunday (unless otherwise stated) by a specified day in the next week. |
| Half-monthly credit | Payment of all supplies made in the period 1st to 15th of the month by a specified date in the second half of that month. Payment of the 16th to month end by a second specified date in the first half of the next month. |
| 10th & 15th | International terminology having the same meaning as half-monthly credit but specifying payment by the 10th of the month covering the 16th to month-end supplies and 15th of the month covering supplies made in the first half of month. |
| Monthly credit or 1MO | Payment of the full month's supplies by a specified date in the following month, quite usually the 7th, 10th, 15th, 25th or last working day. |
| Net 7 prox | International terminology, having the same meaning as monthly credit specifying payment to be by the 7th of the month following. |
| Two-monthly credit or 2MO | As for monthly credit plus one extra calendar month. Three-monthly or longer term are indicated by the appropriate figure. |

*Other credit terms:*

| | |
|---|---|
| Journey terms | Where payment is to be made to the representative or van salesman. |

| | |
|---|---|
| Contra terms | Where payment is dealt with by offsetting the value of supplies ordered on a collateral basis. Periodic reconciliation and settlements are necessary. |
| Stage payments | This is an agreement with the customer for equal or specified payments to be made by bank transfer, direct debit or cheque, perhaps each week through each month. In such cases it is best to arrange that the first payment in the month clears exactly the final balance outstanding for the month before. |

NB: As has already been mentioned, an important point not to be overlooked when deciding credit terms is that cheques take two or three days to clear through banks. This also generally applies to direct debits as, although the banking system has the capability of prompt clearance, transfers are currently regulated to the speed of cheques and incoming credits.

## CASH DISCOUNTS FOR EARLY SETTLEMENT

Cash discounts may offer some benefit to both seller and buyer in special circumstances. In this case, the terminology is as follows:

| | |
|---|---|
| 2%/10 or M30 | In this example, 2% discount may be deducted by the buyer on settling within 10 days. Alternatively, the full amount is to be paid in 30 days. Similar discount on monthly credit terms might appear as '2% Net 7 prox, or Net 15 prox', depending on the intention. |

The main considerations for discounts for early payment are, first, the relative financing costs saved to the seller by the early payment versus the cost of the early settlement discount; and, second, the degree of the seller's need for earlier payment due to cash-flow problems.

Whatever the circumstances regarding these matters, early payment discounts will only have a point when the seller can identify clear benefits through their use. To obtain maximum impact, such discounts should, as a principle, be introduced dramatically in the form of a campaign to improve credit. Alternatively, they can be introduced as a customer benefit at a time when prices have to go up, thereby helping to counter a bad effect.

One problem which should not be overlooked about early settlement discounts is that when such a facility does operate, there is a tendency for customers to take the discount whether their payment qualifies or not. It is, therefore, necessary to plan the follow-up policy and procedures very precisely in advance of the introduction of the system.

## CHARGES FOR LATE PAYMENT

There are two views about charges for late payment. The first is that to lay down such charges could be construed as an authority to pay accounts late and be charged for the facility. Where credit exposures and risks are high, this could be the opposite of the impression which a seller will wish to give to the customer. In such cases it may be better to avoid providing for such charges and to insist upon prompt payment.

The other view is that, as there will always be some accounts overdue, the customers concerned should be charged partly to influence them to return to terms, and partly to cover the costs of the unauthorised credit.

The decision to charge or not is a matter for management judgement, and the factors mentioned on pp. 48–50 will all directly bear upon the decision. Normally, charges for late payment are based upon the cost of money plus an additional element for administrative costs.

It is necessary that the arrangements for charges for late payment will have been agreed with the customer in advance, and for the convenience of proof, they should be confirmed in writing preferably in the contract. It is also desirable for a clause to be included in the invoice as a reminder.

There are, nevertheless, instances where an account has become overdue for a substantial sum and no standard arrangements have been made for charges for late payment. In such a case a supplier may for special reasons decide to permit a further period of delay but require an interest charge to cover the additional period of delay. Clearly this would be very reasonable and would be quite regular but should be confirmed and acknowledged in writing.

Generally speaking, on the subjects of both early settlement discounts and late payment charges, a logical approach would be to make provision for both and to introduce a sliding percentage scale based upon the higher discount for very early settlement and the highest charges for very late payment. This concept however would mainly be applicable to sales where there is a high profit margin. Also, computer calculations would be necessary.

A final point concerning charges for late payment is the question of compounding interest charges. This would be a reasonable arrangement provided the basis is clearly established in advance. Otherwise it is usually better when making such charges to open a separate 'late charges' or 'interest' account so that the position will always be clearly understandable and reconcilable.

## PROGRESS PAYMENTS

Progress or stage payments are a means by which a series of part payments can be arranged for major transactions involving considerable outlay of capital and a long period before delivery. The building and heavy-machinery manufacturing trades are good examples where stage payments are appropriate, and they are normally supported by Independent Architect or other certification.

## RETENTIONS

Again, these relate mainly to the building and heavy-machinery trades and involve the retention of a percentage of the purchase price for a period. The purpose is to arrange for the builder or manufacturer to accept a continuing responsibility for the building or machinery he has provided, for a warranty period.

## CONSIGNMENT ACCOUNTS

This term is used to cover the physical transfer of supplies but to leave legal title or ownership with the consignor. By this arrangement the consignee acts as the consignor's agent. There may be good permanent reasons to operate trade on this basis is special conditions and the system also provides a safe way of ensuring security when the finances of the customer are particularly weak. In these circumstances there is a benefit to both parties, as consignment supplies enable the consignee to continue trading and obtain profits, and the consignor to keep alive his supply position and at the same time improve the prospects of a successful outcome in the face of temporary customer difficulties.

A variation to consignment accounts is the 'depletion contract'. The purpose of this is for the seller, as an ongoing arrangement, to agree to keep the customer 'topped up' to an agreed level of supplies, but for the customer only to pay for the amounts used during the period agreed for invoicing. Another variations is the 'stock maintenance contract'. In this case the supplier will maintain an agreed level of stock at the customer locations, based upon a single 'blanket' order, each new consignment being invoiced at the time and payment being due according to the credit terms agreed. It is important to be clear about the moment when title transfers in such cases from the seller to the buyer.

## METHODS OF PAYMENT FOR OPEN-ACCOUNT CREDIT

Whether written into the credit terms or not it is necessary that the method of payment will be acceptable to the seller. Indeed it is often wise to stipulate the form this should take, or to identify those forms it may not take. Settlement by third-party cheque for example is usually not considered a satisfactory arrangement. The normal long-established instruments of payment are, of course, hard cash, cheques and postal orders. These are well understood. In recent years, however, other methods have been added including the direct debit system, the bank telegraphic and telephonic transfer system, and the National Giro. It is appropriate that some comment should be made about these, and indeed about other systems which have already existed for many decades: certified cheques and banker's drafts.

## Direct debit

By this system the seller, with the written authorisation of the buyer to his bank, claims payment direct from the buyer's bank account. It is in effect rather like the cheque system except that the action is carried out by the payee instead of by the payor. It can be operated either on the basis of a fixed amount paid at regular intervals of time like the bank standing order, or the debits can be for varying amounts as and when they become due. In sophisticated computer conditions, the seller can gear up the whole process by the use of magnetic tape passed to the bank instead of having to prepare vouchers for the purpose.

Direct debits completed manually may be preprinted with all the constant information, leaving only the date and amount to be inserted in writing at the time of banking. The direct debit thus made can then be banked with cheques covered by a bank deposit slip. They are in fact no stronger in effectiveness than cheques, since they can be returned due to insufficient funds. The buyer may also stop direct debits not yet presented or withdraw authority at any time for the continued use of the system.

The direct debit system in fact relies on the seller exercising great care and being very conscious of a sense of considerable responsibility. The buyer, by authorising the system to be used, is placing total trust in the seller not to abuse authority and to operate it efficiently within the spirit of the authorisation. The system, provided it is not abused by the seller, offers immense benefits to both sides. The seller is able to obtain payment when due and can release sales representatives to get on with their job of giving better marketing service to their customers. The benefit for the buyer, provided there is no argument about when payment is to be made, is that there is no longer a need to worry about the clerical burden of gearing up payment to his supplier, or to suffer embarrassing encounters with company representatives about slow payment.

The whole system is painless and particularly flexible if it is handled correctly by the seller. The direct debit system is potentially excellent provided the seller operates it in precisely the way authorised by the buyer and provided the buyer is given good opportunity to make contact to deal with accounting queries before the debit is put through.

## Bank telegraphic and telephonic transfer

These systems may appear to those outside banks, to be one and the same as their difference lies only in the method of transmission within the bank communications. There is a minimum sum which may be transferred by the system, currently £10 000, but there is no upper limit.

The customary way to arrange the service is for the buyer to speak to the bank, sending confirmation in writing, to organise that payments will be transferred to the seller's bank account according to the buyer's order from time to time. After the original instruction to the bank, it is not usually necessary for each payment to be actioned by letter, but to follow telephoned instructions. The precise arrangements however depend upon the people immediately concerned and clearly the bank will require complete and safe arrangements. The great value of telegraphic/telephonic transfers is that such payments are for immediate irrevocable value.

## National Giro

This is the banking branch of the Post Office. The service operates a central accounting system but makes full use of all the post offices across the country for the receipt and issue of cash. National Giro caters for the private person and for businesses of all sizes and character. Basically, it operates in much the same way as the banks, with which it has working arrangements, including the deposit of cash in post offices for the credit of bank accounts, and the handling of bank cheques in the same way as banks handle Post Office postal orders.

The service is comprehensive in that it has a Giro cheque system, operates standing-order payments, automatic debit transfers similar to the bank direct debit system, and enables customers to withdraw cash at will from post offices around the country. Currently, it has two strong claims of customer benefit. The first is that post offices are open on Saturdays and for longer periods than the banks. The second is that the transmissions of cash deposited in any branch of the post office are made within twenty-four hours to the customer's Giro account regardless of amount. In the case of banks, unless the system of direct transfer is used (which applies only for major cash movements) the clearing time is from two to three working days except where the place of deposit and account to be credited are local to one another. The National Giro, therefore, has considerable attractions to multiple retail stores where large volumes of cash are handled and where they have central bank or National Giro accounts.

## Certified cheques and banker's drafts

The normal bank cheque is only as good as the financial standing of the person or organisation issuing it. Also, when the cheque has been received it will take two to three working days to know if it has been met, unless special clearance has been arranged, in which case earlier knowledge of clearance can be obtained. The risk of cheques being returned is, therefore, very real, particularly when the financial position of the payer is weak. The only truly safe cheques where this situation exists are those where the cheque is either issued directly by the bank as a banker's draft, or where the customer cheque has been 'certified' by the bank.

The system of certified cheques was officially discontinued many years ago by the clearing banks, but there are instances from time to time of banks 'certifying' customer cheques. This certifies that the customer funds have been set aside to meet the cheque on arrival. Such cheques are usually recognised by the bank signing on the face of the customer cheque adding the word 'certified' and normally rubber stamping the bank name under the bank signature.

Banker's drafts are currently the normal way for banks to issue the equivalent of cheques having the banks' full authority for payment. They usually appear as normal cheques issued directly to the bank concerned. Quite often they show no reference to their customer. One of the problems in the handling of certified cheques and banker's drafts is that they come in a variety of somewhat different forms. This factor may not be difficult for the seller's treasury or credit staff to recognise, but difficulty of recognition is often experienced by delivery men, van salesmen and other field employees.

## OTHER DOCUMENTARY INSTRUMENTS OF CREDIT

The methods of payment so far discussed have been those particularly in use for open-account credit arrangements. Separate from these, however, are transactions involving substantial amounts, particularly for overseas business, which are quite often not dealt with on an open-account basis; or, if they are, require special arrangements for payment other than the normal cheque-type payment.

For this type of transaction a number of other documentary instruments are more suitable in the effecting of payment. The most important of these are promissory notes and bills of exchange. Although the vast majority of credit transactions, particularly inland, are dealt with on an open-account basis, these other documentary instruments of credit cover substantial sums and, therefore, have a significant bearing on the choice of credit terms.

### Promissory notes

This term is self-explanatory. They are usually somewhat similar to postdated cheques and simply comprise a promise on the part of a person or organisation to pay a specific sum which may be of any size, on a specific date. Depending upon the financial standing of the issuer, they have a degree of negotiability in the same way as cheques may have. Promissory notes have two advantages: first, they comprise a specific and unconditional undertaking to make a payment on a future date; second they establish once and for all that the amount involved is in fact due from the buyer.

Promissory notes are mainly used in connection with bank loans. In trading circles their principal value lies in the handling of substantial overdue sums to crystallise such positions and establish future undertakings when a debtor is not currently able to clear a commitment. Promissory notes, incidentally, can be supported by some form of security; in which case they are usually known as 'collatoral notes'.

### Bills of exchange

Unlike a promissory note, which is given by a debtor to the creditor, a bill of exchange is made by the creditor and presented for acceptance to his debtor. The debtor makes the bill effective by his signature after writing 'accepted' across it. Until accepted, it of course has no value. In the same way as in a promissory note, a bill of exchange unequivocally promises payment on a specified date and establishes the payee's entitlement to the sum involved.

The main value and use of bills of exchange these days occurs when they are supported by the guarantee or endorsement of a third party of high financial standing. When this has been obtained they are much more suitable as negotiable instruments and can be discounted with merchant or other banks, or with other commerical concerns having investment finance available. Bills of exchange are widely used in overseas trading or as stage payments for major commercial transactions.

## CONCLUDING CREDIT TERM OBSERVATIONS

Business is always on the move, no matter how difficult or easy the current climate of trading may be. Commerce is alive and active and the influences are continually changing and require different emphasis in handling. The credit manager, therefore, who simply accepts the apparent credit-term practices of the past, or the apparent practices of industry without question, fails to exploit the full value and potential of the responsibilities of credit management, and fails to make important opportunities to advance the credit effectiveness of the company and thus obtain a healthy and beneficial edge over competition.

The credit manager should always keep in mind the options open to the company regarding credit terms, and the way in which they can be deployed to secure full advantage both to the buyer and to the seller. The credit manager should remember that, whether the company is a manufacturer, distributor or retailer, it is not in the banking business. Credit terms granted are always costly and it is, therefore, of considerable importance that they should be the minimum necessary to secure profitable business. The correctness of the credit terms the credit manager allows will undoubtedly be a major contribution to the successful trading of the company.

# PART III

# ASSESSMENT OF CREDIT RISKS

# 5

# Establishing Credit-worthiness

**D. G. S. Williams, Treasurer, Texas Instruments Ltd**

## THE NEED FOR RISK ASSESSMENT: THE INVESTMENT IN TRADE ACCOUNTS RECEIVABLE

The real test of the value of credit management, and that which distinguishes it from mere 'credit control', is its ability not merely to collect overdue accounts or to avoid bad debts, but to enable the company to achieve the maximum overall profitability from trading. To do this in a competitive market environment, it is not usually sufficient for sales to be confined to 'safe' customers, since this by definition excludes the generally significant amount of business to be found from customers who, for one reason or another, are only marginally creditworthy. The credit manager's role in enabling his company to trade successfully with this class of customer, while maintaining financial risk and the consequent losses at an acceptable level, is an essential one if the company is to exploit fully the markets open to it.

In this context it will be apparent that the evaluation of risk becomes of fundamental importance, because without adequate assessment, selective risk-taking in the interests of increasing overall profitability becomes hazardous or impossible. Furthermore, it is an essential prelude to the effective exercise of account collection techniques. No collector, however skilled or experienced, can be fully productive without adequate knowledge of the risks involved in dealing with his customers, since these will largely determine the nature and timing of the required follow-up action. Moreover, provided that risk is properly evaluated before sales commence, it is possible to improve collection prospects by setting terms and regulating shipments in such a way that financially weak customers are not encouraged to become over-extended. Active co-operation between the credit and sales functions to establish suitable terms will do much to facilitate profitable sales, while reducing the likelihood of overdue accounts and an unnecessarily high incidence of bad debts.

## WHO SHOULD BE RESPONSIBLE FOR RISK ASSESSMENT?

It is not uncommon to find companies in which the initial evaluation of customers' credit status and the granting of credit are the responsibilities of the sales or marketing department, while the credit function is left to collect the accounts and to take such steps as may be possible to avoid bad debts when, usually belatedly, an abnormal level of risk is detected. This is obviously a totally unsatisfactory situation, since not only is a sales function generally ill-equipped to carry out financial investigations, but also, since sales managers and representatives are usually measured on the volume of new business generated without regard to ultimate collection of revenue, there is for them an automatic disincentive to operate procedures which may in any way act as a brake on the taking of orders.

The responsibility for risk assessment falls logically into the lap of the credit manager, who will ultimately be held accountable for collection of the debt, and in all probability for failure to do so should the customer become insolvent. These responsibilities must go hand-in-hand, but in order to minimise the conflict which can easily arise between sales and credit through the operation of what can often appear to a marketing man as wilfully restrictive credit practices, it is desirable that there should be a measure of involvement of the sales function in the evaluation process. This applies particularly in cases where the initial assessment by the credit department indicates the likelihood of an above-average risk in trading with the customer. The credit manager's brief must be to find, wherever possible, a way of accepting every potentially profitable order which his company is offered, bearing in mind that profits are made only from business which is taken, and never from that which is turned away.

In order to discharge this responsibility the credit manager must be prepared to work with his marketing colleagues to determine how the customer's requirements can be met within acceptable limits of financial exposure, and this may often require the analysis of prices, profit margins, product availability, competition, etc., in addition to the normal criteria used in assessing credit risk. A credit decision, albeit an unfavourable one, reached with the participation of the sales management, is much more likely to gain acceptance than one arrived at by the credit department alone. The credit assessment should in fact represent a material part of an overall business decision arrived at through a co-ordinated effort between sales, manufacturing, credit, and other company functions, having as its objective an increase in prospective ultimate profit to the company. A credit decision made in isolation and without regard to the other factors mentioned can often, and with justification, be challenged, and the credit manager will always do well to bear this in mind when credit criteria alone indicate the likelihood of a marginal or negative decision.

## SOURCES OF CREDIT INFORMATION AND THEIR USE

The first objective of credit investigation must be to build up as complete and reliable a picture as possible of the customer and his financial condition. To achieve this, information has to be sought from a variety of sources. The extent to which it is economic to pursue credit investigations will obviously be governed by the value of prospective business with the customer, and also by whether it is likely to continue into the future or to consist merely of a single order. Clearly a one-off purchase valued at £150 would not warrant an extended investigation, but should such an order be accompanied by indications of further and larger business, then the sooner enquiries are placed in hand to cover the forecast future commitment with the customer, the better. In this connection, the credit function should look to the sales department for guidance.

### References provided by the customer

Standard practice in the UK, though not by any means universally followed, is to invite a prospective new customer to provide the names of his bank and of two trade referees. This procedure is to be recommended, since it affords the opportunity to obtain from the customer certain additional information which can be of value in setting up the account. It also has the advantage that the supplier's credit department is able to establish its first formal contact with the new customer. It is of course desirable that this should happen at the outset rather than later, perhaps as the result of the account becoming overdue, when the chances of forming a cordial relationship may be less favourable. There is also much to be said in favour of letting the customer realise that the supplier, through his credit department, has both the desire and the means to foster a business-like relationship, and that the matter of granting credit facilities is being given professional attention.

In order to formalise this procedure it is usually desirable to request the customer to complete a form of application for credit account facilities, (see Figure 5:1) in which can be incorporated the supplier's standard credit terms (if any), and also an undertaking signed by the customer that he accepts the terms and will pay in accordance with them. The customer may also be asked to indicate the value of credit (either monthly or overall) which he expects to need. This figure may well differ from the estimate given by the supplier's salesman to the credit department, but in any event it is of considerable help in clarifying the level on which credit enquiries should be based.

### Bank references

An opinion from a British bank can generally be relied upon, and the characteristic wording in which such communications are frequently couched, range from:

'Undoubted'                    —the highest rating normally encountered

To:   (Name and address              Your ref: Credit dept.
      of supplier)

I/We request you to open a credit account in the name of:

. . . . . . . . . . . . . . . . . . . . . . . . . . . . . . . . . . . . . . . . . . . . . . . . . . .
Address  . . . . . . . . . . . . . . . . . . . . . . . . . . . . . . . . . . . . . . . . . .
. . . . . . . . . . . . . . . . . . . . . . . . . . . . . . . . . . . . . . . . . . . . . .

I/We give below the names and addresses of referees of whom the customary trade enquiries may be made.

I/We note your credit terms as set out in your Standard Conditions of Sale and agree to pay in accordance therewith for any goods/services supplied by you.

        Viz.   'All accounts are strictly net and payable
               at the end of the month following the month
               of invoicing.'

Expected maximum            Signature . . . . . . . . . . . . . . . . . . .
amount of credit            . . . . . . . . . . . . . . . . . . . . . . . . . . . .
required    £ . . . . . In all*    (position) . . . . . . . . . . . . . . . . . .
                 Weekly*    (NB: If a partnership, all
                 Monthly*   partners should sign.)
        *Delete non-applicable

Bankers
Name of bank . . . . . . . . . . . . . .    Full branch address
                            . . . . . . . . . . . . . . . . . . . . . . . . . . . . .
                            . . . . . . . . . . . . . . . . . . . . . . . . . . . . .
Trade referees
(1)   Name . . . . . . . . . . . . . . . . .    Address . . . . . . . . . . . . . . . . . . . .
                            . . . . . . . . . . . . . . . . . . . . . . . . . . . . .
(2)   Name . . . . . . . . . . . . . . . . .    Address . . . . . . . . . . . . . . . . . . . .
                            . . . . . . . . . . . . . . . . . . . . . . . . . . . . .

(NB: Trade referees should be in a position to speak for a credit figure comparable with that stated above.)

**Figure 5:1   Request to open a credit account**

*through*

| 'Respectably constituted private (or public) company, considered good for its engagements' | —a good average opinion, suggesting that nothing adverse is known and that the account is satisfactorily conducted |

*down to:*

| 'We regret that we are unable to speak for your figures' | —indicating that the the bank has substantial reservations about its customer's financial situation. |

Needless to say, the intending supplier confronted with the last of these would do well to ponder the advisability of allowing significant unsecured credit, even when other sources indicate a more optimistic view.

In general, the credit assessor must bear in mind that a bank will normally base its report on its own experience only, and that in the context of the customer's overall business activity it may in fact know relatively little. However, on the principle that one source of information complements others, a bank opinion will often help to confirm or otherwise the validity of alternative data, and since it can usually be obtained quickly and at little cost, it should always be sought.

A general question such as 'Is X Ltd good for trade credit?' is likely to be largely a waste of time, being too vague to guide the bank as to what the seller's intention is. Both the proposed amount of credit and the terms should be stated, and if known, the duration of the business, eg:

'Is X Ltd considered good for trade credit of £2500 per month on 30-day terms?'

*or:*

'Is Y Ltd good for credit of up to £15 000 in all on a contract of 12 months' duration with progress payments at 3, 6 and 9 month intervals?'

The bank manager faced with such enquiries as these will have a reasonably clear idea of the commitment which his customer is expected to undertake, and will therefore be in a much better position to give a constructive reply.

If an enquiry is based on a stated amount of credit without indication of the duration involved, the replying banker may sometimes be in a quandary, since he has no means of knowing whether the sum stated will become payable in one amount or over a period. In the case of a customer whose business is a small one, it may appear that the amount is larger than his resources could normally be expected to sustain in a single payment or over a short time, though within scope if paid in instalments over a longer period. In such cases it is customary to give a reply containing an expression such as:

'. . . considered good for your amount if taken in a series'.

*or:*

'. . . preferred in a series.'

This must be taken to indicate some reservations as to the customer's capacity to handle the stated amount at one time or in the immediate future, but with the expectation that the commitment could be met in smaller sums over a period. To avoid any uncertainty to which such a reply might give rise, it is best to clarify the proposed credit terms in the original enquiry as indicated above.

Another commonly found expression in bank replies is the following:

'There are charges registered.'

This statement is frequently made in connection with enquiries on limited companies, and it is an indication that, to the bank's knowledge, its customer has registered with the Registrar of Companies one or more charges over its assets in conformity with Section 96 of the Companies Act 1948. So far as the enquirer is concerned, this may be taken as a reliable indication that the customer has executed a mortgage or other form of charge in favour of a third party as security for a debt.

One final point on bank enquiries; since it is normal practice for banks to reply only to enquiries received from other banks, the usual routine of enquiry and reply is in four stages, as follows:

Enquiry:  Supplier to his bank.
Supplier's bank to buyer's bank.

Dear Sir(s),

We shall be obliged by your opinion, in confidence and without responsibility on your part, as to the suitability of:

(Name and address of prospective customer)

for the following purpose:

Reply may, if desired, be made through our bankers, ABC Bank Limited, (branch address).

Thank you for your assistance in this matter.

Yours faithfully,
For XYZ Limited

Credit Manager

**Figure 5:2    Specimen text of enquiry letter to customer's bank**

Reply:      Buyer's bank to supplier's bank.
            Supplier's bank to supplier.

It is possible to eliminate one of these stages, with probable saving of time and possibly also bank charges, if the supplier sends his enquiry direct to the buyer's bank with an invitation to reply via the supplier's bank, which should of course be named. The text of a suitable enquiry letter for use in these circumstances is given in Figure 5:2.

## Trade references

These, the second source of information usually obtained direct from the customer, are regarded by some credit managers with the same degree of scepticism as bank enquiries, on the supposition that an uncreditworthy customer is unlikely to quote the names of suppliers who are liable to give adverse information. While it has been known for traders with generally bad paying habits to keep one or two suppliers 'sweet' for purposes of obtaining good trade references, the practice is probably not sufficiently widespread to invalidate this source of information. The observation by the enquirier of a few commonsense precautions can result, in most cases, in the gleaning of useful indications as to the prospective customer's payment practices.

If possible enquiries should be confined to referees who allow credit on terms and to a level comparable with that proposed by the new supplier. A suitable reminder in the credit application form (see Figure 5:1) should assist in eliciting suitable names. However, this may not always be possible, and the credit manager will have to determine in each case whether references are likely to be productive or not. The following guidelines should be noted:

1   If the referees named are companies of 'national name' standing or are particularly well-known in the supplier's industry, referencs should always be followed up. The opinion of the credit department of such a company is always worth having, and will not infrequently contain useful background information which may be of value in the overall credit assessment.

2   If a referee is a concern which is unknown to the supplier, it is desirable for its identity and standing to be established with reasonable certainty. The opinion of an unknown referee must naturally be of limited value, and where substantial credit is envisaged it is worth taking some trouble to ascertain whether there is any undisclosed association between the potential customer and the referee.

3   The enquirer should do everything possible to make it easy, quick and economic for the referee to reply, and to ensure that relevant information is obtained. This can best be done through the medium of a reply pro-forma (see Figure 5:3), which should be printed on the reverse side of the enquiry letter. The referee whose task is made easy in this way is more likely to reply promptly and to give the desired information than if he has to expend time and effort composing a letter. Wherever possible alternative replies to questions should be embodied in the pro-forma so that it can be completed in a few moments with the

| | Please reply in the column below, deleting where necessary |
|---|---|
| 1 How long has the subject of enquiry been known to you? | ..... months ..... years many years |
| 2 If a recently opened account, were satisfactory references given? | Yes/No |
| 3 What amount do you customarily allow on credit? | £...... |
| 4 On what terms? | Cash only Weekly Monthly On ..... terms |
| 5 Are payments made regularly and in accordance with your terms? | Prompt Slow Very slow |

6 Please give any other relevant information below:

The above information is given in strict confidence and without responsibility on my/our part.

Date          198 ....     (Signature) ................

**Figure 5:3  Specimen reply pro-forma to customer's referee**

minimum of trouble. In particular, it is a good idea to provide a space for the referee's own comments in addition to the standard questions, as frequently this is used to supply helpful supplementary information. Above all, the enquirer should enclose a pre-addressed, prepaid envelope for the reply. Experience with this type of enquiry medium shows a high percentage of prompt response, and the method is strongly recommended.

## Suppliers other than trade referees quoted by customer

Information from these can be useful as a cross-check on opinions offered by the quoted referees, especially if it is suspected that the latter may for any reason fail to give an impartial report.

## Competitors

This is the third variety of trade referee which is available to the credit manager in his search for information, and it is without doubt potentially one of the most valuable. If proof of this is needed, one has only to consider the wide use made of credit interchange, as it is called, in the USA. In that country, under the auspices of the National Association of Credit Management, hundreds if not thousands of groups of credit managers meet constantly to exchange opinions and experience on conditions and trends within their own industries. The personal contacts so established create a near-perfect environment for the confidential exchange of opinions. As a result, the type of enquiry which in the UK would generally be the subject of a formalised written request for a trade opinion, and in continental Europe is hardly known at all, can in the USA be conducted over the telephone or face-to-face between credit managers who, although working for competing companies in the same industry, are able to converse freely and in the mutual knowledge that confidence will be respected.

There is obviously much scope for British credit managers to derive the same benefits from credit interchange as do their US counterparts, and in fact during the last few years there has been some progress here towards establishing credit groups within specific industries. Every credit manager should try to find out if such a group exists within his own industry, and if so, to join it as soon as possible, although it has to be said that at the time of writing the number of such groups in the UK is still quite small. Even where no group exists, however, it is perfectly feasible for any credit manager to establish contact with his opposite number in competitor companies. A good opportunity to do this may be when a prospective customer offers the name of one of the supplier's competitors as a trade reference. The normal enquiry letter can be sent, but it is much better for the credit manager to telephone his competitor and put the enquiry verbally. This will in all probability prove much more productive than the written enquiry would have done, but even more important will be the chance to establish a useful working contact for the future. The community of interest which can exist between credit managers operating in the same market and facing the same problems is usually not realised until discussion actually takes place. When it does, the benefits of such professional trade contacts are quickly appreciated. The credit manager who is a member of the Institute of Credit Management does of course enjoy a special advantage in this respect, since through this professional body he has a ready-made channel of introduction not only to his fellow members in the same industry, but to those in many others as well.

## Credit reporting agencies

It follows that where sources of information are meagre, as with a very recently established business, one cannot expect a reporting agency to produce a comprehensive report, since the material to do so is just not available. The subscriber should therefore tend to think of agency reports as either:

1 A reasonably quick and easily accessible summary of some (but probably not all) obtainable information; or

2 One of several channels which can be tapped to ensure maximum visibility and to cross-check other sources, particularly in cases where a large sales volume is anticipated, and extensive coverage is therefore necessary.

The first of these, if taken in conjunction with bank and trade references supplied by the customer, may be considered sufficient to justify a decision to allow credit up to a relatively modest level (perhaps £3000/4000) provided that the desired amount appears within scope, none of the sources consulted reveals any adverse indication, and there are no material inconsistencies between the opinions given. When large business is expected, it is better to have some duplication of information than too little, with the consequent risk that some vital factor may be overlooked. The prudent assessor will in such cases call for an agency report, which, although in much of its content may merely confirm what is already known, may provide some unique information or indicate the need for further enquiry in certain directions. The section below, which indicates the likely content headings of an agency report, will when taken in conjunction with other parts of this chapter show how the report can help to supplement and cross-check other data, and vice versa. The agency report usually contains some of the following elements:

1   Full name and registered address of subject.
2   Names of proprietors, partners, or directors.
3   Nature of business. Location of branches, factories, etc.
4   Authorised and issued capital.
5   Whether associated with other companies as parent, subsidiary or as part of a group.
6   Main features of latest annual report (usually for publicly quoted companies only).
7   Annual turnover.
8   Abbreviated balance-sheet details including profit and loss account balance.
9   Secured charges registered including dates and names of secured parties.
10   Amounts and dates of any recently registered county court judgements or other distresses.
11   Opinions of a selection of known suppliers detailing amounts of credit allowed, terms and payment experience.
12   Banker's opinion (normally indicated as that of 'a usually reliable source').
13   Agency's suggestion as to amount of credit which would appear within scope, and comment on figure (if any) proposed by enquirer. Recommendation as to advisability of assurances or care in dealings with subject.

It may be thought that the above range of information should be sufficient in itself to enable a credit assessment to be made without recourse to other sources. This might be so (at least for credit up to a moderate level) were every agency report to contain all the quoted data in a complete, accurate and up-to-date form. Regrettably, experience has shown that this is often not the case. Because of the varying availability of information, notably (as mentioned above) on recently established concerns, some reports will be found to be quite comprehensive, while others, even from the same agency, will contain little more than name, address and registration information. For purposes of credit assessment such reports are, of course, almost useless, and the credit analyst will be obliged to turn to other channels if he is to carry out his task effectively.

Probably the most serious shortcoming of the agency reporting system arises from inaccuracies due to inadequate or superficial updating of information retained on file from previous reports. The reproduction of such material in a currently dated report can sometimes go undetected except through cross-checking from other sources. As an example, cases have occurred where suppliers' experiences given in a report furnished one or two years earlier were repated verbatim as if they had resulted from current enquiries. More seriously, a company which was formerly a subsidiary of a well-known and financially impeccable parent was still quoted as such, although in fact ownership and control had passed to a much less creditworthy concern more than two years prior to the report date. The implications of errors of this kind to the subscriber who relies exclusively on agency reports for his credit information hardly need stressing, and underline the need for multiple lines of enquiry wherever a major credit decision has to be taken. The recipient of an agency report who detects such material errors should of course draw them to the attention of the agency concerned immediately, and should insist not only on a fresh report, but also on an explanation as to why he should have received potentially misleading information. Unless both are promptly forthcoming he should give serious consideration as to the advisability of changing his agency.

**Agency rating books**

This is an additional service of one or two major reporting agencies, which provides a valuable fund of immediately available credit-status information, albeit of an abbreviated nature. The best known of these is the *Dun & Bradstreet Register,* which covers the whole of the British Isles in several large volumes each relating to a particular geographical area; the subscriber may take one or more volumes according to his need. Within each volume, the area is subdivided, usually by town or city, and under each such heading are listed in alphabetical order the names of numerous trading concerns operating in that location. Information provided includes address, trade, date of formation or registration, authorised and paid-up capital and indication of any registered charges (if a limited company), name of the proprietor or parent company, name and branch of bankers, and finally a code letter from which the subscriber may form a general estimate of whether the amount of credit which he is being asked to provide is within the normal scope of the subject's known operations. Periodic supplements are mailed to subscribers giving additions and amendments to the main body of the Register.

The principal value of agency-rating books is the immediate availability of information, as for example where an order is received from a new customer and prompt delivery is required leaving insufficient time for the normal process of credit enquiry. In such cases, if the initial order is relatively small, it may be sufficient that the value is seen to be within the credit rating indicated in the rating book, or perhaps that the customer is identified as being associated with a larger company of substance. If it is then decided to release the order, this will have a positive value in that the customer's immediate requirements will have been satisfied, and subsequent enquiries may be pursued without undue haste. It is a good plan to follow up the initial shipment with a letter to the customer, advising that his order has been executed and inviting him, if he expects to place further business with the seller, to apply for credit facilities in the usual way. This should convince the customer of the seller's good faith, and co-operation in providing any desired credit-status information is more likely to be forthcoming than if the first order had been held pending full enquiry.

## Company annual and interim reports (public companies)

This is one of the most easily accessible and least expensive sources available to the credit investigator seeking information on a company whose shares have a Stock Exchange quotation. The report of any publicly quoted company may be obtained at no cost merely by requesting it from the company secretary or registrar, or (if it is desired to conceal the identity of the enquirer) through the medium of a bank. Many such reports not only contain the expected financial statements and accompanying data, but are also useful books of reference to the overall operations of the companies and their subsidiaries. It will often be found that, for a company of this kind, the published annual report will be a more comprehensive basic source of information than an agency report, which itself will usually consist largely of information gleaned from the company's own publication. It may be considered better to obtain the latter in full and free of charge than to pay for an agency report containing only a small part of it.

## Press comment

While a company annual report may be obtained at any time, it is of course most relevant when newly published, and some companies issue interim reports at half-yearly intervals to give their shareholders an account of progress. These may also be obtained in the same way as annual reports. Both annual and interim financial results of major companies are usually published in the daily press, and the *Financial Times,* or the business section of some other responsible daily paper, is required reading for the credit manager. While the publication of company results on the day after their issue is valuable, even more significant is the informed comment which often accompanies them, and this may well still be relevant for several months after is actually appears. It is good practice to extract such material (taking care to annotate it with date and source) and place it on file for future reference together with other status information relating to the customer.

## Historic financial data on companies

Where significant or substantial credit is to be extended, it is usually desirable for the credit analyst to have knowledge not merely of the most recent financial status of the company under investigation, but also of how this compares with the performance of earlier years. The published accounts of publicly-quoted companies contain profit and loss account and balance sheet information both for the year being reported and for the immediately preceding year. This, however, is not always sufficient for purposes of perceiving longer-term trends which may be of greater importance in assessing credit status than variations between one year and the next.

The task of comparison is greatly facilitated when, as is sometimes the case, the company report includes tables showing sales volume and related financial information over a period of five or ten years prior to the date of the current report. Where these are not given, a useful alternative source is the statistical card service of Extel Statistical Services Ltd (a subsidiary of Extel Group plc). These cards provide in a concise form the principal features of the published annual reports for the current and past several years of almost all companies quoted on the British and Irish Stock Exchanges, those traded in the unlisted securities market, and also a large number of the leading unquoted companies. Interim figures, where published, are covered by the card service, as are details of noteworthy events which take place between the issue of one formal company report and the next, e.g. a takeover of or by another company, or a rights issue to shareholders. Cards may be obtained on a subscription basis for a selection of named companies, by geographical location, or by industry. Updating is frequent—many cards are updated daily, and the remainder weekly, so that the subscriber is automatically provided with regularly revised information on the companies in which he is most interested.

## Stock Exchange opinion

While it is generally possible to obtain a good idea of the company's overall financial condition from its annual report, it is helpful in some cases to have informed comment from an independent source. One of these, though not generally available as a public service, is the opinion of a stockbroker, particularly one who has frequent dealings in the shares of the company concerned and may therefore be expected to have a degree of specialised knowledge. The stock market and those who operate in or close to it are very sensitive to information which may cause movements in share prices, and a credit manager who has access to a stockbroking firm may occasionally be able to obtain a useful and expert opinion as to the fortunes of a quoted company in which he has an interest. Where no such contact exists, it is worth asking a banker to obtain an opinion through its head office stock and share department. Most of the UK joint stock banks deal on behalf of their customers with a range of broking houses, and although a broker will normally give an opinion in the expectation that some business may result, a good customer of the bank will normally be accorded this service on an occasional basis without demur. It is worth mentioning that some specialist stockbrokers periodically issue excellent surveys of quoted companies in which they have a special interest, and although these usually have a restricted circulation, a helpful bank may be able to secure one on request. Such a publication can provide a valuable addition to the credit investigator's information dossier on his customer.

## Companies Registry search

The quest for financial information on the smaller limited company is frequently more difficult than in the case of larger enterprises. Prior to the 1967 Companies Act, many smaller limited companies qualified as 'exempt private companies' which, *inter alia*, meant that they were not obliged to file annual accounts with the Registrar of Companies, and were thus able to keep knowledge of their financial status secret from the world at large. With the passage of the 1967 Act, this privilege was lost, and since the accounts of all limited companies, irrespective of size, are required to be lodged with the Registrar each year with the annual return and thus become a matter of public record. It is therefore possible, in theory at least, for the credit investigator to have access to the latest annual report and accounts of any limited company by means of a search at the Companies Registry. However, with the passage of the Companies Act 1981 to meet the EEC Fourth Directive on accounts, new company reporting and publication requirements were introduced. These clearly defer to continental practices in that, if a company meets certain criteria, it may omit some information from its published accounts which it was previously required to include, although a second set of accounts must still be prepared for shareholders which must contain all the statutory information. The following is a brief guide to the exemptions:

1   Public limited companies and those involved in banking, shipping or insurance, either directly or through subsidiaries, are not eligible for any exemption.
2   For other companies, the following are the criteria which may qualify for exemption:

Small—Turnover up to £1.4m. Balance sheet total up to £0.7m. Average employees per week up to 50.
Medium—Turnover up to £5.75m. Balance sheet total up to £2.8m. Average employees per week up to 250.

To qualify, a company or group must satisfy at least two of the criteria for both the current and the previous year. In such cases, accounts filed at the Companies Registry may be found to omit certain information, most notably the profit and loss account and/or the analysis of turnover. From the credit analyst's point of view this can limit the value of a Companies Registry search. Furthermore, a proportion of searches may in any case prove abortive because many companies, either through oversight or as a matter of policy, delay the filing of their annual returns for so long that for credit assessment purposes the information when found is too out-of-date to be of real value. Despite these reservations, the Companies Registry can still provide some valuable information in addition to the published accounts, such as the names of directors and principal shareholders; the names of other companies in which the directors may have an interest; and in particular, details of mortgages and charges against the company's assets which are required to be registered in accordance with the Companies Acts. These usually constitute the best evidence of the existence of secured creditors whose claims would, in the event of the company's being placed into receivership or liquidation, have to be met in full before any distribution could be made to unsecured trade and other creditors.

## Company accounts

A study of the final accounts—profit and loss account and balance sheet—of a limited company can provide the credit analyst with an extremely valuable insight as to its likely creditworthiness when taken in conjunction with other sources of information. The higher the credit figure which is in prospect, the more desirable it is to have some direct financial knowledge of the customer, and as a rough guide it can be said that for amounts above £15 000/£20 000, irrespective of trade, the examination of balance sheets should be standard practice. For smaller amounts, balance sheets should still be scrutinised if readily available, as their possession can only help to make the results of risk evaluation more accurate. As with other sources of credit information, however, the credit· investigator should be warned against reading too much into a balance sheet alone; other data, and in particular some knowledge of the customer and his business, are usually necessary to add perspective to the view which the balance sheet offers.

As already mentioned, it is usually not difficult to acquire current and past balance-sheet information on public companies, but because of the delays which sometimes occur in the filing of returns at the Companies Registry, it can be less easy to obtain reasonably up-to-date accounts of private companies, particularly the smaller ones. The importance of seeing accounts while they are still current cannot be over-emphasised, and because of this it is often preferable to make a direct request to the customer for balance sheets, using the Companies Registry search only if the customer is unco-operative. The direct approach also gives an opportunity to ask for a full set of final accounts, rather than the abbreviated ones which (as mentioned above) some smaller companies may file at the Companies Registry by virtue of the statutory exemptions. It may be pointed out to the hesitant customer, first, that any information furnished, including balance sheets, will be treated as strictly confidential; and second, that disclosure is in the customer's own interest since with the evidence of a sound financial footing before him the credit manager can generally take a more positive and flexible attitude to the granting of credit than would otherwise be the case. A reasoned approach will often persuade the customer unless, of course, his financial status is such that a sight of the balance sheet would tilt the scales firmly against him. As a last resort, it is worth reminding the customer that since all companies must by law file accounts with the Company Registry, he has nothing to lose by disclosure.

## INTERPRETATION OF ACCOUNTS

It is desirable that the credit investigator should be reminded of the indicators which the balance sheet and profit and loss account can provide to the financial health of a business and which, when placed alongside data obtained from other sources, can help materially in the assessment of the overall risk involved in granting trade credit.

The value of balance-sheet analysis lies in the comparison, first, of various figures relative to the business at a particular date; and second, of the same figures with those for preceding years in order to ascertain the trend, whether favourable, static, or unfavourable. It must always be kept in mind that a business is a dynamic thing in which changes are constantly occurring, while a balance sheet shows the financial position at a single point in time. It can therefore be misleading to deduce too much from a single year's figures without knowing whether they compare favourably or unfavourably with those of earlier years. Nevertheless, even a single audited balance sheet (which will always show figures for the immediately preceding period) is better than nothing, and gives some opportunity to assess the soundness of the underlying situation.

The statistical result of the comparison of one final account figure with another is termed a 'ratio'; the comparison of any ratio with the same ratio for a different accounting period indicates a 'trend'. Both ratios and trends are important to analysts, but for the trade–credit investigator some are more important than others; a few, which we may term 'key ratios', are sometimes sufficient in themselves to establish a favourable or unfavourable verdict for the purposes of credit risk assessment, irrespective of the remainder. Listed below are some of the ratios commonly studied by analysts, with an indication of those which are usually key ratios for purposes of trade credit management.

### Profit/net assets

Indicates the management's degree of success in utilising assets to generate profits, i.e. in running a viable business. The profit figure should include both operating profit and other income, after depreciation charges but before interest and tax (note the importance of obtaining both balance sheet and profit and loss account, as without both, this and the next few ratios cannot be calculated).

### Profit/sales

Indicates efficiency or otherwise in running the whole business (manufacturing, selling, administration) and in particular in keeping overheads under control. Especially significant in a period of declining sales, when it may require skill and determination on the part of management to reduce overheads in the same proportion as the reduction in sales, and so avoid a worsening in the profit/sales ratio.

### Sales growth

Current year's sales as percentage of prior years. A figure less than 100% (decline in sales) may be significant in relation to a worsening of profit/sales.

### Profit growth

Current year's profit as percentage of prior years. Compare with sales growth.

### Sales/net assets

Indicates effectiveness in use of assets to generate sales. Generally, an improving ratio between one year and the next is favourable— but only if the sales are profitable.

### Sales/fixed assets

Can indicate efficiency in utilisation of premises, plant, equipment in the business. A high ratio can also suggest a labour-intensive rather than a capital-intensive business, and may help to explain a profit/sales ratio (see above) which is lower than expected for the industry.

### Sales/net current assets (key ratio)

A measure of success in employment of working capital (net current assets = current assets less current liabilities). However, an excessively high ratio, or a very rapid rate of increase, may warn of overtrading, i.e. selling on a scale for which the working capital base is inadequate. A business operating under these conditions has above-average vulnerability to slowing down of payments by trade debtors, reduction of bank overdraft facilities, or an unexpected downturn in sales, any of which may leave the company with insufficient liquidity to pay its own creditors. The prudent credit manager will always beware of over-commitment to such customers.

### Sales/net worth (key ratio)

Another important indicator in detecting overtrading (Net worth = total assets less liabilities other than to the company's own proprietors; in other words, the total of paid-up capital plus reserves.) When estimating net worth it is important to discount the book value of any intangible or fictitious assets, for instance goodwill or formation expenses, since in all probability these would realise little or nothing, particularly in a forced break-up of the company. It is also desirable to ensure that a conservative valuation is placed on inventory (stock) as in a break-up situation this might realise only a fraction of its book value.

### Sales/inventory (or stock)

Gives a rough guide to the period for which inventory is held (e.g. a 4:1 ratio indicates a three-month inventory turn); but this may not be uniform through the year due to seasonal and other variations.

Should be judged according to the nature of the trade. A higher ratio than average for the type of business suggests success in moving stocks quickly. Bear in mind that slow or non-moving inventories tie up funds and erode profits.

### Fixed assets/total assets

In general, fixed assets are those which create sales and therefore should be viewed as profit generators. This ratio will normally be higher in a manufacturing than in a non-manufacturing business not using plant, machinery, etc. Compare with profit growth to judge if fixed assets are being used productively.

### Inventory/net current assets

Important in assessing whether too much working capital is tied up in materials, work-in-progress, finished goods. Needs to be adequate in relation to the nature of the business and to sales volume, but not excessive compared with other current assets. May be subject to seasonal variations in certain businesses, but a constantly inflated stock level makes inroads into both available funding and profits. A rising trend may denote an accumulation of obsolescent stock or poor control over acquisition of raw materials and components.

### Current liabilities/net worth (key ratio)

Since net worth represents the value of the proprietors' stake in the business, this ratio is a measure of the protection offered to outside creditors. If current liabilities are several times covered by the net worth, there would be reasonable prospects in a break-up of all creditors being paid in full. However, it must be remembered that some creditors may be secured, and that their claims must be fully met before the unsecured trade creditors receive any distribution at all; thus this ratio must be considered in the light of any available information about the company's secured indebtedness. Also, to be fully valid, the net worth must be assessed on a conservative basis (see section on sales/net worth).

## Trade debtors/sales (key ratio)

This gives a guide to the average period taken to collect money due from customers. It must be construed in the light of the terms of business customary in the particular trade or industry, e.g. a ratio of 1:4 representing debtors of one-quarter of a year's sales, or a three months' average collection period, would be acceptable in a trade where terms of 90 days are normal practice, whereas in a business with standard terms of 30 days, a 1:4 ratio would indicate a severe over-investment in trade receivables. For the prospective supplier this kind of situation can be a sign of possible trouble, since it is common for businesses with poor control of their trade debtors to try to redress the balance by taking long credit from their suppliers. Where this ratio appears adverse, note should be taken of the trend over two or three years. If it is static or deteriorating, the prospective supplier would be well advised to be satisfied as to how he will control the account before entering into any substantial commitment.

## Current assets/current liabilities

An index of the company's available working capital—the so-called 'current ratio'. A ratio of 2:1 or more is usually considered satisfactory, but anything less needs further scrutiny. It must be remembered that not all current assets are equally liquid, and the constituents may need to be assessed individually. If a high proportion is represented by cash or near-cash items, this is encouraging, but in practice this is not often the case. A current ratio which at first sight appears adequate can sometimes prove illusory because some or most of the current assets either could not readily be turned into cash or are shown in the balance sheet at a valuation which is unlikely to be realised. The most common example is a high stock figure, which on investigation can be found to reflect overlarge inventories of raw materials or parts, or of slow-moving finished goods; or even of work-in-progress which cannot be completed due to lack of some essential component or because of order cancellations by customers. When examining the current ratio it is also worth considering the possible effect of the different current liabilities. It is as well to assume that most trade creditors will have to be paid in the near future—say within 60 days. A bank overdraft, although generally repayable on demand, may in the case of a healthy business be allowed to run on indefinitely, but where the overall financial picture is weak this should not be relied upon. Corporation tax may not have to be paid for a year or more—but it is as well to be sure that the tax figure does not include any arrears. It will be seen that the current ratio can pose a number of questions, and it may be unwise to rely too much on the ratio alone in any particular year's figures. The trend is probably a more useful indicator to an improving or worsening working capital situation.

### Liquid assets/current liabilities (key ratio)

The most important ratio for the credit assessor in determining company liquidity, and more valuable than current assets/current liabilities for this purpose. (Liquid assets = current assets less stock and any other items which cannot or may not be readily turned into cash.) If a high proportion of the remaining current assets represents trade debtors, it is important to ensure that an adequate reserve for bad or doubtful debts has been allowed. If short-term loans are included, the identity and status of the borrower should be known before the figure is regarded as readily realisable. Provided a conservative view is taken of all such items, this ratio is the best guide to the company's ability to pay its way on a short-term basis, and as such is of critical interest in the overall credit assessment.

Most of the ratios commonly examined in the course of balance-sheet analysis are covered by the above categories. The credit assessor will be well advised to pay particular attention to the key ratios first, as it may often be found that these will be sufficient in themselves to allow a constructive evaluation of the customer's financial position to be made and in consequence the remainder need not necessarily be analysed in detail.

## CUSTOMER VISITS

As the credit assessor reviews the information which he has gathered from various sources, and particularly after the final accounts have been analysed, it can happen that he is still unable to arrive at a satisfactory conlusion as to the customer's credit-worthiness for the amount of business proposed. It may be that there are relevant facts unascertained or questions arising from the balance-sheet analysis unanswered. In such cases, especially where a worthwhile volume of business is at stake, a visit by the credit manager (or by an experienced assistant) to the customer's premises can be of immense value in the interpretation of the assembled data and in filling any gaps which may exist. Even more important is the opportunity offered by a visit to view the reality of the business itself and to meet the people running it. However comprehensive the information supplied by reporting agencies, banks, etc., and however up-to-date the financial picture shown by balance sheets, there is no substitute for the personal visit in enabling the credit manager to acquire the overall impression of a business in action, and above all the confidence factor which can be so greatly influenced by meeting with the directors and management, particularly of a company still in the early stages of its development.

When arranging to visit a customer for credit-status evaluation purposes, the credit manager will sometimes do well to invite the sales manager to accompany him. This can be beneficial in a number of ways, the most important of which is that the sales manager will have the opportunity to observe for himself the scenario at which the credit manager will be looking, and will therefore be in a position not only to understand the reasons for the eventual credit decision, but also in many cases to contribute to it himself. It need hardly be said that such a decision is much more likely to gain acceptance by the sales department as a whole than one arrived at unilaterally by the credit manager, particularly if the verdict is less favourable than had been hoped for. Another significant benefit of the joint sales/credit visit is the demonstration to the customer that both sales and credit managers are working together in order to facilitate the granting of credit appropriate to his needs. This can be good from the customer relations aspect, and can also forestall any attempt by the less creditworthy customer to exploit in his own favour what might otherwise be seen as a division between the sales and credit functions of the supplying company. Lastly, the sales manager can often be of assistance to his credit colleague in confirming details of pricing, delivery dates, etc., as well as providing technical information about products, which might sometimes be relevant to the discussion but with which the credit manager himself may be unfamiliar.

Much of the benefit of a customer visit can be lost if the meeting takes place wholly in the office of a director or one of the management. The credit manager should make every effort to see as much for himself as possible, bearing in mind that in addition to the specific questions which he may wish to ask, it is also desirable that he should carry out a realistic appraisal of the business as a whole. With this as his objective, he will be looking at, for example, the following:

1  Are the customer's premises situated in an improving, static or declining area?
2  Are they new or old, in good repair or dilapidated?
3  Is there good access to main road and rail links, and are there any indications that these may improve or worsen in the foreseeable future?
4  Do the premises have adequate space to allow for expansion if necessary?
5  Is the visitors' reception area adequate and are visitors dealt with expeditiously?
6  Is the administration area adequate in size for the number of staff, and do working conditions appear satisfactory? Does the area give the impression of being well organised; it is well lit and heated/ventilated, and is office equipment of good standard?
7  Does the production area seem well organised and does the workforce appear to be employed productively? If machinery and equipment are used, is it modern or old, well-maintained or otherwise?
8  Does the production process seem to flow smoothly, or is there evidence of bottlenecks? Is it possible from an inspection of work in progress to judge the quality of workmanship or materials used?
9  Is the finished goods area well laid out? Is there evidence of any significant accumulation of obsolete stock, or of shortage of current production? Does the finished product look to be of good quality?
10  Are finished goods shipped out by the customer's own transport? If so, are the vehicles hired or owned?

11 If the latter, are there adequate maintenance and parking facilities? Are the vehicles modern and adequate for their purpose?

12 Do management and directors work in suitable office accommodation, and does the standard of this contrast greatly with that of the remainder of the office area?

The above list is not exhaustive, but is indicative of the kind of information which a customer visit can readily produce, and which can give overall a useful impression as to whether the business is in good shape or otherwise.

One final comment on this important aspect of the risk-evaluation programme: whom should the credit manager endeavour to meet during his visit? The answer will be determined to some extent by the size of the customer's organisation. In the case of a sole trader or partnership, obviously no one but the proprietor(s) can be expected to provide adequately all the answers to the questions which are likely to be asked. If the customer is a small limited company, the interviews will probably all need to be at board level and should normally include one with the managing director. Moving up the scale, the usual choice in a medium-sized company will probably be at the company secretary/financial director level, possibly also including the purchasing director or manager if terms of business have to be discussed. In the largest companies, the interviewing need not necessarily be at board level, but the credit manager should aim at meeting those who are likely to be able to give both reliable information about the company and also, where desired, firm commitments about the manner and timing of payments. Probable candidates would be the financial controller, chief accountant, or treasurer (should the company have one). The most important single need, especially with the smaller or recently-formed company, is to gain a feeling of confidence in the people running the business. The customer may be a limited company, but a successful business relationship depends on people, and unless confidence in them is established, the prudent credit manager may remain unconvinced about committing his company to the granting of substantial trade credit, irrespective of the amount of favourable comment which he may have obtained from third-party sources.

# 6

# Credit Limits and Risk Categories

**D. G. S. Williams, Treasurer, Texas Instruments Ltd**

## WHY HAVE RISK CATEGORIES?

When all the available information on the prospective customer has been assembled, the decision regarding the amount and terms of credit will have to be taken. It is common practice for a financial credit line or limit to be established which attempts to reflect simultaneously the overall level of confidence in the customer's capacity and intention to meet his obligations, and also the amount of credit which, taking into account the payment terms, may have to be extended in order to accommodate the orders likely to be placed. At times these two considerations can conflict, so that neither is properly satisfied. The better course is to classify each account, dependent upon the overall assessment, into a risk category which should be quite independent of the actual amount of credit to be granted. This procedure has the following advantages:

1  Credit limits can be fixed initially, and if necessary be subsequently changed according to the needs of sales, and to the amounts which the selling company is prepared to have outstanding in the various risk categories from time to time. No change in credit limit need, however, denote an increase or diminution of the risk factor.

2  By establishing a range of risk categories according to various definitions, the different levels of risk recognised by the company

are clearly codified and may be easily understood by anyone familiar with the system. This is far superior to the vague and ill-defined descriptions of risk which are commonly found where no formalised system of categories exists.

3    The identification of graded levels of risk by means of a series of single digits or letters means that the information can readily be stored in computer files both for record purposes and to facilitate selective reporting. Thus it is a simple matter to produce, from a computerised sales ledger, exception reports showing not only accounts which are in an overdue or overlimit condition, but also (as separate reports if necessary) those of such accounts which fall into the higher-risk categories, and which therefore represent an unacceptable degree of financial exposure. Such reports can be a valuable management tool for controlling the overall levels of risk in the receivables portfolio.

4    Since accounts representing various levels of risk demand different follow-up and control procedures, it is convenient to establish a standard procedure for each risk category. The credit manager will then know that a follow-up timetable and controls on (for example) the acceptance of new orders and shipments against existing ones, are operative for each category; and those of his staff responsible for handling the accounts will be aware of the limits of their authority. This is a very desirable refinement of the more normally practiced methods of account control, which generally give little or no recognition to degrees of risk beyond an occasional 'watch' instruction on the account record.

## HOW MANY RISK CATEGORIES?

In order for the system to be effective, there must be sufficient categories to allow an adequate grading of risk, but not so many that the distinction between one level of risk and another becomes unclear. In practice this will usually mean not fewer than three risk categories and not more than five, unless for some reason it is desired to subdivide one category into two or more parts. The following is a suggested range of categories, with the definition of each:

### First category ('A' or '1'): negligible or zero risk

Government or municipally owned organisations fully financed from public funds; nationalised industries; publicly financed universities, colleges and other educational establishments; hospitals, medical schools or research establishments; 'national name' commercial companies of undoubted credit standing and financial strength. NB: The last-mentioned need to be selected with care and in full knowledge of their financial capability. Recent business history is filled with the names of major public companies which have foundered or come close to doing so. An august name is, of itself, no guarantee of perpetual solvency, and any commercial customer placed in this risk category should, in common with those lower down the scale, be subject to regular and careful financial analysis.

Beware also of the limited liability company which derives its principal finance (usually on the security of a debenture) from a government department, or a majority of whose equity is held by such an organisation. Such companies *must* be regarded as normal business risks and be evaluated for credit purposes on the usual commercial criteria. They can become insolvent and sometimes do so, to the discomfiture of trade creditors who ill-advisedly rely on the government association in the mistaken belief that it offers them some special kind of security. Any limited company must be judged on its own financial merits, and one which (albeit with government connections) fails to satisfy the supplier's requirements in this direction should be asked to furnish acceptable guarantees, or be allocated credit facilities only within the compass of its assessed financial capability.

### Second category ('B' or '2'): ordinary trade risk

Companies, partnerships or sole traders of good reputation and financial status, having no known record of payment delinquency with suppliers.

This category will, in most businesses, probably encompass at least 50% of all customers. Those who for any reason are initially rated in a higher (i.e. worse) risk category should be expected to graduate to this one after a period of satisfactory trading, and subject to the later provision of more favourable information to outweigh the earlier reservations.

### Third category ('C' or '3'): potentially slow payer

Customers believed financially sound but with a known history of slow payments, either with other suppliers or in earlier trading with the supplier carrying out the assessment.

This rating is based on the normally justifiable expectation that a buyer who takes extended credit from one or several suppliers will do so from others if given sufficient latitude. Recognition of this tendency from the outset of business will give the new supplier the opportunity to begin as he intends to continue, which should be by stating in an unequivocal manner his terms of payment and by enforcing them. Failure to do this will almost certainly result in the account becoming overdue at an early stage, a position from which it is often more difficult to recover than to prevent it from arising in the first place.

It is sometimes thought that this type of customer, by definition financially as sound as those in the second category, does not for this reason represent a higher degree of risk. However, the additional risk lies in the probability that the customer will, if permitted to do so, allow his account to assume a more or less permanently overdue condition, with a consequently higher balance outstanding than if payments were made on time. If for any reason the customer should later run into unforeseen financial difficulty, the supplier might find himself with a higher amount at risk than if the account had been more regularly conducted. Because of this it is correct to acknowledge an additional degree of risk and to create a suitable category to cater for it.

It should be noted that exporters to certain countries where a high level of political or economic uncertainty exists run the risk that payments, even by a financially sound customer, may be subjected to delay in transit. For this reason it is desirable to place customers operating in such territories in a special risk category which may conveniently be the third category as described above.

## Fourth category ('D' or '4'): significant or high risk

Customers of known or suspected financial weakness.

This is the area of receivables from which the majority of bad debt losses may be expected to arise, and as such it deserves special attention. At the same time it is not uncommon to find that business with this type of customer can be potentially more profitable than that with less risky accounts, and it is therefore reasonable to expect a proportion of the customers of most companies to fall into the fourth category. Early identification of this level of risk is of paramount importance, as is the estabishment of effective procedures to control the level of financial exposure at all times.

## Fifth category ('E' or '5'): unacceptable risk—cash terms only

This category embraces the outer fringe of customers who are so financially weak, or so chronically unreliable in payment habits, that there is no option but to impose prepayment terms and control procedures sufficiently watertight to ensure that no order is executed until payment has been received.

The above range of five risk categories should be sufficiently comprehensive for most businesses, and for some it may be found that fewer will suffice. A possible simplification is as follows.

| | | |
|---|---|---|
| 1 | First category | } = Average to minimum risk. |
| 2 | Second category | |
| 3 | Third category | } = Above average risk. |
| 4 | Fourth category | |
| 5 | Fifth category | = Unacceptable risk—cash terms only. |

Where control procedures include (as must be the case in most businesses) the possibility of withholding shipments to customers whose accounts become unduly delinquent, it is sometimes an advantage to distinguish between the 'no credit' condition temporarily imposed on customers in the fourth and lower categories, and that permanently applied to accounts in the fifth category. This is particularly so where changes in the customer credit status have to be placed on a computer file. In such circumstances it is probably inappropriate to change the customer risk category from (for instance) third to fifth merely in order to implement what may be a temporary restriction. A convenient solution is to add to the letter or digit which designates the normal risk category a suffix (possibly 'X' or '0') to signify a temporary credit hold condition, e.g.

B   = Second category
BX = Second category—credit temporarily withdrawn

The suffix can of course, if entered on to a computer record, be used to activate special exception reports, e.g. a listing of all customers subject to credit withdrawal at the report date.

It is good practice, when risk categories are used, to arrange that category and credit limit are normally reproduced together on reports and internal account records, etc., so as to provide a concise indication of the credit conditions under which each account operates, e.g.:

B   10 000 = Ordinary trade risk account with £10 000 credit line.
or:
D   1000   = High risk account with £1000 credit line.

There is no doubt that the use of suitable risk categories together with financial credit lines greatly improves the quality and effectiveness of credit management.


## RISK, BAD DEBTS AND PROFITABILITY

It is a demonstrable fact that some companies (and indeed some credit managers) tend to regard the avoidance of bad debts at all costs as the key factor in their credit policies. It must however be accepted that any business enterprise involves the taking of risks, and whatever credit is given there must always be some expectation of bad debts. Where over a protracted period the bad debt losses of a business are fewer and smaller than average *for the industry* (and some industries are more productive of failed businesses than others), the likelihood is that over-restrictive credit policies are being followed, and that a high proportion of the more risky business which presents itself is being turned away either through outright refusal of credit facilities, or because the terms granted are insufficient to allow sales to develop. The probable consequence of this over-cautious approach is that, as the price of avoiding some bad debts, the seller is also losing the turnover and consequent profit on those orders which, although of above average risk, could with proper skill and judgement have been turned into productive sales. It may well be that the profit so lost is greater in total value than that of the additional bad debts which would have been incurred had a more entrepreneurial attitude been adopted towards credit extension. This fact often escapes the notice of management anxious to minimise bad debt losses but forgetful of the possible costs of so doing, and is a cogent argument in favour of the selective and calculated acceptance of a proportion of higher risk business.

## RISK AND CREDIT LIMITS

The purpose of a credit limit (or as some prefer to call it, a credit-line) is to establish the level of financial involvement which the seller is prepared to support as a result of credit sales to his customer. As mentioned above, the credit limit should not itself be used as an indicator of the assessed level of risk; this function is better performed by the use of risk categories. Credit limits are sometimes set according to an arithmetical relationship with one or more of the financial measures shown in the customer's final accounts, e.g. 10% of net current assets, or 20% of net worth; or by means of a formula derived from a weighted aggregate of several financial ratios. However, although these methods may suit particular circumstances none of them is capable of sufficiently wide application to be recommended here for general use. Moreover, since they are admittedly directly linked to the customer's financial strength, they are in effect more an indicator of risk than of an acceptable level of trading.

In setting a credit limit, the credit manager should never overlook the fundamental purpose of granting credit facilities, which is to assist and encourage customers to satisfy as far as possible their requirement for the seller's products or services, and in so doing give the seller the opportunity to maximise profitable sales. Given two customers of equal financial strength (or weakness), a credit limit which is appropriate for one selling situation may be entirely unsuitable for the other. For example, customer X may wish to buy a standard product which is readily sold in large volume at a modest profit margin to a wide variety of customers, most of whom are regarded as 'safe' (i.e. risk category A or B). The seller's incentive to incur a significantly above-average risk in order to add to his sales of this product is therefore low, since the profit reward will be no greater than on average sales, and the goods will in any case soon find an outlet elsewhere without the additional risk. Customer Y, on the other hand, may be a potential buyer for another product of which the seller has large slow-moving stocks, or which is obsolescent, seasonal, or on which there is an unusually high profit margin—or possibly a combination of these factors. Clearly in this case the seller's incentive is greater, and in these circumstances the credit manager would usually be justified in allowing a higher credit limit to customer Y than to customer X, even though on financial criteria alone the risks of trading might appear similar. This general example may serve to indicate the need for the credit manager to become fully involved with his sales and marketing colleagues in order that all significant business opportunities may be adequately evaluated on the basis of potential overall benefit to the company. It is important that 'rule-of-thumb' methods of establishing credit limits are not allowed to inhibit business unreasonably or to become a cause of conflict between the credit and sales functions. The credit decision should in fact form part of an overall business decision to be made in the best interests of the company, and should not be regarded in isolation, as an end in itself.

There is a case to be made for a strategic approach to the management of credit risk. If it is accepted, as a basic premise, that since most business involves risk and that at any time, a company which sells on credit terms will have in its accounts receivable a proportion of above-average risk accounts, then it is a relatively straightforward business decision to decide what that proportion can most advantageously be. From this, an overall financial target level of higher-risk exposure can be established. For example, if it is decided by management that the company's best interests will be served by having 10% of its total accounts receivable derived from sales to higher-risk customers, then if the total receivables portfolio is £1 000 000 the target level for higher risk accounts will be £100 000, and pro rata should total receivables increase as a result of sales growth.

As a result of this management decision, the credit manager will have clear terms of reference as to how far he may go in granting credit to higher-risk customers. He will more readily appreciate the need to spread the risk by not allocating too high credit limits to a very few risky customers, and also that in order to accommodate the accounts receivable arising from fresh sales, existing accounts must be collected as soon as possible; available capacity within the target level should be directed towards supporting new business and not to allowing extended credit on that which is past. After a suitable period of trading, a decision may be made to increase or decrease the high risk target level depending on the company's bad debt experience during the initial phase. A strategic approach to risk management of receivables can do much to improve visibility and help to ensure that, where above average risks are accepted, they are properly controlled and result in an acceptable improvement to overall company profitability.

# 7

# Automated Insolvency Risk Assessment

**Howard Tisshaw, Managing Director, Performance Analysis Services Ltd**

## INTRODUCTION

The high incidence of corporate bankruptcy in the 1980s has only emphasised the importance of objective and precise financial analysis. The conspicuous absence of going concern qualifications and the high levels of creditors associated with failing companies demonstrates only too clearly that risk assessment is no easy task. Hence the need for a simple, quick and accurate method for identifying failing companies and, just as important, for confirming that there is no risk has never been greater.

One way of overcoming this problem is to use a solvency model derived from the Z-score technique. Such models are now extensively used in the USA and the UK by various groups ranging from bankers and credit managers to auditors and investors. Where there is a need to avoid high risk business, minimise bad debt exposure and anticipate problems then there is a role for a solvency model to aid the decision-maker in his judgement.

## DEVELOPING A SOLVENCY MODEL

The Z-score technique for forecasting corporate failure is now well established and because of its ability to measure both profitability and balance-sheet strength it provides a very powerful index of financial performance. In order to understand why the Z-score approach is so accurate it is necessary to appreciate the way in which a solvency model is developed.

The first stage is to compute over 80 ratios for a sample of failed companies and a sample of solvent companies. Then, by using a technique called multiple discriminant analysis, it is possible to create a solvency model based upon a subset of those ratios which best separate the two groups of companies, and thereby produces the best correlation with financial health.

At the end of this analysis the chosen ratios are computed, entered into a formula and a Z-score is generated. If the Z-score is below the solvency threshold, i.e. negative, then the company is at risk, that is, it has a similar financial profile to previously failed companies. If the Z-score is positive then the company is not at risk. Obviously the greater the value of the Z-score, the healthier the company and vice versa.

## HOW WELL DO SOLVENCY MODELS WORK?

The track record of the Z-score technique is quite remarkable. Whilst the accuracy of such models does vary depending on how they are developed, the statistics published by Performance Analysis Services Ltd clearly demonstrate their predictive nature. In fact they show that no company has failed without warning since 1972 and there has usually been three years notice of pending financial distress.

Furthermore this warning can be extended by transforming the Z-score into a PAS-score (Performance Analysis Services score) which then permits a company's relative performance to be tracked through time. By reading the trend in the PAS-score, both above and below the solvency threshold, the momentum of a company's decline or recovery can easily be determined.

## THE PAS-SCORE

The PAS-score is quite simply a relative ranking of a company based upon the Z-score on the scale 1 to 100. For example a PAS -

score of 50 indicates that a company's performance is average, whereas a PAS-score of 10 says that only 10% of companies are performing less well (not a happy situation). Thus having computed a Z-score for a company it is now possible to transform what is an absolute measure of financial health into a relative measure of financial performance. In other words the Z-score tells you whether a company is at risk or not whereas the PAS-score puts the trend and current performance in perspective.

The power of this approach is derived from its ability to combine the key characteristics of both the profit and loss account and balance sheet into a single performance rating. Thus a company with strong profits but a weak balance sheet can be directly compared with a company with weak profits but a strong balance sheet. Hence, having calculated the PAS-score anyone who has little or no financial training can immediately assess the underlying financial risk attached to a particular company and can then vary his terms of trade accordingly. In essence it works on the principle that the whole is worth more than the sum of the individual parts.

## AN EXAMPLE OF THE Z-SCORE APPROACH IN PRACTICE

Figure 7:1 shows the trajectory for Scotcros plc, a company operating in several areas ranging from food to engineering, which failed in October 1983.

What is quite remarkable about this company is that it did not produce a pre-tax loss in the four years prior to its failure and had a strong stock market performance due to its pre-tax profits rising from £200 000 to £420 000 in the year to 31 March 1983.

The trajectory of the company's PAS-score, however, tells a different story. The graph shows how Scotcros rapidly declined in performance to a point where only 4% of companies were performing worse. Furthermore, for the last two years, prior to failure, its trajectory was below the solvency threshold indicating that it was at risk of failure. In essence, whilst there may have been some strength in the profit and loss account, the large debt (be it from the bank or from trade creditors) in the balance sheet was more than sufficient to show that this company was in danger.

In addition, the use of a 'risk rating' provides further insight into

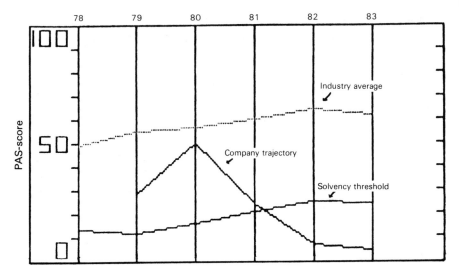

**Figure 7:1   Scotcros plc—the Z-score approach**

the underlying risk. The risk rating is calculated only when a company has a negative Z-score and is based upon the trend of the trajectory, the size of the negative Z-score and the number of years the company has been at risk. By using a 5-point scale, with 1 showing only a 30% chance of failure in the next 12 months and 5 indicating the company is unlikely to survive in its present form for much longer, risk measurement is easy. For Scotcros the risk rating was 4!

## CONCLUSION

The Z-score approach to assessing company solvency is being increasingly used in credit management in the UK. By simply calculating a small set of financial ratios from a firm's published accounts and entering these in a simple formula it is possible to calculate a Z-score. This Z-score will then reveal whether a company is at risk or not, and can then further be transformed into a PAS-score which will highlight a company's relative performance. This analytical approach is a practical tool for assessing the risk attached to a debtor ledger and when armed with this knowledge the professional credit manager knows when to vary terms of trade, can avoid high-risk business and is able to direct the sales force towards healthy companies. In essence it can be an invaluable credit management aid.

# 8

# Insolvency Signposts

**John Argenti, Lecturer and Consultant**

## TWO METHODS OF FORECASTING FAILURE

There are essentially two methods of predicting failure. One rests upon financial data and includes: the well-known ratios (dealt with elsewhere in this handbook); the increasingly well known Z-scores of Altman in America, Taffler in the UK, and others elsewhere; and the age-old skills of 'reading the balance sheet'. The second lists all those features of companies that have failed in the past and compares the items with what can be observed in a suspect company.

The first method, although unquestionably effective in predicting trouble, suffers from three very serious defects. Firstly, companies in trouble take good care to delay publishing their accounts and while such a delay is in itself often a cause for anxiety the fact is that vital figures are not available to the worried observer often for months, sometimes for years. Secondly, even when the figures do become available, they may have been the subject of 'creative accounting'. It should be noted that it is a rule, not an exception, for companies in difficulties to indulge in this practice—sometimes to the point of fraud. It requires some skill, even on the part of an experienced observer, to detect whether a set of accounts has been dressed up and if so to what extent. The third difficulty is that while some of the ratios of a company may be signalling insolvency other ratios of this same company may appear neutral or even reassuring. It may be difficult to interpret the true state of a company in such circumstances.

For these three reasons it may be useful to turn to the second method of detecting approaching failure by listing and comparing features of companies that have failed in the past with the company under suspicion. Many such lists have been published in the past 50 years. Some of them contain dozens of items (some plainly trivial and unreliable). Unfortunately, most of the lists do not rank their items in importance and none of them place the items in any sort of sequence. The A-score is an attempt to correct these three defects.

It starts with the assertions that (a) there is a process of failure, (b) that this process takes years to complete (or, restating these briefly, companies take many years to fail and they do so in a broadly similar sequence of events) and (c) the process can be divided into three stages:

1  *The defects.*   Companies that are going to fail display a number of defects for years before they actually collapse.
2  *The mistakes.*   It is because of these defects that a company will eventually make a mistake that leads to failure. (Notice that companies which do not display the defects *do not* make the mistakes that lead to failure.)
3  *The symptoms.*   Having made the mistakes the company will then begin to display all the familiar symptoms of approaching insolvency—deteriorating ratios (hidden by creative accounting) signs of stringency, etc. These symptoms occur in the last two or three years of what is often a five to ten year process of failure.

## THE A-SCORE

The A-score requires the observer to visit the suspect company (something one should do even if up-to-date accounts are available), to ask a number of questions and to score answers on the lines suggested below. It is a deliberately subjective approach in contradistinction to the objective nature of the financial aspects. These are the questions and scores in each of the three phases of the failure process:

## The defects

1   *The autocrat.*   Companies run by autocratic chief executives are inevitably more liable to dismal failure (and to soaring success) than those run by the more pedestrian (but reliable) professional managers. Where an observer identifies the chief executive as an autocraft (i.e. dominating colleagues) then score 8 marks. (Score nil for all other styles of management.)

2   *Chairman–Chief executive.*   A rare, but essential, duty of every chairman is to dismiss an inadequate chief executive. Where these two duties are performed by one man, especially if he is also an autocrat, which often is the case, the danger is such as to warrant a score of 4.

3   *Passive directors.*   If the other directors do not normally contribute to the discussion of major decisions score 2.

4   *Unbalanced Board.*   If the directors on the Board do not reflect a wide spectrum of knowledge score 2. (For example if 4 out of 6 members of a board of an engineering company are engineers.)

5   *Finance director.*   Score 2 if the finance director is not a strong enough personality to make his views clearly known to the board.

6   *Management depth.*   Score 1 if there is no depth of professional managers just below Board level.

7   *Accounting defects.*   Score 3 if the company does not employ a system of budgetary control, a further 3 if it does not have a cash-flow planning system and 3 also if it does not have a costing system for products, departments, etc.

8   *Response to change.*   Score 15 if the company is old-fashioned in some significant area (e.g. out of date products), or if it has not responded to some significant change (e.g. has not cut back in a recession).

Total possible score for defects = 43.
Pass mark for defects = 10.
Thus if a company scores 10 or more in this section the observer is entitled to some anxiety, for it is sufficiently defective to allow it to make one of the fatal mistakes and if it does it may not know how to correct it.

## The mistakes

1  *Gearing.*  Any company that allows its gearing to rise to a level at which its future is placed in jeopardy by a stroke of ill-fortune is asking for trouble. Score 15.
2  *Overtrading.*  Companies that expand faster that their capital funding (or that contract slower than it) are in danger. This is a mistake which well-managed companies can make with impunity for long periods but which catch the defective company unawares. Score 15.
3  *Big project.*  Score 15 if the company has recently launched a project of such a size that, should it go wrong, the company will be crippled.

Total possible score for mistakes = 45.
Pass Mark for mistakes = 15.
Thus if a company scores 15 or more in this section the observer is entitled to some anxiety. If, in addition, the score in defects exceeds 10 his anxiety should be acute.

## The symptoms

1  *Financial signs.*  Score 4 if the financial ratios, the Z-score, the balance sheet, etc., show signs of deterioration.
2  *Creative accounting.*  Score 4 if the observer detects any accounting tricks designed to dress up the accounts (low depreciation, overvalued stocks or assets, low repairs and maintenance, etc.).
3  *Non-financial signs.*  Score 3 if there are such signs of stringency as a decline in product quality, fall in market share, offices needing repainting, etc.
4  *Terminal signs.*  Score 1 if there are writs, rumours and resignations.

Total for the A-Score = 100.
Pass mark = 25.
Thus any company scoring more than 25 may be deemed to be a candidate for failure. The higher the score the more likely the failure and the sooner.

In practice most non-failing companies score well below the danger mark of 25, typically only 5–18. Any well-run, professionally-managed company scores nil (e.g. Marks and Spencers). But companies in trouble often score far in excess of 25, typically 35–70.

The reader is invited to score two companies that are well known to him; one should be a very successful company, the other very unsuccessful. The A-scores will fall well below and well above 25.

The A-score is intended as a method of predicting failure that is complimentary to the methods based on financial data. It may be equally effective in identifying companies that are in trouble but which are taking action to effect a recovery—in their case, of course, the A-score will be moving down to below 25.

# PART IV
# SALES LEDGER

# 9

# Sales Ledger Administration

**Ann Westoby, Credit Manager, Avdel Ltd**

## WHAT IS THE SALES LEDGER?

The sales ledger is the detailed record of the unpaid sales transactions which in total comprise the debtors or receivables asset of
the balance sheet.

As a straightforward record the sales ledger displays the debit and
credit entries which have been made on each customer's account. It
is useful, therefore, to show how much is owed by each customer, in
addition to the total debtors figure. However, it has many other uses,
and should never be dismissed as just another audit statistic. If
properly used it is a ready-made means of setting collection targets,
forecasting future cash receipts, and identifying the prime areas for
chasing. Used in conjunction with other financial information it is
also a major tool in the management of the company's cash flow.

Aditionally, because it is a chronological record of sales to and
payments from customers it provides a wealth of statistical information. For instance, if analysed by region or product it can be of great
value to the marketing department when researching market trends.
Similarly, it can be used to plot the sales and payment history of
particular accounts, thus helping credit managers to assess the
customer's worth.

The debtors (or accounts receivable) balance often represents 30%
of total assets, and therefore this very important area of business
management must be properly maintained and properly controlled.
After all it is the asset which can most easily be turned into liquid

funds. Therefore, the quality of the balances contained therein will have great influence on the decision of banks and trade creditors to lend or not to lend; and on the saleability of the business in a merger or liquidation.

As has become very obvious during the recession of the late 1970s, early 1980s one prime cause of company failure has been poor credit management, resulting in unwise selling coupled with an inability to collect outstanding debts. The information contained in a properly maintained sales ledger can be a signpost to danger, and can ring all the necessary warning bells to prompt remedial action. On the positive side it also identifies the better customers, those who have proved themselves to be reliable and prompt, to whom one would be happy to increase sales. Sales ledger information given to a sales representative can often help him to plan a more profitable selling programme.

The objectives of a sales ledger, therefore, are manifold, but to be of any value at all the ledger must be in a workable format, and be accurately and efficiently maintained.

## LEDGER FORMAT

At one time it was standard practice for the sales ledger, in common with all other accounting, to be kept manually. For some small businesses this can still work very well, and can be in the form of a handwritten bound book, or a handwritten or typed looseleaf ledger. As it is usual to send customers a written statement of account at regular intervals, a looseleaf ledger would be more practical for all but the smallest businesses.

When accounting first became mechanised many companies transferred their ledgers to machine cards. This was almost a motorised version of the manual system, and relied on an operator to enter invoices and cash on to the card on a daily basis, thus speeding up the handling of the sales ledger, and providing a carbon copy of the card to send to customers as a statement of account. There are still many companies using this tried and tested method of accounting. The paperwork produced on an accounting machine is unmistakeable, and in common with the majority of handwritten systems operates on a brought-forward system.

A.B.C. Ltd,
High Street,
Anytown

⌐ NAME AND ADDRESS ¬

X.Y.Z. Ltd,
The Broadway,
Sometown.

**STATEMENT**

| ACCOUNT No. |
| --- |
| 1140 |

| DATE | REFERENCE | GOODS | VAT | CASH | BALANCE |
| --- | --- | --- | --- | --- | --- |
| 1.12.83 | B/FWD | | | | 442.66 |

E.& O.E.

| OVERDUE ACCOUNTS | | | | BALANCE NOW DUE |
| --- | --- | --- | --- | --- |
| 30 DAY | 60 DAY | 90 DAY | 120 DAY | |
| 3.02 | 34.64 | 0.00 | 0.00 | 442.66 |

somepress 20939    Terms:— 2½% CASH DISCOUNT IF PAID DURING THE MONTH FOLLOWING
THE MONTH OF DELIVERY — VAT STRICTLY NET.
Remittances received after the end of the month are not included in this statement.

A.B.C. Ltd,
High Street,
Anytown

⌐ NAME AND ADDRESS ¬

X.Y.Z. Ltd,
The Broadway,
Sometown.

**STATEMENT**

| ACCOUNT No. |
| --- |
| 1140 |

| DATE | REFERENCE | GOODS | VAT | CASH | BALANCE |
| --- | --- | --- | --- | --- | --- |
| 1.01.84 | B/FWD | | | | 442.66 |
| 13.01.84 | 19338 INV | 80.34 | 13.98 | | 543.92 |
| 20.01.84 | 13588 INV | 51.52 | 7.53 | | 602.97 |
| 26.01.84 | 13683 INV | 13.45 | 1.97 | | 618.39 |
| 31.01.84 | 22 CSH | | | 442.66— | 175.73 |

E.& O.E.

| OVERDUE ACCOUNTS | | | | BALANCE NOW DUE |
| --- | --- | --- | --- | --- |
| 30 DAY | 60 DAY | 90 DAY | 120 DAY | |
| 0.00 | 0.00 | 0.00 | 0.00 | 175.73 |

somepress 20939    Terms:— 2½% CASH DISCOUNT IF PAID DURING THE MONTH FOLLOWING
THE MONTH OF DELIVERY — VAT STRICTLY NET.

Remittances received after the end of the month are not included in this statement.

**Figure 9:1    Machine Card statement—brought-forward system**

A brought-forward statement shows the balance remaining at the close of the previous month, the current month's transactions, and the new closing balance.

As computers have become cheaper and more readily available more and more companies are computerising their sales ledgers.

**STATEMENT**  OF ACCOUNT WITH

A.B.C. Ltd,  
High Street,  
Anywhere.

X.Y.Z. Ltd,  
Broadway,  
Somewhere.

| ACCOUNT No. 1234567 | | STATEMENT DATE 29 FEB 84 | | |
|---|---|---|---|---|
| ITEM DATE | ITEM REF. | DESCRIPTION | AMOUNT | BALANCE |
| 20DEC83 | 033641 | INVOICE 20DEC83 | | 53.75 |
| 11JAN84 | 035341 | INVOICE 11JAN84 | | 171.07 |
| 27JAN84 | 040425 | INVOICE 27JAN84 | | 57.18 |
| 09FEB84 | 043568 | INVOICE 09FEB84 | | 71.69 |
| 20FEB84 | 045934 | INVOICE 20FEB84 | | 62.96 |
| 20FEB84 | 045935 | INVOICE 20FEB84 | | 174.70 |

***OVERDUE AMOUNTS TOTAL...£297.00***  
***PROMPT PAYMENT WILL BE APPRECIATED...THANK YOU***

TERMS — NETT CASH PAYABLE BY 20th OF THE MONTH FOLLOWING THE DATE OF INVOICE.  
NOTE — PAYMENTS MADE BUT NOT SHOWN ABOVE SHOULD APPEAR ON NEXT STATEMENT.

TOTAL NOW DUE £ 606.35

**Figure 9:2  Computerised statement—open-item system**

Even very small companies, with only a few accounts, can afford a micro-computer on which to run their accounting systems.

Most computerised sales ledgers are on an open-item basis. This lists only those items which are still outstanding, and can include an 'ageing' to alert both customers and credit staff to any overdue items.

## OPERATING THE SALES LEDGER

The sales ledger has two main uses, to facilitate maximum use of the credit limits and to collect sales proceeds as fast as possible. It comprises invoices, credit notes and cash which go to make up the individual customer balances, and the total accounts receivable.

### Prompt and accurate postings

Invoices, credit notes and cash should be posted to the ledger on a daily basis. This will adjust the balance for purposes of order-vetting.

Cash should be allocated immediately whenever possible to clear paid items. Sometimes, however, the customer does not supply sufficient information to allocate the payment accurately. In such cases payments should be applied 'on account', i.e. not related to specific items. However, correct allocation should be achieved as soon as possible. If the customer pays a round sum, he should be asked to approve allocation against the oldest items on the ledger.

### Statements

Prompt posting aids prompt month-end closure, which facilitates the early issue of statements.

Many customers pay only items listed on a statement, and this document provides a useful reminder that payment is due. It follows that the sooner statements can be issued, the quicker cash can be collected.

### Account queries

It is often when payment is made that queries are first notified. The customer may deduct a debit note, or merely comment on his remittance advice that a certain item is disputed.

Except in very small companies it is unlikely that the person responsible for cash allocation will also be reponsible for account queries or chasing. A good system is therefore necessary to allow the sales ledger section to alert the chasing section, and possibly the customer service department, to any queries.

It is essential that disputes and debit notes are not allowed to accumulate. If they are not cleared accurately and promptly they can cause undue interruption of payment, besides creating an atmosphere of ill-will. Although the credit staff may not be active in clearing disputes, they must be as vigilant in chasing the party responsible for action as they are in chasing customers for payment.

## Order vetting

If there is to be a true credit control system, as opposed to simple cash collection, daily vetting of orders against credit limits and overdue accounts is essential. Which is why the importance of prompt ledger updating, both of invoices and cash, cannot be over emphasised. Where the product being sold has a lengthy lead time order vetting should be carried out on receipt of the order, and again immediately prior to dispatch.

The subject of stopping supplies is a highly emotive one, so it is useful to have some method of annotating queries or disputed items on the customer's record to avoid sanctions being applied unjustifiably.

## COMPUTER SYSTEMS

The need for prompt update of the sales ledger has already been explained. It is in this area where computerisation is at its most valuable.

With the increased availability of 'user-friendly' machinery more and more credit personnel are able to decide what they want from their sales ledger system. The innovation over the last ten years of on-line, real-time systems has added considerably to the credit manager's armoury.

For example, if a payment is received in the morning post it should be possible to input the payment details on-line, and update the account on a real-time system. The credit manager is then immediately able to look at the revised statement of account on screen. With the additional real-time update of invoices and credits, he can have an account picture which is literally only minutes old. Such a facility is of immeasurable value, both for order-vetting purposes and for chasing payments. Because it enhances the credit department's efficiency and knowledge it also enables them to create a better customer relationship. Nothing can be more embarrassing than a credit clerk, chasing with incomplete information, to be told by the customer that he has just received a credit note which clears the outstanding balance.

## Cash matching

It is possible nowadays to have a package or a programme which will allow automatic cash matching. This entails the operator posting only the customer's identification, i.e. account number, and the total payment received. The computer will then attempt to allocate the cash using a number of pre-set algorithms. The most common of these are payment against:

(a)   total account balance;
(b)   total overdue balance;
(c)   overdue balance less debit notes;
(d)   overdue balances less subsequent credit notes;
(e)   overdue balance less unallocated cash;
(f)   single item.

There are obviously many more, and they will vary according to the requirements of the user.

If a perfect match can be found the computer automatically clears the items. Otherwise the cash will be posted on account, and an exception report will be issued to enable the clerical staff to reconcile the payment and complete the allocation.

This system is extremely useful to companies who have a high volume of straightforward accounts. Such accounts can be easily incorporated into an automatic system, which releases the clerical staff to deal with the more complicated receipts.

## Debit notes

To ensure complete accuracy any system should include the facility to create debit entries to agree with the customer's debit note deductions. Ideally it should be possible to give such items the customer's own debit note reference. They will then be easily identified on the statement. For the purposes of ageing it is desirable to flag queries in such a way that their presence is ignored. When chasing and order-vetting, queries items should be excluded from the balance. This assumes even greater importance on systems which impose automatic credit sanctions.

## CASH COLLECTION AIDS

In order to achieve maximum chasing efficiency the sales ledger stands as the credit clerk's most useful tool. From the input created during the course of a month a statement of account is produced showing the individual balance on each account. Although different companies choose different formats the message should always be the same. How much is outstanding? How is it made up? What value is overdue? By how much is it overdue? What are the terms prevailing on the account? When should payment be made? Coupled with the detailed statements should be an aged receivables analysis.

### Aged receivables analysis

This will show an on-line balance for each account, aged in days or months. If the ledger is divided into more than one working section, there should be an aged sub-total for each section.

For the purposes of cash collection this analysis highlights the oldest items which need attention, and it can be used very efficiently as a chasing document to record payments received and promises made. Additionally, it identifies the collectable items which need to be received in order to meet the pre-set cash targets.

ANALYSIS OF CUSTOMER DEBTS   MONTH ENDED 29 FEB 84   PAGE 353

| CUSTOMER ACCOUNT NO. & NAME | OVER 4-MTHS | 4-MTHS | 3-MTHS | 2-MTHS | 1-MTH | LATEST | TOTAL | L1" PTTN (%CR CHANGE) |
|---|---|---|---|---|---|---|---|---|
| Acc. no. 1 Customer name. | | 0 | 39 | 0 | 10837 | 12450 | 23327 | 017 |
| Acc. no. 2 Customer name. | | 0 | 0 | 0 | 962 | 735 | 1698 | |
| Acc. no. 3 Customer name. | 1721  05 | 1263 | 4242 | 2327 | 2435CR | 2756 | 9875 | |
| Acc. no. 4 Customer name. | | 0 | 0 | 0 | 3835 | 4537 | 8372 | |
| Acc. no. 5 Customer name. | | 0 | 0 | 0 | 0 | 1062 | 1062 | |
| Acc. no. 6 Customer name. | | 466 | 0 | 2042 | 752 | 870 | 4132 | |
| Acc. no. 7 Customer name. | | 0 | 0 | 681 | 0 | 92 | 773 | |

Acc. no. 1 — CREDIT REF 0 LIMIT 20000 / GRADE A / PAYMENT TERMS 045

Acc. no. 2 — CREDIT REF 1 LIMIT 3000 / GRADE X / PAYMENT TERMS 30 DAYS

Acc. no. 3 — CREDIT REF 2 LIMIT 10000 / GRADE / PAYMENT TERMS 60 DAYS

Acc. no. 4 — CREDIT REF 0 LIMIT 15000 / GRADE A / PAYMENT TERMS 30 DAYS

Acc. no. 5 — CREDIT REF 0 LIMIT 5000 / GRADE A / PAYMENT TERMS 30 DAYS

Acc. no. 6 — CREDIT REF 1 LIMIT 12000 / GRADE D / PAYMENT TERMS 045

Acc. no. 7 — CREDIT REF 0 LIMIT 5000 / GRADE C / PAYMENT TERMS 60 DAYS

**Figure 9:3   Aged receivables analysis**

## Statements and invoices—file copies

Although the aged receivables analysis highlights the collectable balances it is the statement of account which shows how those balances are comprised. It is useful, therefore, to have a copy statement available to the collection staff. With on-line computer systems this may be in display form on a visual display unit (VDU), or produced and stored in hard copy.

Because customers sometimes mislay altogether, or query the detail on invoices, it is also necessary to have copies available in the office, both for reference by the chasing staff, and for supply to customers. These copies will take many different forms, depending on the system in use. On the simplest form of manual system there may be carbon copies of a typed item. At the other end of the scale it is now possible to have computer-produced invoices on microfiche.

The advantage of the microfiche system is ease of filing, and reduction of paperwork. A 6in × 4in sheet of fiche will hold 270 A4 documents which eliminates the need for vast areas of filing. The system entails sending a magnetic tape, bearing all items to be copied, to a microfiche bureau. The tape will be run through a computer which operates a camera and photographs each item, and produces a microfiche. Retrieval is quick and efficient and by means of a fiche reader–printer photocopies can be produced.

## SALES LEDGER CONTROLS

### Invoice numbering

Some companies allocate invoice numbers either when the order is first received and entered, or when it passes the order-vetting system in the credit department.

Ideally, when an order is received it should be recorded and given a transaction number which will appear on all documentation prior to invoicing. This will include order acknowledgements, advice and packing notes and order amendments. When the goods are dispatched, or the job completed, the invoice should be created and given a unique sequential invoice number. For the customer's benefit the invoice should show both the invoice and transaction numbers. However, for accounting and credit purposes the invoice number should be used.

It is possible with many computers to have invoice numbers allocated automatically in sequential order. Where this is not possible the number allocation should be the responsibility of the credit department.

Great care must be taken to ensure that no number is missed, and that no number is duplicated. To achieve this it is necessary to keep a record of numbers used. This may be simply a book containing a pre-list of numbers which are then crossed out as they are allocated, or may be in the more comprehensive form of a day-book. In this case it will give invoice details against each allocated number. These rules apply to all systems whether manual or computerised.

## Cash book

Where possible cheques should be handled by a cashier who operates independently of the credit department. On receipt, cheques and remittance advices should be totalled separately to ensure they agree. A handwritten or typed list should be prepared showing the payer details and the amount received. The original list should be retained by the cashier, and a copy passed to the sales ledger with the remittance advices.

Once the cash has been allocated the cleared items should be totalled to ensure the value agrees with the total receipts. It is advisable that either the cashier or, preferably, the credit manager checks and initials the cash allocation documentation, the receipts listing and the bank paying-in book to ensure all balances agree.

## Nominal ledger reconciliation

The entries which are posted to the sales ledger must also be posted independently to the nominal or general ledger. With a completely integrated computer system there will be an interface which performs this task automatically. Whether this is the case, or whether the items are transferred manually, a complete reconciliation of sales to nominal ledgers must take place at the end of each accounting period. Any differences should be investigated and corrected immediately. The nominal ledger is the basis for the company's profit and loss account and balance sheet, and must be accurately kept. The sales ledger section of the nominal ledger shows on the balance sheet as 'debtors'.

## Audit trail

Each year the books of a company will be audited to ensure their accuracy. As part of their duties auditors will need to prove that invoicing is happening correctly, that credit notes are properly authorised, and that cash is accurately applied and balanced. They will also wish to plot the sequence of events from the initial placing of an order, right through to the eventual payment receipt. This detail is known as the audit trail. Any company wishing to change its sales ledger system, especially when changing to computerisation for the first time, should ask their auditors to check the new procedures. They will then satisfy themselves that the audit trail is adequate, or suggest any modifications necessary to make it adequate, before the system is installed.

## CREDIT MANUALS

Good administration of a sales ledger requires several areas of control, i.e.:

1 processing of documents;
2 knowledge of staff;
3 training of new staff;
4 communicating new systems or changes;
5 observance of company policies;
6 meeting parameters and financial controls;
7 liaison with other functions, especially sales staff.

Whatever the size of business, it is worth producing a credit manual, thick or slim, for the guidance of all concerned.

This provides the opportunity in a single document to set out general policies and detailed procedures, with sample forms and documents, so that there can be no misunderstandings, either in the credit department or in other functions in collaboration with credit.

### Suggested contents of a credit manual

1 Credit objectives and policy, comprising:
  (a) a clear statement of objectives and policy which can be quoted publicly and used by staff;
  (b) details of other affected functions, e.g. production and marketing;
  (c) industry standards and competitors' practice.

2 Credit organisation, comprising:
  (a) organisation chart, stating reporting responsibilities;

    (b)  job descriptions;
    (c)  qualifications required for each job;
    (d)  training systems;
    (e)  staff reviews.

3   Budgets and reports, including:
    (a)  budget planning, with required data from sales and others;
    (b)  reporting requirements, with forms and instructions.

4   Credit approval procedures, comprising:
    (a)  credit information sources;
    (b)  method of applying credit limits and categories;
    (c)  alternatives for payment terms;
    (d)  credit insurance requirements;
    (e)  order referral system;
    (f)  stop-shipment policy and system.

5   Invoicing procedure.

6   Collection procedures, including:
    (a)  responsibilities for timing and frequency;
    (b)  timetable for standard procedures;
    (c)  systems for special ledger groups, e.g. government;
    (d)  rules for using third-parties, collection agents and solicitors;
    (e)  bad debts and write-off procedures;
    (f)  handling of disputes and debit notes.

7   Appendix of forms and reports, including samples of:
    (a)  order acknowledgement;
    (b)  invoices;
    (c)  sales conditions;
    (d)  packing notes;
    (e)  statements;
    (f)  collection letters;
    (g)  computer tabulations;
    (h)  regular reports;
    (i)  budget forms and instructions.

**Credit manual preparation and updating**

The credit manager should ensure that the manual is kept updated with changes as they happen. The best way to ensure this is done is to have the manual in daily use.

All sales ledger credit and collection systems should be reviewed periodically in any business and most managers compile their own checklist of all important features. The same checklist and its answers can be used for developing the credit manual, as well as for management information purposes.

## CHECKLISTS FOR SALES LEDGERS, CREDIT AND COLLECTION SYSTEMS

In attempting to produce an ideal checklist, there is the danger of throwing in a multitude of hair-splitting details plus a number of questions quite inapproriate for some businesses.

Obviously, flexibility must be applied, but the following suggested checklist may prove useful as a basis for producing shorter, tailored versions for any one company:

1   Do you have a separate person or department responsible for credit and collections?
2   Is there a credit manual or equivalent written guide and are all credit staff familiar with it?
3   Has it been circulated to other departments?
4   Do staff understand the real meaning of ratios, i.e. that you borrow funds at 12% p.a. and make 4% on sales, so that overdues cancel profit after four months and a bad debt of £1000 requires further sales of £25 000 to cover it?
5   Is there a check on the credit approval operation to ensure that over-strictness is not losing sales and that liberal approvals are not losing profit?
6   Are all credit limits reviewed regularly and increased/decreased for maximum sales and profit effect?
7   Is there a reliable customer list, with all static information reliably recorded and updated?
8   Is there a budget or plan for debtors? Does it make proper allowance for normal overdues, special terms and projected bad debts?
9   What is the working capital available for debtors? If it is ever

adequate, how will credit sales be allocated, e.g. large accounts, or prompt payers, or long-term prospects?

10 How are customers checked out on first orders?

11 Is credit insurance available, desirable and properly used?

12 What is the relationship with credit reporting agencies? Do you insist on specific information?

13 Are salesmen used for information-gathering? If so, is it reliable, or uneconomic to use them?

14 For important accounts, is Companies House used for data?

15 Have you developed a system of reliable interchange of credit information with other suppliers?

16 Do you use the DSO system to measure the average collection time for a credit sale?

17 Can a credit staff member authorise terms longer than standard? If so, how much and will it affect the price?

18 What is the policy for asking for guarantees or otherwise dealing with sub-marginal accounts?

19 Are payment terms shown clearly on quotations, order acknowledgements, invoices and statements?

20 Is the ledger system (handwritten, typed, machine or computer) adequate to meet the credit and collection parameters?

21 Are invoices, credit notes and cash posted daily to the ledger?

22 Is a regular review made of the efficiency of the cash-receiving and cash-application function?

23 Are statements produced and dispatched within five days of month-end?

24 Is there a system for comparing balances with credit limits and referring excess items for attention?

25 Do invoices show data designed by credit manager to speed payment?

26 Are overdue accounts recorded promptly enough to allow timely follow-up?

27 Is the follow-up of overdue accounts firm enough at the right time? Do persistent 'takers of extra credit' receive only standard treatment?

28 Is interest charged on overdue accounts?

29 At what stage are significant overdues or customer emergencies reported upwards?

30 Is the correct approval system used for writing-off bad debts?

31 Have you checked the performance of collection agents and solicitors against others, to see if you can get a cheaper/faster service?

32 Are debtors, or bills receivable discounted? If so, is there an efficient system for ensuring due payment by customers, since such accounts are 'off' the ledger?

32 Would factoring be a more efficient means of improving cash flow?

It is often interesting to write yes/no answers to the right of these questions. Even a well-ordered credit operation may find that it overlooks some areas which were once satisfactory but are now weaknesses and represent a profit drain.

## CONCLUSION

In conclusion, the sales ledger is a definitive record of sales made, payments received and balances outstandings.

Some companies regard the sales ledger as the Cinderella of the accounting functions, but as has been illustrated many other functions rely on the sales ledger information. Not least of these is the credit department whose efficiency will be greatly affected by the quality of the sales ledger.

# 10

# Computer Aids and Innovations

**A. S. Loveland, formerly Group Credit Control Manager, Carreras Rothmans Limited**

## INTRODUCTION

In the modern business environment there is a paramount need to have absolute control over sales ledger activities and functions. The advantages in this are to:

1   Obtain the most accurate and timely management information concerning the cash flow of the business.
2   Limit trade risks inherent in the business.
3   Decrease investment in trade debtors.
4   Increase cash flow inwards.

These objectives can be attained using a variety of methods depending upon the scale of the business. Where large volumes of data are involved, however, the most significant development affecting the control, and, through it, the efficiency of sales ledger administration, including the management of credit, has been the introduction of computer systems for processing data electronically.

Computer systems are simply a collection of procedures which are integrated as a whole and depend upon and interact with each other. They are controlled by operating instructions in a logical sequence, known as programmes, and depend upon data which are the known facts concerning an object or event. In its raw state, data is virtually unusable, and cannot produce results of itself, but when subjected to a series of logical processes within a system it can be manipulated to provide significant information and lead to the next stages of the business functions. Data consists of facts which are either fixed or variable.

Much data will be common to a number of systems which may need access to it simultaneously: for this reason corporate data

---

### Sales ledger and credit management data per account

| *Fixed data* | *Variable data* |
|---|---|
| Account number | Current items on ledger |
| Trading name | account |
| Accounting address | Transactions in current |
| Delivery address | trading period |
| Telephone number | Value of order on hand |
| Telex number | Value of orders rejected — |
| Date account opened | Itemised by reason code |
| Sales region/division | Overdue items |
| Frequency of call | Payment history |
| Terms | Floating credit limit |
| Credit category | Actual currency conversion |
| Order limit | rates |
| Fixed credit limit | Salesman's next call date |
| Geographic co-ordinates | |
| Routing instructions | |
| Supply depot | |
| Packaging instructions | |
| Shipping marks | |
| Shipping documentation | |
| requirements | |
| Export/import licence | |
| requirements | |
| Currency for transactions | |
| Budget currency conversion | |
| rates | |
| Special declarations | |
| Special instructions | |

---

**Figure 10:1 Fixed and variable data.** The examples are not meant to be comprehensive. Much of the data will be represented in each customer's file area by codes.

bases, or data banks, have been developed for retention on storage media, such as magnetic discs or tapes, for processing by the computer. Figure 10:1 gives examples of the types of data which could fall within the categories of 'fixed' and 'variable' for use within UK and export sales ledgers and credit management systems, whilst Figure 10:2 shows how this could be held within a corporate data bank for processing simultaneously within a number of systems.

The advantages of using a computer to process such data are:

1   immense speed;
2   absolute accuracy;
3   integration of data common to a number of functions;
4   minimisation of the time-scale of sequential operations;
5   simulation of business activities by the creation of complex mathematical models.

## SALES LEDGER ADMINISTRATION

Certain basic records are generally maintained by the sales ledger department, including:

1   the customer account index;
2   debit and credit documentation;
3   price tables/tariffs;
4   sales ledgers;
5   statements of account;
6   daybooks.

Where these are produced by clerical or simple machine methods they are invariably prone to inaccuracies and are both difficult and expensive to maintain because of their labour-intensive nature. Where copies are required at more than one location the problems are multiplied. Within a computer system these hurdles can be overcome effectively.

### Basic account data

Traditionally this could be maintained, for example, on typed or

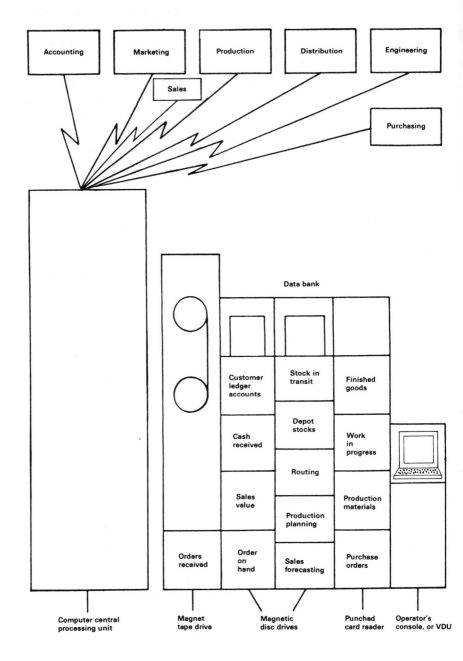

**Figure 10:2 How orders received interact with customer ledger accounts.** The ledger accounts contain fixed and variable data, and relate to a range of mainstream systems.

manuscript strip index in Kardex type units, with amendments carried out by typing or by hand, or on index cards retained in filing wheels or in box files. Much of the data would have to be repeated, often many times, on associated records involving the re-creation of the data clerically. Computer applications allow the data to be created once only on a prime verified document, such as an account information form, and from that source of input to the computer to be repeated automatically on all associated documentation. The indices referred to can be replaced by index cards produced from perforated fanfold stationery, with the relevant data printed horizontally by the computer on them. When burst out the cards form an easily visible record, which can be regularly spaced in accessible containers to show the computer-produced data at an angle of 45°. Any missing index card shows up immediately in the system, any slave index is controllable from the master index to show identical data, and amendments are effected by the computer reprinting the cards when fixed data in the data bank is amended. Figure 10:3 illustrates this application.

Once data has been input to the computer it is available for reproduction on a variety of documentation, as in Figure 10:4, and can be retained on a variety of storage media depending upon access and retrieval requirements.

Certain refinements such as check digits and validation routines can be built into the data itself and computer processes in order to guarantee levels of accuracy unattainable by other methods. This is the basis of the high level of efficiency required in the maintenance of the sales ledger records referred to earlier. For example, a code number in any coding system—whether numeric, alphabetic or alpha-numeric—is liable to be transcribed incorrectly. Another digit, which might also be equated to an alphabetic character, may be derived from the code number by an arithmetic process and added back to the code number as a prefix or suffix or in the body of the code number. A six-digit account number with a check digit might therefore appear as 249827 E.

Whenever the computer processes the account number it will carry out a similar calculation. If it arrives at the correct digit it will accept the number as correct and continue to process the transaction to that account number within the parameters of other validity checks. If any check is failed the transaction will be rejected,

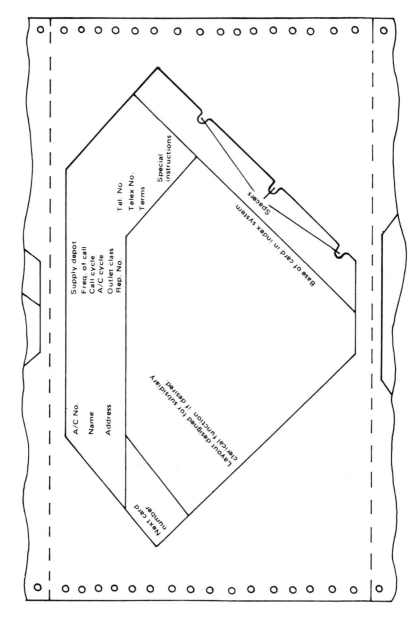

Figure 10:3    Visible index card. The card is mounted on sprocketed fanfold computer stationery

136

| Data | Customer index | Invoice | Delivery note | Credit note | Statement | Account update |
|---|---|---|---|---|---|---|
| Account number | * | * | * | * | * | * |
| Name | * | * | * | * | * | * |
| Accounting address | * | * | * | * | * | * |
| Delivery address | * | * | * | * | — | * |
| Terms | * | * | — | — | * | * |
| Supply depot | * | * | * | — | * | * |
| Packaging instructions | — | * | * | — | — | — |
| Special delivery instructions | * | * | * | — | — | — |

**Figure 10:4  Application of computer-held data to a variety of output documentation**

the reason being shown, for clerical or management judgement, amendment and reprocessing as necessary.

### Sales ledger systems

Two main systems are in use for sales ledgers—closed balance brought forward and open item.

#### Closed balance system

The use of the closed balance system is extremely widespread in consumer-oriented businesses, which may have influenced its introduction into industrial systems. It presupposes that there are no variable credit terms applicable to invoices, that cash received is posted simply as a credit to clear the oldest part of the balance outstanding, and that it is only necessary to list as individual credits and debits on statements those items which occur in the current accounting period. Any reconciliation of an account depends entirely upon a clerical examination of items uncleared by cash received, with outstanding items being brought forward clerically to the current copy statement, and so on in each successive period. It is almost impossible for any large-scale ledger reconciliation to be effectively supervised, and any, other than the most elementary, analyses of outstanding debts are effectively prevented. It is small wonder that the use of this system has resulted in disastrous consequences in some industrial systems. It can, of course be computerised—but the power of computer-processing techniques is more applicable to open-item systems, to which the considerations which follow are related.

Open-item system

A manufacturing company may well apply different terms to different invoices. For instance, transactions in a business-building environment could attract lengthy credit terms, which might be shortened subsequently if economic considerations justified their renegotiation. The ledger could then contain entries of the nature outlined in Figure 10:5, taking into account transit time.

Transaction number 3 would be payable sooner than the earlier dated items numbers 1 and 2, which is extremely important to the maintenance of the ledger. Care must be taken when posting cash to clear the appropriate items and such action ensures that the reconciliation of accounts is as up-to-date as the cash posting itself. Any

| Transaction number | Invoice number | Date | Draft number | Terms | Date due for payment |
|---|---|---|---|---|---|
| 1 | 2389 | 30 Jan 1984 | ME281 | Sight+90 days | 9 May 1984 |
| 2 | 2520 | 10 Feb 1984 | ME328 | Sight+90 days | 20 May 1984 |
| 3 | 2834 | 1 Mar 1984 | ME421 | Sight+30 days | 10 Apr 1984 |

**Figure 10:5  The open-item system**

deviation from normal can immediately be highlighted in exception reports for management action.

The open-item computer system should allow for the most comprehensive data possible to be taken into account at the systems design stage. This might well appear to be costly in terms of size of the system and design time, but it is surprising how difficult it often is to expand some systems later on if the data fields or facilities upon which the enhancements depend are not already available.

Assuming that the computer will produce invoices, credit notes and statements, it should also produce remittance advices to simplify the allocation of cash received to the correct account. With the open-item system the computer can take this a stage further by printing on the remittance advice outstanding items as per the statement. Even if the customer does not return the remittance advice dispatched to him, an office copy should be available. This will assist considerably in the identification of items paid. It also serves admirably as the cash-input document, merely by annotating the items paid and making appropriate adjustments for currency differences and bank charges, etc., if applicable, see Figure 10:6.

## Order processing

Sales ledger administration may include the processing of orders. If this is the case they may be handled centrally or at decentralised locations and remotely from the computer installations. If a supplier's own computer-produced order form has been completed it should contain computer-produced account data. This can be accepted as correct and the order can be encoded for the invoicing routine without delay, unless additional vetting of specific considerations such as deferred delivery dates is necessary. If a form other than the supplier's own computer-produced order form has been used it will be necessary to determine or vet the account data against the sales ledger customer index to establish its accuracy for processing to the correct account. The advantage of the computer-produced central customer index, with slave indices at decentralised locations, is now immediately apparent.

When the order has been checked for acceptability it must be punched or encoded, for processing by the computer. On site, batch-

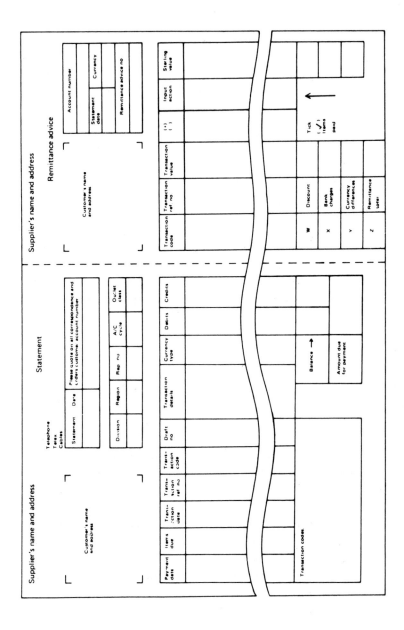

Figure 10:6  Computer-produced combined statement of account and remittance advice for open-item system permitting cash input and allowing exhaustive analysis

processing methods will normally be used, with the data-preparation department encoding on to magnetic tapes or punching cards or paper tape. After verification the data is input to the computer, which generates output. Communication systems enable orders to be encoded remotely, at stockholding depots for example, by means of devices known as terminals which are capable of transmitting data to the computer and receiving back output from it. Types of terminals which operate on-line are:

1  *Teletypewriter.*  This operates like a typewriter producing on to a paper roll a copy of the data keyed, and can have the capacity to punch paper tape. It transmits data to the computer and receives back transmitted output. It can also print hard copy from output transmitted to a visual display unit (VDU), but is only useful for commercial systems where the printed output at remote locations is low, mainly because of its low speed.

2  *Termiprinter.*  This has a typewriter-style keyboard but has a print belt which moves across the paper roll at high speed, enabling output to be printed three times as fast as a teletypewriter. A typical speed is 300 characters per second. It transmits data, can read and punch paper tape and can print data from a VDU. It also has the advantages that it is quieter than a teletypewriter, can print more copies, has improved tabbing facilities and is more reliable.

3  *VDU.*  These incorporate video screens displaying say, 25 lines of 80 characters on the screen as they are keyed. The computer can transmit to the VDU a screen format for a particular function containing data which the VDU operator cannot alter, with blank areas where the operator can key-in the required data. This corresponds exactly with filling a form. Data keyed in is validated and accepted by the computer. Errors can be flashed on the screen, enabling the operator to key-in the correct data.

The detail of the order may then be checked by the computer against other data, as follows:

1  customer credit category;
2  customer credit limit;
3  account balance;
4  order value limit;
5  product brand/pack availability.

This results in its rejection if unsatisfactory, or in the required printed output for packaging, dispatch and invoicing, either on-site or remotely. In cases where stock shortages exist, priority or 'rationing' sequences can be introduced, and/or details of items not supplied can be written away automatically to subsidiary files for release when stocks became available. In these cases, messages would invariably need to be created on the documentation by the computer explaining to the customer the action taken.

Apart from the printed output, all related computer files would be updated within the sales–accounting and stock-control suites of programmes, creating further data for the production of statements and analyses of information.

## CREDIT MANAGEMENT

### Basic data processing

The credit control department will be responsible for establishing credit data concerning new accounts, adding these to the main computer files, amending data in the light of trading experience, and deleting from the files, or making dormant, those with whom trading is discontinued.

These details should be entered into the data bank by means of an account information form which could be written out either partially or completely by:

1   the customer;
2   the sales representative;
3   the credit executive.

The design of the form should enable it to serve as a direct input document to the computer, thus reducing the clerical work involved. Figure 10:7 illustrates a section of such a form which would be suitable as an encoding document, but it must be borne in mind that other input methods exist which could be equally suitable, depending upon the machines available for other systems operated within the computer installation, e.g.:

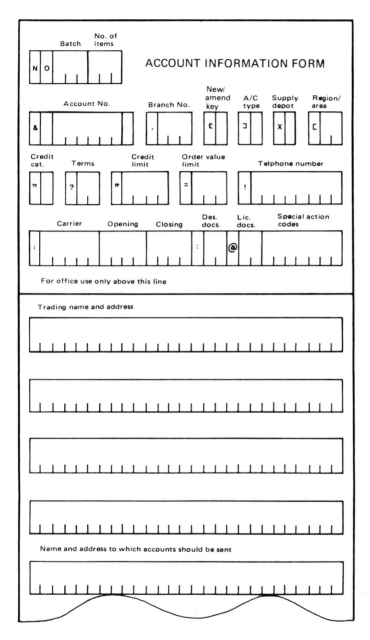

**Figure 10:7 Format of an account information form.** The form serves for encoding basic data to create or amend a customer's main computer file

1   Optical character recognition:

    (a)   Mark sensing. Small black marks representing data created manually or mechanically, as in Bardata typing or computer printing systems, enable documents to be read at speeds of 300 pages a minute, operating either off-line or on-line.

    (b)   Document reading. This is normally limited to one or two lines per document of characters in standard founts, printed within very close tolerances.

    (c)   Page reading. A full page of OCR characters can be read at operating speeds of up to 500 pages a minute.

2   Automatic typing.
3   Keyboard accounting systems.

> Output on punched paper tape, magnetic tape or magnetic card can be processed on-site or via communication systems into the computer.

The main advantage of this approach to basic credit management systems is that clerically maintained records can be dispensed with. As each amendment to the basic data occurs the computer can update not only its internal files, but reflects the changes in all relevant processes immediately and amend the data in all output documents and records. For example, it is perfectly feasible for the computer to be programmed to calculate and reset credit limits based upon trading levels and prompt-payment records, with variable tolerances also taken into account in the establishment of the revised credit limits. Similarly, credit categories could be changed depending upon payment record. These changes could then be reflected in management reports, revised indices and potted credit data printed on office copies of statements. This enables a total breakaway to take place from records such as manually maintained credit-sanction cards and allows the information to be made available more generally. Invariably, clerical records contain errors and present misleading information upon which to base credit judgements. Even valid information can easily remain hidden within such records. Within a computer system, however, the latest data can be applied more efficiently to the latest circumstances of an account. Queries and rejections can be channelled to appropriate levels of management, and control over the judgements made can easily be developed.

## Systems advantages

The employment of a computerised credit system brings new dimensions of efficiency into the control of the receivables investment:

First it demands that an agreed credit policy is defined. In a broad sense this concerns:

1 The parameters defining credit classifications of customers. For example, what will be the considerations defining category 1 accounts whose orders may bypass all credit restrictions, or what considerations will automatically relegate accounts to a cash with order trading basis.
2 The authorities to which queries will be referred for clearance.
3 The financial limits of staff involved in the credit process.
4 The procedures and authorities for holding orders or stopping shipments.
5 The internal systems for following up overdue receivables.
6 The external systems for taking legal action.
7 The nature and recipients of management information, e.g. debt duration, aged debts analysis, doubtful debts analysis.

Second, it provides the most powerful mechanisms for the following functions:

1 Establishment, revision and operation of credit limits and checking.
2 Cash collection and updating of current accounts.
3 Automation of overdues procedures.
4 Updating historical records and reconstructing accounts.
5 Controlling adjustments.
6 Production of management information.
7 Analysis of accounts to identify the need for, and nature of, appropriate controls.
8 The operation of selective controls and special actions.

To assist in the understanding of these applications some specific examples will be considered.

Credit categories

These could be represented by a simple code. Any number of options are open and may be related to circumstances such as:

CAT 1   Customer whose worth is such that no restrictions whatever will be applied.

CAT 2   Normal account whose credit limit will be the moving average of his trading value in each of the last six trading periods, plus a variable percentage business-building tolerance, and whose order value limit will be a fixed percentage of the credit limit.

CAT 3   New account subject to special surveillance routines and fixed credit limit.

And so on.

Credit authorities

Two points must be borne in mind:

1   No account would be opened unless authorised and counter-signed by two nominated executives. The authorised signatories would be defined in relation to the initial limit of the new account.

2   All rejections could be referred to nominated executives depending upon the financial limits assigned to them, e.g.:

| *Executive responsible* | *Orders, which together with current balance of the account exceed credit limit by value:* |
|---|---|
| Credit executive | —up to £500 |
| Credit supervisor | —between £501–£1500 |
| Credit manager | —over £1500 |

Orders held

Separate agreed procedures could exist for holding orders. It might be acceptable for an order to be held without reference to any authority if R/D cheques had been received from an account in two successive trading periods. But where an international key account was concerned this action might only be acceptable after the sales executive responsible had been alerted to a specific problem as agreed but had been unsuccessful in resolving the difficulty. In both these cases the established procedures might require print-outs of the accounts and the orders concerned to be considered jointly by both credit and sales management.

## 'Overdues' systems

The prime considerations are the tone, method and frequency of internal hasteners. Policy might dictate a series of warning or reminder letters concerning late payment to be sent, coupled or not with the production of reminder/overdue statements and the writing back of prompt settlement discount. Generally speaking, too many reminders cloud the issue and positive early action produces best results. In this application the computer could have initially calculated the value of prompt settlement discount and entered it on both invoices and statements. If it needed to be written back on grounds of late payment, care would need to be taken that any subsequent credits were taken into account. Any warning or reminder letters sent would need to be recorded in the trading history of the account, thus generating a different sequence of actions in relation to future problems. The computer printing of overdue letters could follow rapidly after the due date for payment, and could be extended into an automatic transfer routine to an agency or solicitors used to process the debt externally. Incidentally, not all collection agencies or solicitors are as effective as they would wish clients to believe; there could be more than a little merit in running controls on debts transferred to them for processing as well.

Copies of hasteners generated by the computer on multipart stationery could be formatted specifically for different simultaneous purposes. A hastener for an overdue overseas payment could serve a quadruple purposes in this manner using one set of data:

1  Top copy—to bank asking them to contact their correspondent by cable, telephone or airmail (depending upon amount involved).
2  Second copy—to area representative, requesting details of any known reason for delay in payment.

3  Third copy—to customer as above.

4  Fourth copy—for office use to progress the transaction.

A further significant computer feature for processing outstanding items is the use of Datamailer stationery. This comprises a multipart set of documents which could include a pre-printed reminder letter and remittance advice enclosed within an envelope in continuous stationery form with a top copy for office purposes. All the data printed by the computer would appear on the top copy, but only the required data would appear on the successive parts of the stationery as determined by the position of backing carbon on each part. Routine clerical and post-room functions which would otherwise be carried out are automatically obviated.

Analysis

This is perhaps the most intriguing aspect of computer systems in sales-ledger administration and credit control. Ledgers can be extremely complex in relation to numbers and types of accounts, and trading patterns. Computer techniques are ideal for identifying the nature and scale of problems within the ledger and for monitoring the effects of changes devised to eliminate them. They enable a disciplined approach to be brought to bear upon these problems and replace what can be a muddled, mystical art with science.

In 1897 Vilfredo Pareto investigated the distribution of wealth and income in Italy and discovered that a very large percentage of both were in the hands of a very small percentage of the population. In recent years a similar inequality has been found in many fields of business, typically:

1  80% of the revenue may come from 20% of the customers.

2  20% of items transferred to doubtful debts may result in 80% of the value of bad debts written-off.

This type of relationship appears so frequently that the phenomenon is known as Pareto's Law, 80/20 distribution or ABC analysis.

In practical terms, 80% of customers will conduct their business in a perfectly straightforward manner. So who are the 20% who will not? Where a sales ledger of many tens of thousands of accounts is concerned, the manager controlling it must know the constitution of the 20% currently and be able to predict with some degree of certainty which accounts will fall into that group in the near future. If he does not have that information his control is illusory—he can only react to events as they occur, at best. Computer techniques allow problem areas like this to be probed. When certain characteristics have been determined a simulated situation based upon them can be developed and the entire ledger can be scrutinised against these parameters. In this manner accounts can be detected whose characteristics are a potential cause for concern, and the computer can produce relevant data on a continuing basis for management scrutiny and initiation of remedial controls. The nature of these early warnings can be changed as the nature of the business itself changes.

## Reports

Within the closed balance brought-forward systems, reports tend to be elementary, but the following ones are of great value:

1  Debt duration—overall, and by region and compared with targeted durations.
2  Analysis of outlets by classification/region—to identify the nature of the types of outlets with which business is transacted, and shifts in the emphasis.
3  Value of sales by outlet classification/region—to be related to costs of servicing the outlets, by region.
4  Analysis of sales by outlet credit risk category.
5  Analysis of overdue debt hastening action—to identify number of:
   (a)  First stage hasteners          ⎫ By outlet classification/
   (b)  Second stage hasteners        ⎬ region/territory
   (c)  Transfer to agencies/solicitors ⎭ salesman.
6  Analysis of late payment—to identify point at which cash is received from major accounts in relation to due dates for payment. This can only be continued each period until the account is closed off. Nevertheless, it is an extremely powerful

tool to identify the customer's use of the supplier's capital, and can be linked with rapid progression systems.

7　Analysis of credits issued—by outlet classification/territory salesman/region.

8　Daily cash flow report.

Within the open-item system, not only are all the reports listed above feasible, but the following can also be generated:

1　Aged debt analysis—to indicate by customer within region the age of overdue items. The value of loss of interest represented by the overdues can be calculated and the accounts ranked in terms of total interest lost.

2　Analysis of aged unadjusted deductions and open credits.

3　Analysis of invoices in dispute.

4　Analysis of unearned discounts taken.

It is obvious that because the computer can process vast quantities of data against any required parameter at immense speed an entire range of reports can be generated to cover all the aspects of sales ledger administration and credit management which are relevant and important to any individual business. Often such analyses are extremely voluminous, which is necessary at the working level, but summaries of all reports can also be created providing pertinent information for successive levels of operational management and for incorporation in board reports.


**Advanced systems**

Visual display units (VDU)

These have been referred to earlier in the context of order processing. They also have an extremely important part to play in the development of on-line credit management systems. They create the facility for the computer to be interrogated remotely to determine the exact status of an account at a point in time and for unprotected data to be amended by direct input. If required, back-up files can also be accessed to determine past history.

Delays in obtaining information, or in updating records, as in more conventional systems are thereby eliminated. Paper output is reduced by the facility to obtain information direct from the cathode-ray tube screen display, but where it is necessary back-up hard copy can also be printed. In summary, the benefits to be derived can be:

1   Reduced documentation.
2   Faster information input and retrieval.
3   More accurate data for the basis of decisions.
4   Faster decision making.
5   Improved control and customer relationships.
6   Cost reduction.


## Hand-held terminals

These devices incorporate a small keyboard and mini-VDU, and are able to be linked via a domestic telephone handset to a remote mainframe or mini-computer. They have been in use in the USA for the past 12 years or so for order taking by salespersons and have been introduced only comparatively recently into the UK. Typical information which they accept when it is transmitted from the computer to a salesperson's home telephone, and which the salesperson can play back and read on the screen, two lines at a time, include for each account:

1   Account details in sequential order (call sequence) of calls to be made in the next and subsequent working days.
2   Average volumes by brand code/period over the last '$n$' number of call cycles.
3   Suggested current order to be taken by brand code/volume.
4   Current credit status.
5   Current credit limit.
6   Amount/date due.
7   Account/duration overdue.

Orders taken and cash collected can be keyed into the hand-held terminal and transmitted direct into the company's computer via the salesperson's home telephone automatically the same day or overnight, following which the next day's and subsequent day's calls are updated in the hand-held terminal by the computer.

Computer output microfilm (COM)

The use of microfilm has helped to solve many business problems through its inherent advantages of:

1 space saving;
2 fast reference;
3 security;
4 weight reduction;
5 lower carriage costs;
6 inexpensive duplication;
7 accuracy of filing;
8 computer compatibility.

Computer line printer output can be microfilmed in the same way as any other document, but the COM process converts data held on digital computer magnetic storage media directly on to microfilm in a single operation without the creation of paper output.

Computer printing speeds are slow, even at 1500 lines, or approximately 24 pages, a minute. COM transfer speeds can be typically 120 000 characters a second creating 300 frames a minute, each frame equating to a page of computer-printed output. Data can be presented within a form outline by means of a form overlay being optically superimposed over the text. A general application would present 270 pages of text on a small sheet of film (fiche), 4in × 6in. Real time advantages cannot be obtained through COM, and it is not practical to amend microfilm after it has been produced. Nevertheless, since the cost of reproducing copies of microfilm is nominal, with no deterioration in quality between successive copies, this medium is eminently suitable for widespread dissemination of computer data. Consider its applicability to the circulation of credit information from a centralised headquarters to 1000 regional offices.

COM installations are expensive, but this disadvantage can be partly overcome by the use of bureau services; a growing business, as evidenced by Eurocom Data Ltd, a jointly-owned subsidiary of the National Westminster Bank and the US National Bank of Oregon, whose UK operation alone now involves 10 centres providing services to 500 companies.

Postal delays are eliminated, and the latest possible sales ledger financial information is made available to management.

## VDU/COM combinations

The Kodak KAR-4000 Information System is based on a powerful mini-computer which links with a Kodak microimage terminal. As documents are micofilmed they are allotted a code number. This code number is fed into the mini-computer, through a VDU, together with other information from the document—addresses, dates, invoice numbers. This provides the index to the file. When information is needed, the operator requests it via a VDU. The VDU then locates and displays the information on its own screen, or, should it be requested, locates the document image itself and displays that on the screen of the microimage terminal.

This system is capable of being developed so that:

1  Each document produced by the computer, e.g. invoice, credit note, statement, could be given by the computer a prefix and unique serial number starting at '0' within each group of documents.
2  The data could be assembled on magnetic tape for COM production on microfilm rollfilm daily, with an index created as one or two leader frames for each group of documents.
3  COM rollfilm could be held in cartridges in a carousel in date order.
4  Copies of the COM rollfilm could be produced for simultaneous use, if necessary, and for security purposes.
5  The existence of a specific document could be identified on-line via the VDU giving date, type of document, value and serial number—information generally adequate for answering most queries.
6  In instances where the document had to be accessed for fuller information, or to enable a copy to be taken, the relevant dated cartridge would be loaded into the microimage terminal. The computer would automatically drive the film on to the exact address of the document to display it in full on the screen.
7  In the event of a systems failure, the film could be accessed via conventional microfilm reader/printers.
8  It would be practical to house the COM equivalent of approximately 2 million documents in one carousel, taking up little more space than the filing pedestal of a conventional clerical desk.

Predictive systems

The data base at Companies House is computerised and it is possible to obtain from specialised agencies, e.g. Extel Statistical Services Ltd, details of statutory documents as soon as they have been filed. Relevant financial ratios can then be fed into the computer models to predict, where appropriate, potential insolvency—the Z-score factor. Academic work in this field, originated in the late 1960s by Prof. Edward Altman of New York University, has been translated into the UK business environment by Dr Richard Taffler of the City University Business School, from which the Microcomputer Credit Control System of Performance Analysis Services Ltd, Eastcheap, has been developed. This is based on an analytical technique known as multiple discriminant analysis which determines from the financial ratios for a company under examination its solvency threshold and financial track record. This is then compared with the average performance of companies in the same industry. Additional analyses enable a credit analyst to formulate a sound prognosis on the financial health of the subject company.

## CONCLUSION

Computers have been around for many years, and all the techniques described have been used successfully in sales ledger and credit management systems. But computer aids and innovations do not of themselves solve problems—the key to success is people and those who:

1 identify the need for systems;
2 design systems;
3 operate the machines;
4 interpret the results;
5 implement judgements.

It is therefore essential in a computer-oriented environment that a sound understanding of computer systems is developed in all of those who have a role to play with them in sales ledger and credit departments, and that their awareness of developments resulting from fast moving computer technology is continuously updated.

# PART V
# CASH COLLECTION

# 11

# Collection Practices

Herbert Edwards, Managing Director, Jardine Financial Risk
Management Ltd

## THE IMPORTANCE OF CASH

'The sooner you ask, the sooner you get paid' is an excellent
approach to the slow-payment problem which cripples companies
and hinders national growth. Other apt mottoes are 'A sale is not
complete until the cash is in the till', and 'Net income is depleted
more by the cost of slow debtors than by bad debt losses'. What is
today's situation?

Most business commentators and credit analysts are obsessed by
bad debts and ignore the effects of slow trade payments. Countless
businesses are stunted by lack of liquidity rather than lack of sales.
Managements today avoid increasing bank borrowing by delaying
payments to creditors. Consequently, other firms suffer a lack of
funds. There is a mass of inertia between the invoicing of sales and
the release of cash to settle them. Elsewhere, e.g. in Germany where
payment discipline is stronger, commercial expertise is employed in
the pre-contract negotiating of payment terms, related properly to
costs and prices, rather than engaging in cat and mouse games to
avoid subsequent payment. Strangely, in the UK many managements have been content to balance slow income by delaying
outgoings, instead of finding ways of speeding up incoming cash.
Payments today remain slow, inefficient and usually in complete
violation of contracted terms.

Why this situation? How can the inertia be shifted? Cynics say that trade creditors on the balance sheet are free and simple to increase whereas bank finance or share capital costs money and brings external interference. This is only part of the truth. The rest is founded in history when Britain's financial strength was so vast that the availability and cost of credit was simply not a factor to concern businessmen. Payment was delayed to tradesmen and shopkeepers for as long as the customer required. The view of 'don't worry, they will pay in the end, they're all right' was a compliment when money cost only 2% p.a. There was no need in the business structure for a specialist manager to stoop so low as to demand repayment of overdue debts. That was a task for bailiffs and the like when final dishonour struck.

But when the UK was left with massive debt obligations abroad while imperial wealth melted away with colonial independence, bank funds became expensive and restricted. The cost of money became a factor in pricing and profitability yet many companies were still dominated by attitudes bred in the past. Old-style managers frowned upon being 'as tough as the Americans' over debts. There seems little doubt that industrial reinvestment in Germany was aided by fast movement of money between companies to produce their 'economic miracle'.

In recent years, more senior persons in UK management strata have found it necessary, yet surprisingly possible, to discuss debt implications with customers. Sheer volume growth has seen the appointment of specialist managers to keep cash flowing back into the business at a planned rate.

Significantly, recent business failures have invariably been companies where no specialist credit function existed or where it was too junior to be effective. Rather sadly, there are still companies that believe it will upset business relationships to ask for overdue debts to be settled. Lucky clients! Their benefit of extra free credit can be as much as a 5% straight addition to net income plus the beneficial use to which the 'creditor finance' is put. Progressive companies now pay as much regard to the payment term in the contract as to the price and date.

So, back to the motto, 'the sooner you ask, the sooner you are paid'. Quite clearly, if the customer genuinely cannot pay, the sooner you find out, the greater are the chances of rescuing your funds.

There is no magic formula for 100% cash collection of credit accounts. It is essential, however, to use timely and competent methods for collection. It is your money. The debtor has merely borrowed it. He must repay it as agreed. So ask him to do so. How you ask is an art, not an exact science.

## CASH COLLECTION POLICY

The function of trading companies is to supply goods or services, not working capital. Sales must be turned into cash at a rate which enables current liabilities to be met promptly. A collection policy should, therefore, be designed to achieve the maximum sales value permitted by working capital available.

The development of a well thought-out collection policy, whether simple or sophisticated, will indicate the degree of importance placed on cash by management. A collection policy will indicate that the company has moved from simply accounting for debtors to cash-planning in line with marketing needs.

Whilst accurate ledger-keeping is also essential, the key word on collections is 'commitment'. The progressive company increases its competitive edge by planning to obtain all cash due, using the most advanced methods economically possible. It must consider the quantities and calibre of staff required as well as their seniority in the hierarchy. It is essential that customers, as well as company staff, come to know that the collection manager is as senior as the sales manager.

Similarly, adequate accounting machinery or computer time is essential to achieve timely statements, reminders and reports. Delay can result in slower cash, at a cost which is measurable at current borrowing rates.

The collection policy should include reference to priorities, e.g. favoured accounts, key customers, special terms, marginal sales, cash-only business and so on. The use of credit risk categories on all accounts aids this. With the objective to maximise debtors for the shortest possible time, resources should be organised to cope with varying priorities, rather than having a standard collection system for all accounts from A to Z.

Adequate liaison with production, sales and dispatch departments should also be built into any collection policy, particularly where credit limit observance is required and where marginal (i.e. normally undesirable) business is necessary to achieve sales volume.

Hardly any business remains at the same level of sales activity for long. As sales boom or decline, sensible management will adjust its collection policy to achieve planned objectives, just as marketing tools are changeable.

## Basic rules for collection policy

1 Involve all affected departments in policy discussion.
2 Produce a clear, precise policy document (even the smallest business can do this).
3 Ensure that all staff, particularly sales, understand and implement the policy.

## Checklist for preparation of the collection policy

1 How much working capital is, or will be, available for financing credit sales?
2 What credit terms, e.g. monthly, 90 days, etc., should be granted? What is the industry norm? What do your competitors allow?
3 What amount of current debt, i.e. credit limit, will be allowed on each customer?
4 Regardless of unused credit limits, when will credit facilities be withdrawn, if debts are overdue?
   NB: When these questions have been answered the approximate sales value possible for the business can be calculated.
5 Will interest be charged for credit, or for overdue accounts?
6 As payment terms must appear in Conditions of Sale and on invoices is there any conflict with other conditions?
7 Can the planned collection systems enforce the policy adequately?
8 What expenditure on staff and equipment is available for collections?
9 What measurements and reports are required by the collection function and by management?

### Using collections to increase market share

In a competitive industry, two companies look for ways to increase their market share.

The competitive situation causes product quality, prices and deliveries to be similar. Sales are £5 million and net margins approximately 3% before tax for both companies. Payment terms are standard at net monthly and debtors represent 75 days' sales unpaid. Company A reorganises its collection activity to eliminate weaknesses. The cost is an extra £8000 a year in staff and equipment. The result is a running level of debtors at 62 days' sales unpaid.

*Results:* Company A, paying 12% p.a. interest on overdraft, borrows less and saves £22 000 per year, adding £14 000 (i.e. £22 000 less £8000 costs) to net income and raising the return to 3.3% before tax.

Company B remains as before and looks a worse bet to its lenders.

Company A generates £182 000 more funds to use in the business (13 days' sales at £14 000 per day). It uses the funds to increase marketing strength and R & D. It thus increases market share.

Company B then takes desperation measures (=price-cutting, longer terms, marginal business) and as a result:

1    loses market share;
2    suffers bad debts;
3    incurs crippling interest expense.

Company A has used cash flow to strengthen its market position.

Figure 11:1 indicates the variety of factors affecting collections.

### CASH COLLECTION—TIMING

Most companies still request repayment of debts too slowly but it is also possible for demands to be made too early or too frequently to be effective. The timing of collection actions is important to their success.

First, consider all the methods available, e.g. by letter, telephone, telex and visits. How appropriate are they for the accounts on the books? The need to collect from prompt payers on time and from

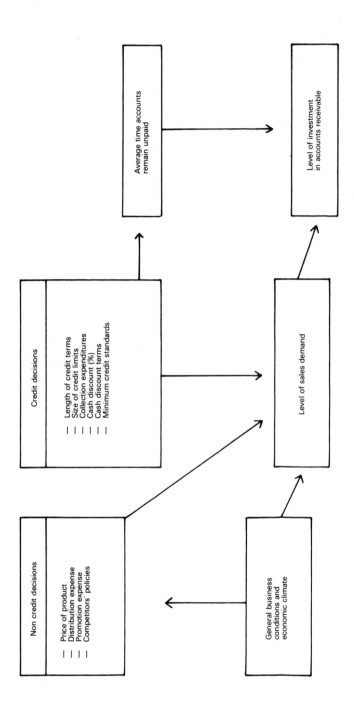

**Figure 11:1  Factors affecting investment in accounts receivable**

162

delinquents by a certain deadline will indicate the timing required for the methods used.

For normal commercial businesses the following parameters may prove useful:

1   Invoice: send this on the same day as the goods, or at the latest within 24 hours of dispatch. *Do not accumulate just to save postage.* It will be a long time before mail costs are as expensive as payments missed because of invoices not booked.
2   Statement of account: allowing time to include all invoices and cash on the ledger, send statements no later than the 5th working day following month-end.
3   First reminder action: no later than 7 days after sending the statement.
4   Next reminder action: no later than 14 days from the first reminder.
5   Final routine reminder: not more than 14 days later.

The standard system should thus be completed in 6–8 weeks from due date. Thereafter, more specialised action is needed.

There is no point in dragging out a reminder system over a longer period, such as once a month for six months, particularly on a continuing account. It makes no sense to apply 30 days' credit terms, then send a series of polite requests for overdues whilst still supplying further goods. This amounts to condoning longer credit which, if acceptable to the seller, should be formalised by changing the terms to 90 days, thus saving the time and expense of pointless reminders!

Normally, everything that is to be said to a customer, concerning non-performance on payment, can be said in the critical first month following due date.

From the first to the last collection reminder, each step should recognise the previous ones and increase in strength.

When the routine system has expired, the remaining failures should pass to a senior person for specialised action. The alternatives then available depend upon the company policy but should still be completed in less than one month. For example, a specially prepared letter, a legal threat, a visit or a telephone call to the managing director can be made and followed up within one month.

If the routine system and the specialised referrals are completed as suggested, the following advantages will be apparent:

1 All delinquent accounts will receive timely attention.
2 Problems and errors will be revealed earlier, giving the opportunity to correct them more efficiently.
3 A pattern will develop of prompt, slightly late, very slow and extremely bad paying accounts. This knowledge can then be used to attack particular weak areas, over a longer period.
4 The effectiveness of the various collection actions can be measured.
5 Customers will learn, over a short period, that if payment is not made promptly, they will receive a thorough approach on the subject, which will be difficult to resist without appearing to be bloody-minded or impoverished.

A slack, spare-time approach to collection or a widely-spaced reminder system will not reliably indicate any of the above. Rather, it will tell the customer he can get away with payment timed to meet his own needs.

## COLLECTION METHODS

1 Analyse ledger into size of accounts.
2 Collect largest accounts by personal visit (as many as time permits).
Collect all other accounts above a certain value by telephone.
Collect all smaller accounts by routine letters.

*Example:* Ledger has 2500 accounts, totalling £5 million, average balance £2000. There is the usual 80/20 pattern, i.e. 1/5th customers buy 4/5th sales value.

A 36 accounts in excess of £20 000, total £3 300 000, average £92 000;
B 460 accounts between £1000 and £20 000, total £865 000, average £1900;
C 2004 accounts below £1000, total £835 000, average £400.

A = Personal visit each month, if required.
B = Telephone twice per month, if required.
C = Printed letter series.

The company's basic documentation of order acknowledgement, invoice and monthly statement may not be regarded as collection tools, yet their effectiveness can reduce subsequent collection expenditure.

## The order acknowledgement

Customers' orders should always be acknowledged by a formal document which states very clearly the conditions of sale. These give the opportunity to quote payment terms and related conditions.

With same-day or very rapid delivery, there is little point in mailing separate order acknowledgements, as conditions of sale can be printed on the packing slip/dispatch note and included with the goods.

The subject of payment terms and conditions of sale is covered at length elsewhere in this book, but their useful effect on collections is in defining clearly:

1 the payment terms;
2 cash discount qualifications;
3 the carriage and packing charge basis;
4 the retention percentage and due date, if applicable;
5 the penalty interest basis for payment delays;
6 the dates by which non-receipt or shortages must be notified.

More than anything else, the conditions of sale give the seller the opportunity to countermand any onerous conditions of the buyer's order. This avoids subsequent disputes due to the buyer applying his own conditions.

*Example:* Buyer's order states, *inter alia:*

1 Payment will be made net at 90 days from receipt of complete set of equipment, or at 30 days less 2½% cash discount.
2 Packing and carriage at seller's expense.

Seller's terms are: net 30 days net from invoice date (not the same as receipt of goods), including part shipments, no discounts allowed, and packing and carriage invoiced at cost.

Deductions and delays will occur on payment if the buyer's terms are not corrected at time of receipt of order.

Normally, it is accepted that the seller's conditions supersede those of the buyer's order, unless the buyer comes back with a variation to the acknowledgement. In other words, 'the last document applies'. However, recent legal judgments have required the two parties to come to agreement where 'major discrepancies exist' between buying and selling conditions.

This emphasises:

1    Buyer's conditions should be checked by the seller and changed if in conflict with sales conditions.
2    The confirmation of order is the place to emphasise payment requirements.

Thus, a whole area of subsequent collection difficulty is abolished. Because of the potential impact on net income, the credit manager should participate in establishing conditions of sale.

## The invoice

The sales invoice should be designed by the credit manager and not by lawyers, dispatch departments or accountants, or, worst of all, left to the printer!

The prime purpose of the invoice is to secure payment.

It is not intended as a vehicle for conveying general information to customers, such as:

1    names, addresses and telephone numbers of depots and branches;
2    carbon-copy data from 'other parts of the set';
3    technical descriptions in unnecessary detail;
4    advertising data.

All such clutter detracts from the main purpose and is better placed on other documents.

The credit manager should produce a clear, simple invoice document showing:

1    invoice number and date;
2    customer's order number/date;

3 dispatch method and date;
4 quantity and description of goods;
5 price and value per item and total;
6 any technical data which is unavoidable;
7 VAT, packing and carriage amounts;
8 the payment terms.

If the invoice achieves the ideal of being sent within 24 hours of dispatch of goods, it is not necessary to quote a dispatch date. Too many different dates disguise the important date—that of the invoice itself, which usually determines the payment due date.

## The statement of account

Collection begins in earnest with the statement, prepared and issued monthly as a summary of the trading activity.

Opinions differ on the necessity for statements as many debtors ignore them and require only invoices which are duly approved and paid.

However, if invoices are mislaid, such a policy puts them outside the terms of the contract and there is clearly a wide discrepancy at any given date between debts shown in a seller's sales ledgers and buyers' bought ledgers.

Majority opinion remains that statements usefully provide: a regular summary of transactions; a medium for collection of accounts; the only 'bought ledger' available to some debtors. Most systems for goods received have a built-in delay factor for inspection and clearance, so that inventory reserves are made prior to posting to the bought ledger. In recent years, debtors who previously claimed no use for statements have become dependent on them for reconciliations, also when pursued for overdues and undoubtedly when making-up accounts for the balance sheet creditor's figure.

The statement enables the seller to answer customers' queries before they are asked by listing individual unpaid items clearly without historical 'clutter'.

An open-item statement is more effective than a carried-forward balance statement because no paid items or blanket balances are shown.

Carried-forward balance statements, commonly used on mechanised or handwritten ledgers, attract time-wasting questions, such as 'how is the opening balance made up?' Whenever a customer disputes a balance instead of paying it, two to three months' extra credit, at a cost to the seller, is automatically obtained.

Statements, to be most effective, should show the following data for each open item:

1   date;
2   reference (e.g. invoice number);
3   order number;
4   value.

The juxtaposition of these items helps the customer's bought ledger department to identify with their own paperwork.

Statement items should be in strict date order, with cumulative balance and a clear total. The total can be split to show post and packing and VAT elements if required but it is not normally necessary to show these for each invoice listed.

If possible, the statement should include an ageing block, to show the customer at a glance the condition of the overdues as to 30, 60, 90 days old, etc.

All overdue items and certainly the overdue total should be highlighted in some way on the statement.

The first collection message should be printed on the statement, for both overdues and current debts, e.g.

> Statement 31.8.1984
> Current total £xxx. Please pay by 30.9.1984
> Overdue total £ XX. Immediate remittance by return, please.

Statements should always carry an escape clause for recent cash, e.g. 'Payments made in the last 7 days may not be included'. This simple measure reduces hostile telephone calls and letters from customers whose payments crossed with the closing date for statement input data.

Statements should be aimed at individuals where possible. Whereas later we will discuss aiming personalised collection efforts only at financial decision-makers, statements are required by individuals within bought ledger departments. The objective is to help them find their way swiftly and directly to the person handling the account.

Having produced an accurate and timely statement, with a polite request for overdues to be paid immediately, the way is clear for a vigorous follow-up to be made, if payment does not arrive within a few days.

Mention should also be made of the use of statements in cash application. After all, fast matching of cash received is a direct aid to collecting the remainder.

There are two main pressure points in cash application:

(a) Identifying the detail of what has been paid.
(b) Inputting the data to the ledger/computer/machine.

Both problems can be eased by encouraging customers to return statements with their remittances. One successful method is to repeat the statement data on a two-sided perforated document, whereby the customer returns the left-hand page as a remittance advice. Duplicate copies are retained by the sales ledger staff.

When the remittance advice portion of the statement is received back it is easy to identify the paid items marked by the customer.

Various computer systems exist for accepting direct input of the original statement, or the retained copy, or a tabulation-style copy, either by optical mark reading or by simplified punching of the data already held on the sales ledger file.

Where the customer uses his own remittance advice, the copy statement retained in the sales ledger helps with identification and conversion of the customer's data.

## Collection letters

There is a mass of conflicting opinion on collection letters, due to the varying attitudes to enforcement and also to the wide range of debtor response to a standard letter.

Ideally, any customer who does not pay on time should be visited, to analyse his cash problem. But there is not time to visit all customers and there is not always a cash problem.

The next best solution is to telephone for payment. At least the customer must reply in some way. But telephone calls are expensive and time-consuming.

So, we are left with the least efficient of all collection methods—the reminder letter. It is inefficient because it is one-sided. The customer can ignore it. Even if he reacts in some way, the reaction cannot be dealt with until some further time has elapsed. So a great industry has grown up to design more effective debt collection letters. The spectrum contains the whole range of polite reminders, gentle persuasion, tough words, threats of further action, 'backing down again' letters, apologetic letters, number $n$ of a series, special coloured paper, special-sized printing, humorous wording, legalistic jargon, and so on.

For what purpose? There is an initial period between due date and seriously overdue, when we cannot afford to visit or telephone, yet we must do something to bridge the gap of silence. So we send a letter. Or several.

The nonsense is compounded by the fact that for overdues up to, say, 60 days, the customer will pay when it suits him. Only if we can personalise or specialise the collection action will that routine be broken.

As the period for collecting debts by printed letters should not exceed 60 days, there should be not more than three letters sent. Furthermore, the wording should be simple and direct. Politeness is always essential but firmness is justified also. The debt is your money. The debtor has merely borrowed it. He has contracted to repay it on a certain date and has failed to do so.

When payment does not arrive, you do not know whether:

(a) The customer cannot pay, for lack of funds.
(b) The customer can pay, but prefers not to, for some reason.
(c) The customer has a dispute with another department.

So, it would be wrong to assume the worst. The object of the letters is to extract a response of some kind. Whether the response is in the form of a partial payment, a letter or a phone call, it should be seized upon and dealt with, and not just allowed to slide into the clerical chore-mass.

*First reminder.* This should refer to overdue amount and date as indicated on the statement and ask for payment by return or the reason for non-payment.

*Second reminder.* This should refer to lack of response to the first letter, repeat the overdue debt amount and date and conclude with a mention of specialised action failing receipt of payment or the reason for non-payment.

*Third (final) reminder.* This should refer to the lack of response to two previous letters, give details of the debt and notify the customer that the matter has been passed to a third-party for collection, with the proviso that *seven days* will be allowed before that action proceeds.

Do not make empty threats. If you achieve an efficient series of letters ending in a threat of, say, a collection agency, you must then use a collection agency. If you promise dire action, then revert to yet another 'ordinary' letter, all credibility is lost and the customer will not take future threats seriously.

There are many, many ways of wording the three basic collection letters and examples follow. It is important however, to vary the wording from time to time and to keep a collection history file to show when customers pay and which letter produced the payment.

If a customer is determined to pay at 75 days on terms of 30 days, even the most thorough letter programme would accommodate him on the basis shown in Figure 11:2. In this way, the customer will accumulate a set of 36 (12 x 3) letters every year!

|  | Day from end of delivery month |
|---|---|
| Statement | 35 |
| No 1 letter | 42 |
| No 2 letter | 56 |
| Final letter | 70 |
| Payment received | 75 |

**Figure 11:2   Collection history documentation**

A continuing pattern of slow payment by a substantial customer must be interrupted by special action, such as a visit or telephone call to discuss compliance with payment terms.

Many companies have now eliminated the No 2 reminder and go

from a polite reminder at say 7 days overdue to a final threat at say 21 days. This normally brings most overdues in by the close of the first overdue month, instead of the second.

*Samples of overdue messages on statements.*   These can be rubber-stamp blocks, eye-catching stickers, typed or computer printed:

> 'Overdue £168.50. Please pay by return.'

*Or*

> 'Payment terms are net monthly account.
> As at date 30.9.84, overdues total £2468.36
> August £1234.18. July £905.20. June and prior £328.98.'

*Or*

> 'Current            £4296.30
> 30 days            £6136.32
> 60 days            £ 884.63
> 90 days            £1239.20
> Over 90 days       £3018.63
> Please pay all non-current items *immediately*.'

*Or*
Brightly coloured stickers saying:

> 'I'm Miss Jones. I look after your account.
> Please let me have a cheque for the overdues shown or give me a ring to talk about it.'

*Or*

> 'Overdues spoil your credit record. Please pay.'

*Or*

> 'Do it now! is a slogan we are borrowing to ask you to pay the overdue amount shown here. Pay it now (Please).'

*Samples: first reminder letters*

Dear Mr Paine,
   Our last statement showed in detail the amount of £1645.39 which
is OVERDUE for payment to us.
   Will you please make immediate arrangements to pay this
amount or alternatively let me know your reason for non-payment.
   Yours sincerely,
      D. Marks, Credit Department (Ext 211)

*Or*

'We cannot trace your payment for the August account of £652.00
which became overdue two weeks ago.
   Please pay this to us without delay or let us know if there is any
problem affecting payment.'

*Or*

'It may be useful to remind you that our contractual credit terms
are net 30 days from invoice date.
   On this basis your account shows £689.26 overdue and we look
forward to your payment by return mail.
   We enclose a stamped, addressed envelope to help you.'

*Samples: second reminder letters*

Dear Mr Paine,
   We wrote to you two weeks ago about your overdue account for
£1645.39. Details appear on the last statement sent to you.
   So far, we cannot trace your payment nor any reply. If we do not
hear from you by return, we shall transfer collection action to
————— (solicitors, collection agency or whatever).
   We look forward to your response.
   Yours sincerely,
      D. Marks, Credit Department (Ext 211)

*Or*

'We have now sent you a detailed statement of overdues and a
polite request for payment, yet we have not received the courtesy of a
reply.

Can we please have your payment of £652.00 by return, in order to avoid passing the account to a third-party for collection, with extra costs?'

*Or*

'As there has been a regular business between us for a long time, we are concerned that you have not responded to our previous requests for overdues to be paid. They now total £432.23.

Please send us either your remittance for this sum or let us know what is preventing your settlement being made.

If we do not hear from you this time, all we can do is hand the matter to a specialised agency to resolve.'

*Samples: final reminder letters*

*For the Chief Accountant*

Dear Sirs,
  *Re: OVERDUE ACCOUNT: £1645.39*
We regret to note that you have not responded to our previous reminders about the above debt.

As we mentioned in our last letter, your account is being transferred to ———— for collection, with any additional costs chargeable to you.

Receipt of your payment in full by return will avoid this expensive and distasteful action.

Yours faithfully,
A. Benson, Credit Manager (Ext 127)

*Or*

*For attention of Chief Financial Executive*

Dear Sirs,
  *Re: FINAL DEMAND: £652.00*
Our last statement detailed the overdue debt shown above, representing goods dispatched to your order.

We are not aware of any query or dispute on the debt and have received no reply to the payment requests sent to your bought ledger department.

Our next step is third-party collection action without further referral to yourselves.

Your immediate payment of £653.20 will prevent this action which will involve extra costs for your account.

Yours faithfully,

A. Benson, Credit Manager (Ext 127)

## Partial payment letters

Partial payments are a useful trigger for further action. Having received less than the required payment for overdues, it is important to notify the customer immediately of the discrepancy.

*Example:*

Dear Mr Hudson,

We thank you for the payment of £356.00 received today in respect of your overdue account.

As notified to you on recent reminders, the amount we actually require is £1577.00.

Your payment is, therefore, short by £1221.00 and we would appreciate advice of the reason by return. A pre-paid envelope is enclosed for your fast reply.

Yours sincerely,

M. Baker, Credit Department (Ext 169)

There are several possible reasons for a short payment and it is wrong to assume that the customer is short of cash. Other reasons could be:

1   deduction of a disputed amount, not explained;
2   an instalment only, agreed with other staff;
3   deliberate slow payment to suit own terms or systems;
4   (most frequently) invoices not yet cleared.

When the short-payment problem has been settled, remaining arrears should be dunned with the *next appropriate stage of letter,* so that the debtor does not successfully side-step the dunning procedure by making part settlement.

## Stopping supplies

If the customer cannot pay £100 how can he find £200? If the policy is to discontinue supplies at, say, 60 days overdue, it will be necessary to warn the customer of this by 45 days at the latest, to allow time for a payment to be generated.

Insert a Stop-Warning letter, or a paragraph on a standard letter, at that date stage, and SEND IT TO THE BUYER.

Copy it to the sales manager. He is also involved in the 'failure' situation.

Buying staff today carry a lot of financial weight. Rather than see production stop or incur sales difficulties, the buyer will probably ensure that payment is brought up-to-date. Properly approached, the buyer can also ensure compliance by his bought ledger staff with the contracted terms in future.

Once supplies are stopped, collection having failed, it is important to:

1  Notify all possible 'order takers'.
2  Decide whether to accept orders or not, with shipments held. (This will probably depend upon the risk category of the customer.)
3  Actually receive payment or a written acceptable settlement plan before resuming supplies.

*Sample: Stop-Warning letter*

Sent at due date plus, say, 45 days.

ABC Nuggets Ltd,
14 Long Lane,
Heymouth, Barset.                                   15 September 1984

For the attention of Chief Buyer.

*Copy:* J. Friend, Sales Manager
XYZ Ltd

Dear Sirs,
  *Re: Stoppage of supply*
Despite reminder letters to your financial staff, we can trace no payment of the debt of £1620.93. Details have already been supplied.

This letter is to remind you that our policy is to discontinue supplies to customers with seriously overdue accounts.

Please help us avoid this distasteful measure by arranging payment of this amount by return mail.

Yours faithfully,

for XYZ Ltd

J. Brooks, Credit Department (Ext 626)

Note on J. Friend copy: Will allow until 30.9.84 before stopping.

## Interest for late payment

Similarly with penalty interest charges (also known as service charges, carrying charges or credit surcharges) it is necessary to give written warning. In this case, as the penalty will apply sooner, e.g. at due date plus 15 days, the best place for the warning is on the statement of account.

In a suitable space, on each statement where overdues exist, the following note should be highlighted:

'Chief Accountant please note:

Interest will be charged at (2%) per month on any overdue amount not received 15 days after due date as per clause 4 of conditions of sale.'

## Personalised correspondence

There is also the critical area of special correspondence of which there are two kinds:

1  replies to incoming correspondence;
2  finalising the more serious overdue situations.

It is unlikely that adequate form letters can be pre-prepared to cope with all incoming mail except for a well-designed acknowledgement card to use when a delay in reply cannot be avoided. It is essential to give priority to incoming letters since most will relate to disputes which cause unpaid accounts until satisfactorily answered.

Persons authorised to generate non-standard correspondence

should be properly trained in effective letter-writing, to meet the following parameters:

1   See the customer as an esteemed outlet for the sales function.
2   Identify the salient points needed to settle the matter.
3   Deal with decision-makers only.
4   Be courteous but accurate, polite but firm.
5   Achieve all that must be said on one sheet of paper. (Copy evidence if necessary to be attached.)
6   Sign the letter personally.

There are many psychological ploys available to letter writers. Having identified the customer's problem and ensured that the recipient of the letter is the person who matters, the credit writer has a choice of several approaches. A large measure of empathy is needed to put the writer in the other person's position, in order to resolve the problem in the most efficient way.

There are no prizes available for literary masterpieces or for flowery waffle. The only acceptable measure of success is the speed with which the customer is satisfied enough to make payment, with goodwill maintained.

## Telexes

The use of telex messages for collection work is still largely under-developed, despite their being cheaper to send than dictated letters. It is probably their comparative rarity that gives telexes their sense of urgency, similar to that of telegrams.

Simple telexes to customer's senior staff can have a very stirring effect, when brilliant letters have no impact at all. This is probably because the defensive 'filters' of secretaries and assistants protecting chief accountants and directors seem to let telexes through to the great men's desks. Telexes can often replace special letters to good effect, if used selectively.

## Collecting by telephone

This is by far the most cost-effective way of collecting accounts and Chapter 12 is devoted to this subject.

Whilst not quite as good as personally confronting the customer, there is the compensating advantage of being less inhibited on the telephone than in a face to face interview.

The telephone should be used for collecting debts above a certain value or beyond a certain age. The timing of calls should follow the same patterns as letters, so that a high volume of fairly standard calls can be made each day. As soon as the customer responds with excuses or problems, the call becomes non-standard and skill is required in concluding the conversation successfully.

The telephone collector must be sure to have available: ledger details; file notes and correspondence; previous promises, with dates and amounts. The collector should pause to plan the call properly, be sure to speak to the correct person and conclude by obtaining a precise date and amount for a promised payment.

For difficult accounts and for calls to the giant corporations, two calls will probably be necessary, as the sheer size of the account or the problem may require 'leaving it with them' for a while. The collector should allow an agreed time for investigation then conclude the matter on the second call.

The notation of telephone results should not be skimped. A clear record should be made of important points stated by either side, plus the promised amount and date. Wherever possible, a letter should be sent confirming the agreement made.

## Personal visits

Personal collection of accounts falls into two categories: a special visit to a senior person to discuss a problem, and a routine visit to a paying centre to assist in clearing invoice queries and reconciliations. In both cases, obtaining the required cheque saves postal and system delays, and helps to achieve financial deadlines.

Special visits should never be made 'cold'. A meeting should be properly arranged with the appropriate senior person to review business between the companies. This provides an ideal opportunity to update credit ratings by obtaining more recent financial data than exists with external sources. The credit-conscious customer will normally recognise the worth of justifying a good credit rating and will be aware of the interchange of credit data between suppliers. The credit manager will have the chance at first-hand to pick up complaints from the customer, probably as to prices and deliveries (take the marketing man with you!) and possibly as to payment terms or documentation errors. It is often useful to provide the customer with a list of his recent payment dates and amounts, alongside the correct due dates, to demonstrate his non-compliance with payment terms.

Such a visit is an excellent opportunity to build goodwill and develop personal contacts in case of future needs.

A letter should always be sent immediately on return to base, to confirm accurately the points agreed, especially as to corrective action being taken by the credit manager.

Routine visits to paying centres have a special place in the collection system. The investment of resources in employing specialist staff, probably with company cars, to spend say 80% of their time visiting key customers, will be a brave decision by most managements. However, there is a distinctly measurable pay-back, when comparing salary and other costs to the interest saved by collecting massive accounts 30–60 days earlier than would happen if left to normal methods.

Consider the monolith corporations. Payment terms are, say, 30 days but the diverse receiving depots, the checking of goods and clearance of invoices all lead to an elapsed time of say 65 days before payment can be made. Then the bought ledger computer only prints out on the 20th of the month, and the cheque finally arrives after 90 days. The cheque is for only 83% of the account total, because some invoices are mislaid. At no point is there any malice or ill-intention. The delays are purely bureaucratic. Bought ledger staff themselves are often just as fed up as suppliers with the system's imperfections, since they are harassed by dunning letters and phone calls.

This is an excellent opportunity for an account representative to visit the beleaguered bought ledger to bring reinforcement and relief. He can take the monthly statement, identify uncleared invoices, provide copies, pick up errors and queries, seek out buyers or other payment-approvers and generally maximise the volume of invoices going through the computer for payment.

By careful negotiation he can also achieve 'special' payment of overdues, or payments on account. Meanwhile, no pressure is applied by letter or telephone and both parties are happier with the improved account 'atmosphere'.

## Special ledgers

For collection purposes at least, sales ledgers should be sub-divided between key, ordinary trade, associate company, government and export accounts, etc.

1   *Key accounts:* these have a significant effect on debtors totals, overdues and cash collection and deserve special treatment, i.e. visits and phone calls.

2   *Ordinary trade:* representing usually the vast majority of accounts by number but not value, the whole range of collection methods apply. They can be sub-divided numerically or alphabetically but it is vital to complete the collection cycle for the entire ledger. It is a strange fact revealed in audits that A–M accounts are usually in better condition than N–Z accounts. This is simply because collection programmes run out of time halfway, then start at the beginning again the next time. If there is a shortage of staff or time, begin ledger review from the back, or 'Z's', on alternate occasions.

3   *Associate company:* these debts are settled variously:
    (a)   by book entries by both parties;
    (b)   by a central ledger centre;
    (c)   by normal payment on mandatory terms.
    In all three cases, overdues are unusual. Where overdues exist, it is normally for group reasons as a means of financing one unit out of another. Unauthorised overdues should be collected by reference to a senior central authority, since it is nonsensical for subsidiaries to obtain such unauthorised finance without the knowledge and approval of group treasury/finance functions.

4   *Government:* some sales to ministries and public corporations require special billing forms, which are only authorised after inspection and approval of the goods or services.
    Normal collection procedures are quite pointless in these cases, since payment is made immediately (or within a timing cycle of up to 21 days) once the approved forms are received (e.g. Ministry of Defence Forms 640).
    The ledger collection system should be devoted to producing the required paperwork as efficiently as possible.
    Where it is certain that the correct forms have been submitted

more than one month earlier, then submission of copy details to the government paying centre concerned will invariably bring payment or details of the error delaying payment.

Credit managers sometimes hear customers say: 'We can't pay you yet. We sell to the government and, as you know, they never pay in less than 90 days.' The truth is probably that billings are recorded upon manufacture, instead of at date of submission of approved forms. Inspection delays may be the fault of government departments but are often within the control of suppliers who simply do not notify inspectors or make consignments available on time. Documentation delays are invariably the fault of the supplier. Audits have revealed government debts *more than one year old,* where the supplier recorded the sale in the ledger but never got around to submitting 640 Forms to the Ministry.

There is a large area which can be influenced by credit departments in the field of government debts.

5   *Export:* a separate chapter deals with this specialised subject. Suffice to say here that routine letters sent to domestic customers have little effect on foreign accounts. Documentary terms require a follow-up system to the bank. On receipt of bank advice of non-payment by the customer, telex or letter follow-ups direct to the customer can safely be made. Better still, if a local agent is employed, he can be incentivised to earn his commission by only being paid when the customer debt is paid. Telephone calls are rarely satisfactory, in view of costs and time differences, but the use of external agencies such as banks, agents and subsidiaries compensate for the remoteness.

## CASH TARGETS

The best-organised collection department 'doing its best' will possibly collect 10% less cash each month than one working to a prescribed cash target. There is a distinct incentive effect in establishing in advance the amount of money which is available from a set of customers. The total required and the monthly deadline combine to encourage more effort and resourcefulness from the staff concerned.

## How to calculate the cash required?

Using the debtors forecast or budget for any future period, obtain the days' sales outstanding figure (DSO). If there isn't one yet, begin by calculating the DSO for previous periods, then establish the likely pattern for the future. Calculation of cash targets needs the DSO figure and actual sales for previous months.

*Example:* You have just ended August with debtors equivalent to 75 DSO. Now calculate cash needed in September to achieve budgeted 72 DSO.
August 75 DSO comprised:

| | | | | |
|---|---|---|---|---|
| August | 31 days | Sales | £ 468 000 | |
| July | 31 days | Sales | £ 529 000 | |
| June | 13 days | Sales | £ 221 000 | (= 13/30 of £510 000) |
| | 75 days | | £1 218 000 | Debtors |

To achieve 72 DSO in September will require a result of:

| | |
|---|---|
| September | 30 days |
| August | 31 days |
| July | 11 days |
| Total | 72 days |

So, September cash must be equivalent to:

| | | | | |
|---|---|---|---|---|
| June | 13 days | = | £221 000 | |
| July | 20 days | = | £341 000 | (= 20/31 of £529 000) |
| | | | £562 000 | |

Therefore if £562 000 is collected, September DSO must be 72.

Other methods of cash targeting:

1 Historical basis of percentage of aged debtors:
   e.g. 78% of current: 86% of 1–30 days: 95% of 31–60 days: 99% of 61 days +
2 Examination of ledger to identify collectable amounts.
3 Allocation of lump sum required by management.

None of these methods is as accurate as the DSO method, but they still have the incentive effect of a predetermined target.

**Visual aids for cash targets**

The incentive effect on staff is continued by displaying progress in some visual way. Many systems exist for wall-charts, displays and tabulations but require adaptation to suit a particular operation. In general terms, two items are required:

A  A large cash graph, for the collecting month or period.
B  A collection progress sheet, for listing the accounts.

*Example: Cash graph* (see Figure 11:3)

1 Graduate the cash (e.g. £562 000) on the vertical.
2 Graduate the days available (e.g. 30) on the horizontal.
3 Draw a diagonal 'par line' from 0 to £562 000 at 30 September (this indicates the approximate daily collections required).
4 Highlight on the horizontal any special actions, e.g. letters sent, accounts stopped, 60 days overdues phoned, staff sick, etc. (this helps to explain peaks and troughs).
5 Mark DAILY the cash *and firm promises* on the graph. (The progress of the 'snake' creates genuine motivation when allied to well-organised collections to beat the deadline.)

*Example: Collection progress sheet* (see Figure 11:4)

1 Regardless of ledgers and tabulations, make a separate list of collectable accounts over a certain figure (e.g. 80% of total).
2 Show amounts current and overdue.
3 Have a column for promises as well as cash received.
4 As the month progresses, focus attention on remaining gaps in promises or receipts.
5 Use total results at month-end as a guide for next month's activity.

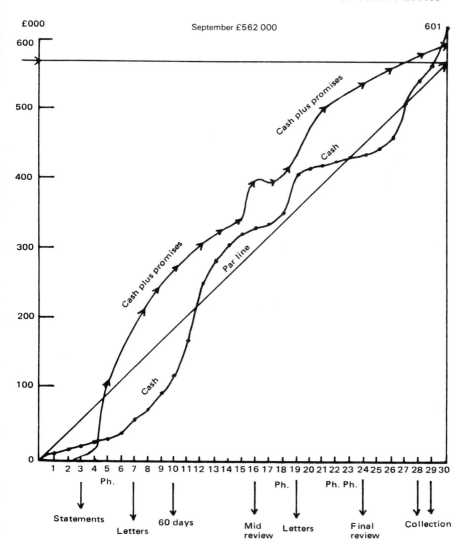

**Figure 11:3  Specimen cash graph**

## COMPUTER AIDS TO CASH COLLECTION

The management principles should be to put as much basic work on to the computer as possible, leaving the expensive humans free for customer contact and exceptional problems.

**185**

| | | | | | |
|---|---|---|---|---|---|
| For September: £562 000 | | | | | |
| *Account* | *Current* | *Overdue* | *Total* | *Promised* | *Received* |
| Black Brothers | 38 129 | 2 296 | 40 425 | | |
| White & Co. | 627 | 2 016 | 2 643 | | |
| Brown Ltd | 10 123 | 3 838 | 13 961 | | |
| Grey-Grey Ltd | 11 009 | 201 | 11 210 | | |
| Blue-Black & Son | 1 768 | — | 1 768 | | |
| Scarlett Ltd | 990 | 630 | 1 620 | | |
| etc., etc., | etc | etc. | etc. | | |
| Accounts below £500 | 122 126 | 38 011 | 160 137 | | |
| Total | £559 909 | £63 197 | £623 106 | | |

**Figure 11:4  Collection progress sheet**

Excellent service bureaux exist to provide computer facilities where there are none, or inadequate ones, at present, with well-tried software programmes for several collection procedures. Many software packages now exist for purely local minis and micros for credit and collection work.

The credit manager should make a study, initially and at intervals, of the tasks to be done by computer, both as to layout and frequency, then decide on the cost/effectiveness.

**Examples of aids**

1   Invoices: Can be produced either on-line as part of dispatch system or by punching dispatch paperwork.
    Easily produced and dispatched daily and easily input to sales ledger, with low error rates.
2   Statements: Can be produced when required on open-item basis as soon as last data has been entered. Can include an ageing block automatically and generate the first printed reminder message.

3   Collection reminders: Programmes can be set for output of prescribed letters or tabulations for all accounts in certain ageing conditions at certain dates, e.g.:
(a)   Overdues 7 days after statement date: No 1 letter.
(b)   Overdues 14 days after No 1 letter: No 2 letter.
(c)   Overdues 14 days after No 2 letter: final reminder.
(d)   Overdues 7 days after final reminder: list to credit manager.
(e)   Overdues partly paid at any stage: partial payment letter.
(f)   Overdues 7 days after partial payment letter: list to credit manager.
(g)   Stop-Warning letters when list input by credit department.
The letters should always be edited by credit department for idiot-errors prior to dispatch, but all file-searching and production work by staff will have been eliminated.

4   Action tabulations: Parameters can be set for the production of useful listings to aid collection, but care must be taken to avoid consuming computer time with badly planned or not-really-needed reports. Useful tabulations include:
(a)   Monthly aged analysis of all accounts.
(b)   Detailed list of overdues over say £5000 and 60 days.
(c)   Accounts in excess of credit limits (for collection purposes).
(d)   Stop list.
(e)   List of overdue actions, showing date and type of last letter.
(f)   Monthly open-item list, listing chronologically all items open on the ledger, showing account number.
(g)   Sales last 12 months, by customer.
(h)   Orders on hand, by customer.
It is important to think in terms of 'exception' reports, since the computer can do the scanning of thousands of items and select only the data needed, once the parameters are set by the credit manager.

The use of visual display units (VDU) is now increasing, whereby any data held on computer tapes or discs can be accessed and displayed live on a screen at the user's desk. Thus the delay between the 'need' and the 'response' is cut to a minimum and the collector can talk to a customer by telephone whilst looking at a screen showing billings or cash input only minutes earlier. The same screen displays can be used for reconciling accounts by searching and calculating with a cursor.

In most cases, data is input to the computer file by the keyboard on the VDU, thus eliminating punching operations and delays.

## BILLS OF EXCHANGE

These are clearly defined in the Act of 1882 as:

> A bill of exchange is an unconditional order in writing, addressed by one person (A) to another (B), signed by the person giving it (A), requiring the person to whom it is addressed (B) to pay on demand, or at a fixed or determinable future time, a sum certain in money to or to the order of a specified person (C), or to bearer.

A bill is used to facilitate payment where a customer requires longer than normal credit terms. For example, a supplier of raw materials to a manufacturing customer requiring credit draws a bill of exchange to the value of the debt payable, e.g. 3 months later. The customer accepts the bill by signing it, so obtaining 3 months in which to turn the materials into finished goods and sell them avoiding the need to use working capital. The supplier can sell the bill to a discount house, at an agreed rate, for immediate cash. A bank bill provides the same facility, where a bank lends its name in place of the buyer, to strengthen the bill for discounting. Discount houses buy bank bills at the finest rate (published daily in the financial press) but the cost is increased by the bank's charge for adding its name.

First-class trade bills (i.e. with two good names) carry a higher discount rate than bank bills, but no bank charge is incurred.

*Advantages*

1   Ideal for covering short-term credit extensions.
2   Interest (or discount fees) are easily calculated for passing on to or sharing with the customer.
3   Rarely dishonoured, because of customer's bank's knowledge.
4   Can be 'guaranteed', by endorsement by a third-party.
5   Immediate legal evidence of the money debt, actionable at law.

*Disadvantages*

1   Some customers regard bills as an adverse credit opinion.

2   Credit limits must include all unmatured bills subject to recourse to the seller if dishonoured.

Promissory notes are similar to bills drawn by the supplier but are drawn by the buyer promising to pay a precise value on a fixed date.

Both bills and notes are commonly used in revolving credit facilities where a continuing loan is renewed at regular intervals, say quarterly, by accepted bills or notes, instead of repayment to the lender.

## DIRECT DEBITING

This method of transferring funds is promoted by the clearing banks as a means of reducing cheque handling. Previously used mainly for consumer instalment payments and for fuel-oil and brewery debts, it is now rapidly spreading as an efficient way of collecting varying amounts of trade debts.

The seller must obtain his customer's agreement to debit their bank account on agreed due dates with monthly debt values. The banks insist on a standard wording for such debit authorities, to eliminate dangerous small-print, and the customer's bank must also sign it. Customers must be creditworthy for the amounts involved, otherwise debits can 'bounce' in the same way as cheques.

The system requires the supplier to send the usual monthly statement to the customer with a request to notify any errors by a certain date. On the due date, all debts not disputed are debited by the supplier's bank to the various customer banks, with a single credit to the supplier. This saves the customer time, paperwork, postage and bank charges. The bought ledger system is reduced, no remittance advice is needed and the monthly debt is simply picked up from the bank statement.

Suppliers wishing to operate a direct debit system should consult their own bank and plan the promotion very carefully. Initial customer resistance is based on 'fear of the unknown' and the best approach is to offer a trial period only. Experience proves that customers' fears are invariably groundless as the benefits are realised. Nevertheless, the supplier must be recourseworthy enough to give adequate indemnities to banks and customers against error.

## CASH DISCOUNTS FOR PROMPT PAYERS

These require very careful management to be effective, otherwise they become a much abused trade discount.

Suppliers already granting cash discounts have the advantage of earlier payments but the per annum cost is high (e.g. 2½% 14 days, net 30 is equivalent to 57% per annum) and they must disallow late payments and chase customers for repayment of unauthorised deductions. If the cost is already comfortably included in prices and margins, the per annum rate can be ignored for the sake of cash flow. However, if margins are critical, it would be far cheaper to retain the 2½% and collect net in due course. After all, it is better to wait 30 days for £100 than to receive £97.50 in 14 days!

Suppliers not already giving cash discounts cannot afford to start offering them without a compensating price increase, unless they are desperate for cash at any price. If the credit manager wishes to offer a cash discount to tempt his slow-payers to come into line, he must remember that the discount will also be taken by all those customers paying promptly already.

The ideal time to introduce a cash discount structure is when an across-the-board price increase is announced, when the effect of the increases can be 'softened' by the offer of a discount. Whereas a seller can rarely afford to offer a cash discount, a buyer cannot afford to ignore it.

## SETTLEMENT REBATES

More efficient than cash discounts, these are schemes whereby the seller agrees to rebate part of the price, say 5% on 31 December, or quarterly, on the total sales value to a customer, provided that payments have been prompt to terms, say 30 days, and that a certain target sales value has been exceeded.

The agreement can specify that the rebate will be reduced either by the interest cost of overdue payment at say 12% p.a. or by the value of overdues being deducted from the qualifying sales figure. Specific negotiation is required for each customer, but the advantages are clear for all parties, i.e. sales, credit and buyer.

## PENALTY INTEREST

This technique is used by some trade suppliers as a deterrent to slow payment rather than as an income item. Interest charges are only legally enforceable if the right to charge them exists in the conditions of sale accepted by the buyer. Even then, the rate is critical. A low rate, say 1% per month (12% p.a.) would be very attractive to a buyer as a means of finance, whereas 3% per month (36% p.a.) would probably be rejected by a court as usurious. Penalty interest charges are booked by most companies as a memo item, whereby they are not taken into income until actually paid and are usually written-off if the principal debt is paid without interest. It seems logical that, where prices are carefully costed to include 30 or 60 days' interest for credit, an extra charge is justified if payment is not received by that date. However, the imposition of penalty charges involves a marketing decision as well as the credit resources to control the scheme.

## CASH COMPETITIONS

While these are commonplace for sales staff, they are comparatively rare for credit staff. Yet, it is just as hard or harder to increase the share of the market's liquidity as it is to increase sales market share. If cash targets provide incentives, then competitions certainly do. Prizes take the form of cash bonuses, percentage commissions, company products (difficult for makers of gas turbines or rubber grommets!), foreign holidays or attractive hardware. Schemes can be for any period, although longer than 3 months appears to lose impact, and can be between individuals, sections or departments, either in one unit or on an inter-company basis. Typical subjects for cash competitions have been:

1  Highest total cash received by a target date.
2  Largest reduction of overdues, value or percentage.
3  Largest reduction of overdues exceeding 60 days.
4  Combined scheme (to balance all activities) for:
   (a)   best reduction of DSO in the quarter;
   (b)   largest percentage reduction of 1–60 days' overdues in the quarter;

(c)   largest percentage reduction of 61+ days' overdues in the quarter;

(d)   lowest percentage bad debts to debtors in the quarter.

The latter scheme allowed plenty of time, i.e. 3 months for actions to mature, and did not allow overdues to improve at the expense of cash or bad debts.

If there are clear anomalies between staff, such as difficult ledgers and easier ones, weightings must be introduced and accepted by competitors. In all cases it is advisable to have an extra allocation of marks for 'manager's assessment', so that exceptional actions can be rewarded or penalised as required. Competitions can also be extended to customer bought ledgers, with lucky draw prizes for payments received by certain deadline dates.

## USE OF SALES FORCE

There are good arguments for and against allowing sales personnel to handle debt collection. In favour, they are usually numerous and well-organised to cover all accounts. They have a greater opportunity for personal contact. They are sometimes more articulate. They have product leverage to exert. Against these points, they usually do not have the time to do the cash job properly, see it through and follow it up. They have a split loyalty to avoid alienating a sales prospect.

Whereas it is essential to keep the sales function informed on all difficult customer account situations, they should only be asked to take the lead when senior access can best be handled by a sales person or where there is a combined marketing/credit problem and the business is at stake.

Where collections are the responsibility of the salesman, the finance director must ensure compliance with full credit reporting and performance requirements.

In many organisations only the sales function is authorised to talk to customers, with credit staff in a subservient role. If financial targets are being met satisfactorily by this method, there is no problem, but progressive companies today expect a high degree of sales effort from sales staff, leaving them insufficient time and expertise for credit and collections.

## FIELD WAREHOUSING

This US technique has not yet developed in the UK as some predicted it would. The concept is that warehousing companies hold secure stocks of suppliers' products in regional areas and release them locally to customers against prescribed credit limits or cash payments. Suppliers pay storage costs and service fees, but in return sales can be increased to marginal risk accounts due to very efficient local deliveries, rapid use of available credit lines and, if required, collection of accounts.

## FACTORING

A finance plus credit service offered by several firms who are usually subsidiaries of the main banks. Two facilities are available: invoice discounting, whereby monthly billings are sold to the factor with or without recourse; or the full service whereby the factor allocates credit limits and buys the sales value within the limits without recourse and outside the limits with recourse. Cash is paid to the seller either immediately, less an interest charge and a retention amount, or at an agreed interval, based on the seller's previous collection period. A service charge is levied as a percentage of sales. Most suppliers find they can run credit operations for less than the factor's charge but factors claim an efficient cash flow service, which clearly appeals to many suppliers.

## COLLECTION AGENTS

A credit manager may decide that after a certain time, say 3 months overdue, it is cheaper to pass accounts to an outside third-party than to give them specialised treatment in his own busy department.

Most collection agents have an excellent performance record, but a few are complacent and tardy. Careful selection must be made, probably by giving a few trial cases to more than one prospective agency and negotiating the lowest possible percentage collection fee. It is vital that cash collected by agents is passed to the client without delay and that the agent is bonded, in case of his insolvency, while holding unremitted funds.

The reason collection agents succeed where a sophisticated credit department has failed is probably due to the third-party effect on a customer plus the concentration of effort on only a few defaulters.

## CREDIT INSURANCE

This is a facility to reduce losses when collection fails and the customer goes into insolvency. Trade Indemnity Ltd is the leading company providing home trade cover but there are now several insurers and a specialist broker will aid in finding the best cover available, then in negotiating the finest terms. Premium is a very low percentage of sales for 85% (normally) cover of prescribed credit limits. The reason for the supplier taking a 15% loss is to discourage overselling to risk accounts. Some companies regard the credit insurance premium as an unnecessary expense and prefer to allocate funds to cover bad debt reserves. Insured suppliers regard the cover as any insurance, i.e. a budgeted expense to guard against an unbudgeted loss or expense. In addition to the actual cover, the facility provides free credit assessments and an internal discipline effect on credit limit observance.

## THE CREDIT ARMOURY

To conclude, the credit manager should arm himself with adequate details of all the credit services available from banks, brokers and specialist companies, plus, of course, data available from credit interchange within industries and through the Institute of Credit Management. There will always be occasions when finger-tip knowledge is required for a particular situation and there is no excuse for the introverted credit executive to miss profit opportunities (or loss-savings) through not being up-to-date on current practice.

# 12

# Telephone Cash Collection

**Pauline Malindine, Independent Telephone Communication Consultant**

## INTRODUCTION

### The role of telephone collection

In the light of the present-day economic climate, the use of the telephone in cash/debt collection continues to grow. As a medium of communication it has a substantial role to play in vital cash flow situations that are becoming so critical if businesses are to survive.

Its cost effectiveness lies in its immediacy and effectiveness at stimulating the necessary response in most cases on the first call, thus helping to eliminate the increasing cost of face-to-face cash collection.

It also has the flexibility that can bypass or interlink with the normal pattern of computerised reminder letters and statements. It thus offers an unscheduled, spontaneous, and persistent method of cash chasing.

### Telephone limitations

There are, however, certain limitations in telephone collection, especially to the untrained and the timid! It is easier to use put-off excuses, complicated explanations, lies and in some cases downright rudeness on the telephone because the collector is unseen and therefore appears impersonal. The telephone alone cannot win over all the hardened slow debtors, but used together with written reminders and personal cash collections it can be a most effective method. Even the most hardened 'keepers of the purse' can be persuaded into at least a discussion of the overdue debt situation by a well-trained, professional, persistent, yet friendly account controller.

There is no way that the telephone can produce or become a substitute for documentation, i.e. invoices, statements, legal letters, etc., but linked with these, and with up-to-date communication between relevant departments, it can be seen to be highly sophisticated and accurate.

### Impact of telephone collection

So often there is no guarantee that a written communication—a chasing/reminder letter—ever actually reaches the appropriate desk to be glanced at in the 'in' tray by the decision-maker. The telephone therefore has a more immediate impact and feedback.

In some industries there is a natural reluctance to accept requests for settlement over the telephone more because of the traditions of the industries than personal prejudice. It is therefore very important that the collectors are familiar with the type of market and the personality types that fall within the framework of that market.

There has been in the recent past less urgency and a less aggressive process of debt chasing, and credit limits and lead times have inclined to be rather lax. Now the survival of a company depends very largely on its cash flow situation and cash/debt collecting has become a major activity. It would, therefore, seem prudent for companies to take advantage of the 'good' financial boom years to organise their collection systems, including telephone methods, in readiness for the leaner years when money is tighter.

### METHOD

To utilise to the full the telephone as a positive and meaningful medium for cash collection, it is necessary to look closely at the following three main headings:

1   staff selection and control mechanisms;
2   training methods and disciplines;
3   telephone cash-collection techniques.

The final heading is by far the most important but cannot be isolated from 1 and 2 as these have a direct bearing on the need for, and success of, 3.

*The importance of trained specialists.* The telephone is an important instrument of communication often taken for granted and often misused. Its strength lies in its economic swiftness of contact and time-saving immediate feedback. To maximise its effect, therefore, appropriate staff must be selected who can effectively cultivate and maintain a high level of cash collection at all times and be able to communicate with all appropriate levels of management. To ensure that the correct approach is always adopted, the correct choice of staff is vital. Staff need to be selected and effectively trained in the techniques of cash collection—and the cash-collection task seen as an area of activity needing specific expertise, carried out by trained staff, not just handled by any spare body in the office whose regular work load has spare capacity and the job of telephone cash collection is gradually slotted in!

As with telephone selling, specific techniques need to be introduced to increase the likelihood of meeting every call objective, and to overcome persistent objections. These must therefore be carried out by the right calibre of staff.

A clearly-defined job specification and personality profile must be discussed and prepared prior to final selection. This enables the company recruiting to form a clearly defined picture of the type of person needed. Some questions to consider could be as follows:

1   To whom is he/she responsible?
2   What daily volume of telephone activity is expected?
3   Is it necessary to be a good team member?
4   At what level of responsibility within the existing establishment would he/she be?
5   Is this a new post? Does the title describe the authority intended in the job?
6   Is there sufficient cash collection activity to utilise all working hours?

7   What training should be given? And by whom?
8   Is there a meaningful method of control/motivation?
9   What is the likely/possible career path?

*Recruitment.* Once the above criteria have been discussed and the priorities set, then recruitment can begin. The interview must be carefully structured and a telephone interview is essential before a shortlist of probables is drawn up. Although it is always ideal to find people who have plenty of telephone expertise, it is likely that their experience will be limited to one area of activity and they may have little or no relevant experience with telephone cash collection. Once the base level has been set, then with the right training and encouragement the cash collector will develop along the lines expected by the company.

*Control mechanisms.* For any method of telephone activity to be seen to be a success, whether it be a pilot scheme in one area or a complete organised national activity, a control must be kept. This may take the form of a simple daily sheet or a complicated computer form. Whatever method is adopted, it must be in essence simple. The best control methods are simple in design and seen as a guide to personal development and motivation for the cash collection staff, not just meaningless forms filled in and passed up the ladder, or chewed up by the computer, never to be discussed or seen again!

The telephone collector's ability will be judged on the number of payment commitments obtained each day/week. Therefore, the control must be in line with these objectives and seen to be straightforward and factual. Linked with the pre-research list, a daily tally of activity will:

1   stimulate constant interest to achieve the daily work load;
2   motivate continually to produce more than the previous best;
3   develop confidence and pride and increase responsibility towards the job in hand;
4   keep a constant record of names/dates/times and results of telephone contacts;
5   act as a guide to time control during the day;
6   increase liaison with management concerned and stimulate interest in the development of cash collection;

7   ensure that the collector keeps a regular note of conversion rates of success;
8   give an added check on the amounts promised/collected;
9   ensure ongoing job satisfaction.

Once these control sheets are collected at the end of each day/week/ fiscal/calendar month, the telephone collector must be aware that these documents are being analysed and constant interest being shown either as a judgement of results or as a discussion point during personal training.

An example of a daily activity sheet is seen in Figure 12:1.

## Training methods and disciplines

As with all types of telephone activity, management very often miscalculate or misunderstand the importance of telephone training. The telephone seems such a straightforward instrument, used for conversation, it is often forgotten that telephone training in business is as important as training the face-to-face salesperson—more important, when we consider that in an average day a salesperson in a large town may only successfully contact about ten customers. A professional trained telephone collector can make four times that number in a day, and the capital cost to the company is almost half that of a salesperson and car! No salesperson would consider meeting a client without planning the call, checking up on names, previous correspondence and invoices. Armed with this, the telephone collector can then begin the presentation. The technique used will finally decide success or failure.

The interview may take a few minutes, it may take an hour, but the telephone collector has only a few seconds in which to stimulate sufficient interest and confidence in the listener to establish contact and hold their attention. Therefore, a slap-happy 'dial and try' type of approach on the telephone is doomed before it begins.

A three-tiered telephone training approach is highly recommended:

1   Induction training.
2   Ongoing individual on-the-job training.
3   Team motivational training.

Telephone cash collection     Outgoing call record sheet     Name _____     Date _____

| No. of calls | Company name | Title/name of decision-maker | Date and value of last payment | Outstanding balance | Payment secured | Promised date | | Company name | Title/name of decision-maker | Date and value of last payment | Outstand-ing balance | Payment secured | Promised date |
|---|---|---|---|---|---|---|---|---|---|---|---|---|---|
| 1 | | | | | | | 15 | | | | | | |
| 2 | | | | | | | 16 | | | | | | |
| 3 | | | | | | | 17 | | | | | | |
| 9.30 | | | | | | | | | | | | | |
| 4 | | | | | | | 18 | | | | | | |
| 5 | | | | | | | 19 | | | | | | |
| 6 | | | | | | | 20 | | | | | | |
| 7 | | | | | | | 21 | | | | | | |
| 8 | | | | | | | 22 | | | | | | |
| 10.30 | | | | | | | | | | | | | |
| 9 | | | | | | | 23 | | | | | | |
| 10 | | | | | | | 24 | | | | | | |
| 11 | | | | | | | 25 | | | | | | |
| 12 | | | | | | | 26 | | | | | | |
| 13 | | | | | | | 27 | | | | | | |
| 12.30 14 | | | | | | | 28 | | | | | | |
| TOTALS | | | | | | | | | | | | | |
| | | | | | | | | | | | TOTALS | | |

Figure 12:1    **Daily activity sheet**

*Induction training.* When the new chaser/debt controller is first introduced to colleagues, all will feel strange, so a clearly-defined induction training programme should be implemented. This will ensure clear understanding of the job in hand and the authority and responsibility that is associated with the cash chasing task. Particular emphasis should be given to:

(a) telephone cash collection techniques; and
(b) explanation of cash flow as it affects the company.

In many cases it is highly valuable for the telephone collector to go out with the field sales force to meet a variety of customers. This gives the controller the chance to develop mental pictures of customer types when handling them over the telephone at a later date. Although this is not always possible, it makes the telephone job more worthwhile and meaningful to put faces to names. In a more positive vein this visual contact can often result in higher returns, and be an effective method of maintaining a high level of goodwill when the telephone follow-up is used.

A discussion on the type of market is essential as it will undoubtedly affect the type of approach needed for cash collection. For example: is the customer handling his own money (i.e. his own business)? Is he merely juggling £ numbers belonging to a large combine? Does the debtor work 'unsociable' hours and is the call time to catch him therefore crucial (e.g. in the agricultural market)?

*Ongoing training.* Once the collector is established, training must become personalised to isolate weaknesses and strengths. This has to be done early before bad habits form. This early individual accompaniment training *must* be handled personally by the credit manager or chief cash controller and *not* by another collector with a few more months' experience. During the first few weeks, many doubts and worries concerning the job/environment/relationships may develop and it is only the manager of the department or office who can effectively sort out these problems.

Each collector should have an individual training file containing an appraisal form filled in regularly following each individual training session with constructive suggestions for improvement and with meaningful objectives set to achieve before the next training session (see Figure 12:2). British Telecom are very co-operative in advising on the best possible equipment that enables the trainer to

**Figure 12:2 Example of accompaniment training form**

Name _____  Department _____  Date _____

| | Excellent | Very good | Good | Satisfactory | Below average Poor |
|---|---|---|---|---|---|
| *Personal* | | | | | |
| Attitudes towards (a) Management | | | | | |
| (b) Colleagues | | | | | |
| (c) Training | | | | | |
| Job understanding | | | | | |
| Liaison | | | | | |
| Time keeping | | | | | |
| Overall appearance | | | | | |
| *Administration* | | | | | |
| Desk condition | | | | | |
| Handwriting/figures | | | | | |
| Accuracy if balancing | | | | | |
| Active interest in results (i) Personal | | | | | |
| (ii) Department | | | | | |
| Tidiness of individual filing | | | | | |

| | Excellent | Very good | Good | Satisfactory | Below average Poor |
|---|---|---|---|---|---|
| *Telephone technique* | | | | | |
| Research before calling | | | | | |
| Opening approach | | | | | |
| Listening technique | | | | | |
| Positive presentation | | | | | |
| Objection handling | | | | | |
| Creating new business | | | | | |
| Achievement of call objectives | | | | | |
| Closing techniques | | | | | |
| Voice qualities (include the following when appropriate) polite, friendly, firm/ professional, confident, knowledgeable, positive and enthusiastic | | | | | |

Achievement of objectives set during previous session _____

General comments _____

Date _____ Day _____
Number of calls accompanied _____
Uninterrupted time spent _____

Training objectives set _____

'listen in' during live telephone calls. To train constructively, it is extremely difficult to judge, praise or criticise if only one half of the conversation is heard.

The essence of regular accompaniment training is the regularity—from a motivational point of view—of knowing that every month the collector will have the undivided, uninterrupted attention of the manager/supervisor during a training session. During these sessions the activity control sheets can be examined and points discussed.

Any telephone work can become repetitive and tiresome (by the very virtue of its speed and convenience) and new stimuli should be introduced at intervals to rejuvenate the telephone cash collectors. Ongoing training should be carried out regularly whether there is one member of staff cash collecting or a whole team.

A wall graph showing time spent with individuals and at what interval can act as an excellent control for the manager and be seen by the collectors as part of their regular motivation.

*Team motivational training.* As with any sales force, the need for training is important and must be written in as an integral part of the management activity of the credit manager/supervisor. To achieve the necessary productivity in terms of cash promises and settlements all areas of telephone activity must be tried and monitored.

If the 'team' of cash collectors consists of more than four members, then the most senior or most experienced should be given the task of daily supervision and control. This line of control and responsibility must be clearly defined and be understood by all the team members. It must also be clearly defined to any new member joining the group.

Regular meetings should be held where success and achievement are discussed. To stimulate interest it is an excellent idea to let each member contribute in some way to the meeting with a short planned presentation. This will aid confidence and add substantially to the interest of the meeting.

Incentive schemes

Incentives and motivational aids can be of tremendous value. They must be seen to be fair and carefully thought out and planned in such a way that all members of the team have a fair chance of showing up well. Financial incentive schemes can be valuable occasionally but if they once become accepted as a regular addition to the monthly salary cheque, their incentive power dimishes and in fact becomes a demotivating factor very quickly.

### External training

It is often worthwhile considering the use of an outside source of training. This can take the form of an expert running training sessions on the company premises; or the organising and implementing of appropriate sessions away from the working environment.

Very often the physical presence of a new knowledgeable face, free from the possible internal bias, can be a highly practical and worthwhile investment and can stimulate a fresh look at the subject under training. Many companies use their internal department managers to contribute to training sessions in other departments. This method ensures an excellent cross-fertilisation of ideas, and guarantees good communications within departments.

### Telephone cash collection techniques

It is necessary to understand where the cash chasing activity fits into the overall buying pattern of the customer; and how much the customer *already knows* about the company's payment terms and conditions.

Frequently the sales personnel of a company are so keen to 'make a sale' they are apt to forget to mention to the customer how and when payment should be made for the goods purchased. Sadly this lack of understanding can frequently result in a breakdown of communication at the cash chasing stage, when a firm and positive call is being made to the customer, only to find that he has been 'promised' some unrealistic discount, a free sample, or extended credit by the salesman at the time the order was placed.

Naturally not only does this create a feeling of inter-departmental disloyalty, but worse, the customer loses confidence in the company as a whole.

Projecting a balanced image at all stages to the customer will ensure his brand/company loyalty, help guarantee co-operation, and maintain his custom well into the future (see Figure 12:3).

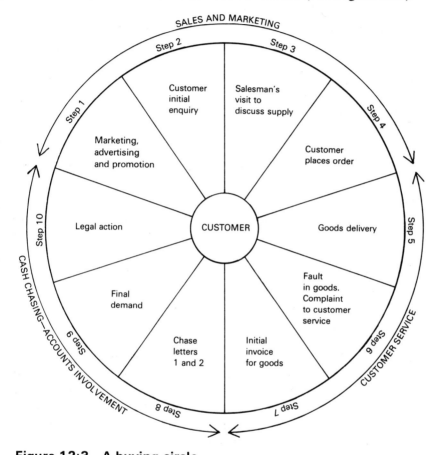

**Figure 12:3   A buying circle**

The telephone cash chasing call plan

*Step One: Pre-call preparation*

Clearly define primary and secondary call objectives. Prepare for likely non-payment excuses. Make call away from distractions. Set own personal frame of mind to harmonise with call objectives.

Plan best time to ring (judge by knowing the customer or his type or business/trade). Be prepared for 'third-party' or alternative contact.

Define precisely who is the decision-maker, by name and/or title, judge what authority he has over the settlement of the overdue debt.

Be clear of own payment terms/discounts as they relate to the call, and understand the payment/credit history of the customer.

What efforts have so far been made to secure settlement?

Is the contact at head office/branch level? Does the company have a 'prompt payment' or manual list and what are the procedures to get on to this list?

Is our system compatible with that of the customer—are computer cut-off points in harmony?

Does the customer know to which address to send his remittance/debt?

Have to hand all relevant documentation, i.e. ledger, computer print out, VDU information, memos, correspondence, etc., applicable to the call, showing details of the overdue debt/invoices/statements, etc.

Above all remember that the call is to establish commitment with the debtor that an amount (stated specifically) is overdue and that the request is for money for goods already received and used.

*Step Two: Reaching the decision-maker*

Be clear how to approach the decision-maker—surname, title, first name(s), etc., and be sure the contact is the correct person with whom you plan to establish a dialogue (e.g. small family businesses often have a number of brothers with the same surname).

A 'third-party' or alternative contact may well help in the commitment process—secretaries, wives, colleagues, superiors, etc.

The first impression at the start of the call will set the scene and show by the tone of voice the firmness and dedication to gain commitment of the overdue debt. So voice projection, tone and emphasis must be correct and reflect the company's image and attitude towards the debt. Sounding casual (by using slang words and phrases—quid, OK, cheers, hi, wotcha, bear with me, dear, etc.) can sound too familiar and dilute the firm professionalism required.

Time the call to catch the debtor at his most unprepared and vulnerable. Often an early morning call at the very start of his working day shows how seriously the situation is taken and it gives the customer all day to send in the settlement or see to the query which has caused the delay in payment.

At no time should the decision-maker be 'left alone' over the phone. Have all necessary paperwork available on the desk. If you leave the contact alone while you go away to check up on information, he may well be thinking up all manner of extra excuses, or worse, 'hang up'!

*Step Three: Developing the dialogue*

Mention the exact amount of the debt at the start of the dialogue and again during the call (and, of course, at the end when confirming the amount promised).

Use questions to ensure and gain facts with open-ended questions, e.g. '*Where* did you say you sent the cheque Mr X?' '*Which* branch was handling your query Mrs Y?' '*When* will you be sending us the cheque Miss Z?'

*Do not answer your own questions.* Use silence at the end of each question to add strength to your point.

Once the information is complete, then 'Yes' step questions can be used to gain commitment from the debtor and lead him logically to the point where he will find it difficult to refuse to settle the overdue account, e.g. 'Can I confirm that you have received goods from us during August?' (Yes) 'I believe my colleague sent you the necessary copy invoices as requested?' (Yes) 'Do you agree that there is an outstanding balance of £500 now due for settlement?' (Yes).

During the dialogue the use of well-timed and planned questions is essential; it implies strength, confirms actions, builds good customer rapport and draws out problems and queries that need prompt attention to prevent further payment delays. Customers rely on put-off excuses and non-payment objections to delay settlement and the professional chaser must be ready to handle these with confidence. The rules for this procedure are as follows:

1   Be sure that your paperwork and support information relating to the debt are accurate and up-to-date.
2   Be sure that the customer has not been promised some 'special' treatment regarding his payment by other sections of your company.

3   Be sure that your planned action is in accordance with your company's credit policy.
4   Be sure that your immediate superiors are in a position to support your verbal instructions and/or threats to the customer.
5   Be sure of your own lines of authority and discretionary behaviour.

To handle an objection, complaint, query or excuse, the best technique to apply is as follows:

1   *Listen* carefully to judge the customer's mood/emotion; to establish the *real* reason for non-payment (many debtors exaggerate their problems). Make notes as the debtor is telling you his 'excuse' and finally plan in your mind how you intend to tackle the comment or situation.
2   *Acknowledge* or appreciate the problem/comment in a way that remains neutral. An argument at this stage will completely destroy any sensible and mature dialogue.
3   *Apologise* if required, if, for example, a promised action has not been carried out (e.g. goods damaged have not yet been replaced, etc.).
4   *Develop questions* to establish that the facts are correct, to extend information given, to involve the debtor and keep call control.
5   Finally, continue in the pursuit of the debt, even if the amount promised is less than the original total first envisaged.

During the dialogue, maintain consistency in controlling the call, retain a calm, level, but firm attitude, and be sympathetic and helpful in overcoming debtors' difficulties for settlement.

Remember—do not leave your decision-maker alone.

*Step Four: Reaching commitment*

Once step three has been completed and a positive dialogue has taken place, it is necessary to reach a final call conclusion.

As the debtor is already costing our company money because of his overdue account, it is important that the cash chasing call should be kept as brief as possible to reduce our telephone costs.

With a clear objective at the call start, the commitment should be based on the debtor's willingness to co-operate in settling his account, but it is sometimes necessary to recap frequently on the figures and the payment time scales to ensure prompt settlement.

Check precisely when the cheque will be sent (not just when authorised, but when actually posted) and confirm address to which it should be sent.

Confirm with the debtor the exact amount promised, cheque dates, signatories, and, where applicable, cheque numbers.

Recap at the end of the call on the amounts and promised postal dates, and confirm that a further telephone call will be made if the cheque does not arrive—in case it was lost in the post!

Sometimes it is a generous gesture, and good for company goodwill, to ring a contact when a cheque does arrive to 'thank' the debtor for settlement.

To summarise, remember that manner and attitude will be reflected in the voice, and adopt the correct 'stance' that is applicable to the style of telephone cash chasing required by the company (i.e. relaxed, firm, threatening, etc.).

Recognise that frequently there are considerable benefits to customers to pay promptly, so do not be shy to mention them, if appropriate. (E.g.: No further cash chasing calls or letters; possible discount for prompt settlement; regular supply of goods without the worry of breakdown in production; long-term expectation of reduced prices because of increased cash flow, etc., etc.

Always be mindful that we are only collecting cash due for items already delivered or used. Do not therefore adopt a defensive or apologetic stance as this shows weakness and the customer will often respond with aggressiveness and will try to control the chasing call himself.

Handle each customer as an individual. It is particularly easy over the telephone to group people together and assume that all their reactions will be the same.

## CONCLUSION

Selling techniques can be applied to all types of telephone calls, not only to calls selling tangible products.

For example, selling appointments, selling image, selling knowledge, selling the concept of a telephone call, selling the benefits of prompt cash settlement, all have specific call handling techniques.

Learning these techniques in theory is useful, but can only really be of value when a practical application is tried within the constraints of each individual company's credit department.

Telephone cash collection, therefore, does not necessarily need to be an aggressive, unpleasant task given to those people who have a reputation for making customers feel belittled and humble. Far better to think of cash collection as part of the overall sales effort of the company—leaving the customer with respect for the collector and willing to begin a new chain of buying activity.

# 13

# Collection Agencies

Bryan D. Watson, Managing Director, Inter-Credit International Ltd

## WHY USE AN AGENCY?

The use of a collection agency as an aid to the credit manager introduces for the first time a third-party element to the collection of a debt. The value of this approach can only be recognised when one compares the collection work carried out prior to passing the account to an agency, and the activity conducted by an agency on receipt of the debt.

The credit manager who uses his agency wisely will know that most agencies operate on a 'no collection—no charge' basis, whereas his own department's efforts are a total cost to his company. He will also be aware that an agency's efforts are concentrated over a three- to four-week period, their only incentive being the successful collection of a debt. Most credit departments will include debt collection as only one of the many duties they are expected to perform.

The other advantage to be gained from the use of a good collection agency is that it can offer a total collection service, including account reconciliation, tracing of absconding debtors, confirmation of registered offices and eventual legal action when required.

## WHEN SHOULD DEBTS BE PASSED TO AGENCIES?

The age at which a debt should be passed to an agency is a variable, dependent upon current trade practice. However, if one recognises that the true value of an overdue account at 60 days is approximately 85% of its total, and this drops to 80% at 90 days, it is in this area that one must consider external action.

## ACTION TAKEN BY AN AGENCY

On receipt of an account for collection, an agency will immediately send to a debtor an initial letter intended as a 'debt qualifier', whereby the debtor is made aware that the creditor has placed the account with a collection agency and that the creditor requires payment by return. This has the effect of bringing to light disputes which have not been previously notified to the creditor, reasons for non-payment, and in many cases full settlement of the account. This latter fact mystifies many experienced credit managers who, whilst utilising every collection technique they know, fail to understand the psychological advantage an agency has in intervening between creditor and debtor in a positive manner.

Should no reply be received from a debtor within a reasonable period, a telephone call is made by an experienced collector to the most senior executive responsible for payment within the debtor company. The agency's role is now that of motivating some form of positive payment action or a promise from the debtor without being side-tracked by non-availability or other issues. All activity is recorded by the agency and payment promises diarised to ensure that follow-up telephone calls are made to those debtors whose payments are not received on time.

## REPORTING BACK TO THE CREDITOR

During the three-week collection cycle, there is a continuing flow of correspondence and telephone calls between the agency and debtors including reconciliation of accounts and settlement of disputes. At the end of this period all accounts passed to the agency are reported on to the creditor, including those accounts which the agency consider will only respond to some form of legal action. This report should be acted upon immediately, as the accounts which have not responded will now be moving into the 100 to 120 days overdue section, and should be carefully examined with a view to taking legal action.

## LEGAL ACTION

An agency with an active collection policy finds that only 1% of overdue accounts passed for collection ultimately require some form of legal action before payment. At this stage it is worth examining the performance and charges of solicitors retained by an agency as opposed to company solicitors or an outside practice. In many cases the solicitors acting for an agency will handle the total legal debts for that agency. They will, therefore, specialise in debt collection procedures for county and High Court actions, and due to the volume of cases will be able to act for lower fees than can be expected from an outside practice. They will also be motivated by the agency with the urgency of obtaining legal action, together with keeping the creditor informed at each stage of the process. The biggest single factor for the use of agency's solicitors is the preparatory work undertaken by the agency prior to recommending legal action. It is no coincidence that agency solicitors have a far higher success rate in the recovery of overdue accounts than ordinary solicitors. This is mainly due to the fact that all circumstances surrounding a debt have been explored, and the validity of the debt established prior to recommending legal action.

## THE COST OF USING COLLECTION AGENCIES

The cost to a company using a collection agency varies with the type of service required and the agency selected. There are three distinct areas in the collection field, each with its own system of charges and collection methods.

### Trade associations

The non-profit making trade associations usually charge an annual subscription fee together with a percentage of the value of accounts successfully recovered.

## Voucher system

During the past ten years a North American system has been introduced into the UK whereby the agency sells books of collection vouchers to companies, in return for the agency sending a series of letters to effect collection of a debt, irrespective of the value of the debt. The creditor purchases by prepayment books of vouchers entitling him to submit one debt per voucher. On receipt of the voucher, the agency commences a series of letters to the debtor for a fixed period of between three to four weeks. If the debt is not collected within the period, the creditor then has the option of leaving the debt with the agency for telephone collection for a further fee, usually consisting of a percentage of amounts successfully collected. Alternatively, they can proceed to legal action or write off the debt.

## Commercial agencies no collection—no fee

The most common form of collection charge and certainly the most economical is the contingency fee, whereby the agency charges a percentage of debts successfully recovered with no charges made for unsuccessful cases. The main advantage of this system is that it involves a creditor in no prepayment of subscriptions or vouchers, and the agency is motivated to effect swift recovery of all accounts passed for collection. The scale of percentages offered to a creditor is dependent on the type of debts to be collected, and centres around the average age, invoice value and total volume of debts to be passed to the agency.

## ASSESSING THE AGENCY

A credit manager, using his experience of his company's debtor situation, can assess the value of a collection agency as an effective aid in his department's collection effort. It should be stressed that, when passing accounts to a collection agency, the title to the debt remains with the creditor at all times, with the agency acting on behalf of the creditor. It is important, therefore, that a creditor should satisfy himself concerning his choice of agency and its financial standing. The minimum requirement would be the same as for any new customer requiring credit, bearing in mind that at any one time an agency could be holding the funds of debts successfully recovered. A copy of the agency's latest audited accounts together with details of employee bonding is essential to establish a firm business relationship. This should be followed by a selection of letters to be used on behalf of the creditor, together with an agreed cycle of telephone calls to debtors. Finally, details as to the frequency of reports and advices of payment received should be agreed.

The recovery performance of an agency should always be monitored by the creditor over a minimum period of six months, allowing for recognised trade fluctuations of payment and the general economic pattern.

An agency can only be as effective as the creditor allows it to be, and the speedy reply to the agency's request for information, together with accurate details concerning all aspects of the debts to be collected, allow for an efficient and harmonious collection effort.

## AGENCY CREDIT REPORTS

Some credit decisions ultimately result in bad debts, partially predictable from information available at the time of assessment. A good collection agency will include a credit reporting department within its services, both for UK and overseas companies. The use of this facility, together with the gathering of trade information, is worth more than any number of selected trade and bank references. Some agencies will include a credit limit together with an up-to-the-minute report collected from trade sources and other creditors. Information taken from Companies House can be historical in many instances, and can only be of use as a reference point. Trade information gathered by an agency, together with the documented credit worthiness of companies kept on file by an agency, will assist many credit managers to form an assessment easily and confidently.

## HOW TO FIND A COLLECTION AGENCY

The ideal method is the recommendation of a satisfied user. In the absence of this, two or more agencies should be given a trial with a few cases to handle and be judged on:

1   efficiency of handling;
2   time taken to collect/resolve;
3   total cost involved.

There follows a list of some established agencies.

ATP International Ltd,
Sutherland House,
70–78 Edgware Road,
London NW9 7BT
Tel: (01) 202 8212

British Mercantile Agencies
   Ltd,
Sidcup House,
12–18 Station Road,
Sidcup, Kent
DA15 7EH
Tel: (01) 300 6815

Commercial Credit
   Consultants Ltd,
Unicredit House,
2 Cotton Street,
Liverpool L3 7DY
Tel: (051) 207 5777

Credit Aid Ltd,
16–18 New Bridge Street,
London EC4V 6AU
Tel: (01) 353 7722

Dun & Bradstreet Ltd,
26–32 Clifton Street,·
London EC2P 2LY
Tel: (01) 377 4377

Inter-Credit International
   Ltd,
Inter-Credit House,
205–207 Crescent Road,
New Barnet,
Herts EN4 8SW
Tel: (01) 440 8532

Jardine Credit Management
   Ltd,
Lloyds House,
Lloyds Street,
Manchester M2 5WL
Tel: (061) 831 7021

NB: This list is not intended to be all-inclusive. It is acknowledged that there are some 215 registered collection agencies in the UK.

## FURTHER READING

Paul Rock, *Making People Pay.* Routledge & Kegan Paul, 1973.

# 14

# Budgets, Ratios and Reports

**Herbert Edwards, Managing Director, Jardine Financial Risk Management Ltd**

### THE NEED FOR COLLECTION PLANS AND REPORTS

Most company plans begin with the sales budget, normally for 12 months ahead. Detailed budgets then provide costs to arrive at net income and cash flow for the financing required to achieve the planned sales. Cash planning requires a debtors (or receivables) budget and the credit manager is the person best qualified to produce it. The ratio between sales and debtors is decided by credit terms and collection performance which combine to give the collection period, or days' sales outstanding (DSO) ratio (sometimes expressed in weeks or months).

The DSO ratio is the prime tool to measure credit efficiency. The current DSO performance, plus or minus known or forecasted business changes, can be applied to the sales budget to produce an accurate debtors budget.

Once the debtor budget, with all its accompanying details, has been accepted by management, the credit manager has a published yardstick by which to be measured. Staff and resources must then be organised to achieve budgeted levels each month.

By budgeting, organising, then achieving the planned debtor level, the credit manager is contributing to profit assurance by 'guaranteeing' the planned cash inflow.

Increasingly these days, the seller is competing for limited customer liquidity with other suppliers, so collection performance against budget may vary, favourably or unfavourably. The monthly reporting system should provide analysis of the reasons for variances (e.g. changed customer habits) to aid marketing and general management.

Monthly reports should be as analytical as time allows, both as a means of improving credit management (by identifying weaknesses to be dealt with) and to amplify the basic figures to top management.

So, the pattern for good budgeting and reporting should be:

1 Obtain sales budget, by class of debtor.
2 Apply collection period (DSO) plus or minus expected changes.
3 Produce debtors budget by monthly total and DSO.
4 Calculate total overdues value from planned percentage.
5 Report monthly actual results versus budget.
6 Explain variances.
7 Identify actions to eradicate weak areas revealed.

## RATIOS

The credit manager should select the ratios most useful to him from all the data readily available. He should avoid demanding accounting data just to produce ratios which are not then used. Instead, he should spend the time analysing variances from planned results, in order to improve them.

Most companies supplying goods on credit terms find the following ratios useful:

1 Days' sales outstanding.
2 Overdue percentage to total debtors.
3 Aged analysis of overdues within total.
4 Disputes and claims, as DSO and percentage of total.
5 Debtors as percentage of sales.
6 Cash collected as percentage of cash collectable.
7 Bad debts and provisions for doubtful accounts, as percentage of sales.
8 Sales by class of customers as percentage of total sales.

### Days' sales outstanding

Expressed in days, weeks or months and sometimes called collection period. It expresses debtors as being equivalent to a number of days of sales. It is not affected by sales volume, but is affected by credit terms and collection efficiency.

*Method 1.* See Figure 14:1.

Since debtors normally relate to the latest sales made, the ratio is best calculated using actual latest sales rather than annualised or average figures.

*Method 2.* This is another method of calculating DSO if monthly sales figures are not available:

$$\frac{\text{Debtors}}{\text{Sales last 3 months}} \times 92 = \text{DSO or collection period}$$

This averages sales per day for the most likely sales period relating to the debtors and is slightly less accurate than Method 1 because it levels out peaks and troughs in sales. Example (same figures used):

$$\frac{£1\,200\,000}{£1\,680\,000} \times 92 = 65.7 \text{ DSO}$$

*Method 3.* This is a further method of calculating DSO in the absence of sales figures for the period:

$$\frac{\text{Debtors}}{\text{Sales YTD annualised}} \times 365 = \text{DSO}$$

This method compounds the averaging weakness even further, as in this example:

$$\text{Sales January–August} \frac{£1\,200\,000}{£4\,110\,000 \div 8 \times 12} \times 365 = 71.0 \text{ DSO}$$

The preferred method is Method 1 which requires obtaining actual sales for the period immediately preceding the date of measurement.

## Overdue percentage to total debtors

This is the most commonly used ratio, a typical remark being 'our overdues are only 8%, whereas a year ago they were 15%.' This is, in

| DSO | Plastic Widgets Ltd | | | August 1984 |
|---|---|---|---|---|
| A    Debtors total | | | | £<br>1 200 000 |
| Equivalent to: | | | | |
| Sales | | | Days | |
| August | £650 000 | | 31 | 650 000 |
| | | Balance | | 550 000 |
| July | £430 000 | | 31 | 430 000 |
| | | Balance | | 120 000 |
| June | £600 000 | | 6/30 | 120 000 |
| | | Balance | | — |
| | | Balance | | |
| | | Balance | | |
| | Total days' sales outstanding | | 68 | |

B
Average sales per day £1 200 000 ÷ 68  =  £17 647
Overdues £230 000 ÷ £17 647        =  13.2 days' sales
Therefore current               =  54.6 days' sales

Part A: Can be made as soon as the ledger closes. It shows that debtors are equivalent to 68 days of sales, despite payment terms of net 30 days. This means that tomorrow's sale will be paid, on average, 68 days later.

Part B: Can be added when the overdue total is known.
Expressing overdues as days of sales is more accurate than as percentage of debtors. Current days of 54.6 indicate that some sales are on longer than 30 days terms, that overdues analysis is understated, or the books were closed late.

**Figure 14:1    Ratios: method 1**

fact, quite meaningless, since the ratio has variables. It helps complete the total picture, but is dangerous to use alone. For example:

| | |
|---|---|
| Total debtors | £1 200 000 |
| Overdues | £ 120 000 |
| Overdues = | 10% |

But, if current sales were £750 000 and not £650 000, the table would read:

| | |
|---|---|
| Total debtors | £1 300 000 |
| Overdues (still) | £ 120 000 |
| Overdues = | 9.2% |

An apparent improvement! Yet the overdue debts have not changed at all.

**Aged analysis of overdues within total**

This is more useful as a tool for improving overdues. Taking the overdue total, establish by analysis the values overdue in monthly categories, i.e. 1–30, 31–60, 61–90, 91–120, 120 days and over, then express each ageing category as a percentage of the total overdue as in Figure 14:2.

| Total overdue | Overdue ageing | | | | |
|---|---|---|---|---|---|
| | 1–30 | 31–60 | 61–90 | 91–120 | 120+ |
| £120 000 | £83 000 | £21 000 | £12 000 | £1000 | £3000 |
| 100% | 69.2% | 17.5% | 10.0% | 0.8% | 2.5% |

**Figure 14:2 Aged analysis of overdues within total**

Ideally, if there must be any overdues at all, they should be 100% 1–30 days old. From month to month, collection activity should aim to increase the left-hand percentages at the expense of the right. In comparing quality of overdues, the values are also important, since the percentages are affected by high or low sales. These generate higher or lower 1–30 days overdues, affecting the entire spread of the 100%.

## Disputes and claims

Most businesses suffer a continuing proportion of claims against sales or disputed account balances. Although claims are resolved sooner or later, the distortion of total debtor balances continues because of the inflow of fresh claims. It is important for plans and budgets to take account of the running level of cash not collectable because of unresolved disputes. The effect can be stated either as a percentage of debtors or as a number of days' sales, e.g.:

| | | |
|---|---|---|
| Total debtors | £1 200 000 | or 68 DSO |
| Disputes | £ 48 000 | (4% or 2.7 DSO) |

In other words, up to 2.7 days' sales value could be knocked off the debtors total, if faster action were taken to resolve disputes.

For internal action purposes it is useful to age disputes in the same way as overdues, so that oldest items get the correct priority, as they represent the most serious drain on profits.

## Debtors as percentage of sales

For balance sheet comment and end-of-period reports, it is common practice to express debtors as a percentage of annual sales, e.g.:

| | |
|---|---|
| Annual sales | £6 165 000 |
| Debtors | £1 200 000 |
| Percentage | 19.5% |

It is then quite usual to invert the percentage, or simply to divide the debtors into the sales figure, and express the answer as the 'account turnover period' (see Figure 14:3).

Whereas both measurements are valid for measuring comparable periods, they are too loose to be of value in the credit department where more precision is needed from month to month.

## Cash collected as percentage of cash collectable

This ratio is extremely valuable if the data can be collected without disproportionate effort. If collectable cash can be calculated in

Debtors equal 19.5% of annual sales

$$\frac{100}{19.5} = 5.13 \text{ times per year}$$

or

$$\frac{£6\,165\,000}{£1\,200\,000} = 5.13 \text{ times per year}$$

**Figure 14:3   Account turnover period**

advance, i.e. debts becoming due in the month plus debts already overdue, it is useful, for subsequent budgets and forecasts, to record the actual collections made as a percentage of the collectable figure. The resulting deficit (e.g. 92% collections = 8% deficit) becomes the overdue debt for the following period (NB: not the overdue percentage).

This procedure can be refined, if facilities permit, as an accurate forecasting tool, as follows:

1   Record the collection experience of each month's sales, e.g.:
    August sales 100
    —Collection    August 5         Unpaid 95
                   September 20            75
                   October 65             10
                   November 10             0
2   Build up a historical pattern to show seasonal effects as in Figure 14:4. Unless there are drastic changes in conditions, these trends can be applied to forecasts for future payment of monthly sales.

| % Unpaid | J | F | M | A | M | J | J | A | S | O | N | D | J | F | M | A | M | J | J | A |
|---|---|---|---|---|---|---|---|---|---|---|---|---|---|---|---|---|---|---|---|---|
| Same month | 98 | 98 | 97 | 93 | 95 | 92 | 95 | 94 | 95 | 91 | 92 | 89 | 97 | 98 | 96 | 93 | 94 | 93 | 94 | 95 |
| Previous month | 80 | 77 | 78 | 75 | 72 | 73 | 71 | 73 | 74 | 68 | 66 | 67 | 81 | 78 | 79 | 74 | 71 | 72 | 71 | 75 |
| Two months previous | 16 | 14 | 12 | 10 | 9 | 10 | 11 | 10 | 12 | 7 | 9 | 8 | 15 | 15 | 13 | 11 | 10 | 11 | 10 | 10 |

**Figure 14:4   Pattern of seasonal effects**

We see that collections were heavy in the last quarter, October to December, but fairly poor in the early part of the year.

Payment of any one month's balance can be tracked by the left-to-right diagonal pattern*, e.g. November balances remained 92% unpaid by the end of November, 67% by December and still 15% by January.

## Bad debts and provisions for doubtful accounts

Most businesses experience lost income due to bad debts and a multitude of policies exist for reserving income against future losses.

In the total panorama of debtor planning, the credit manager should take account of projected losses, resulting in reduced gross balances, and the reduction of net balances caused by deducting reserves and provisions.

There are two controlling influences on the amount of bad debt provision (in addition to how much the company can afford); the auditors will insist on adequate provision, so that the written-down debtor balance is accurate, and also the tax inspector will allow only reasonable specific provisions against tax, whereas company policy may require larger provisions as general reserves.

### Sample policies

1　Bad debt reserve established out of income at a level of 1% of debtor balances existing at year-end. Actual bad debts incurred transferred from sales ledger to bad debt reserve.

Recoveries against bad debts credited to reserve, not to sales ledger.

2　Specific bad debts and doubtful debts identified monthly but left in ledger until year-end. Bad debt reserve created monthly to cover cumulative value. At year-end, known bad debts written off to reserve, doubtful debts, not yet lost, transferred to suspense account.

Bad debt reserve at year-end adequate to cover suspense account.

*Harvard Business Review, May 1972*

3   Transfer all bad and doubtful accounts (however defined) from the sales ledger to a bad and doubtful account. Make a cautious estimate of possible recoveries. Maintain a (specific) provision for the net balance of the bad and doubtful account.
4   Reserve specifically known bad debts.
    Make additional general reserve for serious overdue accounts on percentage basis, e.g.:
    Balances overdue 61–90 days—reserve 10%
    Balances overdue 91–120 days—reserve 25%
    Balances overdue 121–180 days—reserve 50%
    Balances overdue over 180 days—reserve 100%
5   Take historical average bad debts as percentage of sales, e.g. 0.8%. Plan monthly reserve through the year to achieve 0.8% of sales value by year-end. Adjust for any exceptional losses occurring.
6   Where customers are divided into classes, or credit-risk categories, establish the bad debt history for each class.
    Apply a reserve policy adequate for each, as in Figure 14:5. This is a particularly accurate method where the sales budget can be split into customer risk categories.

|               | Sales     | Bad debts | %   |
|---------------|-----------|-----------|-----|
|               | £         | £         |     |
| A = No risk   | 1 500 000 | 0         | —   |
| B = Average   | 2 800 000 | 16 800    | 0.6 |
| C = High risk | 750 000   | 23 600    | 3.2 |
| Total         | 5 050 000 | 40 400    | 0.8 |

**Figure 14:5   Debt histories**

7   Where credit insurance exists, any of the above policies can be modified to exclude the insured portion of bad or doubtful balances.


**Sales by class of customer**

For purposes of debtor planning of bad debt reserves, credit granting, and marketing liaison, it is valuable to analyse sales, both

| | Sales £000 | | as % of | Debtors | |
| | August | YTD | total | £000 | DSO |
|---|---|---|---|---|---|
| *Home* | | | | | |
| North | 160 | 1702 | 11.9 | 532 | 72 |
| South | 230 | 2554 | 18.0 | 670 | 65 |
| London | 390 | 4256 | 30.0 | 1170 | 68 |
| Total | 780 | 8512 | 59.9 | 2372 | 66 |
| *Export* | | | | | |
| East | 94 | 521 | 3.7 | 182 | 86 |
| West | 101 | 1609 | 11.3 | 644 | 98 |
| Total | 195 | 2130 | 15.0 | 826 | 96 |
| Government | 130 | 1406 | 10.0 | 334 | 56 |
| Associates | 191 | 2140 | 15.1 | 501 | 60 |
| Total | £1296 | £14 188 | 100% | £4033 | 68 |

**Figure 14:6   Sales/credit analysis**

forecast and budget, into separate classes. According to the purpose, this might be geographical, by product or by credit category.

For example, a company sells to home, export, government and associates, with a regional organisation for home and export, and with credit risk categories for the home trade. The sales/credit analysis for August reads as detailed in Figure 14:6. The figures for home sales in Figure 14:6 are analysed by credit risk, as detailed in Figure 14:7.

## Combined ratios

The foregoing suggested ratios can be permutated according to need. Figure 14:8 uses the four basic items:

1   Days' sales outstanding.
2   Overdues as percentage of debtors.
3   Aged overdues within total.
4   Disputed debtors.

| Area | Sales £000 | | as % of | Debtors | |
| --- | --- | --- | --- | --- | --- |
| | August | YTD | total | £000 | DSO |
| North A | 16 | 170 | 9.9 | 45 | 65 |
| North B | 95 | 982 | 57.7 | 258 | 65 |
| North C | 49 | 550 | 32.4 | 229 | 86 |
| S/Total | 160 | 1702 | 19.9 | 532 | 72 |
| South A | 74 | 744 | 29.1 | 190 | 61 |
| South B | 116 | 1300 | 50.9 | 358 | 66 |
| South C | 40 | 510 | 20.0 | 122 | 76 |
| S/Total | 230 | 2554 | 30.1 | 670 | 65 |
| London A | 80 | 860 | 20.2 | 215 | 62 |
| London B | 210 | 2228 | 52.3 | 590 | 68 |
| London C | 100 | 1168 | 27.5 | 365 | 77 |
| S/Total | 390 | 4256 | 50.0 | 1170 | 68 |
| Total A | 170 | 1774 | 20.8 | 450 | 62 |
| Total B | 421 | 4510 | 53.0 | 1206 | 65 |
| Total C | 189 | 2228 | 26.2 | 716 | 78 |
| Total | 780 | 8512 | 100 | 2372 | 66 |

*Notes*
1 This shows, true to form, that C accounts pay more slowly than B, who pay more slowly than A.
2 There are regional differences (worth investigating).
3 The spread of business between categories shows North has too few 'blue-chip' customers and too many risky ones, requiring greater financing resources. South and London have better spreads. In all cases, a comparative study from period to period will show if the drift is towards better or worse risk customers.

**Figure 14:7   Home sales/credit analysis by credit risk category**

Comparison with budget, last month, *and* last year indicates quality differences for further action.

*Monthly debtors report*  August 1984

Antique Wurzels Ltd

|   |   | This month | Budget | Last month | Last year |
|---|---|---|---|---|---|
| 1 | DSO | 68.0 | 66.5 | 65.0 | 66.0 |
| 2 | Overdues (%) | 18.1 | 12.0 | 12.6 | 11.9 |
| 3 | Overdues (%) | | | | |
|   | 1-30 | 65.2 | 74.0 | 69.0 | 71.0 |
|   | 31-60 | 24.1 | 20.0 | 24.1 | 25.2 |
|   | 61-90 | 7.0 | 5.0 | 3.3 | 3.1 |
|   | 91-120 | 1.1 | 1.0 | 1.2 | 0.7 |
|   | 120+ | 2.6 | — | 2.4 | — |
| 4 | Disputes (%) | 4.2 | 2.0 | 3.5 | 2.5 |
|   | Sales (£000s) | 152 | 200 | 186 | 210 |
|   | Collections (£000s) | 165 | 190 | 188 | 225 |
|   | Total debtors (£000s) | 360 | 410 | 385 | 463 |

**Figure 14:8  Combined ratios**

These give some depth to the planning and reporting of debtors, which sometimes consists of only the total debtor figure, the overdues total and possibly the sales and collections for the period.

## CREDIT BUDGETS

A budget for monthly debtors can easily be constructed from a sales budget for the same period. Its eventual accuracy will depend upon:

(a)  the accuracy of the sales budget monthly values;
(b)  the credit terms granted for the budgeted sales;
(c)  the efficiency of collection operations;
(d)  trade conditions and economic climate.

The credit manager will apply historical trends plus his own foresight and market knowledge to the sales estimates in calculating his debtors budget.

## Approach to a credit budget

1 Make list of assumptions for budget period (DSO approach, overdues, market oddities, etc.).
2 Assess the DSO level for each month in the year ahead.
3 Apply the DSO to the sales estimates for the immediate preceding number of days, to obtain the total debtors figure for each month.
Then, for further refinement (select as appropriate):
4 Assess the days' sales level for overdues for each month. Using average sales per day, calculate overdues value and percentage of total debtors.
5 Split items 1, 2 and 3 between classes of trade, e.g. home and export, and/or regionally or between business units.
6 Assess disputed debtors by DSO value and percentage for each month.
7 Record cash figure for each month, as result of subtracting debtors total from previous month's debtors plus this month's sales.
8 Assess transfers out to bad debt suspense and budget reserve against gross debtors to produce net figure.
9 Trim debtor budget where necessary to meet financial planning requirements.

## Sample forms for debtor budgets

1 Sales budget by class of customer and business unit for January to December (or whatever the budget period is) as shown in Figure 14:9.
This will be produced primarily for marketing or sales purposes and may contain data of no interest to the debtor budget. However, the credit manager should ensure that data he does need is properly incorporated in the sales form.
2 List of credit department assumptions for debtor budget. An example might read:
*Credit manager's assumptions*
  (a) DSO for home trade to be 10% worse than last year, due to longer terms granted and difficult conditions.

Sales budget (including VAT)

| | J | F | M | A | M | J | J | A | S | O | N | D | Total |
|---|---|---|---|---|---|---|---|---|---|---|---|---|---|
| *Customers* | | | | | | | | | | | | | |
| Home: | | | | | | | | | | | | | |
| North | | | | | | | | | | | | | |
| South | | | | | | | | | | | | | |
| London | | | | | | | | | | | | | |
| S/Total | | | | | | | | | | | | | |
| Export: | | | | | | | | | | | | | |
| East | | | | | | | | | | | | | |
| West | | | | | | | | | | | | | |
| S/Total | | | | | | | | | | | | | |
| Government | | | | | | | | | | | | | |
| Assoc. co. | | | | | | | | | | | | | |
| | | | | | | | | | | | | | |
| Total | | | | | | | | | | | | | |

**Figure 14:9   Sales budget by class of customer and business unit**

(b) Export business to remain the same.

(c) Government DSO to be improved by new paperwork system—suggest 25% faster payments.

(d) Major customers to buy less, with marginal customer sales (high risk) increasing by 20%—effect on DSO requires further calculations.

(e) Transfer of staff functions to computer in mid-year could slow up collections for 1–3 months until teething problems cleared. Allow for this in June to September, etc., etc., according to knowledge at the time.

*Sales manager's view of above*
(a) Agreed.
(b) More detailed estimates now available. Less business in USA and France, with increases in Scandinavia and Japan.
(c) No comment.
(d) Do not agree definition of marginal customers. To discuss.
(e) No comment.
(Collaboration then follows to agree on final assumptions to be built into the budget.)

3 *Debtors budget worksheet*
This is prepared for separate customer classes within sales regions or profit centres, prior to consolidation as total debtors. For each sub-budget involved (see Figure 14:10):
(a) Follow procedure outlined earlier.
(b) In applying DSO to sales to obtain debtors, greater accuracy is obtained if sales patterns within the month are known from past experience, e.g.
August 68 DSO means:

| | |
|---|---|
| All sales for August | —31 days |
| All sales for July | —31 days |
| 6/30 (20%) sales for June | — 6 days. |

But, if it is known that sales in a month have a pattern of:
Week 1—10%
Week 2—15%
Week 3—25%
Week 4—50%
then the last 6 days of June will be nearer to 50% than 20%.
(c) There is a simple reconciliation of December 1983 total debtors by taking the opening figure for debtors (i.e. year-ended 31.12.1982 in the sample), adding the sales total for 1983 (final column) and subtracting cash receipts total for 1983 (final column).

4 *Consolidated debtors budget*
The sub-budgets can be consolidated onto a final form, in exactly the same style as the worksheet. However, not every line can simply be added to arrive at a total. i.e.:
Line 1 (sales) and 3 (total debtors) can be grouped, but
Line 2 (DSO) is *calculated afresh*, by obtaining the number of days' sales in the grouped debtor totals.

Debtors budget worksheet     £000     1983

| | Year ended 31.12.82 | Jan | Feb | Mar | Apr | May | June | July | Aug | Sep | Oct | Nov | Dec | Total 1983 |
|---|---|---|---|---|---|---|---|---|---|---|---|---|---|---|
| 1 Sales inc VAT | | | | | | | | | | | | | | |
| 2 Projected DSO | | | | | | | | | | | | | | |
| 3 Total debtors £ | | | | | | | | | | | | | | |
| 4 Overdue debtors — days | | | | | | | | | | | | | | |
| 5 Overdue debtors — % | | | | | | | | | | | | | | |
| 6 Overdue debtors — £ | | | | | | | | | | | | | | |
| 7 Disputed debtors — days | | | | | | | | | | | | | | |
| 8 Disputed debtors — % | | | | | | | | | | | | | | |
| 9 Disputed debtors — £ | | | | | | | | | | | | | | |
| 10 Current debtors — days | | | | | | | | | | | | | | |
| 11 Current debtors — % | | | | | | | | | | | | | | |
| 12 Current debtors — £ | | | | | | | | | | | | | | |
| 13 Cash receipts — £ | | | | | | | | | | | | | | |
| 14 Bad and doubtful — £ | | | | | | | | | | | | | | |
| 15 Reserve — £ | | | | | | | | | | | | | | |
| 16 Total debtors / Less bad debt reserve / = Net debtors — £ | | | | | | | | | | | | | | |

**Figure 14:10   Debtors budget worksheet**

Line 6 (overdues—£) is obtained by grouping sub-budgets, then Line 5 (overdues—%) is calculated by taking line 6 as a % of line 3. Then

Line 4 (overdues—days) is calculated by applying the % in line 5 to line 2.

Lines 9, 8 and 7 (disputes) are obtained in the same way as lines 6, 5 and 4.

Lines 12, 11 and 10 (current) are also obtained in this way. There is a check-back available as:

    lines 4, 7 and 10 = line 2
    lines 5, 8 and 11 = 100%
    lines 6, 9 and 12 = line 3

Line 13 (cash) is obtained by adding line 3 of previous month to line 1 this month and deducting line 3 this month.

Line 14 (bad and doubtful) is the estimate of the total of line 3 which is considered lost or doubtful. It may be in a separate suspense account.

Line 15 (reserve) is the monthly allocation of reserve against line 14, according to the method of reserving adopted.

Line 16 (net debtors) is the result of line 3 less line 15.

5   *Departmental expense budgets*

Whether the credit function is large or small, it is worth budgeting its annual expense to the company. No forms will be recommended here, as they are not specific to credit management, but will follow the company style for all departments.

The subjects which can usefully be included in a credit department budget on a month-by-month basis are:

(a)   Number of staff, part-time or full-time—split as to supervisory or not.
(b)   Salary costs (and total related costs).
(c)   Computer or other equipment charges, as allocated.
(d)   Postal and telephone costs.
(e)   Travel and entertainment costs.
(f)   Credit insurance premiums, if any.
(g)   Bad debt reserves.
(h)   Training and recruitment costs.

The total budgeted costs for credit administration can finally be related, on a standard form, to sales and debtors to provide measurements of efficiency, from one period to the next. For example:

(a)  Credit sales value per staff member.
(b)  Receivables value per staff member.
(c)  Cost of department as percentage of sales.
(d)  Cost of department as percentage of receivables.

## CREDIT OPERATING REPORTS

These should be as frequent and analytical as time permits and only produced if really needed, as:

1  Accurate records of results.
2  Action tools for the credit manager.
3  Means of reporting to top management.

Where good budgets exist, reports should include variances from budgets and, if possible, variance analysis.

Where there are computers or other mechanical aids, programs fit reporting needs and reduce the time and expense of editing results, e.g. due to time lapses, or different customer groupings.

Figure 14:8 illustrates a simple report format combining several credit results and comparing them with budget, previous month and previous year. A multitude of other report styles exist and some examples follow below.

Reports for record purposes should be as full as possible, culling all relevant data and presenting it in an efficient layout.

Reports for action purposes should normally be by exception highlighting only items of interest, to avoid having to scan unnecessary detail which may obscure the 'red flag' areas.

Reporting upwards should show selected information of interest to management normally consisting of basic figures plus variance details with explanatory narrative.

Typical reports produced by industrial companies include:

(a)  Aged trial balance.
(b)  Analysis of debtors.
(c)  Debtor report, with variance analysis.
(d)  Days' sales outstanding reports.
(e)  Analysis of disputed debts.
(f)  Analysis of retentions.

(g)  Suspense account report.
(h)  Reconciliation of debtors to general ledger.
(i)  Debit note analysis.
(j)  Cash analysis by class of customer and interest charge on overdues.

## Aged trial balance

Produced at regular intervals and easily updated with one line per customer and debts aged horizontally. It might display:

Column 1  Account number
       2  Name and address
       3  Payment terms
       4  Sales code(s)
       5  Total debt
       6  Current total
       7  Overdue total
       8  Overdue 1–30 days
       9  Overdue 31–60 days
      10  Overdue 61–90 days
      11  Overdue 91–120 days
      12  Overdue 120 days and over
      13  Credit limit
      14  Credit risk category
      15  Excess of debt over credit limit

The report can be by sales office, geographical area, type of ledger or any convenient breakdown, with a grand total.

## Analysis of debtors

A typical analysis can be summarised monthly from the aged trial balance as detailed in Figure 14:11.

## Debtor report

This report should compare the main debtor items with budget and previous periods. See Figures 14:12 and 14:13.
    The variance analysis detailed in Figure 14:13 shows that the

| ABC Ltd | Analysis of debtors | | | | | Dated: | | | | |
|---|---|---|---|---|---|---|---|---|---|---|
| Item | Accounts | Balance | Current Regular | Special | Disp. | O/Dues | 1–30 | 31–60 | 61–90 | 91–120 | 120+ |
| | 1 | 2 | 3 | 4 | 5 | 6 | 7 | 8 | 9 | 10 | 11 |
| | Trade debtors | | | | | | | | | | |
| 1 | Key | | | | | | | | | | |
| 2 | Minor | | | | | | | | | | |
| 3 | Government | | | | | | | | | | |
| 4 | Export | | | | | | | | | | |
| 5 | Sub-total | | | | | | | | | | |
| 6 | Non-trade | | | | | | | | | | |
| 7 | Assoc. co. | | | | | | | | | | |
| 8 | Total gross | | | | | | | | | | |
| 9 | Less: Discounted | | | | | | | | | | |
| 10 | B/D reserve | | | | | | | | | | |
| 11 | Total net | | | | | | | | | | |
| | Remarks: | | | | | | | | | | |

**Figure 14:11   Aged trial balance analysis**

| ABC Ltd | Debtor report | Date: | | | | | | |
|---|---|---|---|---|---|---|---|---|
| Item | Reference | Actual | Budget | Fav/ (unfav) | Last month | Fav/ (unfav) | Last year | Fav/ (unfav) |
| 1 | Trade—current (£) | | | | | | | |
| 2 | Trade—overdue (£) | | | | | | | |
| 3 | Trade—total (£) | | | | | | | |
| 4 | Retentions (£) | | | | | | | |
| 5 | Non-trade (£) | | | | | | | |
| 6 | Suspense (£) | | | | | | | |
| 7 | B/D reserve (£) | | | | | | | |
| 8 | Discounted (£) | | | | | | | |
| 9 | DSO—current (days) | | | | | | | |
| 10 | DSO—overdue (days) | | | | | | | |
| 11 | DSO—total (days) | | | | | | | |
| 12 | Overdue (%) | | | | | | | |

**Figure 14:12   Debtor report**

|  | £ |  |
|---|---|---|
| Actual debtors | 1 400 000 | |
| Forecast debtors (budget) | 1 200 000 | |
| Excess investment | 200 000 | (poor credit control?) |

|  | BUT | £ |
|---|---|---|
| Actual sales at budget DSO (90 days) | | 1 500 000 |
| Less budget sales at budget DSO | | 1 200 000 |
| Sales volume variance | | 300 000 |
| Add: Debtors at actual DSO (say 84 days) | 1 400 000 | |
| Less: Debtors at budget DSO | 1 500 000 | |
| Credit efficiency variance | | 100 000 |
| Net variance or over-investment | | 200 000 |

**Figure 14:13 Variance analysis showing unfavourable variance due to sales pattern, not credit failure**

over-investment in debtors of £200 000 is, in fact, a mix of credit sales exceeding budget by £300 000, but this excess investment is reduced (improved) by the fact that credit control has achieved an actual credit term of 84 days against a budget of 90 days, so generating an additional £100 000.

Days' sales outstanding reports

As stated previously, there are many ways of calculating the collecting period, or days' sales outstanding ratio. Figure 14:1 gave a sample form layout. The points to remember are:

1   The resultant number of days is the *equivalent* of sales contained in the debtors total and is not the actual sales items unpaid.
2   Discounted debtors and bills receivable, not yet due, should be added back to the net debtors, to obtain a meaningful DSO. They represent credit granted to customers, with a recourse risk.

| ABC Ltd | Disputed debts | | | Date: |
|---|---|---|---|---|
| Above £1000 | Reason for dispute —<br><br>Action taken. | Person<br>responsible for<br>clearance | Expected<br>settlement date | Value |
| A/C customer | | | | |
| | | | | |
| Sub-total | | | | |
| Sub-total of sundries below £1000 | | | | |
| Total disputes | | | | |

**Figure 14:14   Sample form for analysis of disputed debts**

Analysis of disputed debts

This can be produced as either a complete list or an extract of disputes above a certain value or a certain age as frequently as the user needs. The purpose is to pursue settlement of disputes.

The format can be extremely simple (see Figure 14:14).

Analysis of retentions

When companies experience retentions as part of contract conditions, it is necessary to record them accurately, to achieve payment when properly due, rather than treating them as 'under payments' to be corrected at some future date.

Normally, a monthly report of retentions is adequate for control. See Figure 14:15 for a sample analysis form.

Suspense account report

The suspense account is the halfway house for bad and doubtful

| ABC Ltd | Analysis of retentions | | Date: | | | | |
|---|---|---|---|---|---|---|---|
| | | | | | | | |
| Line    Description | Total | Contract numbers | | | | | |
| 1   Total—last month<br>2   + New this month<br>3   − Paid this month<br>4   Total—this month | | | | | | | |

| | | | | | | | |
|---|---|---|---|---|---|---|---|
| Ageing of retentions<br>5   1–30 days<br>6   31–60 days<br>7   61–90 days<br>8   91–365 days<br>9   Over 1 year old | | | | | | | |
| 10   Total (= line 4) | | | | | | | |

| | | | | | | | |
|---|---|---|---|---|---|---|---|
| Reason for retention<br>11   Inspection<br>12   Contract period<br>13   Price investigation<br>14   Other | | | | | | | |

**Figure 14:15   Sample form for analysis of retentions**

debts prior to write-off. It is useful to have a reporting form to show the movement of accounts from the sales ledger into suspense with subsequent collections and write-offs from suspense against the bad debt provisions.

The report is normally produced quarterly or semi-annually. A sample format is shown in Figure 14:16.

Reconciliation of debtors to general ledger

There are many styles of producing this to suit company needs and

| ABC Ltd | | | Suspense account report | | | | Date: | | |
|---|---|---|---|---|---|---|---|---|---|
| Above £100 | | | | | | | | | |
| A/C | Name | Transferred from S/L | | Collected | | Written off | | Balance | |
| | | Previously | Current | Previously | Current | Previously | Current | | |
| | | | | | | | | | |
| | | | | | | | | | |
| Sub-total | | | | | | | | | |
| Sub-total a/c's below £100 | | | | | | | | | |
| Grand total | | | | | | | | | |

**Figure 14:16  Sample form for suspense account report**

240

audit requirements. No special format will be suggested here, but the principles of reconciliation are:

1 Reconcile at the end of each trading period, e.g. monthly.
2 Do not proceed to next month input until previous month reconciled.
3 Keep a running control record of input data.

In theory, reconciliations are simple. During the month, batches of invoices or payments are posted to individual customer accounts and the batch totals (=sales, cash book, etc.) posted to the general ledger. At month-end, the total of customer account balances should equal the debtors account in general ledger. In fact, minor discrepancies in postings occur at any stage so that some fault-finding is required.

For this reason, a reconciliation document should record each separate batch posting, debit and credit, normally in chronological order, to facilitate the search for differences.

Debit note analysis

In a business subject to a high rate of returned goods, quality

| ABC Ltd | | Debit note analysis | | | Date: 31.8.83 | | | |
|---|---|---|---|---|---|---|---|---|
| Date | Returned goods | Price error | Short delivery | Wrong goods | Repair charge | Other reason | Total | % |
| | £ | £ | £ | £ | £ | £ | £ | |
| 1982 | 674 | — | 26 | — | 7 110 | 269 | 8 079 | 9.9 |
| Jan. 83 | — | — | 152 | — | 1 234 | — | 1 386 | 1.7 |
| Feb. | 1 210 | — | — | — | 191 | — | 1 401 | 1.7 |
| March | 265 | — | — | 161 | — | 156 | 582 | 0.7 |
| April | 1 480 | 629 | — | — | 263 | — | 2 372 | 2.9 |
| May | 764 | 1 818 | 1 296 | — | — | — | 3 878 | 4.8 |
| June | 12 136 | 1 990 | — | 5 002 | 2 501 | — | 21 629 | 26.8 |
| July | 18 919 | 4 163 | 623 | — | 1 362 | — | 25 067 | 30.9 |
| August | 12 123 | 2 012 | 42 | — | 1 761 | 763 | 16 701 | 20.6 |
| Total | 47 571 | 10 612 | 2 139 | 5 163 | 14 422 | 1 188 | 81 095 | 100.0 |
| % | 58.7% | 13.1% | 2.6% | 6.3% | 17.8% | 1.5% | 100% | |

**Figure 14:17  Debit note analysis**

| ABC Ltd | Cash analysis by customer class/ interest charge to sales divs. | | | | | Date: | |
|---|---|---|---|---|---|---|---|
| Class | Month's cash | % | YTD cash | % | Overdues £ | Interest @ 12% £ |
| Home: North South London | | | | | | |
| S/Total | | | | | | |
| Export: East West | | | | | | |
| S/Total | | | | | | |
| Govt. Assoc. co. | | | | | | |
| Total | | 100% | | 100% | | |
| | | | | | | |

**Figure 14:18  Cash analysis by customer**

problems or price changes, there is likely to be difficulty in coping with debit notes raised by customers. A delay in investigating customers' claims will confuse customers' accounts and possibly delay collections.

Any reporting style should include an ageing of uncleared debit notes (i.e. claims) and, if possible, an analysis of reasons. See the example given in Figure 14:17. This report should be copied for use by quality control, customer service and marketing functions.

Cash analysis by customer

The purpose of this report is to demonstrate clearly where the month's and year's cash has come from. This is not necessarily in the same proportions as sales, due to longer or shorter payment terms between classes of business, e.g. home and export, or due to better or worse collections by different regional offices. It expresses the varying DSO figures in terms of cash. It can also provide back-up for charging interest based on excess asset value to the various divisions or offices. See Figure 14:18.

# PART VI

# CREDIT INSURANCE

# 15

# Home Trade Credit Insurance

C. C. Mitten, Consultant, Trade Indemnity plc

The main purpose of credit insurance is to reimburse, within defined periods of time, the major proportion of working capital which a supplier loses outright, or ties up indefinitely, when a customer to whom goods have been delivered, or services supplied, on credit terms fails to pay because of his insolvency.

Over the years, credit insurance has been developed to protect suppliers from unexpected bad debt losses and also, by way of early warning, to help them avoid such losses. Apart from protection and information, credit insurance can provide the discipline to produce sounder credit control and improved cash flow; it can also make more financial resources available to a policyholder. Properly used credit insurance is an effective instrument which can give management a measure of confidence and peace of mind in any particular business climate.

## SALES BOOKED AS INCOME ON ASSUMPTION ONLY

Most industrial and mercantile business in the UK is conducted on credit terms. Suppliers of goods or services make deliveries or render services to their customers on the assumption that the customers will pay for the goods or service on, or shortly after, the due date. To a large extent, the period of credit which customers are allowed to take is controlled by the supplier keeping a close watch on the ratio between total receivables and total sales at any one time; as long as the ratio looks good and lies within pre-determined limits, no crises arise and the trade cycle continues. Notwithstanding the credit period involved, however, the overall assumption that customers will pay must be upheld before receivables revert to cash. In the event of a customer's insolvency the assumption is proved to have been illfounded and a bad debt becomes chargeable to the profit and loss account.

## WHY IS CREDIT INSURANCE NECESSARY?

Credit insurance is widely used to provide cover against this contingency of bad debts, in many instances by companies who suffer few, if any, losses by way of bad debts.

So the question arises as to why suppliers spend money on credit insurance if their bad debt write-off to the profit and loss account is negligible. A clue to the answer lies in a close examination of three important aspects of a company's cash flow management: receivables, credit exposure and the weighing of opinion against fact.

### Receivables

It is very difficult to overstate the importance of receivables in any balance sheet. Official statistics show that trade debtors account for 25% of all assets, fixed and current combined, and 40% of current assets.

Receivables—rolling credit at any one time—are the end product of the total manufacturing/selling operation mounted by a supplier for the sole purpose of putting his goods/services at a customer's disposal. All the investment and effort involved in the operation have been made upon the assumption that the customer will pay and that nothing will happen to that customer which will prevent him from paying at the end of the credit period involved.

If the assumption is illfounded and the customer fails, the effort has been totally wasted and the supplier faces a loss situation.

### Credit exposure

The second important aspect to examine is the matter of 'credit exposure' in terms of how total receivables are spread over total active customers, at any one time. In all trading operations based upon selling goods/services on credit terms, the probability is that 70% to 80% of total receivables at any one time will lie with a minority of the total active customers. The remaining 20% to 30% of total receivables will be spread over a much larger number of smaller customers. In other words, a small number of baskets holds most of the eggs.

## Opinions versus facts

Finally, the overall assumption upon which customers enjoy credit terms from their suppliers can only be based on the supplier's opinion that the customers will continue to be in a position to pay.

However, the fact is that on occasions customers cannot pay because they are insolvent. In this case, the supplier suffers a bad debt; his cash is lost outright or is tied up indefinitely. Moreover, if the insolvent customer happens to be a major debtor, the effect of the bad debt on the supplier's cash flow forecasting could be serious, if not disastrous.

## FEASIBILITY OF CREDIT INSURANCE

Once these three important aspects of cash flow management have been closely examined conclusions can be drawn as to the feasibility of credit insurance to any given trading operation. If feasibility can be positively established it is not a difficult matter to assess the amount of cover which it is necessary to apply to the operation in order that credit insurance can fulfil its main purpose. It then becomes a comparatively simple matter to evaluate the cost/effectiveness of credit insurance as a means by which cash flow management can continue to function with a measure of confidence and peace of mind.

Regardless of whatever economic climate prevails at any given time, companies become insolvent for one reason or another. Their major suppliers then suffer bad debts which at best are extremely irritating, particularly so when 'everybody', except the major suppliers, 'knew it was going to happen'. At worst, the major suppliers face problems with their cash flow forecasts and budgets. A credit insurance premium is a budgeted cost to guard against an unbudgeted expense.

Let us now look at the market which supplies credit insurance.

## THE DOMESTIC CREDIT INSURANCE MARKET

For over 60 years, the British insurance industry has regarded the insurance of trade credit as a specialist function best left to specialist underwriting organisations. Therefore it supports the specialist underwriters as shareholders and by providing reinsurance facilities under which the credit underwriters can 'lay-off' the major proportion of the credit risks they underwrite at any one time. In return for a proportion of premium income reinsurers enable the underwriters to accept very substantial credit lines on any commercial risk at any one time.

The extent to which the reinsurers have supported the credit underwriters during the ups and downs of the last 60 years or so is a measure of the confidence placed by them in the individual underwriters' commercial judgement in assessing the credit risk put to them by their policyholders.

At the present time the UK domestic credit insurance market consists of Trade Indemnity plc, Credit & Guarantee Insurance Co. Ltd, The Insurances of Credit Company (a branch of Les Assurances du Crédit SA of Namur) and British National Insurance Co. Ltd. Additionally credit protection, as opposed to credit insurance, is provided by London Bridge Finance Ltd, a subsidiary of Hill Samuel & Co. Ltd, and by some factoring companies.

### Trade Indemnity plc

In 1918 the British Trade Corporation, a government-created body, one of whose aims was 'that arrangements should be made for the insurance of commercial bills', formed Trade Indemnity Co. Ltd, to which was transferred the credit insurance portfolio of the Excess Insurance Company together with its credit underwriter. The

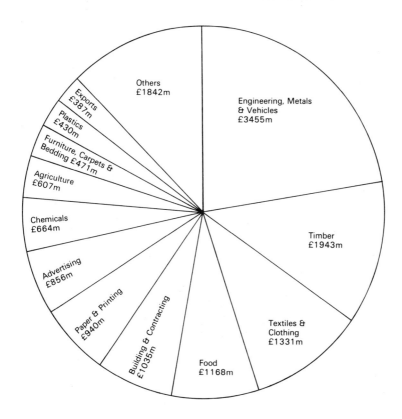

**Figure 15:1 Trade Indemnity plc. Distribution of UK insured turnover by trades (1983 figures)**

company was registered on 5 March 1918 with a paid-up capital of £20 000 and limited reinsurance facilities. Thus started the first specialist credit underwriting company in the UK and the business was gradually expanded until the outbreak of the Second World War. During the war years there was little demand for domestic credit insurance but, nevertheless, Trade Indemnity retained most of its policyholders and emerged in 1945 on a scene set for post-war development.

In 1946, Trade Indemnity earned a premium income of £134 000. By 1950 the income had reached £603 000 at which point the business took off to its present position.

Today the company has an issued and paid-up capital of

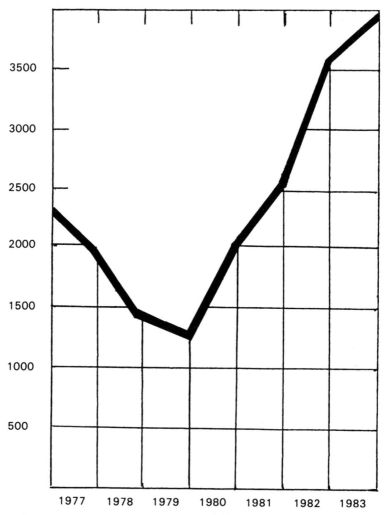

**Figure 15:2 Trade Indemnity plc. Bad debtors and business failures notified**

£1 807 536, the major shareholders being Commercial Union Assurance Co. plc, Excess Insurance Co. Ltd, Guardian Royal Exchange Assurance Group, Prudential Assurance Co. Ltd, Royal Insurance Group and Swiss Re Holding Ltd. In 1983 premium income reached £37 195 415, the estimated volume of turnover insured being £15 128.3m. In the same period claims paid amounted to £24.8m.

Credit & Guarantee Insurance Co. Ltd

Credit & Guarantee Insurance Co. Ltd was established in 1957 by a consortium of vaious Lloyd's brokers, a merchant bank and a mutual general insurance company with the principal objective of underwriting 'whole turnover' credit insurance. In 1960 the company was acquired by the National Employers Mutual and subsequently sold to the Landel Trust in 1965, the reformed 'Credit & Guarantee' being capitalised with an issued capital of £500 000.

In 1968 the Landel Trust reorganised its insurance interest. As a result the original capital of Credit & Guarantee was 'injected' into the Dominion Insurance Company. A new company, Credit & Guarantee (Underwriters) Ltd, was formed to transact credit insurance business in the name of the Dominion. Within 12 months the 'whole turnover' activities were discontinued and the company specialised in specific account business. In 1971 Credit & Guarantee (Underwriters) Ltd paid the largest loss settlement in the history of the UK credit insurance market. This settlement related to the insolvency of Rolls-Royce, the insured supplier being paid within four working days of lodging documentary evidence of loss.

In 1973 N.V. Nationale Borg Maatschappij of Holland, a specialist guarantee company, Dansk Kautionsforsikrings-Aktieselskab (the Danish credit insurance and guarantee company) and the Dominion formed European Bond Underwriters, which appointed Credit & Guarantee (Underwriters) Ltd as underwriting agents with their guarantees issued in the name of the Dominion.

In 1974 the Dominion, the Nationale Borg and the Dansk Kaution, together with The Mercantile & General Reinsurance Co. Ltd (Prudential Corporation plc) decided to become equal participants in the formation of an insurance company for the underwriting of credit, surety and guarantee business. On 1 January 1976, the existing portfolios of Credit & Guarantee (Underwriters) Ltd and European Bond Underwriters were assigned to the new company, Credit & Guarantee Insurance Co. Ltd, and the senior management, the underwriting and administrative executives of the companies, together with essential records, were transferred to the new company. The company has an authorised and issued capital of £800 000.

## The Insurances of Credit Company

This is the United Kingdom Branch of Les Assurances du Crédit SA of Namur which was formed in 1946 and initially engaged in consumer credit insurance made available to hire purchase and leasing companies. In 1951 the company widened its activities to include the insurance of commercial and industrial credit and now has branch offices in Belgium, Holland, Luxemburg, France and the UK.

In 1982 the company's premium income increased by 24.5% to over the 2 billion Belgian francs mark for the first time in its history. One-third of this premium income derived from consumer credit insurance including the insurance of bank and credit cards.

## British National Insurance Co. Ltd

British National Insurance Co. Ltd is wholly-owned by Armco Ltd of the USA. The company has an authorised capital of £30 000 000 of which £18 000 000 is issued and fully paid. It conducts a general insurance underwriting business and since March 1982 has underwritten domestic credit insurance in the UK.

The company also issues credit insurance policies to companies resident in Europe and in the name of North Atlantic Insurance Co. Ltd is licensed to issue policies to French policyholders.

In August 1984 The Continental Corporation (USA), Skandia International Insurance Corporation (Sweden) and Yasuda Fire & Marine Insurance Company Limited (Japan), announced their intention to form a new insurance company to write political, war and credit risk insurance on a world-wide basis. The company, which is to be equally owned by the three venture participants, will be called The PanFinancial Insurance Company Limited, will be licensed as a British insurer and will have its headquarters in London.

PanFinancial, with an initial capitalisation of approximately $12 million, is expected to be fully operational early in 1985. The company will commence operations with a book of credit insurance which it has agreed to purchase from British National Insurance Company Limited, which will continue to be a participant in this business as a reinsurer.

## CREDIT INSURANCE BROKERS

At the beginning of the 1950s, with business in the UK getting back to normal, Trade Indemnity expanded its sales force and at the same time made a determined effort to encourage leading Lloyd's insurance brokers to take an interest in the facilities which it could provide for their clients.

A number of brokers made a positive response but, like the insurance industry generally, viewed credit insurance as a specialist function best left to specialists and formed credit insurance departments to develop this class of business. These departments built up healthy portfolios of clients using both domestic and export credit insurance, the latter facilities being provided primarily by a department of the Board of Trade, as it was then known, The Export Credits Guarantee Department.

In time many of the credit insurance departments became companies in their own right, albeit as subsidiaries of the main broking companies. This comparatively small number of specialist credit insurance broking companies have their own committee, the United Kingdom Credit Insurance Brokers' Committee, within the British Insurance Brokers' Association.

It is the function of the specialist credit insurance broker to explain the facilities available to the prospective client and to advise them if, and how, credit insurance is applicable to their particular business. The broker then gives details of that business before the underwriting market in order to obtain quotations. Having done this, the client is advised as to the quotation which is most suitable, in terms of cover and premium cost, for the business. Once a policy has been issued the specialist broker has a servicing commitment to ensure smooth operation of that policy in all respects. The specialist credit broker is wholly concerned with the insurance of trade credit and can devote time to the benefit of the client on the one hand, and the underwriting market on the other. As in other classes of insurance the broker receives remuneration by way of commission paid by the underwriter with whom the business has been placed.

Let us now consider what the domestic credit insurance underwriting market has to offer and, also, some of the underlying principles involved.

## Basic principles

1 Credit insurance cover relates to trade credit but not consumer credit.

2 Credit underwriters do not guarantee the payment of a debt at the due date; they indemnify following the insolvency or protracted default of a debtor. The indemnity is usually between 75% and 90% of the admitted loss which arises within an agreed limit of credit. It is a condition of normal domestic credit insurance that the policyholder must keep the uninsured percentage entirely at his own risk.

3 Whilst it may be possible to credit insure advances made by purchasers in anticipation of the delivery of goods by a supplier, it is not possible under normal domestic credit insurance to cover financial credit, such as loans or advances made by banks or finance houses.

4 Sales to associated and subsidiary companies, government departments, nationalised undertakings and public authorities are excluded from the scope of any domestic credit insurance policy.

5 The policyholder is required at all times to exercise reasonable care and prudence in granting credit to, and withholding credit from, a buyer.

6 There is insolvency when any of the steps set out below have been taken by a court or by a policyholder:

   (a) An adjudication in bankruptcy has been made against the buyer.

   (b) A receiving order having been made against the buyer, a composition or a scheme of arrangement has been approved by the court.

   (c) A valid assignment, composition or other arrangement has been made by the buyer for the benefit of his creditors generally.

   (d) An order has been made against the buyer for a winding-up by the court.

   (e) An effective resolution has been passed for the voluntary winding-up of the buyer.

   (f) A compromise or arrangement has been made binding on the buyer and all the buyer's creditors.

(g) A receiver has been appointed on behalf of the debenture holders or other creditors of the buyer.

7   There is protracted default when the insured buyer having accepted delivery of goods has failed to pay such part of any insured debt as relates thereto at the end of the period of 90 days after the due date or, if the original due date has been postponed, at the end of the period of 90 days after the postponed due date.

8   When an insured buyer becomes insolvent, policyholders have a claim upon underwriters. The insured claim is payable within 30 days of the debt being admitted to rank for dividend against the insolvent estate of the buyer in favour of the policyholder.

In cases of protracted default the claim is payable within six months thereafter, subject to satisfactory proof of loss.

All claims must relate to amounts which are admitted or which would have been admitted if insolvency had occurred against the insolvent estate of a buyer. Disputed items are not covered, although once the dispute is settled and the debt is admitted or established, cover will become operative.

Any recoveries in connection with amounts owing to the policyholder by an insolvent or defaulting buyer are divisible between the policyholder and the credit underwriters in the proportion of their respective shares of the total indebtedness.

9   The cost of credit insurance and the amount of the indemnity are determined by an underwriting assessment of a policy-holder's business, important factors being the spread of risk and the quality of major exposures, past experience of bad debt losses, terms of payment and the standard of credit management. There is no such thing as a credit insurance tariff. Each proposition is assessed on its merits and in the light of underwriters' experience of the trade concerned.

## TYPES OF DOMESTIC CREDIT INSURANCE POLICIES AVAILABLE

### Trade Indemnity plc

The company's policies cover debts which arise from the sale and delivery of goods, or the supply of services, on credit terms during the period of the policy, which is normally twelve months, against the risks of insolvency or protracted default of the buyer.

Whole turnover policy

This is the most frequently used form of cover and is much more flexible than its name might suggest. It can cover the whole turnover of a company or group or the whole turnover of any separately identifiable trading unit within a company, the indemnity being a percentage, normally 80%, of any insured loss. At the same time it can cover the whole of any particular kind of turnover e.g. including only the larger accounts above a datum line, or excluding a first loss by means of a minimum retention or a threshold.

Whole turnover policies normally have a discretionary limit which enables credit to be granted up to a stated figure without consulting the company provided that an agreed credit procedure is followed. Underwriters' approval of credit limits in excess of the discretionary limit is necessary and their decisions enable accounts to be opened with confidence or can assist in loss avoidance. Of course a policyholder is free to trade in excess of an approved credit limit but the amount by which that limit is exceeded would be at his own risk. A credit limit charge is made at the end of each quarter related to the number of credit limits approved under a policy.

Premium is quoted as a percentage, usually a fraction of 1%, on the turnover of insured sales which is declared quarterly in arrears as a block figure. At inception of cover, and at the beginning of each succeeding quarter, a quarterly deposit premium is payable in advance; premium is finally adjusted when turnover declarations for the policy period have been made.

Smaller business policy

This is a whole turnover policy with specially simplified procedures designed for the business which has a turnover up to £1 000 000. The standard cover is 75% of any insured loss, which may be increased to 80% where turnover is above £500 000. The minimum premium rate is 0.5% of turnover and there is a minimum annual premium requirement of £1000.

Specific account policy

This type of policy can cover a single contract with a named buyer or a series of transactions during a period of not less than 12 months with one or more named buyers. Premium is charged on the insurable turnover declared under the policy.

### Specific account policy—fixed time or balance declaring

The fixed time basis is designed for use when trading with a buyer is so regular that the amount owed by the buyer at any one time during the 12 months does not vary and can be forecast accurately. A premium to cover the credit line is charged at a fixed rate at inception; no declarations of turnover are required.

The balance declaring basis is used where the volume of sales fluctuates from time to time. Premium is calculated on balances owing by the buyer at agreed dates, usually the last day of each month, and declarations of balances are made on this basis.

The company also writes anticipatory credit policies to cover payments in advance of delivery and 'work-in-progress' policies; these policies relate to individual contracts.

## Credit & Guarantee Insurance Co. Ltd

At the date of publication of this book, Credit & Guarantee, apart from its surety activities which are not within the scope of this chapter, specialises in customer default and supplier default insurances.

### Customer default policy (specific account)

This policy relates to a customer who will account for a substantial proportion of total annual turnover, or the same transactions will represent a substantial debt in relation to all the policyholder's debtors. The policy relates to both single contracts and continuous business. Pre-delivery cover is incorporated in the protection followed by the post-delivery indemnity.

The majority of customer default policies issued by Credit & Guarantee are in respect of transactions where the amount or amounts at risk for pre-delivery and/or post-delivery liabilities are in excess of £50 000 at any one time during the period of the contract.

The policy covers insolvency of the buyer during the policy

period, the definition of insolvency being as follows:

> 'There is insolvency when:
> (a) An Order has been made against the Customer for a Winding-up by the Court; or
> (b) An effective resolution has been passed for a Creditors' Winding-up of the Customer; or
> (c) A Receiver for Debenture-Holders of the Customer has been appointed.'

### Supplier default policy (consequential loss)

This type of policy is used by policyholders to protect themselves against the risk of one or more of their major suppliers becoming insolvent and thereby failing to execute their contractual obligations.

The policy covers insolvency of the supplier during the policy period, the definition being as follows:

> 'There is insolvency when an Order has been made against the Supplier for a Winding-up by the Court; or an effective resolution has been passed for a Creditors' Winding-up of the Supplier.'

### Other classes of credit insurance

Credit & Guarantee include consumer protection and a range of contingency indemnities in respect of a wide range of commercial transactions. The company also underwrites 'deposit insurance' relating to deposits with banks, assurance companies, unit trusts, building societies and other financial institutions.

## The Insurances of Credit Company

In the UK the company only underwrites on a whole turnover basis. The policy indemnifies the policyholder against losses he may sustain by reason of the declared or presumed insolvency of a buyer to whom goods have been sold, delivered and invoiced, or services supplied and invoiced, during the policy period. This is initially three years, continuing thereafter for consecutive periods of 12 months. Cover is a percentage, usually 85% in respect of approved buyers in the UK, of the insured loss. Reduced percentages of cover apply to losses where the credit has been granted within the discretionary limit.

Premium is calculated as a percentage of insured turnover. Quarterly deposit premiums are payable in advanced with annual adjustment after receipt of a declaration of insured turnover transacted during the preceding 12-month period. Credit limits in excess of an agreed discretionary limit are submitted for underwriters' approval. There is a charge per enquiry and a small file maintenance fee is payable quarterly in respect of each approved limit.

### British National Insurance Co. Ltd

The company issues a whole turnover policy under which the policyholder retains for his own account and uninsured an annual aggregate sum of qualifying losses agreed at inception, together with non-qualifying losses, i.e. small losses below an agreed figure which do not contribute to the annual aggregate. This deductible is based on an applicant's loss experience, spread of debtors and the size of the largest individual exposures.

The indemnity for qualifying losses in excess of the annual aggregate is 100%. The policy covers insolvency only, such insolvency to occur during the policy period which is normally 12 months. There is a maximum liability of £2 000 000 per policy unless special arrangements are made.

The quality of the policyholder's credit management is a major factor in the underwriting assessment and this is examined prior to the issue of a quotation. The credit control procedure is detailed in an endorsement to the policy and adherence to this procedure for all insured transactions is a condition of the policy.

Premium is payable annually in advance and no declarations of turnover are required. Underwriters do not approve specific credit limits although a policyholder is required to notify them if the amount owed by any one buyer exceeds an agreed level of notification. Although there is no hard and fast rule the company's policy is designed for companies which have a credit turnover of £20m or more per annum.

## DOMESTIC CREDIT INSURANCE UNDERWRITERS

### Trade Indemnity plc

*Head Office:*
Trade Indemnity House,
12/34 Great Eastern Street,
LONDON EC2A 3AX
Tel: (01) 739 4311

*Branch Offices:*
Birmingham (021) 643 8297
Bradford (0274) 732484
Bristol (0272) 299496
Cambridge (0223) 324991
Glasgow (041) 331 1088
London (01) 729 3700
Manchester (061) 832 3676
Newcastle upon Tyne (0632) 855358
Reading (0734) 872615

### Credit & Guarantee Insurance Co. Ltd

*Head Office:*
Colonial House,
Mincing Lane,
LONDON EC3R 7PN
Tel: (01) 626 5846

### The Insurances of Credit Company

*UK Office:*
22 Park Street,
CROYDON,
Surrey CR9 1TX
Tel: (01) 680 1565

### British National Insurance Co. Ltd

*Underwriting Room:*
52/54 Leadenhall Street,

LONDON EC3A 1BS
Tel: (01) 488 3464

**United Kingdom Credit Insurance Brokers' Committee**
**British Insurance Brokers' Association,**

Fountain House,
130 Fenchurch Street,
LONDON EC3M 5DJ
Tel: (01) 623 9043
*Secretary:* Miss Wendy Hotston

## FURTHER READING

Paul Barreau, *Credit Insurance,* 2nd edition. International Credit
   Insurance Association.
Hans Karrer, *The Elements of Credit Insurance.* Pitman & Sons, 1957.
Trade Indemnity plc, *Credit Insurance and Credit Management.*

# 16

# Export Credit Insurance

**Robert A. Rand, Director, Jardine Credit Insurance Ltd**

The dominant force in export credit insurance remains the Export Credits Guarantee Department (ECGD), a government department linked through to the Department of Trade & Industry and operating under the terms of the Export Guarantees and Overseas Investment Act 1978, with the remit to operate at no net cost to the taxpayer.

The credit insurance market, however, has also seen the emergence of new underwriting groups and sources or the adaption of existing facilities designed to meet the specific requirements of exporters as direct competitors to ECGD in both areas of commercial and political risks.

## ECGD AND ITS SERVICES

ECGD provides a comprehensive package of facilities designed to provide protection against a number of stated commercial and political causes of loss.

In addition the Department provides unconditional guarantees of 100% repayment to banks who on such security make finance available to exporters at favourable rates of interest.

## TYPES OF EXPORT CREDIT INSURANCE AVAILABLE THROUGH ECGD

ECGD classifies export trade into two broad categories:

1  Trade of a repetitive nature involving sales of a standard or near standard product. Cover on this trade is provided on a comprehensive basis giving the exporter an overall 'umbrella' protection and ECGD an acceptable spread of risk.
2  Trade involving projects and/or the sale of large capital goods of a non-repetitive nature, usually of high value and involving lengthy credit terms. Such business is not suited to comprehensive treatment and specific policies are negotiated for each contract on either a supplier/credit or a buyer/credit basis.

These are the chief forms of export credit insurance cover through ECGD. A more detailed description of the various guarantees follows.

### The Comprehensive Short Term Guarantee

The guarantee is designed to cover continuous volume sales dispatched on terms of payment not exceeding 180 days and the exporter usually undertakes to insure the whole of his turnover for a 12-month period subject to certain permitted exclusions.

Available to manufacturers, merchants and confirming houses, the guarantee is of a continuous nature subject to a simple annual renewal procedure.

In certain instances ECGD will cover a range of markets selected by the exporter provided that the selection gives them a reasonable spread of risk and that it represents a reasonable proportion of the exporter's total overseas sales.

Cover can commence from either date of contract (the pre-credit risk) or date of dispatch of the goods. If the exporter opts for the pre-credit risk cover an additional premium is payable on all contracts.

### Risks covered

The risks covered under the Comprehensive Short Term Guarantee are as follows:

1   The insolvency of the buyer.
2   The buyer's failure to pay within six months of the due date for goods accepted.
3   The buyer's failure or refusal to accept goods sent, unless the exporter is in breach of his contract. The first 20% of the gross invoice value of the contract is carried by the exporter.
4   A general moratorium on external debt by the government of the buyer's country, or a third country through which payment must be made.
5   Delays in payment due to political, economic, legislative or administrative difficulties arising outside the UK.
6   Legal discharge of the debt in the buyer's country, regardless of the fact that the amount transferred may be less than the debt, due to foreign exchange fluctuations.
7   War or civil unrest outside the UK which prevents fulfilment of the contract, where the cause of loss is not normally insurable.
8   Cancellation or non-renewal of an export licence or restrictions by law on exporting.
9   Failure by a foreign buyer to fulfil terms of a contract when ECGD has confirmed in writing that the buyer is backed by a state authority.

### Percentage of cover

ECGD indemnifies at 90% against losses arising from the commercial risks of insolvency and default and at 95% against the political causes of loss—90% if the loss arises before the goods are dispatched.
   Claims are normally payable immediately on proof of insolvency, one month after disposal when the goods are not taken up, six months from due date for default, and four months from the event causing the loss for political causes of loss. ECGD has the right to extend any of those claims waiting periods subject to the particular conditions which obtain in a market.

### Extensions to standard cover

Cover can be extended to provide for the following:

1   Goods imported into the UK and re-exported (subject to there

being no conflict with a listing of imported goods directly competitive with UK products).

2   Export contracts made with UK merchants or confirmers.
3   Sales to associate or subsidiary companies overseas.
4   Sales of goods held overseas in stock.
5   Contracts made in a number of approved currencies other than sterling.
6   Contracts involving the use of the forward exchange market within defined circumstances.

## Premium

Premium is paid in two ways.

First, a minimum non-refundable premium is payable at the commencement of each year of insurance.

Second, premium is payable monthly on exports declared at the end of each month at a flat premium rate fixed at the commencement of each year of insurance (if pre-credit cover is included the additional flat rate premium is also payable monthly).

This rate may be varied through the year for a particular market where ECGD has adverse experience.

## The Supplemental Extended Terms Guarantee

The guarantee is designed to cover business of a capital or semi-capital nature transacted on extended credit terms (six months to five years) or where the delivery period exceeds 12 months—either individual contracts with overseas buyers or continuous business with overseas distributors and dealers.

The guarantee is only available as a supplement to exporters holding Comprehensive Short Term Guarantees and operates on the same comprehensive principles taking in all of the exporter's eligible business.

The risks covered and the cover available mirror exactly those under the Comprehensive Short Term Guarantees. Each contract is underwritten individually, attracting its own specific premium rate according to the period ECGD is on risk and its assessment of the buyer's country.

Cover can be provided for contracts which include foreign goods elements within defined limits.

## Subsidiaries' Guarantees

This guarantee covers the sale by an overseas subsidiary of goods sold to it by its parent or associated companies in the UK. The guarantee follows the general form and content of the Comprehensive Short Term Guarantee in so far as short credit terms are concerned, and a supplemental extended terms facility is also available. ECGD would normally insist upon covering sales to the overseas subsidiary before covering sales by that subsidiary.

## The Supplemental Stocks Guarantee

This guarantee provides cover against losses arising in respect of goods held in stock as a result of such eventualities as confiscation or measures which prevent the re-sale or movement of the stock.

The guarantee is only available to holders of a Comprehensive Short Term Guarantee who have cover for sales from stock.

## External Trade Guarantee

The External Trade Guarantee provides cover for contracts which relate to the sale of goods of foreign origin where such goods are shipped direct from the country of origin to the buyer's country without being imported into the UK. There is a shortlist of goods directly competitive with UK products for which this cover is not available.

The guarantee is comprehensive and generally follows the form, content and disciplines of the Comprehensive Short Term Guarantee with the exceptions shown below.

1   The failure of the buyer to pay for goods accepted.
2   The failure of the buyer to take up the goods.
3   The imposition, cancellation or non-renewal of export or import licences.

As in the case of direct business the UK seller must offer his whole external trade turnover for cover or such proportion of that turnover as provides an acceptable spread of risk.

Under the guarantee, cover is limited to goods supplied on maximum six months terms of payment. The percentage of loss covered is limited in all cases to 90% and claims are payable 12 months after each cause of loss, except for insolvency (immediately on proof).

## Specific Guarantees

Contracts of sale involving capital goods or projects so large as to make them unsuitable for 'comprehensive' treatment can be covered under a Specific Guarantee subject to individual negotiation.

Cover is available from either date of contract or date of shipment and terms up to five years for acceptable contracts may be considered.

The risks covered are broadly similar to those covered under the comprehensive policies but the percentage of cover, even after shipment, is limited to 90%. Also, no cover is given against the failure of private buyers to take up goods which have been shipped.

In the case of government buyers ECGD will cover the risk of default by the buyer at any stage in the transaction; this replaces the ordinary insolvency and protracted default causes of loss. Erection costs can often be included where they are not covered by a separate services policy.

## The Constructional Works Policies

ECGD provides a 90% indemnity against costs incurred and sums owing under the contract depending on whether engineers' certificates/invoices have been submitted or not.

The normal range of commercial and political risks are covered together with, in the case of public employers, the failure or refusal of the employer to perform under the contract.

## The Services Policies

Cover is available for loss of earnings from services rendered to overseas clients under numerous guises, provided that the services are performed overseas or that the benefit of the services performed in the UK is enjoyed overseas by the client.

Where the services form a continuous pattern of business, the period over which they are performed does not exceed 12 months, and the terms of payment do not involve credit in excess of 180 days, cover is available on the same basis as with the comprehensive sale of goods policies.

The Comprehensive Services Guarantee is the vehicle for such business. The risks covered and indemnity provided mirror the comprehensive sale of goods policies with the obvious exclusion of the post-shipment repudiation cause of loss.

Services performed of a non-repetitive nature can be accommodated under a specific services policy arrangement. The risks covered are equivalent to those in the Comprehensive Services Guarantee but the standard indemnity is 90%.

Cover is available for the various types of leases under either services policies (operational leases) or special 'hiring' policies (full pay-out leases).

## ECGD-BACKED BANK FINANCE

Provided an exporter has an ECGD policy covering contracts for the sale of goods or the provision of services, various export finance facilities are available to him as follows:

### Comprehensive banker's guarantees

Two separate 'roll-over' schemes are available covering business transacted on open-account terms (CAD to six months credit) or involving bills and notes where the credit period is less than two years.

Under these arrangements ECGD provides the exporter's bank with an unconditional 100% guarantee of payment up to an agreed level in respect of sums outstanding. This in turn enables the bank to make 100% finance available on dispatch of the goods at an interest rate of up to ⅝% over base rate.

The extent of the financing facility, which is renewed annually, is fixed by ECGD at inception, based in part on the exporter's own financial standing. The premiums based on that facility level are payable in advance.

The exporter enters a recourse agreement giving ECGD the right to recover from him should the bank claim sums due in advance or in excess of claims payable under the standard ECGD policy.

### Specific banker's guarantee

A further facility is available to accommodate business transacted on extended credit terms (usually two to five years).

The same 100% unconditional guarantee to the exporter's bank is provided by ECGD but each contract is considered separately and specifically in terms of the financing facility required. On the basis of the ECGD guarantee the bank will advance funds on evidence of dispatch of the goods against bills or notes drawn at a fixed rate of interest in line with agreed international guidelines. ECGD's unconditional guarantee can be applied to US dollars, Deutschmarks and Japanese yen financing, as well as sterling.

The premium is again payable in advance with the rate dependent on the credit period involved. ECGD retains the same rights of recourse as with the comprehensive schemes.

### ECGD BUYER CREDIT GUARANTEES

As an alternative to supplier credit financing as previously described in this chapter, ECGD operates a number of buyer credit financing facilities under which the Department guarantees loans made by UK banks to overseas borrowers which enable the UK exporter to be paid on 'cash' terms, credit being extended to the buyer through the loan.

Buyer credit facilities are not normally available from contracts below £1 million. Under the arrangements the overseas buyer is required to meet 15 to 20% of the contract value from his own resources with the balance coming out of the loan made. The loan is guaranteed by ECGD and is repayable over the usual permissible credit period. Interest rates follow the international guidelines. ECGD can guarantee the repayment of loans in US dollars, Deutschmarks and Japanese yen as well as sterling.

Recourse to the exporter in the event of a claim payment by ECGD is only taken in the event of his breach of contract and is usually limited to 10% of the loan value.

### Lines of credit

Lines of credit are an extension of the basic buyer credit arrangements. ECGD supports a loan made by a bank in the UK to an overseas borrower to finance contracts made with a number of UK suppliers. The credits can be used by importers to purchase a wide range of capital goods.

In 'project' lines the goods are tied to one particular project, but with 'general purposes' lines there is no such restriction and any importer can use them to purchase goods for up to 85% of the contract price. The amount and period of credit, interest rates and acceptable contract values are negotiated separately, but generally relatively small contract values are permissible.

Variations on the line of credit mechanism are also available on the back of certain UK finance houses' ECGD policies.

### OTHER ECGD SUPPORT FACILITIES

### Tender to contract cover

For contracts involving a UK element in excess of £5 million transacted in US dollars, Deutschmarks or Japanese yen, ECGD can provide protection against the movement in exchange rates between the date of tender and the award of the contract if the forward exchange rates move by more than a small margin.

In addition ECGD can provide cover for the same type of business against the inability to sell the currencies forward until the forward exchange contracts can be arranged.

## Bonds

For contracts with a minimum value of £250 000 ECGD will consider providing support to banks or surety companies for the issue of bonds (Performance, Tender, Advance Payment, Progress Payment and Retention).

Insurance against the unfair calling of bonds raised without ECGD support is also available on a comprehensive 'roll-over' basis for short-term business (not Tender Bonds) or on a specific basis.

## Projects participants insolvency cover

ECGD can insure a main contractor or consortium member involved in projects in excess of £20 million against losses arising from unavoidable costs, expenses or damages due to the insolvency of a sub-contractor or fellow consortium member.

## Joint and several cover

Under this facility, applicable to contracts over £50 million, ECGD will indemnify a main contractor against loss caused by the default of an insured sub-contractor or unavoidable additional costs incurred as a result of action by, but not recoverable from, an insured sub-contractor.

## Overseas investment insurance

ECGD is able to provide UK investors with insurance for up to 15 years against the risk of expropriation, war damage and restrictions on remittances in respect of new investment overseas.

## ALTERNATIVE EXPORT CREDIT INSURANCE SOURCES

Outside the ECGD arrangements, a number of alternative underwriting sources exist to provide cover against either the political risks or the commercial risks involved in overseas trading.

The following sections summarise the main underwriting sources available in both the political risk and commercial risk areas.

## Lloyd's of London

Lloyd's underwriters are able to provide the exporter with specific protection against a wide range of political risks which prevent performance of the contract either before or after dispatch of the goods.

Risks such as import/export embargoes, non-transfer of monies, war, buyer default (government buyers only) can be covered. The indemnity is usually 90% but premium rates, claims waiting periods and the precise nature of the policies issued are very much the subject of individual discussion and negotiation to reflect the exporter's particular needs.

Also available through Lloyd's underwriters are a number of other covers which in part reflect the emergence and identification of risks in the political spectrum caused through changing trading patterns.

### Barter and counter-trading arrangements

Cover is available through the Lloyd's market for both the export and import contracts in a counter-trade arrangement.

Where 'pure' barter transactions actually take place, it is possible to arrange cover through Lloyd's, provided that the barter contract shows the assumed value in hard currency applying to each set of goods, and that the contracts require the less creditworthy country to supply first. Pure barter cover is normally for loss of profits or extra costs due to the non-delivery or non-acceptance of either party resulting from political events.

### Overseas investment insurance

Insurance is available in much the same way as with ECGD (except for the war risk on land) but cover can be extended to existing investments and there is the possibility of extending the indemnity provided to 100%.

Contingency covers

A wide range of covers are available to provide the exporter with protection against specific events arising in connection with his overseas contracting. Examples are kidnap and ransom insurance, cancellation of exhibitions through political reasons, product extortion, etc.

## American International Underwriters (AIU) and CIGNA

These are American-owned underwriters who also offer the exporter protection against losses arising from political events either on a specific basis or on a more general basis covering total turnovers or an acceptable spread of markets.

Multi-sourced contracts can be covered and the risks insured parallel those covered through Lloyd's. The indemnity is usually 90% and premium rates, claims waiting periods, etc. again reflect the individual requirements of the exporter.

Insurances for risks arising from barter and counter-trading arrangements, overseas investments and other contingency risks are available through these sources in the same way as the Lloyd's market although the covers available are sometimes conditional.

## Black Sea & Baltic General Insurance Co. Ltd

This company provides protection against the risks of non-payment in respect of contracts made with buyers in the Comecon bloc.

Cover is available for either the pre-delivery or post-delivery causes of loss, and is normally provided on the basis of the availability of a central bank guarantee or related security for the contract involved.

The indemnity is usually set at 90% and cover is underwritten on a specific basis for each contract which is reflected in the premium rate set as an assessment of the risks carried according to the market involved, etc.

**Trade Indemnity plc**

Trade Indemnity is the traditional source of credit insurance for UK receivables.

Through its export policies, however, cover is available against the risk of insolvency and protracted default in respect of business transacted with buyers in OECD territories.

The cover available, which is not necessarily limited to UK goods, can vary, ranging from whole turnover through various forms of deductible arrangement to selected buyers. Contracts with government and public buyers are automatically excluded. The maximum acceptable payment terms are usually 180 days but extended credit can be considered on a case-by-case basis.

The indemnity provided can range from 75 to 100%. The policies are issued on an annual basis with premiums payable either quarterly or annually in advance. Claims are payable within 30 days of confirmation of debt (insolvency) and within six months of due date (protracted default).

**British National Insurance Group**

British National has American parentage. The facilities provided are restricted in the main to the EEC and non-political risk territories and indemnify the exporter against the risk of insolvency.

Cover is provided on a deductible basis with the level of self-insurance subject to individual negotiation (i.e. 'catastrophe' cover). The intention is to provide a 100% indemnity against aggregate losses arising above the level of self-insurance within the 12-month policy period, subject to an overall maximum of £2 million. (See also p. 254.)

**AIG Political Risk Inc. Comprehensive Export Credit Policy**

This is a fairly recent addition to the credit insurance ranks and is essentially an extension of the political risk covers already offered through the Group.

Cover is available on a comprehensive basis for contracts of either UK or foreign sourced goods transacted on terms up to five years (exceptionally seven years) against losses arising through the normal range of commercial and political risks of non-payment. Exceptionally, cover may be considered for single buyers.

The policies are underwritten on an annual basis with premiums payable at inception and at the end of each policy year. The indemnity provided is 90% under the comprehensive policy arrangements or 80% for specific buyer cover, both subject to a first loss deductible which is variable according to the exporter's particular requirements. The policies carry a claims waiting period of six months (commercial risks) and nine months (political risks), unless specifically amended by the underwriters.

### Credit & Guarantee Insurance Co. Ltd

This company specialises in specific one-off types of credit protection.

Cover is available for either UK or foreign receivables against the insolvency risk with an indemnity in the region of 80%.

Premiums are individually assessed according to the nature and length of risk involved.

### Insurances of Credit Co. (IOCC)

IOCC is a Belgian-based concern with offices in a number of European countries including the UK. Cover is provided against commercial insolvency for business in a number of world markets but predominantly in Europe.

The cover provided is very similar to that under the trade indemnity schemes but is usually limited to 'whole turnover' propositions.

The indemnity is usually between 75 and 85% depending on the market concerned. Policies are usually of a three-year duration at a fixed premium rate.

## FURTHER INFORMATION

For additional details please contact the following:

American International
Underwriters (London) Ltd,
120 Fenchurch Street,
London EC3M 5BP

Black Sea & Baltic General
Insurance Co. Ltd,
65 Fenchurch Street,
London EC3

British National Insurance
Group,
52-54 Leadenhall Street,
(3rd Floor),
London EC3A 2BS

CIGNA,
26-28 Fenchurch Street,
London EC3M 3DH

Credit & Guarantee Insurance
Co. Ltd,
Colonial House,
Mincing Lane,
London EC3R 7PN

Export Credits Guarantee
Department,
PO Box 272,
Aldermanbury House,
Aldermanbury,
London EC2P 2EL
*and*
Crown Buildings,
Cathays Park,
Cardiff CF1 3NH

Insurances of Credit Co.,
22 Park Street,
Croydon CR0 0HY

Jardine Credit Insurance Ltd,
PO Box 71,
Beaufort House,
15 St. Botolph Street,
London EC3A 7HR

Trade Indemnity plc,
Trade Indemnity House,
12-34 Great Eastern Street,
London EC2A 3AX

## FURTHER READING

Export Credits Guarantee Department and Central Office of
Information, *ECGD Services.* Revised edition, 1982.

# PART VII

# EXPORT CREDIT AND FINANCE

# 17

# Export Credit and Collections

W. V. Adams, Commercial Credit Consultant

## BASIC FACTORS INHERENT IN EXPORT CREDIT

It is a sad fact that most UK companies still have only a small percentage, if any, of their sales value as exports. Increasing the proportion requires the development of extra expertise in both marketing and the practical activities of shipping and documentation. All aspects are differences from domestic trade which are expensive and require special expert pricing.

This careful costing and pricing ties exports closely to the financing of export credit, which must have specialist attention to achieve its full potential.

The same basic principles of credit sanction and collecting apply for the export market as for the home trade. The seller is still investing funds and collecting them later in the hope of maximising sales and minimising risks. There are, however, some built-in factors which make the practice different.

### Distance

Mere geography means it is difficult to visit a client to resolve a problem or to develop the relationship. Visits, when they can be made, become more critical and decisive, so that better planning and sharper negotiation are required. Telephone calls need pre-planning because of time differences and connection or line delays.

Correspondence takes longer, and although telexes are sometimes possible, the remoteness means a greater dependence on second-hand information.

## Language

With all the above forms of communication, there is a problem of understanding due to language differences. Obviously it is an advantage for exporters, including credit staff, to speak other languages, particularly those of the customer countries. The availability of translators or even interpreters is still far short of the facility required for the cut and thrust of commercial and financial negotiation. English is, fortunately, the commercial language of most of the world but even English differs across the hemispheres. It is necessary to make deliberate efforts to keep commercial English free of jargon and 'slick' phrases, both written and oral. Particularly letters should be checked before sending, for ambiguities which could generate delays and expense to clarify.

## National custom

Care must be taken to judge the character of the customer by local standards, not entirely by British ones. There are oddities and courtesies attending trade in different markets which require a lot of experience to understand and accept. For this reason, correspondence should always err on the polite side, rather than the forceful or plain-speaking. Export credit men will always feel frustrated by the *mañana* complex, acceptable locally, which says very clearly that 'tomorrow will do'. Thus in these countries the 'due date' is much more flexible than elsewhere.

## Local legislation

Although exporters are always advised to make their contracts subject to English law, there will always be situations where the customer is protected by local law, or where local legislation is needed initially. In most foreign countries, the law is considerably different from the UK and in most cases, certainly in the less-developed countries, is protracted and costly. Legal action should be avoided if at all possible and if it cannot be avoided, there should never be any assumptions about points of foreign law. They should be properly checked with foreign law experts who will also be expensive and possibly slow. Debt recovery proceedings in the less legally sophisticated countries are very protracted and should be avoided unless the debt has very real consequence.

### Foreign currencies/metric system

The decisions as to the currency of invoicing will include a consideration of the condition of the seller's currency in world foreign exchange markets. A strong seller's currency will produce a request from the buyer to invoice in his local currency (or some other) to provide him with the exchange rate advantage. For the same reasons the buyer will want his suppliers to invoice in the seller's currency when that currency is weak on the world's markets.

Wherever possible the seller should invoice in his own currency in order to ensure no loss arising from the exchange transaction. In those cases where invoicing must be in a currency other than the seller's, the seller will be wise to avail himself of the protection of the forward exchange market to protect himself against exchange movements between contract or invoice date and receipt of proceeds.

The whole subject is fully aired elsewhere in this book but suffice to say at this point that the currency of the sale is an essential difference from the home trade which requires careful handling. Even the preparation of statements and invoices in foreign currencies involves extra clerical and book-keeping work.

Similarly with metric measurements, the invoice details of weights, measurements, quantities, etc., may be expressed in unfamiliar ways which require great care to avoid error and loss.

### Local economic and political conditions

Any country largely pays for its imports from the proceeds of its exports and invisible earnings. Thus the export credit risk of non-payment is always tied in some way to the local economic or balance of payments position. Additionally, political ideology may cause a government deliberately to delay settlement or refuse to trade with a country with which it is not in sympathy politically. Even political actions in the UK can lead to reprisals by a trading partner if not resolved at the diplomatic level. An overnight *coup d'état* can change market conditions, which several recent cases can witness. A prolonged drought or floods or earthquakes can bring a sudden end to a country's staple export commodity and create a shortage of available exchange.

From an export credit view, it is vital to look at the risk to payment prospects on a 'country' basis before assessing the 'client' basis. A common dilemma is to find a thoroughly sound customer in a very risky foreign market. In other words, the customer may well pay on the due date, but his local money will not be converted to sterling, or the currency of the contract, by the national bank. It is for this reason that ECGD provides extensive insurance cover against blocked payments.

In this context it is essential for an export credit controller to keep himself fully up-to-date with political/economic conditions in each of his overseas markets because these conditions have a direct bearing upon his collection performance.

All the major banks issue excellent regular reports on the markets in which they specialise and the better-known financial newspapers should be daily obligatory reading.

## ASSESSING THE RISK AND FIXING CREDIT LIMITS

At the credit sanction stage, not only the status dossier on the prospective client but also the appropriate economic/political reports are needed, plus details of any contract conditions which affect the financial decision. Penalty clauses, performance bond requirements and interest charges would be typical items subject to contractual definition.

### Sources of credit information

1   *Commercial agencies:* provide status reports on overseas clients

in the same way as for home trade but take longer to collate and the report content will be proportionate in quality to the state of industry sophistication of the client's territory, e.g. the same detail should not be expected from Saudi Arabia as from USA.

2  *Trade references:* obtainable on foreign buyers in the same way as for home trade and are frequently more informative because the laws of libel are less onerous for much of the world than the UK.

3  *Department of Trade and Industry:* will provide good basic information on a company via the commercial secretariats in overseas embassies. It will not provide credit reports in the usual sense but will give information on the prospect's local reputation, size, quality of premises, location, nature and scope of business, other agencies held, etc.

4  *Internal information:* from sales or other company staff who may have already visited the client can be useful. Similarly copies of correspondence both ways can help build the picture, after making due allowance for commercial optimism.

## Early warning

Collecting sufficient credit reports takes time and it pays handsomely if sales people can be educated to provide names and addresses of potential export clients as soon as sales enquiries are received or market promotional work begun. Credit enquiries can then be started on all the prospects even though some may prove abortive if sales are not achieved.

## Setting the credit limit

The same assessment has to be made as for home trade customers except that limits have to be proportionately higher for export customers on a comparable sales volume, because once an order has been approved for dispatch it is much longer 'in the pipeline' before reaching the customer.

Alternatively, a dual limit can be set, i.e. one for goods in transit and another for goods which have actually reached the customer. Remembering that export custom allows the right of 'stoppage in transit' if justified by non-payment of previous shipments, the exporter can redirect shipments on the way if the active credit limit gives cause for concern.

A further system adopted by some exporters for a dual limit is to set the normal credit limit for shipment and allow say four times that figure for orders accepted but not shipped. This enables manufacture to proceed whilst awaiting the fate of previous dispatches.

## EXPORT CREDIT DOCUMENTS

The relationship between the credit limit and the possible sales value is more variable in export than in home business because payment terms are vastly different. Terms in turn relate to documents of title, which are well-defined and internationally accepted in world trade. The basic export documents are as follows.

### Invoice

More complex than a domestic invoice. As well as the usual data of buyer's name and address, consignee's name and address, goods, quantity, description, price, discounts and value, it will also refer to the price base of ex-works, f.o.b., c.i.f., c and f, etc., each of which are internationally defined for the benefit of banks and exporters in *Incoterms* published by the International Chamber of Commerce.

The purpose of establishing the price base is to decide, as part of the costing exercise, where the obligations of the seller cease and those of the buyer begin. The invoice may be expressed in foreign currency and there may be an exchange clause that specifies which party is responsible in the event of the exchange rate exceeding stated parities. The invoice will probably show gross, net and tare weights and packing details, probably in metric. The destination of the goods may require a customs declaration, sometimes in a foreign language. In the case of exports to Commonwealth or some ex-Commonwealth countries invoices may bear a combined certificate of value and origin. The export invoice is quite a complicated document but its accuracy is absolutely essential to the successful outcome of the transaction.

## Bill of lading

This historic and famous document of the export trade has its origins in the captains of sailing ships signing a bill to certify the safe-loading of specified goods into their vessels. Again internationally defined and used, the bill of lading is a receipt for goods shipped and is evidence of a contract of carriage. It is usually made out by the exporter or his forwarding agent and must be signed in duplicate or frequently in triplicate by the shipowner or his agent. These signed copies are then known as negotiable bills of lading. The B/L, as it is often abbreviated to, must be produced by the importer or his agent in order to obtain the goods at destination and to process them through customs and into his warehouse. It is international practice that property in the goods passes with the bill of lading. Thus it has become sound practice for the B/L to be handed over only against payment or at least signed acceptance of the debt, so that passing of the title in the goods is regulated by the payment conditions, or credit terms. There is no similar security of title for goods dispatched by air or by post.

## Air consignment note

Issued by the carrying airline, this is evidence of the receipt of goods for air dispatch and is a contract of carriage. However, the airline does not require production of a copy of the air consignment note before releasing the goods at destination as this would negate much of the benefit of air freighting, i.e. speed in getting the goods to the customer.

## Parcel post receipts

Issued by the GPO simply as an acknowledgement of the receipt of the goods for carriage and delivery but there is no security in a parcel post receipt as its presentation is not required by the local post office before delivery is effected.

*NB:* The lack of payment security in both airfreight and parcel post deliveries can be overcome by arranging with the client for goods to be consigned to his local bank. The goods on arrival will be delivered to the bank or its agent and placed in the bank's go-down or warehouse. The bank will be instructed by the exporter to release the goods only when the client has met the payment conditions.

### Insurance policy/certificate

Obviously the foreign buyer requires evidence that the goods have been insured against the perils of the voyage and it is the buyer's prerogative to lodge any insurance claims for damage, loss or pilferage en route. For this reason it is usual to send the buyer evidence of marine insurance in the form of either a policy or a certificate. Most regular exporters have a global or blanket policy with the marine insurance company, under which policy each shipment is given a certificate of insurance for issue to the buyer rather than issuing an individual complete policy in every case.

### Certificate of origin

A document issued by a Chamber of Commerce, certifying the country of origin of the goods. For many destinations, it has also to be legalised by the embassy in the UK of the importing country. All this is because of the increasing volume of multinational trading, whereby a large volume of goods of foreign origin is incorporated in UK exports either by assembly process or, more frequently, by simple resale, e.g. a UK merchant buys goods from Germany but has Germany send them direct to Brazil.

### Consular invoice

A document purchased in blank from the UK embassy of the importing country. It must be completed in every detail with 100% accuracy before being stamped and checked by the embassy against that country's import licence regulations.

Other documents may be required and for each destination exporters should refer to publications such as *Croners Reference*

*Book for Exporters* where documentary requirements for every country are clearly set out and regularly updated.

It cannot be said too strongly that a condition for prompt settlement by an overseas buyer is 100% accurate documentation. It is sound practice, therefore, for a credit department to be sent the set of documents of title for each shipment, prior to dispatch, for checking, since correct documentation is essential for satisfactory collection of sales proceeds. It may also be desirable for the credit department to assemble the payment documents to complete the process for banking purposes.

## EXPORT PAYMENT TERMS

These are listed in order of ascending risk.

### Cash with order

If the client is not creditworthy, or his country has exchange problems, it is prudent to obtain cash before dispatch. All international money transfers are handled between banks on an international banking giro system, i.e. the paying bank debits the customer's account, credits the UK bank in its books, sends the UK bank an advice on receipt of which the UK bank debits the account of the foreign bank and credits the account of the UK exporter. It is a highly efficient system, whereby no cash ever moves, and takes one of three forms:

(a) Telegraphic Transfer, or TT, whereby the advice, hence the payment, are cabled.
(b) Airmail Transfer, or MT, whereby the advice goes by airmail and thus takes longer.
(c) SWIFT (Society for Worldwide Interbank Financial Telecommunications), a computer-based system to facilitate same-day transfer of payments. Not all banks, however, participate as yet.

If the funds are advised in a foreign currency, the receiving UK bank will ask the exporter or beneficiary whether it should 'sell and credit at spot' or hold the currency whilst the exporter hawks it around the banking market to get a more advantageous rate.

In the less usual event that the client sends a cheque on his own (foreign) bank e.g. South American buyers send cheques to UK drawn on a New York bank in US dollars, it is prudent to await cheque clearance before dispatch. This can mean a substantial delay which should be borne in mind when considering dispatch authorisation.

## Cash on delivery

This is only secure if sent by GPO parcel post, for surrender to the client against payment of the total invoice value. The GPO service does not apply to every country in the world and the credit department should check to satisfy itself that the service is available for a particular destination, before applying such payment terms. Some export orders show payment terms as COD when the service does not exist and the buyer means CAD—cash against documents.

Whereas in the UK a COD parcel is delivered to the actual address of the consignee and payment has to be met at that time before the parcel is left with the buyer, overseas post offices will not normally deliver a COD parcel to a client but instead will advise him that the parcel awaits his collection at the post office against payment. Thus, if the client has lost interest in the goods, has obtained them from the competition or simply has no funds available the parcel will wait on the post office shelf whilst the exporter writes to the GPO for news of the sales proceeds. The COD service is a time consuming business in terms of collectability and involves a credit period of at least eight weeks. It is difficult to refuse a client or a sales department COD terms as superficially there is no actual credit risk, but it should be avoided where possible.

## The documentary letter of credit

This method of settlement for exports offers the exporter the highest degree of security and the quickest collection period. It is an authority given by the overseas buyer through his bank to a UK bank to pay for the value of an export consignment or consignments providing that the exporter adheres to certain clearly stipulated conditions. The subject is explored in detail in Chapter 18.

## The documentary bill of exchange

There are two basic types, a sight bill and a time or usance bill. The sight bill is payable 'at sight'—i.e. on presentation to the drawee. The time or usance bill is payable at a later date and on presentation the drawee writes across the face of the bill the word 'Accepted' and signs it. The drawee thereby becomes the acceptor and the bill is sent back to the drawer, who will hold it until the maturity date.

The documents of title are attached and are released to the buyer only when he has paid, if it is a sight bill, or accepted if it is a time bill.

Assuming that 90-day terms apply for an overseas buyer, once the goods are dispatched a 90-day bill of exchange is drawn and a set of documents is attached. The bill, with the documents, is sent to the exporter's bankers accompanied by a bills for collection form, which gives the bank the necessary collection instructions. The UK bank then sends the bill and documents (the collection) to its correspondent bank in the buyer's town. On receiving advice from the overseas bank of the bill's arrival the buyer will call at the bank, accept the bill by signing across its face and take possession of the documents for clearance of the goods out of customs.

When the bill matures after 90 days the local bank will present it to the client for payment, and on receipt of the proceeds the London bank will credit the account of the exporter.

There is always the risk that a sight bill will not be paid on arrival or a time bill will be dishonoured on maturity so that the goods have to be returned to the UK with all the attendant expense and inconvenience. The bank formalities do take time and even a sight bill takes anything from one month to two months to be collected and a time bill will have a similar period added to its terms before the proceeds arrive.

Those particularly interested should refer to 'The Uniform Rules for Collection of Commercial Paper', obtainable from the International Chamber of Commerce.

**Open account terms**

The exporter sends the invoices and the appropriate documents of title direct to the overseas client and hopes that he will pay on the agreed due date.

Prompt payment on open account terms can be obtained by conducting export business with a creditworthy UK export merchant or confirming house. These purchase on behalf of overseas buyers from UK suppliers, attend to the forwarding and documentation requirements and normally require only that the UK supplier sends them the invoice. Experience shows that the UK merchant or confirming house are good and prompt payers. For further information, contact the British Export Houses Association, 69 Cannon Street, London EC4N 5AB.

**ECGD**

It will be seen that there are substantial risks attached to the export credit business. War, civil commotion, bankruptcy, refusal to pay, protracted delay for exchange reasons, withdrawal of an import licence, etc., etc. All of these risks and others can be covered by an insurance policy obtainable from the Export Credits Guarantee Department.

Those interested should obtain a copy of *ECGD Services* from the Export Credits Guarantee Department.

**THE EXCHANGE RISK**

It is frequently necessary to invoice the overseas buyer in his own currency and thus receive in the UK a quantity of foreign exchange.

By obtaining a forward rate before actually quoting the customer on the contract it is possible to price the contract in currency so that there will be no loss between the sterling value required and the sterling value of the currency when sold to the bank on arrival in the UK. If it is not possible for internal reasons to obtain the forward rates before quoting it is essential for the credit department to obtain a forward rate before booking the sterling value of the currency invoice to protect the period of credit allowed. (See p. 283). Forward rates are usually quoted as either a premium or discount on the seller's currency. This complication can be avoided by asking the bank to do the calculation and provide an 'outright' forward rate.

## THE IMPORT LICENCE

One country's export is another country's import. Foreign currency is earned by exporting and is spent by importing. The overall difference between the two represents a country's balance of trade. Most countries control their imports and hence their balance of trade by a form of import licensing. Some licences are freely issued and are available for goods of any origin from any country, i.e. the open general licence. Other forms are the global quota, i.e. for a specific quantity of goods from any source and the specific licence for goods of a given nature from a given source for a given amount. Without the requisite licence no exchange will be made available so payment for the export cannot be made. Because the availability of a valid import licence is essential to the eventual collection success of any one export it is vital that the credit department should check that such a licence has been obtained and its number and date known before any export order is approved for credit.

## FURTHER READING

H. Edwards, *Export Credit.* Gower, 1982.
C. Schmitthoff, *The Export Trade.* Stevens & Sons Ltd, 1969.

# 18

# Export Finance

H. B. Jackson, Specialist in Foreign exchange and documentary credits

## INTRODUCTION

Credit control is intimately bound up with the credit terms to be offered and the means by which payment will be made. Credit terms will basically be determined by the custom of the market and the strength of competition. The method of payment will depend upon the way in which credit is granted. The control of credit by way of preliminary enquiries and limits on outstandings will, in turn, depend on the length of credit granted and the security of the method of payment.

Theoretically, any company should be able to finance all its operations from the resources available to it, i.e. its capital plus whatever it is able to borrow from the bank. Its capital will depend on how much the members of the company are prepared to invest in the enterprise and its borrowing from the bank will depend on such factors as the balance sheet figures, profit and loss, turnover, etc., or on the security it can offer by way of mortgages, life policies, etc. Both these sources then are subject to strict limitations and for a company expanding its export trade they are bound to prove inadequate. With the lengthening credit terms now usual in international trade, a company whose product is sold more and more in overseas markets and, therefore, subject to these longer credit terms will soon face a cash flow problem.

To meet this cash flow problem and finance the credit terms the markets demand, extra sources of finance must be tapped over and above the basic sources of capital and bank overdraft. This finance must be sought through channels relative to the export transaction and in particular to the method by which payment will be made.

## PAYMENT METHODS AND TERMS

The terms and method of payment will usually be agreed between the parties and form part of the sales contract. The more common arrangements and the type of finance linked to them are as follows:

1 Cash with order—this presents no problem either as to finance or to credit control.
2 Sales on open account—here the goods are delivered to the buyer and the terms of payment are stated on the invoice. The exporter is, therefore, entirely dependent on the goodwill of the buyer to remit payment when due. Finance may be obtained by using the services of a factoring company who take over the administration of the sales ledger and may be prepared to advance a percentage of the amounts outstanding. This will be dealt with in more detail in a subsequent chapter. Alternatively, the exporter may be able to obtain additional overdraft facilities from his bank against the debtor item in the balance sheet.
3 Sales on credit terms of up to say 180 days where a bill of exchange is to be drawn on the buyer. Where the terms are payment on delivery, the bill would be drawn payable at sight and the attached shipping documents released against payment of the bill. Where credit terms have been agreed the bill would be drawn at so many days after sight, according to the terms agreed, and the documents released against acceptance of the bill whereby the buyer undertakes to meet the bill when it falls due. Such bills with documents attached are lodged with the bank who forward them to their correspondent bank to be presented to the buyer for payment or acceptance. In these cases extra finance may be obtained by discounting the bill with the bank and the possibility of doing so is enhanced if the export is covered with ECGD.
4 Documentary credit. Where the buyer has established a documentary letter of credit through his bank in favour of the

exporter and this credit is irrevocable then the exporter is assured that provided he ships the goods and presents the documents as called for in the credit he will receive payment. As he will receive payment immediately after shipment, the need for finance is reduced. If, however, the exporter requires help with production finance there is a possibility he may obtain assistance from his bank on the strength of the payment assured under the credit when the goods are shipped.

## ACCEPTANCE CREDITS

Additional finance for exporters may be obtained through merchant banks by means of an acceptance credit facility. The merchant bank establishes its own credit in favour of the exporter providing for bills to be drawn by the exporter on the merchant bank. These bills are accepted by the merchant bank and can then be discounted in the money market at the finest rates. It is usual for such credits to run parallel with the bills drawn by the exporter on his overseas buyers and which he lodges with the merchant bank for collection. The bills under the credit will be drawn at the same term as those on the buyers and in due course the payment received for the commercial bills will meet the amount due to the merchant bank on its accepted bills.

## EXPORT MERCHANTS

The specialised services of export merchants can also be utilised to obtain ready finance. These merchants are very well versed in certain overseas markets and in the marketing of certain products. They are prepared to buy exporters' goods for their account and undertake the sale and collection of payment.

## CONFIRMING HOUSES

Another source of export finance is through the confirming house. These institutions act for the overseas buyer making with him all arrangements for credit terms and payment and sometimes seeking out a supplier for the buyer. When the order has been placed the confirming house confirms it and undertakes to pay when the goods are shipped and the relative documents submitted.

## ECGD-BACKED BORROWING

Special arrangements have been made between the clearing banks and ECGD to facilitate the obtaining of finance by exporters from the banks at a preferential rate of interest. These comprise the short, medium and long term finance facilities. (See p. 311–14.)

## OVERSEAS BORROWING

In certain circumstances especially where the amount of a single transaction is substantial an exporter may find it advantageous to borrow from a bank in the country to which the goods are being sold. This would best apply if the goods are being invoiced in the buyer's currency. The payment received for the goods would be used to pay off the borrowing and, as both transactions would be in the same currency, any exchange risk would be eliminated.

## COST OF EXPORT CREDIT

Because of longer credit terms and increased competition in a buyer's market the cost of financing credit terms is of growing importance, (a) in its effect on profit margins and (b) in its effect on prices (cost to buyer).

 If the exporter absorbs the cost of any finance he may have to obtain to be able to offer the credit terms required then his overall profit will be reduced. If on the other hand he recoups the cost of finance by building it in to the price or claims it from the buyer by, say, an interest clause in the bill of exchange the cost of his goods to the buyer is increased and makes his product less competitive. Where large sums are involved, the cost of this credit could be a deciding factor in obtaining the business.

The rate of interest on overdraft can be anything from 1 to 3% over the banks' base rate and this same rate would be applied to the discounting of bills.

Under the special arrangements with ECGD mentioned above, preferential rates are applied. In this context it is interesting to note how the various governments have instituted schemes to provide their exporters with finance at cheap rates of interest and the attempts being made, especially by members of the EEC, to limit the extent of this credit race.

The use of a factoring company can be relatively expensive but this can be set-off against the saving on administration costs. The factor charges a service fee based on turnover and, of course, interest at normal banking rates on any monies advanced.

Documentary letters of credit cost the exporter nothing but in some countries the bank charges for establishing these credits are high and so prove expensive to the buyer, adding substantially to the cost of the goods.

In the case of confirming houses the costs of credit are again borne by the buyer although occasionally a confirming house may ask for a cash discount from the exporter.

Merchant banks charge a small percentage commission for establishing an acceptance credit and in addition the exporter will suffer the rate of interest at which his bill is discounted in the money market.

## BANKING ARRANGEMENTS FOR EXPORTERS

Any business enterprise will maintain an account with one of the clearing banks through which it will conduct the majority of its financial transactions.

It is to this bank that an exporter will first turn for finance when his business development requires a supplement to the resources which he himself has provided. This additional finance will be provided by way of overdraft and the amount made available will depend upon the type and extent of the business being done.

Once the exporter has reached the overdraft limit set by his bank and his expanding export activities require still more financial assistance he may approach the bank for discount facilities. That is, he can ask the bank to negotiate the bills drawn by him on his overseas buyers against the shipping documents of title attached to the bill. The bank will, in any case, be handling the collection of the bill. Provided the bank is satisfied with the transaction and the report on the buyer and particularly if the export is covered with ECGD it will discount the bill and so provide additional cash to the exporter.

The clearing bank will also enter into the necessary agreement with ECGD to provide cash against bills drawn on foreign buyers or in connection with open account sales under the short term finance arrangement. It will also make all the arrangements with ECGD for financing larger sales contracts with credit terms up to five years under the medium term arrangement and for the very large undertakings with longer term of credit under the long term arrangement.

For the credit manager, the bank provides a useful service in obtaining reports from its overseas correspondents on the credit-worthiness and financial integrity of foreign buyers. Its intelligence reports on various countries give the economic conditions in those areas with details of their payment record, controls and exchange risks.

The role of the clearing banks can, therefore, be summed up as providing all the normal banking services including the provision of extra finance and especially that made possible by ECGD support, and also to make available credit and intelligence information on overseas markets.

The role of merchant banks is to provide export finance outside the usual scope of clearing banks either by acceptance credits or by the provision of special loans for large projects. In cases where a contract involving large sums with long terms of credit is being financed by more than one clearing bank acting as a consortium, a merchant bank may take on the role of manager.

## LETTERS OF CREDIT

The letter of credit with which we are primarily concerned is the documentary credit and the most usual form of this is the irrevocable

---

**Banco de Credito del Vespucci**

Documentary credit. Irrevocable

Lima 6 June 19—
Credit no. E.586

*Advising bank*
Chiswell Bank Ltd
Teal Street,
London, E.C.

*Applicant*
Casa Clubera,
Lima, Peru.

*Beneficiary*
Fabric Manufacturing Co.,
Ashstead, Herts

*Amount*
Not exceeding £4300
sterling.

*Expiry*
28 August, 19—
At the counters of advising
bank.

We hereby issue in your favour this documentary credit which is available by payment against presentation of the following documents: Sterling Draft at sight on Casa Clubera, Lima, clearly marked that it is drawn under this bank's Letter of Credit no.—dated 6 June 19—and accompanied by the documents as stated below.

The draft to be drawn to the extent of 100% of full invoice value.

*Documents required*
Commercial invoice.

Consular invoice which must be legalised prior to shipping date and must mention Partida No. 44—99—1.

Complete set clean on board shipping company's B/lading made out to order of Banco de Credito del Vespucci marked 'Freight Prepaid' and 'Notify Casa Clubera, Lima'.

Insurance will be covered by the buyer.

*Covering*
Shipment of 4800 yards printed cotton fabric.

Shipment from UK port.    Partial shipments    Trans-shipment
To Callao.                Allowed.             Allowed provided
                                               B/L are presented.

Terms C & F.

Description of the goods in the consular invoice and in the relative bills of lading must agree in every respect and must be made out in the Spanish language in order to comply with the consular regulations in Peru.

We hereby engage that payment will be duly made against documents presented in conformity with the terms of this credit.

Banco de Credito del Vespucci.

Manager

---

**Figure 18:1    Advice of opening of credit issued by opening bank**

credit. Apart from cash with order, it provides the most satisfactory method of obtaining payment. See Figures 18:1, 18:2 and 18:3.

This is an arrangement whereby the buyer instructs his bank to establish a credit in favour of the seller. The buyer's bank (the issuing bank) undertakes to pay or authorises its correspondent bank in the exporter's country to pay the exporter a sum of money (normally the invoice price of the goods) against presentation of

---

*Beneficiary*

| Fabric Manufacturing Co. | Establishing Bank Reference |
| Ashstead, Herts | Credit no. E. 586 |
| | Our reference XY 27 |

Amount: £4300

Dear Sirs,

We enclose letter of credit issued by the establishing bank in your favour dated 6 June 19—

Please be guided by the instructions marked (X).

(1)  The enclosed letter of credit is solely an advice from the establishing bank and conveys no engagement by us. Drafts negotiated by us under this credit will be subject to recourse to you.

(2)  Kindly note that this letter of credit must accompany the draft and documents at the time of presentation.

(3)  Documents are to be accompanied by your draft(s) marked 'drawn under credit no. E.586 of Banco de Credito del Vespucci and quoting our reference No. XY27'.

(4)  *

Yours faithfully,
for Chiswell Bank Ltd,
Teal Street, London

Manager

*NB: If the UK bank have been asked to confirm the credit then
item (1) would not be marked and under (4) they would
state that they add their confirmation to the credit.

---

**Figure 18:2   Covering advice from advising bank in UK**

*Points to note on receipt of the credit*

1  The credit is irrevocable but not confirmed by a UK bank.
2  Note the way in which the draft has to be drawn.
3  A legalised consular invoice called for and use of Spanish language.
4  Insurance by buyer. If the beneficiary is not happy with this arrangement he may wish to take out supplementary cover on his own account.
5  Can shipment from UK port to Callao be arranged?

*Points to check on receipt of any letter of credit*

1  Goods and packing are exactly as in the sales contract.
2  The voyage is one for which shipping can be arranged.
3  Expiry date and last shipment date can be met.
4  Trans-shipment and/or part shipments are allowed if required.
5  Insurance called for is reasonable and available.
6  No documents called for are not available.

*Presentation*

(a)  If you employ a shipping or forwarding agent, let him have a copy of the credit to know exactly what is required.
(b)  When assembling documents for presentation check that they conform with one another as to description of goods and also with the credit specification.
(c)  If a draft is to be drawn, ensure that it is drawn on the name specified in the credit.

**Figure 18:3   Points to check on letters of credit**

shipping documents which are specified in the credit. It is a mandatory contract and completely independent of the sales contract. It is concerned only with documents and not the goods to which the documents refer.

When the credit is irrevocable it cannot be cancelled or amended without the agreement of the beneficiary and all other parties. This means that, with a credit opened by a reputable bank in a sound country, the exporter can rely on payment as soon as he has shipped the goods and produced the documents called for. The security in the credit can be further enhanced by the British bank, at the request of the issuing bank, adding its confirmation. The exporter then has a confirmed, irrevocable letter of credit (known as CILC) and need look no further than the British bank for payment. With a credit which is not confirmed, however, payment is made by the issuing bank and the local bank negotiates with recourse.

The credit will set out in detail a description of the goods with price per unit and packing, name and address of the beneficiary (the exporter), the voyage, i.e. port of shipment and port of destination, whether the price is f.o.b., c & f or c.i.f., whether part shipments are allowed and trans-shipment allowed, details of insurance (if c.i.f.) and the risks to be covered. Sometimes, the ship will be nominated. The credit will also have an expiry date, which is the latest date for presentation of the documents, and it may also have a latest date for shipment.

The basic documents which are usually called for are:

*1  Invoice.* The amount must not exceed the credit amount. If terms such as 'about' or 'circa' are used a tolerance of 10% is allowed (in respect of quantity the tolerance is 3%). The description of the goods on the invoice and the packing must be exact and agree with the credit. An essential part of the description is the marks and numbers on the packages and these must appear on the invoice. The invoice should be in the name of the opener (buyer).

*2  Bills of lading.* The bill of lading is a document of title to the goods and without it the buyer will not be able to obtain delivery from the shipping company. The credit will call for a full set (they are usually issued in a set of three). They must be clean, i.e. bearing no superimposed clause derogatory to the condition of the goods such as 'inadequate packing', 'used drums', 'on deck', etc. Unless the credit has specifically permitted the circumstances contained in the clause the negotiating or paying bank will call for an indemnity. The bills of lading must show the goods to be 'on board'—'received for shipment' bills are not acceptable. They may, however, have a subsequent notation, dated and signed, which states the goods to be 'on board' and they are then acceptable. Under the regulations set out in the 'Uniform Customs and Practice for Documentary Credits' which came into operation on 1 October 1975 the following bills of lading will be accepted:

(a)   Through bills issued by shipping companies of their agents even though they cover several modes of transport.
(b)   Short form bills of lading which indicate some or all of the conditions of carriage by reference to a source or document other than the bill of lading.
(c)   Bills covering unitised cargoes such as those on pallets or in containers.

Unless specifically authorised in the credit, bills of the following type will not be accepted:

(a)   Bills of lading issued by forwarding agents.
(b)   Bills which are issued under and are subject to a charter party.
(c)   Bills covering shipment by sailing vessels.

The bills of lading must be made out to the order of the shipper and endorsed in blank. If the sales contract is c.i.f. or c&f, then the bills of lading must be marked 'freight paid'. The general description of the goods including marks and numbers must match the invoice. The voyage and ship if named must be as stated in the credit. Unless trans-shipment is expressly prohibited in the credit, bills indicating trans-shipment will be accepted provided the entire voyage is covered by the same bill of lading. Part shipments are permitted unless the credit states otherwise. Although credits must stipulate an expiry date for presentation of documents, they must also stipulate a specified period of time after the issuance of the bills of lading during which the documents must be presented for payment. If no such period is stipulated in the credit, banks will refuse documents presented to them later than 21 days after the issuance of the bills of lading.

The Uniform Customs and Practice for Documentary Credits No. 400 came into operation on 1 October 1984. The UCP only apply if the operating banks, particularly the issuing bank, make the credit subject to the UCP. The UCP do not have the force of law but most banks operate their credits expressly under the UCP. When the 1983 revision comes into operation banks and exporters will have to pay special attention to ascertain whether the credit operates under the old 1974 revision or the new 1983 revision.

The changes are due to the transport revolution which has led to the use of transport documents other than the traditional bill of lading. A much wider number of transport documents has been made acceptable to the banks.

There is an important new provision which introduces three new terms: the nominated bank; the accepting bank; and the negotiating bank. If the seller is resident in a small place in which the advising bank has no branch office the issuing bank may then nominate a local bank to pay, accept or negotiate. If the nominated bank accepts these instructions and the documents tendered are in order it is now laid down that the nominated bank which will be the paying, accepting or negotiating bank will receive reimbursement from the issuing bank.

When documents other than transport, insurance and commercial invoices are called for, the credit should stipulate by whom such documents are to be issued. Where the issuing bank instructs the advising bank by telex to inform the beneficiary of the opening of the credit and then later sends a letter confirming the credit the issuing bank should make it clear in the telex that it considers the confirming letter as the operative document. If the issuing bank does not make such a reservation the telex itself will be regarded as the operative document.

These new provisions refer to transport documents indicating loading on board, dispatch, or taking in charge. Unless the credit calls for a marine bill of lading covering carriage by sea, a post receipt or certificate of posting, the banks will, unless otherwise stipulated in the credit, accept a transport document which appears on its face to have been issued by a named carrier, indicates dispatch or taking in charge and consists of a full set of originals issued.

It should be borne in mind that these documents are not documents of title and that goods dispatched by this means are tantamount to sold on open account. They will be delivered to the addressee without his having to produce any document and as such do not provide any security.

*3   Insurance.* The document must be as stated in the credit (policy or certificate) and issued by an insurance company or its agent. Cover notes issued by brokers are not acceptable.

The details on the policy must match those on the bills of lading— voyage, ship, marks and numbers, etc. It must also be in the same currency as the credit, and endorsed in blank. The amount covered should be at least the invoice amount—credits usually call for invoice value plus 10%. The policy must be dated not later than the date of shipment as evidenced by the bill of lading.

The risks covered should be those detailed in the credit—usually institute cargo clauses W & SRCC. If cover against all risks is called for (which is unobtainable) a policy which states that it covers all insurable risks will be acceptable.

4 *Other documents.* Other documents which may be called for under the credit according to circumstances are: consular certificate, certificate of origin, quality certificate, railway consignment note, airway bill, PO receipt, etc.

Not only must the documents be presented not later than the expiry date of the credit, but if a last shipment date is mentioned, the bill of lading must show shipment by that date. Extension of the shipment date automatically extends the expiry date but not vice versa.

It is very important that exporters when they receive advice of a credit opened in their favour should check it immediately to see that the goods and terms agree with the sales contract, and that they can comply with all the terms and provide all the documents as called for. If any amendment is required, they can then take it up with the advising bank in good time for action to be taken before expiry.

Where a buyer wishes to provide his supplier with the security of payment by documentary credit but at the same time requires a period of credit, he may instruct his bank to issue a credit calling for a bill drawn at so many days after sight instead of the usual sight draft—this would still be an irrevocable credit. In this case the beneficiary when presenting the documents would not receive cash as under a sight credit but would have a bill accepted by the bank which would still receive payment immediately but the opener would not be called upon to pay until the bill matured.

## REVOCABLE LETTERS OF CREDIT

Besides the basic irrevocable credit (confirmed or not) are revocable credits which as the name implies can be cancelled or amended at any time without notice to the beneficiary. They do not constitute a legally binding undertaking by the banks concerned. Once transmitted and made available at the advising bank, however, their cancellation or modification is only effective when that bank has received notice thereof. Any payment made before the receipt of such notice is reimbursable by the issuing bank. The value of these credits as security for payment is plainly doubtful.

## TRANSFERABLE CREDITS

These arise where the exporter/seller is obtaining the goods from a third-party (say, the actual manufacturers) and as a middleman does not have the resources to buy outright and await payment from his buyer. The credit is established in favour of the seller (the prime beneficiary) and authorises the advising bank to accept instructions from the prime beneficiary to make the credit available in whole or in part to one or more third-parties (second beneficiaries). The credit is advised in the terms and conditions of the original except for the amount and unit price and perhaps the shipment and expiry dates may be reduced. The original credit is for the price the buyer is paying to the prime beneficiary but the latter will be obtaining the goods at a lower price and so the credit will be transferred for a lower amount. When the second beneficiary presents shipping documents he obtains payment for his invoice price and the prime beneficiary is called upon to substitute his own invoice and receive the difference. The negotiating bank then has documents in accordance with the original credit.

Where there is more than one second beneficiary the credit must permit part shipments. If the prime beneficiary does not wish his buyer and supplier to be aware of each other, he may request that his name be substituted for that of the opener on the transfer credit and that shipping documents are in the name of a third-party blank endorsed.

## BACK TO BACK CREDITS

These arise in circumstances similar to those of the transferable credit and particularly where the supplier as well as the buyer is overseas. In this case, the middleman receives a credit in his favour from the buyer and asks his bank to establish a credit in favour of his supplier against the security of the credit in his own favour. These credits can give rise to problems with the matching of documents and credit terms.

## REVOLVING CREDITS

These are used where there is a continuous programme of shipments at intervals and the parties wish the programme to proceed without interruption. A credit is established for a certain sum and quantity of goods with a provision that, when a shipment has been made and documents presented and paid, the credit automatically becomes re-available in its original form and another shipment can be made, and so on.

## RED CLAUSE CREDITS

Red clause credits (sometimes called packing credits) are mainly encountered in connection with shipments of wool from Australia, New Zealand or South Africa. A clause (in red) inserted into the credit authorises the negotiating bank to make an advance by way of loan or overdraft to the beneficiary to enable him to purchase the wool, collect and warehouse it and prepare it for shipment. When the shipping documents are presented under the credit, the payment received is used to repay the advance.

## ACCEPTANCE CREDITS

As already described, the merchant bank lends its name by way of an accepted bill to enable the exporter to obtain finance at the best rate. This facility may be used to obtain short term finance as a supplement to clearing bank finance or to obtain it cheaper where the merchant bank's commission plus the money market rate work out to be lower than overdraft rates. It should be mentioned that clearing banks also offer acceptance credit facilities as well as merchant banks.

## CONFIRMING HOUSES

A very old established method of promoting overseas trade, these institutions provide a simple and convenient way of selling to foreign buyers. Although their business developed in the first place on the trade with the Dominions and the Far East they have now extended their activities worldwide.

They operate as principal for the buyer, making all arrangements for credit terms, interest and commission with him. In some cases they will seek out for the buyer a possible supplier of the goods which the buyer requires. Once a sales contract has been established and the order placed, the confirming house will send their confirmation of the order to the seller undertaking to make payment against specified shipping documents. As they have all the necessary facilities and expertise the confirming house will, if required, handle the packing and shipping on behalf of the seller. Although confirming houses normally act for the buyer and commence operations at his behest, there is no reason why an exporter should not approach a confirming house first and ask it to offer its services to the buyer.

When an export order has been confirmed by a reputable confirming house, the exporter is in a similar secure position as if he had received a documentary credit in his favour.

## DISCOUNTING BILLS OF EXCHANGE

The long established universally accepted method of collecting payment for exports is for the exporter (seller) to draw a bill of exchange on the buyer (see Figure 18:4). It is common practice for these bills to be 'documentary', that is, each bill has attached to it the documents of title relating to the export transaction in settlement of which the bill is drawn. In some cases the documents are not attached, having been sent separately to the buyer, in which case the exporter draws a 'clean' bill on the buyer. Bills may be drawn in sterling or in foreign currency.

When the sales contract provides for payment on delivery the bill of exchange will be drawn at sight with instructions for the documents of title to be released to the buyer against payment of the bill.

No. 1234

12 August 1984 for £5000

At 30 Days' sight Pay this First of Exchange
Five thousand pounds sterling ................. to the order of
ourselves .............................................
Twelve china teasets—assorted colours per *SS Iolanthe* from
Liverpool to Lagos.

Value received          which place to account.

To: African Traders Ltd,                    Stoke Potteries Ltd
    PO Box 100,
    Lagos, Nigeria                          John Smith

**Figure 18:4    Specimen bill of exchange**

When, on the other hand, a term of credit has been agreed, the bill is drawn at tenor, i.e. stating in the opening words the period of time granted to the buyer for payment. This can run from the date of the bill or from the date it is presented—sighted.

In this case, the documents of title are released to the buyer against his acceptance of the bill. When the bill matures, it is re-presented to the buyer for payment.

These bills are lodged by the exporter with his bank for collection who in turn forward them to their correspondent bank in the buyer's country for presentation. The fact that a bank on the spot is presenting the bills for payment or acceptance and ultimate payment makes the bill of exchange an excellent method of collecting payment.

A bill of exchange is a legally recognised instrument on which action may be taken in the courts. This right of action can be strengthened by the 'protest' procedure. If a buyer refuses or fails to accept or pay, as the case may be, on presentation, the presenting bank can, if requested by the exporter, protest the bill for non-acceptance or non-payment. This is done by asking a notary to present the bill and record the presentation and non-payment. A document is then available which enables an action to be taken in the courts without further preliminaries.

The exporter has, through the bill of exchange, not only a recognised and controlled method of collecting payment from his buyers but also a means of raising additional export finance. He may in other words approach his bank to negotiate the bills and the bank, if it agrees, will purchase or discount the bills subject to the right of recourse to the exporter if the bills are dishonoured by the buyer.

Bills are said to be discounted when the exporter (drawer) pays the interest, i.e. interest on the period up to payment is deducted from the face amount of the bill. They are said to be purchased when the buyer (drawee) pays the interest—this is usually done by inserting a clause in the bill that it is payable with interest. In providing accommodation by way of negotiation of bills, the bank has a certain security in the documents of title and, therefore, the goods, but it will at the same time be interested to see if there is a good geographical spread of risk and how far the bills are drawn on one large buyer. The bank will on its own account make enquiries on the buyers and take into account the exporter's record of efficiency ensuring that the collection of bills goes smoothly. It will, of course, be influenced by whether the transactions are covered with ECGD.

An alternative method of providing accommodation against bills for collection is, instead of purchasing or discounting individual bills, to make loans up to a percentage of outstanding bills for collection.

It will be clear that an exporter may not necessarily obtain all the extra finance he may require against the bills he draws on his buyers and, in any case, the cost will be about the same as overdraft facilities. To meet this problem, special arrangements have been made by the banks with ECGD as follows.

## ECGD-BACKED SHORT TERM FINANCE

This is an agreement between the banks and ECGD, whereby the banks provide export finance against ECGD's guarantee to the bank at special rates. It is available for transactions where the credit terms are not more than two years. (No longer rigidly applied.)

There are two separate schemes:

1   Where there is an instrument, i.e. where the exporter draws a bill of exchange on the buyer or receives from him a promissory note.

The bank advances 100% of the face amount of sight bills and unaccepted bills but purchases accepted bills. This means that, until the bills are accepted by the buyer, the bank has recourse to the exporter if the bills are not met. Once the bills are accepted the bank's recourse is to ECGD. In the case of non-payment of an accepted bill, the bank recovers from ECGD but ECGD retains recourse to the customer for the difference between what is paid to the bank and what is due to the customer under his ECGD policy. It is required that shipping documents should be attached to the bill.

2   Open account scheme—where there is no bill of exchange and the sales terms are up to 180 days from receipt of goods or cash against documents. Under this scheme the exporter issues his promissory note to the bank for 100% of the invoice value of the goods exported and falling due for payment in any one month. The due date of the promissory note will be the last day of the month when settlement is due. The bank advances the face value of the promissory note at once and the note must be paid at maturity whether or not the proceeds of the invoice have been received. The bank only has recourse to ECGD if the customer fails to honour his note. Copy shipping documents are required.

The interest rate charged under both these schemes is ⅝% over the bank's base rate.

## ECGD-BACKED MEDIUM TERM FINANCE

The short term arrangement described above is to assist the exporter of consumer and consumer durable goods with relatively short terms of credit. The medium term arrangement is designed to assist the exporter or producer of capital or semi-capital goods where credit terms may be up to five years.

In this field, the exporter is faced with not only the longer wait for payment but also the cost of financing the credit period and the possibility of changes in interest rates. To meet these problems the following scheme has been arranged by the banks and ECGD.

The bank provides post-shipment finance to the exporter selling on credit terms of from two to five years from date of shipment against a specific unconditional guarantee from ECGD. Finance at a fixed rate (at present 7½%) is available only to the extent of the guaranteed amount.

It should be noted that the ECGD guarantees are normally effective from the date of shipment and any finance required before that stage must be taken within the customer's normal banking arrangements.

ECGD has laid down certain conditions:

1   The goods must be deemed to be capital goods or of a category acceptable to the department.
2   The period of credit is generally limited to five years but in certain cases six or even seven years have been agreed exceptionally.
3   ECGD usually requires the buyer to put up a deposit on the order being confirmed and a further percentage when shipment is made—a fair average is 10% in each case.
4   The cover provided under the guarantee is now 100%.
5   The exporter will be expected to arrange to draw bills of exchange for acceptance or obtain from the buyer promissory notes covering the instalments of principle and interest spread over the period of credit. These are usually drawn in series payable at six-monthly intervals and bear an interest clause.

When negotiations have been made between the exporter, the bank and ECGD, the bank draws up a facility letter addressed to the exporter setting out the terms and conditions under which it will make funds available to him on a non-recourse basis. Agreement in principle for finance under this scheme is usually given for three months to enable the customer to complete his negotiations with the buyer. If at the expiry of this period the negotiations are incomplete a new approach by the customer must be made.

## ECGD-BACKED LONG TERM FINANCE

For exports of heavy capital equipment and ships which call for even longer terms of credit than the medium term five years, ECGD has introduced the 'Financial Guarantee'. This is to provide buyer finance as opposed to supplier finance as under the short and medium term arrangements.

The guarantee covers direct loans made by a bank to the overseas buyer and so enable the supplier to be paid on cash terms.

The buyer is expected as a rule to put up from his own resources 20% of the purchase price, the remaining 80% being paid to the supplier out of the loan made to the buyer. The loan is guaranteed by ECGD as to 100% of capital and interest.

The pattern is for the bank to purchase the buyer's promissory notes covering repayment and claused to cover interest. The exporter is paid irrevocably out of the proceeds of the purchase of the notes after presentation to the bank of the documents set out in the supply contract and the financial agreement. The buyer has full responsibility for repayment of the finance irrespective of the supply contract.

Preliminary discussions with ECGD and the bank must be commenced by the supplier as soon as negotiations start with a buyer.

These guarantees are designed to take care of very large capital projects. Contracts for less than £2 million (£1 million for ships) are not usually considered.

This procedure is ideally suited to cases where there are several suppliers to the one contract. Where the amounts are considerable and the credit terms correspondingly long the loan may be put up by a consortium of banks often with a merchant bank acting as manager.

Where the buyer is also seeking means to finance the 20% which he has to provide himself, it is sometimes possible for one of the banks or merchant banks to arrange a Euro-currency loan which would, of course, be outside the guarantee arrangement.

The principle of buyer finance may also be applied to provide finance to say a State organisation for a 'basket' of purchases whereby the foreign buyer stipulates the classes of product he wishes to purchase and the bank and ECGD agree that the total list and value are suitable for the facility required.

**FURTHER READING**

BOTB, *Export Handbook.*
HMSO, *British Financial Institutions.*
Institute of Bankers, *The Finance of International Trade.*
International Chamber of Commerce, *Uniform Customs and Practice for Documentary Credits.*
International Chamber of Commerce, *Uniform Rules for the Collection of Commercial Paper.*
W. W. Syrett and R. F. Pither, *Sources and Management of Export Finance.*
Whiting, *Finance of Foreign Trade and Foreign Exchange.*

# 19

# Foreign Exchange

M. H. Warmsley, Chief Dealer (Training), Barclays Bank
International Ltd

## THE HISTORY OF FOREIGN EXCHANGE

The modern foreign exchange market is very much the product of
the twentieth century. It just could not function to its present extent
without the telecommunication systems and technological developments that are available today.

Nevertheless, the basic conception of dealing in a store of value—
gold, coin, money, bills of exchange, is a very old one; the
profession of money dealer probably started in Roman and biblical
times. The first markets, in coin, were in the Middle East, but these
gradually moved westwards into Europe and eventually, in about
the twelfth century, coin gave way to bills of exchange which were a
much more convenient way of transferring wealth.

Markets developed in Italy, with the church playing an important
part, and later, as the New World was opened up, in Spain, and
governments found bills a useful way of raising finance. Later the
principal trading centres moved to Antwerp, and in the seventeenth
century, to Amsterdam. Paper money was by then coming into use,
and markets were established, but, due to the problems of forgery,
storage and transport, remained small and were overshadowed by
the more flexible bill markets.

Until the latter half of the eighteenth century, all the markets were
very much 'physical' markets. Something—notes, coin, gold, pieces
of paper—actually changed hands. About 1880 it improved and

more rapid means of communications caused a market to develop in 'balances'. A buyer and a seller of a currency, in any country, would decide on a price, or rate, for the exchange and then rely on each other to deliver, in the relative countries, the requisite amount from the balance of one account to the balance of another on a given settlement date. There was no need for the two parties to such a deal to be in physical contact, or even in the same city or country, and as telecommunications improved, so did the market-place, so that today it is worldwide and also one of the fastest moving international markets in existence.

## PRESENT-DAY FOREIGN EXCHANGE MARKETS

### World markets

Because of the almost instantaneous means of communication now available by telephone or by teleprinter between all the major cities of the world, a physical meeting place for dealers, or traders, as they are also known, is no longer necessary. In some centres, however, such as in Paris, there is a room set apart for exchange dealing in the Stock Exchange, or Bourse, where dealers stand around a ring, or corbeille, and trade with each other for certain hours during the day. This semi-public meeting place has some advantages as a meeting place for dealers and it enables the central banker, who is always present, to be well aware of what is happening, but it is rather cumbersome and has drawbacks. There is obviously a limit to the number of participants; traders must make their wishes known publicly, and contact with the outside world must be made at secondhand through telephone booths on the periphery of the room.

Most markets consist of organisations linked by national and international telephone and telex networks and as such can function at any time or in any place in the world. There is no need for a dealer to be physically located in any particular market, or for him to adhere to any particular 'office hours'. For convenience, ease of staffing and to keep communication costs down however, trading tends to follow local business hours, and because of this world markets are split into zonal markets.

## European markets

The major zonal market covers the European area, which coincides at the start of the day with the end of trading in the Pacific basin markets of Singapore, Hong Kong and Australia, covers a good part of the rapidly growing Middle East markets, and overlaps the major part of the American Eastern seaboard markets, and for an hour or so the West Coast Market.

With such a massive global coverage and with a multiplicity of national markets, the European zone has become the biggest and most important of the world markets. Within the area there are major dealing centres in London, Frankfurt and Zurich, and also very active are Paris, Brussels, Amsterdam, Copenhagen and Stockholm. In some countries (e.g. Switzerland with Zurich, Geneva, Basle, etc., and Germany with Frankfurt, Hamburg, Dusseldorf, Munich, etc.,) there are several market centres in the same country, whilst in others, e.g. France and Great Britain, dealing is virtually confined to a single centre.

## The London foreign exchange market

At one time there was a meeting place for bill traders in the London Royal Exchange, but since this died out in the 1920s, the exchange market in London has been entirely telephonic. The market rapidly developed after the First World War, as sterling became less acceptable as an international currency. No controls existed in those days, and the market was free for all, with brokers, bankers, commercial concerns and private citizens able to engage in operations and to compete for business without restriction.

In the mid 1930s, at the instigation of the Bank of England, some order was introduced, and the principal foundations of today's market were laid by an agreement that brokers would not pass foreign and commercial names, and that bankers would not deal direct with each other within the UK.

## Foreign exchange brokers

In the late thirties, there were as many as 50 exchange broking firms in London; there was no control, apart from the agreement mentioned above, over their establishment or activity, and the number was really far in excess of market requirements. When markets reopened in 1951 after the Second World War, the number of brokers (who then had to be authorised by the Bank of England) was restricted, at first to nine, which number sufficed for over 20 years, and only recently has it been allowed to increase.

Since the post-war reopening of foreign exchange markets, dealing has been restricted to banks authorised by the Bank of England. The market today comprises of 290 recognised banks and 308 licenced deposit takers (LDT's) and the majority of these will have private direct lines to one or more brokers, who supply the banks with a constant stream of information, advice and indicative and dealing rates. This service is provided to the banks throughout the working day, entirely at the broker's expense. The brokers solicit and undertake buying and selling orders, never passing the names of interested parties until a deal is actually completed. Complete confidentiality is ensured—the great difference between this type of market and the 'open' exchange—providing member banks with a service they could not get any other way. The trading information a broker gives is based on his knowledge of a large proportion of the banks in the market. Without brokers it would be impossible for one bank to 'do the rounds' of the others. For the service, a broker makes no standing charge, but levies a commission from each party to each deal.

## A dealing room

A modern dealing room provides its dealers with some of the most up-to-date communication systems available. Every desk will have telephone lines, both of the general and private circuit types, between its customers, brokers and correspondent banks, together with Reuters and AP Dow Jones VDU's, supplying them with the latest rates and news information on a worldwide basis. Telex and teleprinters will also be within the room relaying other essential information as well as accepting and agreeing orders with correspondent banks and customers alike. The foreign exchange dealer needs every bit of the communication to operate successfully.

A dealing room can be of any size—employing from one dealer to upwards of 70 to 80 dealers. In a small room, business will be somewhat restricted and each dealer will probably be involved in every type of business. In a larger room, activities will become more specialised, with individuals having responsibilities for various currencies, but all working as a team under a chief dealer.

Business comes to a dealing room from several sources: basically from customers and correspondents, or by the banks themselves acting as principals. A small operation may just seek to cover its customers' requirements—or it may take dealing positions in an endeavour to create and increase its business and profits. A larger operation must always participate fully in the market so that the dealers are conversant with events and can provide a competitive service to customers and correspondents.

In the UK banks are generally restricted in the positions they can run by the Bank of England, which keeps a watchful eye on operations in the London market, and which has by its actions since the last war ensured the continuing development of an orderly, efficient and reasonably trouble-free market in London.


## DEALING OPERATIONS

### Rates of exchange

A rate of exchange is the price at which one currency can be exchanged for another. It can be expressed as so many units of currency A being worth one unit of currency B, or conversely as one unit of currency A being worth so many units of currency B. For example, the USA/sterling rate can be expressed either as, for example, (a) US$1.45 equalling £1 sterling, or (b) as $1.00 being equivalent to £0.69 sterling.

It is always of prime importance to be aware of how a rate is being quoted—mistakes can be costly, but fortunately, in the UK rates are usually quoted as in (a) above—so many units of a foreign currency to the pound sterling.

A rate of exchange will usually be quoted by giving a pair of rates—e.g. US$1.4510-1.4520 to the pound. The first rate is the selling rate, i.e. the rate at which a bank will sell to a client, giving

1.4510 dollars for each pound. The second rate is the buying rate, i.e. the rate at which a bank will buy from a client, demanding 1.4520 dollars for each pound that it gives. The difference between the selling and the buying rate, called the 'spread', is not always the same, and varies according to the amount being dealt and the state of the market. The basic rate quoted is for 'marketable' amounts on the inter-bank market, say for around one million dollars or their equivalent. When quoting for smaller amounts, a bank will widen the spread to allow for possible fluctuations before it accumulates sufficient funds to go into the 'market'.

## Spot rates

As the name implies, spot rates are quoted for spot, or immediate delivery. In fact, market usage defines spot as being for delivery two working days from the day on which a deal is transacted. This is to allow time for instructions regarding the payments of the two currencies concerned in every deal to be exchanged and the payments to be made. Particular regard has to be given to the latest times by which payments must be made in various countries. In practice, as long as settlement can be made in the relevant countries, deals can be completed for any reasonable value date. Deals can be arranged to switch, or 'swap', delivery value from the spot date to the date required. The margin by which a spot rate is adjusted for delivery on another date is known as a forward margin.

## Forward rates

The forward market is entirely separate from the spot market; forward margins can move in entirely different fashion from the spot rates. It is, between banks, only a 'swapping' market. Rates are quoted for the margin, or price, at which delivery for one date is switched or 'swapped' for delivery on another. But, from a client's point of view, what is required is an actual or 'outright' rate. This is obtained by combining the spot rates and the forward margin as in Figure 19:1.

| | |
|---|---|
| Spot rate | = $1.4510 = £1 sterling |
| One month forward margin | = 0.0075 premium |
| Outright price for one month | = $1.4435 |

**Figure 19:1 Forward rates: combining spot rates and forward margin**

A forward margin will be at a premium or a discount compared with the spot rate, or on rare occasions at par—the same as spot. The example above illustrates a premium rate—the premium is deducted from the spot, giving fewer currency units forward for the pound. Thus the foreign currency is more expensive forward—it is at a premium.

If the US dollar were at a discount, in other words cheaper forward, the margin would be added to the spot rate, giving more units to the pound for forward delivery, as detailed in Figure 19:2.

For simplicity, only one rate has been shown in the examples given in Figures 19:1 and 19:2. In practice, as with spot rates, banks quote forward margins in pairs, and the same remarks apply about 'spreads' as for spot rates.

A full example with forwards at a premium would be as follows:

Quotation: Spot 1.4510–1.4520
Forward margins (a) One month: 0.75–0.50 cents premium
                   (b) Three months: 2.00–1.75 cents premium

| | |
|---|---|
| Spot | $1.4510 = £1 sterling |
| One month discount | 0.0075 |
| | $1.4585 = outright rate for one month forward |

**Figure 19:2 Forward rates: discount added to spot rate**

|  | Selling | | Buying |
|---|---|---|---|
| (a) Spot | 1.4510 | — | 1.4520 |
| less one month premium | 0.0075 | — | 0.0050 |
| | | | |
| Outright rate | 1.4435 | — | 1.4470 for one month |
| | Selling | | Buying |
| (b) Spot | 1.4510 | — | 1.4520 |
| less three months premium | 0.0200 | — | 0.0175 |
| | | | |
| Outright rate | 1.4310 | — | 1.4345 for three months |

**Figure 19:3   Outright rates**

Remember that selling margins are deducted from the spot selling rate and buying margins from the spot buying rate. And that selling and/or buying always refers, in the context of 'market quotations', to what the bank is doing. The outright rates work out as set out in Figure 19:3.

If the forward margins were at a discount, the examples would be as follows:

Quotation: Spot 1.4510–1.4520
Forward margins (a) One month 0.50–0.75 cents discount
                    (b) Three months 1.75–2.00 cents discount

If the selling margins now are added to the spot selling rates and the buying margins to the spot buying rate, we get the result set out in Figure 19:4.

## Option forwards

On the inter-bank market, forward dealing is arranged for delivery on a fixed date. Good markets exist in most currencies up to six months, a number up to one year, and in some cases longer than this.

From the commercial point of view, a fixed monthly period, for

| (a) Spot | 1.4510 — 1.4520 |
|---|---|
| Add one month discount | 0.0050 — 0.0075 |
| Outright rate | 1.4560 — 1.4595 for one month |
| (b) Spot | 1.4510 — 1.4520 |
| Add three month discount | 0.0175 — 0.0200 |
| Outright rate | 1.4685 — 1.4720 for three months |

**Figure 19:4   Selling and buying margins added**

delivery only on a stated date, is often not a great deal of use since the exact timing of a commercial payment is impossible to forecast. In such cases a bank can offer an 'option' contract which will give the customer the opportunity of choosing the date on which he takes delivery.

The 'option' element relates solely to the date of delivery—in all other respects the contract must be fully used in accordance with its terms. The option period may run for the whole period of a contract or for a shorter, pre-defined period, and with this facility it is possible for the customer to take delivery in more than one stage.

Because a bank can only cover in the market for a fixed date, it is often at some risk in providing cover for an option period and may wish to include in the rate a margin to compensate for this risk. Naturally, when there is a forward margin in a customer's favour, it can only be given to the starting date of an option period.

### Euro-currencies

A word or two here about Euro-currency markets would be appropriate, as these operations are closely concerned with exchange markets, although to cover the subject adequately would require at least another chapter.

The prefix 'Euro' is simply a short way of identifying the market. One is referring to a money market (i.e. borrowing or lending money) in any currency other than that of the country in which the trading is taking place. The market was started by banks in Europe trading in US dollars, hence the pre-fix 'Euro' (e.g. Euro-dollars). Nowadays, trading is worldwide, and in the Pacific area one hears the expression 'Asian' dollar and so on. There is nothing different about the currency itself—it is exactly the same as the freely convertible dollars, Deutschmarks, Swiss francs, sterling and so on, which are traded in exchange markets. Although the concept of banks seeking to borrow or lend funds they hold abroad and do not immediately require, is not new, the huge explosion in dealing in Euro-currencies, which is now an invaluable source of finance for all manner of international trade and finance, dates from the mid 1950s. A number of factors combined to start this rapid development.

1   Communist countries were, at that time, reluctant to maintain balances in America for fear of sequestration, but as they did not wish to sell the dollars, they sought to lend them outside the USA.
2   In the 1957 UK crisis, the finance of multi-lateral trade in sterling was prohibited, and the dollar gained in importance.
3   At that time, in the USA, Federal Reserve Regulation Q (since amended) restricted the rate of interest payable by American banks for deposits, and foreign depositors therefore sought higher rates elsewhere.
4   The cost of borrowing dollars from European banks was usually a lot cheaper than borrowing domestic funds especially by the recovering countries of Europe and Asia.

The development of the market, at first mainly in dollars, but later in other major currencies, was fuelled by the accumulated USA trade deficit with, and aid to, other countries, and caused many USA banks to establish offices in Europe to tap the supply. The size of the market is impossible to gauge, and this coupled with the inability of any one nation to 'control' the market, causes concern in some quarters. There is no lender of last resort, and no means of ascertaining who is the ultimate borrower, even when funds are placed with a first-class name (usually without security). There is an ever-present danger of a chain reaction leading to default. However, given the present political will aimed at underpinning the stability of world credit markets, until now, such dangers appear to have been contained.

The markets are predominantly in USA dollars, but other major

European currencies are marketable, often by means of an exchange swapping operation. Although long-term deposits and loans are frequently negotiated, the bulk of day-to-day business is concentrated on periods of up to six months and sometimes to a year.

## EXCHANGE RISKS

### The risk

Whenever a businessman commits himself to make or to receive a payment in a currency other than his own, he incurs an exchange risk, unless he can effect his payment at once. If his business is expressed in his own currency, he has no worries—any exchange risk is then the responsibility of his counter party. However, the task of conversion and the assumption of the risk may be something that the other party does not wish to get involved in, and useful business might thereby be lost.

It is important to recognise when there is an exchange risk and to know how it can be covered. A merchant can quite easily see that the costs of some merchandise abroad—or the yield if he sells exports—is quite reasonable at today's exchange rates, but by the time goods have moved and payment is due, those rates may have moved, making the transaction entirely unprofitable. Certainly the rate may have moved in the merchant's favour, but the very real risk of loss is there, and should not have to be taken by the merchant.

Events in the foreign exchange markets continue to demonstrate how impossible it is to try to forecast the trend of rates. True, economic factors may suggest that rates should move in a certain direction, but these cannot allow for any sudden large commercial order, or unexpected political event, or, perhaps, an unanticipated interest rate change, which might swing rates in an entirely unpredictable manner. To try to make a prediction one must bear in mind possible happenings in at least the two countries concerned, and often nowadays because of their influence on markets, in USA and Germany as well (unless, of course, one of these is the trading currency concerned). This task regularly defeats governments, politicians and economists alike, not to mention many 'expert' foreign exchange dealers.

**How to cover the risk**

Today there are a number of ways of covering exchange risks and these are outlined in the following sections.

Forward costs or yields

A merchant could make use of the forward exchange market. In buying or selling his currency requirements at the outset, as soon as his commercial commitment is entered into, the merchant fixes his exchange rate. He then knows precisely how much he will receive or pay on the ultimate delivery date, no matter what might happen to the exchange rate in the meanwhile.

As explained earlier, the forward margin over or below spot can be either at a premium or a discount. The determination of this margin depends on a number of factors. The market in forwards is quite a free market and as such is subject to all manner of pressures of supply and demand for all sorts of commercial, political or economic reasons. However, the principal factor which determines forward margins is the differential between the Euro-interest rates of the two countries concerned. For example, if say the six month cost of borrowing US dollars was 7% per annum and sterling 10%, it would in theory be profitable to borrow dollars, convert to sterling and lend sterling. However, an exchange risk would be incurred for the whole period, which prudently must be covered by a forward exchange contract. Market forces will soon ensure that equilibrium is reached and the cost of that necessary forward cover will equate to the interest differential between dollars and sterling, i.e. 3% per annum.

In fact, the expression of the cost or yield of a forward margin as a percentage per annum is a very useful aid for the merchant—and it can readily be calculated by a bank. It is more readily understood that forward cover will cost, for example, approximately 3% per annum rather than 'a margin of 1½ cents under spot of 2.20, i.e. an outright rate of 2.18½'. The businessman can immediately calculate his costs, knowing that three months forward will actually cost three-quarters of one per cent of the value of his currency.

Conversely, if the forward margin is in the customer's favour, the forward margin will show him, in percentage terms, the benefit he will receive compared with the spot rate, and he can use this benefit either to increase his profits or to make a more competitive price for his merchandise. This is of particular advantage to exporters, as the forward margin for an exporter selling forward to his bank is frequently in his favour.

Quite often an exporter who has hitherto quoted in sterling can improve his returns, and his market, by switching into the foreign currency concerned (providing there is a good forward exchange market in it) and himself accepting and, of course covering, the exchange risk.

### Currency accounts

Currency accounts can be established these days enabling companies to offset payments and receipts in a like currency thus helping to reduce their exchange exposure.

### Borrowing foreign currency

Exporters may wish to consider borrowing a foreign currency rather than using the forward exchange market mechanism. On occasions foreign currencies can be borrowed more cheaply than sterling. Thus if a UK exporter is invoicing his goods priced in Deutschmarks terms and the cost of raising Euro-Deutschmarks is cheaper than its sterling equivalent, he can: borrow the Deutschmarks, sell the Deutschmarks for sterling immediately, thus having full use of the sterling equivalent for the period in question and repay the Deutschmarks loan from his export receivables.

The net effect is of course to finance his export contract at a cheaper interest rate and avoid an exchange risk.

In general, it is advisable to only take advantage of borrowing in a foreign currency at a cheaper interest rate provided you have income in the like currency to repay the loan at a future date, otherwise an exchange risk will be incurred.

### Foreign currency options

Foreign currency options were first formerly introduced on the Philadelphia Stock Exchange in December 1982. The flexibility offered by options was quickly perceived by major commercial banks and an 'over the counter' service is now (1984) in the process of developing.

An option is an agreement between two parties viz, the 'writer' and the 'purchaser' (generally speaking a bank and a corporate customer) that for a fee, the writer confers upon the purchaser the right to exchange one currency for another at a fixed rate throughout a predetermined period of time. The option writer's initial benefit is the fee; his potential cost being open-ended in that it is for him to decide whether or not to cover the obligation in the foreign exchange market. Conversely the option purchaser has a quantifiable loss (the fee) but has unlimited potential for benefit in that he may exercise the option if it has moved favourably but need not do so if it has moved adversely.

---

1 October 1983 A corporate customer purchases an option from his bank (the writer) to buy US$1 500 000 against sterling at an agreed 'strike price' of 1.5000 (the current spot level) for 3 months for a non-returnable fee of £17 500.

*Result 1.* The customer requires his US$ on 10 December 1983 when the spot level has moved to say 1.4200.

The customer therefore exercises the option and buys from the bank US$1 500 000 @ 1.5000 = £1 000 000 + £17 500 (fee).

Compared with cost of dealing in spot market $1 500 000 @ 1.4200 = £1 056 338.03—gives an overall saving of £38 838.03.

*Result 2.* The customer requires his US$ on 10 December 1983 when the spot level has moved to say 1.5800.

Customer 'walks away' from the option and deals on the spot market buying US$1 500 000 @ 1.5800.

|  | £ |
|---|---|
| Cost | 949 367.09 |
| + cost fee | 17 500.00 |
| Total cost | 966 867.09 — saving of £33 132.91 |

---

**Figure 19:5   Usage of a foreign currency option**

It is a major feature of currency options that the purchaser has no obligation to deal, but the writer is virtually certain that when an exchange rate moves against him through the agreed option price that option will be exercised on or before maturity. (See Figure 19:5.)

In summary, the option user can select an exchange rate level for a currency which, when adjusted by the option fee, will give a base exchange rate at which his exposure is covered, whilst retaining flexibility to take advantage of any favourable exchange rate movement by 'walking away' from the option and dealing independently in the foreign exchange market. Generally the cost of an option will decline as the perceived risk of its being exercised reduces.

## FURTHER READING

M. J. K. Warmsley, *The Foreign Exchange Handbook and Users Guide.* John Wiley & Sons.

# PART VIII
# CONSUMER CREDIT

# 20

# Retail Credit Management

**P. G. L. Mudge, Credit Controller, Currys Group plc**

The final sentence of the covering letter sent to the Secretary of State for Trade and Industry by the Crowther Committee with their report on consumer credit, reads thus:

> We urge that reform of the existing legal tangle is badly overdue, and that liberation of the consumer credit industry from the antiquated provisions, and from the official restrictions, that hobble it will enable it to make an increasing contribution to the efficiency of the national economy and to the standard of living of the public.

Some three years later, happily, a positive attempt was made to embody these sentiments in the Consumer Credit Act 1974. The Act has been accepted and applauded both by the retail credit trade and by responsible credit management.

The Regulations which implemented the changes made by the Act were introduced over a period of years, and the final regulations regarding documents, rebates, default notices, etc. were set to come into effect in May 1985, 11 years after the Act itself.

However, although details of consumer credit may change, the fundamentals do not and this chapter is devoted to explaining these fundamentals.

## CREDIT AS AN AID TO SALES

The fundamental purpose of every commercial business is to make a profit. Usually a trader makes more profit when the volume of sales is increased.

The introduction of carefully prepared and advertised credit facilities by properly trained sales and credit staff, can achieve an increase in turnover for the following reasons:

1 More new customers are attracted 'through the door and on to the floor'. The increase in floor traffic is itself a morale booster to any sales force.
2 Sales can be made to those customers who cannot immediately pay cash, and impulse buying is encouraged.
3 Customers are more likely to consider buying better quality, higher-priced merchandise and sales staff will encourage this by 'selling up'.
4 Special credit terms can be arranged to assist in the promotion of any 'slow moving' line, or during a period of poor trade.

There is also an important additional benefit to the trader in increasing sales as more favourable trading terms or bulk discounts may be available from the supplier or manufacturer of the goods sold.

In accepting the obvious advantages of credit trading care must be taken to ensure that the business acquired is additional to that which is usually sold for cash.

There is nothing to be gained by creating a debtor instead of putting money in the bank and a weekly analysis of new business statistics is recommended so that any significant change in the sales mix can be investigated and, if necessary, quickly adjusted.

### FINANCING THE CREDIT OPERATION

The credit operation will be financed by:

1 Funds raised by the trader from within the business or by bank loans, debentures and share issue; *or*
2 credit facilities from outside the business; *or*
3 resources from within and outside the business.

The main advantages of internal finance are:

1 The trader establishes his own credit policy and makes the credit

decisions thus ensuring the maximum growth of the business.
2   The trader retains personal contact with the customer and has a better opportunity of building up goodwill.
3   Special credit terms can be arranged to promote particular sales campaigns for specific periods.
4   A number of different credit schemes can be made available geared to the type of merchandise offered for sale and the individual preferences of the customer.

However much a trader may wish to supply internal credit facilities it is usually only the larger retail organisations that can raise sufficient working capital to do this. The majority of consumer credit is provided by banks and finance houses, and it is from these sources that traders seek the most advantageous credit schemes.

Such facilities are not easily obtained and traders should anticipate a detailed examination of their accounts before credit facilities are made available.

In addition the finance company will impose conditions as to whom facilities can be offered and the amount of credit granted. The trader will also be required to provide a satisfactory volume of profitable new credit business each year or credit facilities are likely to be withdrawn.

Commissions may be paid by finance houses to motor car dealers so as to secure the introduction of this particularly profitable new business, but the financing of small unit merchandise does not normally attract this benefit.

## LIAISON WITH FINANCE HOUSES

Most finance houses make arrangements with traders to provide consumer finance by means of hire purchase, credit sale, conditional sale and personal loan agreements, and, in addition, some finance companies have the authority to make personal loans.

In most cases the trader acts as an intermediary between the customer and the finance company, and although this three-way relationship can take various forms the basic procedure is as follows:

A customer pays a deposit and requests credit facilities to pay the balance by instalments.

The credit documents are completed by the trader and signed by the customer and the trader submits the credit applications, usually by telephone, to the office of the finance company or a credit enquiry agent appointed by the finance company.

If the application for credit is approved, the trader sells the goods to the finance house to whom he sends the VAT sales invoice together with the credit documents and possibly the agent's credit status report.

The finance company then pays the balance of the cash price to the trader and accepts the agreement. Thus the goods are purchased from the trader by the finance company and are then let on hire or sold to the customer under the terms of the agreement.

The financial arrangements between trader and finance house are contained in a master agreement which will be of a recourse or non-recourse nature.

A recourse agreement requires the trader to pay any loss arising from the transactions accepted by the finance company, and to safeguard against the loss the finance company creates a reserve fund by retaining a percentage of the monies due to the trader.

Against this retention fund are charged the balances outstanding on all bad or slow paying accounts and the agreements are assigned to the dealer who then becomes responsible for any further collection effort. Normally the collection of accounts is undertaken by the finance company and the trader is advised of potentially bad accounts so that early action by the trader may prevent write-off.

A non-recourse agreement makes the finance house responsible for such losses, but the charge for credit is usually substantially more and this may not be in the best interests of the business if the customers go in search of better credit terms.

Block discounting is another form of credit offered to traders by some finance companies. In this system the trader enters into the agreement with the customer and collects the instalments as they fall due and these agreements are sold to the finance company in weekly, fortnightly or monthly batches—at a discount.

The finance company retains a percentage of the money due to the trader until it has received in full the payments due under the terms of the agreement, so that the trader receives initially the amount to be paid by instalments less the retention fund deduction and discount charge.

By arrangement with the finance company, the trader may recover the retention over a period by deducting an agreed percentage of the instalments collected before remitting to the finance company.

## THE TYPES OF CREDIT AVAILABLE

When deciding the types of credit facility to use, the trader must bear in mind that government chooses to restrict or expand the purchase of consumer durables by the statutory control of credit terms. Indeed ever since legislation was first introduced during the Second World War, apart from a period of seven months in 1954–1955, there has been terms control of one sort or another, until the 27 July 1983 when all controls on hiring, hire purchase and credit sale were revoked. However, a change in either government or policy could see a return of controls and when these are in force, they fix the minimum deposit and the maximum period of credit according to the type of consumer goods offered for sale. So, not only must the type of credit satisfy the needs of business and customer it must also satisfy the law.

The types of credit generally available are:

### Monthly current account

The trader provides goods or services throughout the month, usually up to a credit limit, and the customer pays the full amount on receipt of a monthly statement. This form of credit attracts additional business, but as no charge for credit is made, the profit margin in the sale price must be sufficient to provide this facility.

Although milkmen, newsagents and some garages and department stores offer this facility, this type of credit has been largely replaced by credit cards and budget or option accounts.

### The budget or subscription account

The customer pays a fixed amount each month and is allowed to make purchases up to a fixed limit. This limit is usually 20 or 24 times the monthly payment, but some companies will go as high as 30 times, although this greatly extends the payment period.

As the credit balance is reduced by monthly payments so the customer is allowed to make further purchases up to the credit limit. A charge for credit, calculated as a percentage of the purchase price, is added to the purchase price or is calculated as a percentage of the outstanding balance and added to the account each month-end. Naturally this form of credit is extremely popular in the retail tailoring trade and is well advertised to attract additional business. It also builds customer loyalty to the company issuing the card.

The credit status of all new customers must be carefully checked and some form of identification provided by the customer to ensure that the current balance of any account can be quickly examined before new purchases are added to the account.

Increasingly this identification takes the form of a plastic card, bearing the customer's signature, the account number and a date of expiry, and sometimes the name and address. This card is used to impress the account number and name on to a sales document which is then signed by the customer and compared by the sales assistant with the signature on the card. The original of the document is given to the customer and the copies are used to post the various ledgers. This card/imprest system is used for credit cards and most revolving credit schemes.

As the monthly instalment is fixed, payment by bankers order or direct debit should be encouraged and statements sent to customers each month.

## Option accounts

This type of credit combines the features of both current and budget accounts.

Each month a statement of account is sent to the customer listing the purchases in the previous month. The customer then has the option of paying the balance in full or paying part of it and having the balance brought forward.

If the option account covers the supply of consumer goods protected by any control orders, then a statutory minimum monthly payment may apply.

A charge for credit is calculated as a percentage of the balance outstanding each month-end and added to the balance so that any customer not paying the previous monthly instalment has to pay more interest.

Again, this is a very popular form of credit offered by department stores and other retailers, attracting additional business, and providing in-store credit facilities very similar to those available to credit card users.

**Credit cards**

Another way in which credit terms are made available to customers is by the trader agreeing to accept credit cards. This is a three-party arrangement whereby the trader receives payment from the credit card company and the customer repays the credit card company by instalments.

Usually the trader has to obtain approval from the credit card company by telephone before supplying goods above a previously agreed value, but given this approval, the customer is allowed to make purchases up to the limit set by the credit card company for each individual card holder.

The credit card details are impressed on to the sale document which is signed by the customer and to establish identification this signature is compared with the signature shown on the credit card.

The trader benefits by way of additional business, but a charge for this facility is made by the credit card company in that an agreed discount is deducted from the price shown on the sale document before payment is made to the trader.

A statement is sent to the cardholder by the credit card company listing the purchases made in the previous month and the cardholder has the option of paying the balance in full, in which case no credit charge is made, or paying the balance by instalments.

In this event a charge for credit calculated as a percentage of the balance is added each month and the cardholder makes monthly repayments subject to any statutory minimum imposed by current control orders.

### Check and voucher trading

This credit operation is basically the same as the credit card system in that the check trader obtains income from both retailer and consumer in the same way as the credit card company.

In the first place the customer applies to the check company for a check or voucher which can be used at certain shops and stores to purchase clothes and goods. The customer pays a deposit to the check company and repays the balance of the check or voucher, to which a charge for credit is added, by instalments.

The retailer accepts the check or voucher from the customer instead of cash and the check company pays the retailer the value of the check or voucher—less a substantial discount.

The collection of trading check accounts, which are usually for relatively small amounts covering the supply of clothing and house-hold fabrics, is undertaken by collector/salesmen who encourage further purchases as the original amount is repaid.

In recent times check vouchers were used extensively for the purchase of high value consumer durables because apparently check and voucher trading was not restricted by government credit control regulations and therefore lower deposits and longer repayments periods applied. It is not surprising, therefore, that a number of the large retail organisations formed separate companies for the specific purpose of making check or voucher credit schemes available to their customers.

### Hire purchase

Hire purchase is the traditional form of credit still most used to finance the purchase of consumer durables. It is the subject of extensive legislation, providing a fair measure of protection to both the trader and the customer, much of which has now been included in the Consumer Credit Act.

Inevitably, dependent on the type of goods purchased, any government credit control orders in force regulate the initial deposit the customer is required to pay when entering into a hire purchase agreement and the maximum period of credit available.

A hire purchase contract is an agreement to hire with the option to purchase. The customer, while having the option to purchase, need not do so and may terminate the agreement and return the goods at any time subject to the terms and conditions of the agreement and the provisions of the Hire Purchase or Consumer Credit Act.

The purchaser, however, does not get title to the goods until the total hire purchase price, which includes a charge for credit, has been paid and in the event of there being default in payment the owner may commence legal action for the return of the goods and or claim the amount of arrears outstanding at the time the agreement was terminated.

The form of the agreement is determined by Act of Parliament, and such was the extent of the legislation that in the Hire Purchase Act even the size of the print was defined. However, the Consumer Credit Act Regulations only require the lettering to be 'easily legible'. (See Chapter 22 for information on the new form for hire purchase agreements, valid from May 1985.)

The Statutory deposit, which may include any trade-in allowance, is paid by the customer on signing the agreement. This initial payment is deducted from the cash price of the goods and to the balance is added the charge for credit, calculated as a percentage of the cash balance. The charge will vary with the period of credit required.

The cash balance plus the charge for credit makes up the hire purchase balance and represents the amount to be repaid by instalments over the length of the agreement.

The total amount the customer will eventually pay for the goods is the cash price of the goods plus the charge for credit and this total is known as the hire purchase price.

After the credit status of the customer has been approved, the agreement will be accepted and signed on behalf of the trader or finance house and the customer given a statutory copy of the agreement with details as to how payment is to be made.

This can take the form of a payment card or book containing slips showing the customer's account number. It is essential that the customer supports each remittance with a payment document so that the account can be readily identified and credited.

In common with other fixed term credit contracts early settlement rebates may be available to customers on request and must be calculated to conform with the Regulations under the Consumer Credit Act from May 1985.

Used properly, hire purchase facilities will greatly expand any business engaged in the sale of consumer durables, but it is strongly recommended that facilities are only made available where the balance, after deducting the deposit, is above a fixed limit so as to ensure that the charge made for credit adequately covers administration and finance costs.

## Conditional sale agreements

A conditional sale agreement is a contract covering the sale of goods in which title does not pass to the buyer until the total purchase price, including the charge for credit, has been paid.

It differs from a hire purchase agreement in so far as the buyer may be committed to payment of the total purchase price without the option of terminating the agreement before the price has been paid.

This distinction, however, only applies if the total purchase price exceeds the limitations of the Hire Purchase Act, currently £5000. If less than £5000, the transaction is bound by the same rules as would apply to a hire purchase agreement. Under the Consumer Credit Act, the figure will be £15000 from May 1985.

## Credit sale agreements

A credit sale agreement is a contract of sale in which title of the goods passes immediately to the buyer, so that the trader or finance house cannot demand the return of the goods in the event of default in payment and the buyer has the right to resell the goods at any time.

In the past, this type of agreement was most used to promote non-durable goods which were likely to depreciate fairly quickly or where there would not be sufficient benefit for the trader to consider repossession and resale.

Many agreements covering the supply of merchandise such as bedding, clothes, furniture and carpets fall into this category, but more recently some finance companies and retail stores have made available credit sale instead of hire purchase facilities for the purchase of consumer durables, including motor cars and marine craft.

As it is sometimes very difficult to repair and dispose of repossessed goods at a profit, some credit companies prefer not to be involved in that way. Instead more emphasis is placed in properly assessing the credit application before offering credit facilities to the customer so that there is a better chance of the account being paid in accordance with the agreed terms.

Credit sale agreements may be subject to government credit control orders in the same way as hire purchase or conditional sale agreements. The initial deposit and maximum period of credit available may be regulated according to the type of merchandise offered for sale.

During periods when governments severely restrict the amount of credit buying by increasing the statutory deposit requirement, many retailers promote short term credit sale agreements, not normally covered by controls, for expensive merchandise, such as colour television sets. The amount of weekly or monthly instalments can be very high and extreme care needs to be taken when assessing the application for credit if a significant bad debt increase is to be avoided. Nonetheless, the short term credit sale agreement is a useful tool for the credit trader when economic policies try to reduce consumer spending by imposing very high initial deposit requirements.

**Trade association**

The growth of the consumer credit industry saw the formation of the Hire Traders Protection Association, which progressed through being the Hire Purchase Trade Association to its present title of the Consumer Credit Trade Association (CCTA). The CCTA now represents the interests of those businesses involved in the various aspects of instalment credit. Nowadays it is not unusual to find traders offering several different types of credit facilities to their customers and the association provides an excellent service to its members by supplying information on all forms of consumer credit.

In addition, different credit documents and contracts are designed and printed for purchase by members of the association and a quarterly trade magazine is also produced.

However, perhaps the most important contribution of the association has been to establish a reputation of such integrity and authority that it is able to represent the interests of the instalment credit trade at all levels with its opinion sought by government departments responsible for legislation affecting the credit industry.

## THE CREDIT POLICY

All too often one learns of retail organisations offering credit facilities without proper regard to their implications. There are businesses where the only thing the sales force have in common with the credit staff is a complete distrust of the other. When the right hand never knows what the left hand is doing because each goes its separate way. The result is often annoyance to the customer and almost always detriment to the business.

The responsibility for allowing this kind of frustration lies with senior management in that the marketing, sales and financial executives have either not established a credit policy at all, or, more likely have not ensured that the correct procedures are being followed by their respective staffs.

It is essential when a retail credit policy is formed, that carefully documented instructions are issued to each part of the operation, whether sales, credit administration or delivery service, so that each knows its own precise involvement and responsibility.

### The choice of credit facilities

Full consideration should be given to the various types of credit available, with the joint aim of satisfying the needs of customers requiring credit and to achieve maximum benefit for the business. The choice of credit facilities will depend largely on the type of merchandise being offered for sale. If, by tradition, the customer is used to the credit facilities and collection methods of the check trade, some resistance might be expected if the retaileer only accepted credit card or budget account customers. The aim should be to offer facilities which are flexible enough for the needs of the market in which they will operate.

## The credit application

The manner in which the customer's application for credit is dealt with will depend on the type of business being conducted. A department store might get the customer to complete a credit application form for careful vetting before a budget account, option account or any fixed term instalment account is opened. The application could be discussed with the customer in the discreet surroundings of the credit office and the decision regarding future purchases could be made by easy reference to a credit limit or historical record of payments on an existing account.

Such is not the case when a previously unknown customer walks into a retail shop demanding instant credit from an inexperienced shop assistant during the manager's lunch break.

The training of shop staff must be such that the salesman knows a credit application will always have to be completed, although it might form part of the agreement itself, and that a credit status enquiry may be made before the agreement is accepted and the goods supplied.

An example of a credit application form is shown in Figure 20:1.

## The credit decision

If a credit application is made at a department store the credit decision will be taken by the staff of the credit office. If the application is made at a retail shop or garage using the credit facilities of a bank, finance company or check trader, then naturally enough the organisation providing the finance will usually insist on checking the credit status of the applicant before approval.

However, when the credit terms are offered by shops financing their own facilities, it may be too restrictive for credit applications to be sent or telephoned to a central office. Instead the credit decision may be taken by the shop staff from information obtained by telephone from a credit reference bureau. In this event, it is essential that the credit instructions given to the shop staff are very explicit and above all *kept very simple* if confusion is to be avoided. An example of a simple credit policy instruction would be:

The credit application would be rejected if:

---

Surname ................................................................................

Christian names ..............................................................

Age ..........................................................

Single/married/widowed/divorced/separated?

Number of dependants ......................

Present address ...............................................................

.............................................................................................

Home telephone number ..................

House/flat/furnished rooms/owner/tenant?

How long at present address ..............

If less than 3 years give previous address ..........................

.............................................................................................

Employer's name and address ..........................................

.............................................................................................

Occupation .....................................

Works or clock number .....................

How long employed ..........................

Employer's telephone number ............

Buyer's bank ......................................................................

.............................................................................................

Give details of current/previous credit transactions:

Account number ..............................

Name and address .............................................................

.............................................................................................

Private reference ..............................................................

.............................................................................................

I certify the accuracy of the above statements and authorise you to
make any enquiries which you consider necessary.

Date ............................... Signature ......................................

---

**Figure 20:1 Application for credit**

(a) The applicant is bankrupt; *or*
(b) County Court judgments have been recorded against the
applicant or immediate family; *or*
(c) the applicant does not have an earned income and cannot
provide a substantial guarantor.

Where shop staff are allowed to make the credit decision it is recommended that proper vigilance is exercised by management. An examination of monthly arrears statistics would pinpoint, very quickly, those shops opening high risk business in which event the credit policy could instruct that all credit applications made at those shops be submitted to the credit office for approval.

The policy could also require all credit applications above an agreed limit to be dealt with in the same way.

### The credit reference bureau

The credit policy may require information to be obtained from a credit reference bureau, detailing how the enquiry is to be made. Bureaux may file information in different ways and unnecessary telephone charges will be incurred if the retailer is not certain of the correct procedure.

Basically bureaux provide details of county court judgments, bankruptcies, administration orders and supplement this information with information from other traders or their own debt collection agencies. In addition, most reputable bureaux purchase copies of electoral rolls should evidence as to residence be needed by the enquirer.

The type and extent of the enquiry made is usually determined by the amount of credit required so that the credit policy should define the type of information needed and the bureaux best able to supply it.

### Delivery of goods

It is sound practice to deliver the goods and obtain a signature from, or on behalf of, the customer as proof of delivery.

The delivery note should be retained at the store or attached to the credit document for easy reference in the event of dispute.

However, with the advent of many retailers offering 'instant credit' facilities, it is often impossible to insist on delivery. If a customer wishes to take the goods away, some form of identification should be seen, such as a bank or credit card, and signatures carefully compared.

## Payment and collection

The credit policy will establish the methods of payment open to the customer and the responsibility for the collection of the account in the event of default. It is very important that the date from which payments are to commence and the different ways of paying the account are properly explained to the customer at the point of sale and stressed again when the credit documents are sent to the customer.

Increasingly customers are given a choice as to the way in which their account can be paid and the remittance slips or monthly statements are usually designed to accommodate a variety of payment methods, such as:

1 Direct at the shop or store.
2 By post to credit office, shop or store.
3 By bank credit transfer.
4 By National Giro.

Payment by banker's standing order or direct debit should be encouraged in preference to any of the methods listed above.

The overall responsibility for collection of the account lies with the credit office, but the policy must define at what stage, if any, the sales staff will be involved.

Calls may have to be made on the customer to request the return of the goods, collect instalments which are in arrears or to obtain evidence of means prior to the commencement of legal action. These are the sorts of activity which retail sales staff may object to, thus creating a conflict between sales and credit personnel. Most successful collection calls are made in the evening and retail staffs do not always consider such calls to be part of their duties, so that increasing use is made of collection or enquiry agents instead.

The credit policy must take any argument out of this most important area by a clear definition of duties for all staff.

## Rebates for early settlement

If the type of credit scheme used, for example credit cards and budget accounts, is such that interest is regularly added to the outstanding amount, then, after deducting the payments, the balance remaining represents the amount required to complete the account.

However, in the case of the usual instalment credit agreement the credit charge is added initially for a prescribed length of credit and if the customer wishes to pay off the balance earlier, a rebate for early settlement may apply.

The rebate Regulations under the Consumer Credit Act lay down the minimum rebate that can be given for early settlement of fixed sum credit, and this applies from May 1985. The Regulations provide the formula to ensure correct calculation of the early settlement rebate, taking into consideration the substantial cost incurred in setting up the account.

There is nothing to prevent a retailer allowing more than the Act provides, and a credit policy may well offer higher settlement discounts to obtain a better cash flow and to promote new business.

In some instances the charge for credit is waived altogether during specific trading periods or if the balance of the cash price is paid within a specified time. This arrangement is sometimes referred to as 'free credit', but usually the financing is paid for by inflated cash prices, reduced part exchange allowances or a manufacturer's subsidy. Nonetheless, some retailers find that this type of scheme attracts additional business and thus offer 'free credit' or high early settlement rebate as an aid to selling.

The above points represent only some of the points to be included in a credit policy. The manner in which credit terms are advertised and the presentation of repayment tables is also important as is the efficiency with which customer correspondence is dealt with.

Above all, the policy should be flexible and reviewed regularly so as to achieve its prime objective of obtaining additional and profitable new business.

## AIDS IN ASSESSING THE CREDIT RISK

Different businesses have different credit priorities and standards. A bank or finance company, relying entirely for profits on credit charges may assess credit applications differently from a manufacturing company looking for maximum sales volume with credit facilities through its own chain of retail stores.

Whatever criteria apply, applications will almost certainly be assessed from information provided by one or more of the following sources.

## A credit reference bureau

The main function of a credit reference bureau is maintaining records to assist in assessing the credit status of would-be borrowers. The information available through the larger reputable credit bureaux includes:

1 Record of all registered county court judgments and decrees in the last six years.
2 Information supplied by other traders with regard to bad debts, slow paying accounts and repossessions.
3 Records of bankruptcies and administration orders.
4 Bills of sale.
5 Satisfaction of judgments and bills of sale.
6 Voters roll information.

Some credit bureaux also file details of all satisfactory credit transactions reported to them by other users.

Credit bureaux will either keep their records in alphabetical surname order, by address or by a combination of name and address.

Bureaux files are usually very accurate, but both methods of storing information have their weaknesses. A persistent debtor could use different names with a correct address and leave a trail of unpaid bills at previous addresses. It is for this reason that most companies require customers to state previous addresses within the last three or even five years.

It is not usual for such complete information to be obtained by telephone so to ensure a relatively fast reply, telex is recommended.

It is not always possible to confirm residence details by reference to the voters roll because the customer may not be eligible to vote.

Information is increasingly being obtained from bureaux files using terminals, either on dedicated lines or through the normal telephone systems. In this way, information is now obtainable in seconds rather than minutes.

## The enquiry agent

In recent years the conduct of some enquiry agencies has not always been above reproach, but now the Consumer Credit Act requires anyone engaged in debt collection, debt counselling or credit reference information to be licensed so that a careful check will now be made.

An enquiry agent is sometimes used to supplement credit reference bureaux, for example to confirm that the credit applicant is in full-time employment and to check the references given by the applicant. Perhaps he will visit the customer at home to examine documents relating to other credit transactions and may make enquiries of a landlord or building society before submitting his report.

Sometimes the credit policy of a finance company may require an enquiry agent to provide a complete status report, to include information obtained from a credit reference bureau, and make the credit decision on their behalf. This is to take the credit decision out of the hands of shop staff and to provide a quicker service than that available by submitting the application by post to a central credit office.

Some agents link their credit reference activities with tracing and/or repossession work thus providing a complete service to the retail credit industry.

## References

One of the basic beliefs of modern credit management is that there should be a full and complete exchange of credit information. While there has been a strong move in this direction, difficulties which remain in obtaining adequate references include:

1 Applications are not dealt with quickly.
2 Banks and many other credit grantors will not give a reference over the telephone.
3 Many large retailers will no longer give credit references on their customers.
4 Other account numbers are not quoted.

Most members of the United Association for the Protection of

Trade, one of the most respected credit reference bureaux, provide the association with details of existing and completed credit transactions, so that independent reference information is readily available on file.

A credit applicant will seldom provide unacceptable references and if independent reference information is not available the importance of checking references provided by the applicant must be questionable.

*A  Bank references.*  As bankers are by profession a cautious lot, and rightly so, it is not surprising to find their credit reports worded in a similar manner. Brief comment without further explanation must usually suffice, such as:

| | |
|---|---|
| Undoubted for your figures | Wonderful but rarely seen |
| Good for your figures | Good risk |
| We do not think he would enter into, etc. | Be very careful |
| Capital fully employed but we do not think, etc. | Too heavily committed already |
| Cannot speak for your figures | Do not touch this customer |

Each credit grantor must make his own decision as to what emphasis is to be placed on the qualified reports.

*B  Credit references.*  Seldom will a would-be borrower provide an unsatisfactory credit reference. However, if the credit grantor insists on reference to an existing or fairly recent credit transaction, at least some idea is obtained of payment habits and the amount of credit which has been repaid in a satisfactory manner.

An example of this type of enquiry is shown in Figure 20:2.

*C  Personal references.*  References may be obtained from private individuals who know the applicant. Again it is not likely that the applicant will provide an unacceptable reference and in practice such references prove most useful in the event of the debtor having to be traced. It is a good policy always to write or call on private references if the credit customer absconds, thus saving the expense of a tracing agent. The types of credit references available are as follows:

The Credit Controller


Dear Sirs,
       Your ref:               Our ref:
       Name and address:

The above named has referred us to you for a credit reference and your assistance in completing and returning this letter will be appreciated.

Your reply will be treated in the strictest confidence and we enclose a business reply envelope for your use.

Yours truly,


Credit Department


Would you please advise:
1    How long you have known the applicant?       ..........
2    Whether or not payments have been made promptly  Yes/No
3    From your experience would you consider the
      applicant able to make monthly payments of £
4    Any other particulars you consider relevant.


Signed:              Company stamp
Position:

**Figure 20:2   Specimen letter for credit reference enquiry**

Hire Purchase Information Ltd—HPI

This company maintains a register of private and commercial motor vehicles, caravans, motor cycles, etc. which are subject to credit transactions, to establish whether any vehicle offered in part exchange or as security is subject to an existing credit transaction. The company also records and advises on motor vehicles reported to police as stolen or subject to a total loss insurance claim.

Where motor vehicle finance is concerned it is essential for such enquiries to be made.

## Confirmation of employment

Perhaps the most obvious and possibly the most important reference is that which confirms the credit applicant's employment. Provided the employer is not required to divulge confidential information concerning earnings, information will normally be provided regarding the nature and length of the employment. Limited information is very often made available on the telephone and almost always supplied in writing.

## Use of credit scoring

Where a substantial number of credit applications are handled at a central point each day, credit grantors may choose to introduce a points scoring scheme to assist in assessing the credit risk.

A credit scoring system is based on the proposition that society is changing sufficiently slowly for a company to be confident that the behaviour of their customers over, say, the last two years, will be good enough to predict their behaviour over the next two years.

Such a system is developed by using a range of sophisticated sampling techniques. Most systems are built by a small number of companies specialising in such work, and as they are fairly expensive, they tend to be limited to the larger credit grantors.

The score chart is produced from information in the credit company's own records with an analysis made of the personal characteristics contained in previous credit applications, and a points value calculated from the way the accounts have been paid. The benefits of such systems are:

(a) A uniform standard is set for checking new credit applications.
(b) Management can easily adjust this standard by altering the total of points needed before the application is accepted.
(c) Management can reduce or increase the acceptance rate—at will—without having to rely on the judgement of credit staff.
(d) Extensive training of credit sanction staff is avoided as the system does not rely on staff expertise and a reduction in staff required may be achieved.
(e) Substantial savings can be made on bureau costs.

An example of a points scoring system is shown in Figure 20:3.

| 1 | *Age* | | *Marks* |
|---|---|---|---|
| | Under 18 | | 0 |
| | 18-29 | | 10 |
| | 30-49 | | 30 |
| | 50—59 | | 20 |
| | 60+ | | 10 |

| 2 | *Residence* | | |
|---|---|---|---|
| | Owner | 2 years + | 30 |
| | | Less than 2 years | 15 |
| | Tenant of | 10 years + | 25 |
| | unfurnished | 5-10 years | 20 |
| | accommodation | Less than 5 years | 5 |
| | Tenant of | 10 years + | 15 |
| | furnished | 5-10 years | 10 |
| | accommodation | Less than 5 years | 0 |

| 3 | *Bank references* | |
|---|---|---|
| | Undoubted | 50 |
| | No reservations | 30 |
| | With reservations | 10 |
| | Fully committed | 0 |
| | Bad— | reject the application |

| 4 | *Marital status* | |
|---|---|---|
| | Married | 10 |
| | Single | 5 |
| | Divorced | 5 |

| 5 | *Employer* | |
|---|---|---|
| | With employer 3 years + | 20 |
| | With employer 1-3 years | 10 |
| | Less than 1 year | 5 |

| 6 | *Occupation* | |
|---|---|---|
| | Skilled | 20 |
| | Semi-skilled | 10 |
| | Unskilled | 5 |

Top
mark     160

Over 80 accept

60-80 Obtain bureau report and then refer to credit sanction
supervisor for decision
Less than 60 decline

**Figure 20:3   Credit scoring system**

Credit is a valuable asset and should not be given away but only granted after sufficient knowledge of the customer has been obtained to justify confidence in his ability to pay. Obtaining and using that knowledge is really what is meant by assessing the credit risk.

## COLLECTION OF ACCOUNTS

The education of the customer should begin at the point of sale, when the credit application is accepted, by emphasising that payment is required on the due date. The customer should be told exactly how and where payments are to be made, with this information again stressed in the guidance literature sent to the customer with the payment book, credit card or monthly statement.

### Update of customer accounts

Whatever the accounting methods, the basic requirement of successful collection operations is accurate book-keeping. Insist that all customer remittances are properly recorded before reminder notices and statements are produced by the credit office or computer centre. It matters little if the account is maintained by the most sophisticated computer system or engraved on blocks of stone, the customer expects the account to be accurate and is justified in complaining if it is not.

Nothing destroys confidence in the credit operation so much as a sales staff having to cope with irate customers who may have been sent unnecessary reminder letters—especially when the shop is full of potential customers. In such circumstances the sales assistant may try to get the complaining customer out of the shop quickly, without investigating the complaint, by using phrases such as 'it is always happening', 'the computer went wrong again' or worst of all 'don't take any notice'. From that point on, the credit office has a problem because the customer may not take seriously any further collection letters.

The collection effort will deteriorate if slow paying accounts cannot be followed up with authority because information is not up-to-date.

It is vital that accounts are updated regularly and accurately. Just as in a manual system the credit department is responsible for posting the ledger so in a computer system it should be the credit department's responsibility to provide and reconcile the input to the computer.

It is the credit staff who have to answer letters and telephone calls from disgruntled customers and sales managers and it is in their own interests to keep complaints to a minimum by achieving a high standard of accuracy when preparing the computer input which should *always* be agreed with the sales and remittance totals *before* being sent to the computer for processing and reconciled immediately *after* it has been processed. A well-tried computer input procedure for remittances and enquiries is shown in Figure 20:4.

## Collecting

Although most customers pay without having to be reminded to any great extent, it is not easy to correct a serious default situation.

The series of collection letters sent to overdue customers should begin sufficiently early and increase in strength to avoid a serious situation developing by neglect. There is nothing difficult in asking customers to pay money that is owed, and the methods employed will vary with the type of credit scheme in use, but to be successful the collection effort *must* be *consistent* and *persistent.*

It is usual for the first reminder letters to be sent about 15 days after the due date and for the sequence to continue at 15-day intervals. The number of letters sent will depend on the nature of the transaction and the amount involved, but for those accounts which miss the first instalment—the *first payment failure*—a personal call should be made *immediately* and the account referred for special attention until it is brought up-to-date or the merchandise is repossessed.

Another good collection practice is to *ask* for payment *when* the customer is *most likely to pay.* The whole point of a collection letter is to induce payment and should be timed to arrive as near to pay day as possible—before the wages are spent, not after.

When overdue accounts have got beyond the routine reminder stage the attention given by the credit office must be positive and the

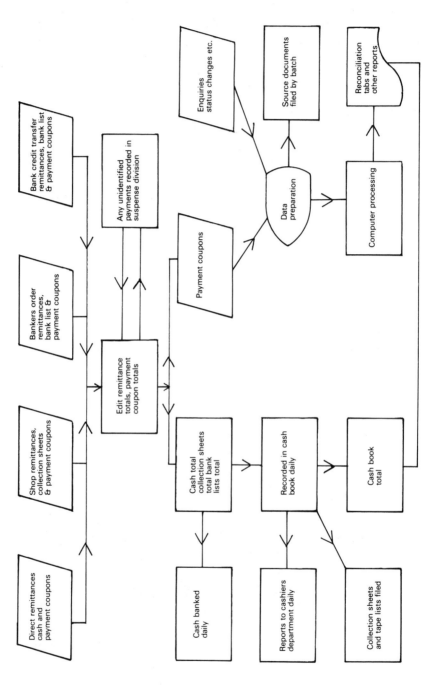

**Figure 20:4  Computer input for remittances and enquiries**

person following up the account should not threaten action unless it is intended to take that action if the account is not paid. The customer will not take collection letters seriously if the credit office does not mean what it says.

Rather than having specially dictated letters the use of facsimiles or letters produced on a word processor which look like specially dictated letters is recommended so that the customer thinks that his account is being given personal attention.

Another problem common to most collection offices is slow paying accounts where the balances are very small and where legal action would not really be economic. The collection of such balances should be achieved by getting the customer who cannot afford to pay £15 or £20 all at once to sign a declaration agreeing to pay by weekly instalments.

The following is an example of a simple collection procedure incorporating some of the points raised above:

1   First reminder—produced on first Wednesday 10 or more days after instalment due date.
2   Second reminder—produced on Wednesday immediately prior to next instalment falling due.

   At this stage if the customer has not paid the first monthly instalment due under the agreement further computer reminders should be suspended automatically and the account listed for special attention. A first payment failure form can be sent by the credit office to the local shop or enquiry agent to establish why the account has not been paid.
3   Third reminder—produced on Wednesday following second monthly instalment falling due.
4   Fourth reminder—produced on Wednesday immediately prior to next instalment falling due—seven days notice of default.

If the account is not brought up-to-date by the next reminder date it should be automatically included in those accounts requiring special attention by the credit office.

Such special attention accounts should be followed up every two weeks using:

(a)   Printed letters.
(b)   Automatically typed letters.
(c)   Specially dictated letters.

The computer system must enable credit staff to suspend or reinstate the reminder sequence at any time.

There are some customers who do not respond to letters at all and if the point comes when expensive legal action must be considered, it is essential that the right type of summons be issued. It is no good entering an action for the return of property which may have been sold or given away nor does it make sense to issue a summons if the customer has absconded.

So a personal approach needs to be made.

## Personal approach

If the customer is on the telephone, this should be used for the first personal approach about the time of the second overdue instalment. If the customer can be contacted personally, it may be possible to find out the reason for non-payment and arrangements may be made for the account to be brought up-to-date.

If this fails, or if the customer is not on the telephone, a personal call will be required. The great advantage of the personal call is that the credit representative can have a face-to-face discussion with the customer and arrive at some definite result. Payment of full arrears or voluntary surrender of the goods is the ideal result but failing this it at least will confirm that the debtor still lives at the address and may establish the real reason why the account has not been paid properly.

If the customer refuses to pay or return the goods voluntarily the collector should try to obtain details of the debtor's employment and income and if possible check the condition of any goods which may need to be repossessed. Although the personal call is relatively expensive, it is probably the most effective method of collecting delinquent accounts and is always recommended prior to legal action being commenced.

Should the enquiry agent or credit representative establish that the debtor no longer lives at the address enquiries should be made of the immediate neighbours, referees and employers. To avoid the need to refer back to the credit office it is recommended that these details are made available to the agent at the time he is instructed.

## Court action

Needless to say, legal proceedings should only be taken as a last resort, but if necessary the creditor will usually be able to obtain judgment against a debtor without employing the services of solicitors or even attending the county court hearing. Action can be taken by:

(a)  the return of the goods, when a fixed date summons is applied for;
(b)  a money judgment when a default summons is applied for.

When a fixed date summons is issued and served on the defendant, a date is fixed by the court for the hearing of the claim. The defendant may decide not to attend the hearing or dispute the details of the claim, in which case a sworn affidavit can then be sent to the court giving more precise details and requesting the court to enter judgment in the plaintiff's favour. A copy of the affidavit must also be sent to the defendant advising that the evidence is being submitted by affidavit form.

When a default summons is issued for a money judgment, if no defence or offer is received from the defendant within 14 days, a written request is then made to the court for judgment to be entered in the plaintiff's favour.

Having obtained judgment, if payment is not then made, enforcement action can be taken by way of Warrant of Execution, minimum £50 (unless of course the original claim was below this amount) or by applying to the court for an attachment of earnings order, when an amount, determined under the order, is deducted by the employer from the wages of the employee and paid to the court on a weekly/monthly basis.

It is important to follow up litigation accounts regularly, to avoid any delay in taking the next positive step should the debtor default in payment.

More detailed information on court procedures can be obtained by applying to any county court for booklets EX50 and EX50C which are free of charge.

## ORGANISATION

In concluding, it is right to mention the organisation required in a credit department if it is to operate on the lines above.

In the first place, the credit manager should be part of the management team and should fully participate in policy decisions which affect the credit function. Either he or his immediate superior should be a member of the board and should for preference be part of the financial rather than the sales team.

The credit department should have:

(a)　an acceptance section;
(b)　an accounts section;
(c)　a query, correspondence and follow-up section;
(d)　a legal section;
(e)　a secretariat and typing pool section.

In addition, the credit manager should liaise with the systems department so that computer routines can be established to the maximum benefit of the user and under no circumstances should any systems be foisted on the credit office.

The credit office staff should as far as possible be interchangeable and job descriptions should ensure that, for example, accounting machine and input operators can do other work when the peak posting operations are over.

The credit profession is an exciting one because from day to day one never knows exactly what is in store. 'There is now't as queer as folk' and it is worth remembering that accounts are real people, sometimes with real problems who look to the credit manager and his staff to relieve what could be a very worrying time ahead.

The credit job is dealing with that most demanding of commodities—people, and all the consumer legislation in the world will not change that.

# 21

# The Effective Use of Computers

**R. G. Haskett, Data Processing Manager, Dytecna Ltd**

The effectiveness of a computer will be judged on its capability to produce the required information at the right time. This capability will depend on:

1   The members of the organisation being able to precisely state what those requirements are, identifying those which aid management decision and those which monitor the business.
2   The ability of data processing staff to translate those requirements into operational computer systems.
3   The accuracy of information held on the computer files from which the reports will be produced.

It is not the intention of this chapter to discuss how the requirements of an organisation should be determined by management, nor how these would be translated into computer systems by data processing staff. The need for accuracy, however, will be a continuing theme, particularly in this first section which deals with aids to credit approval for it is from this process that customer account details are established and thus the major information base which supports management reporting.

## AIDS TO CREDIT APPROVAL

The credit approval or passing process ultimately determines whether or not credit will be granted by the finance house, and regardless of the type of credit being sought or the method used, will be seeking to answer whether the customer can pay and whether it is commercially sound to lend the money. For this process to be effective is dependent on accurate customer details being established at the very outset of the transaction. Unfortunately, these details are seldom originated under the direct control of the finance company concerned with granting the credit.

The setting up of an account starts when the customer makes the decision to obtain credit and an agreement or proposal form is completed. Who will complete this form? Do they understand the need for accuracy? Are they at all concerned? Comparing the hire purchase of a new car in a prestige showroom where the salesman is dependent for his commission on good documentation, against that for a television set in the High Street on a Saturday with the salesman impatient to serve his next customer, reveals two very different circumstances for the origination of forms. In both instances and beyond the direct control of the finance company, information is being created which must be accurate if it is to lead to the correct decision being taken at the time of credit approval.

### Categories of customer

Where a computer is used to aid the approval process then passing the agreement form through computer checking routines should be the first stage of that process, the approval procedures being designed so that the computer carries out all possible checks first with any clerical routines, including the final authorisation, at the end of the process. The prime aid which a computer brings to this process is speed of search and collation of information, grouped according to the criteria established by credit management. In this respect, proposals fall into two categories:

1 Those customers having current or previous transactions with the finance company.
2 Those customers which are entirely new to the finance company.

It is for management to determine what routine checks may be carried out within the confines of the finance company for each of these categories.

## Existing and previous customers

For those customers for whom there have been previous transactions, the most readily available source of information should be
the historical files of customer accounts. If a customer has been
satisfied with previous dealings it is possible that he will return to
that same source when next requiring credit. When this happens,
the computer system must be capable of searching its files and
reporting the details of previous transactions. As the customer may
be requiring a different form of credit, it is important to maintain
cross-references which will trace and report on all types of business
for a given customer in order to give the fullest picture. Examples of
the type of question which computer information can help to
provide answers for are, was the previous transaction discharged in
full? On time? Without constant reminding? Is the customer living at
the same address? Is he asking for a higher level of credit?

Even more relevant is any current experience of a customer and
whether the computer files contain any other running agreements
for him. If so, how does this new proposal increase the total liability
of that customer? Is the finance company part of a larger organiza-
tion, if so, can group liability be determined in respect of that
customer from information exchanged within that group? Is the
finance company part of a bank group and has the customer
indicated having an account with that bank? The presentation of
this type of information to credit management enables them to have
the fullest detail on which to make their decisions of approval or in
indicating further areas of search if necessary.

## New customers

For those customers who are entirely new to the finance house other
sources of information must be utilised. In certain types of credit
business, and hire purchase is a good example, the finance
company is unlikely to see the customer personally and the credit
assessment is based on the business acumen of outside agencies. In
the main these will be accredited dealerships who propose their
customers to a finance company for credit. It becomes important
then to maintain performance statistics for those agencies against

which proposals can be compared. Does that agency provide first-class business? How much have they provided? What percentage of that business resulted in bad debts? Were those bad debts related to a particular class of business or type of merchandise? Is this new proposal connected with that class or type? Is this proposal in a value range or geographical area which is particularly prone to bad debt situations? All new proposals should be matched against such statistical information, and not only that which can be built up within the finance company but also against national trends which are published from time to time.

## Personal credit

In the case of personal credit or running account credit limits being granted to individuals, the credit scoring method (see p. 355) can be used as an assessment aid to creditworthiness. Where no current or previous experience is available, the point scoring method may give a general guide to the expectations from the individual. In this respect a computer can rapidly assess a customer against the points system laid down by the organisation, and can also determine any relationships between sections of that assessment, for example, trade A might score 8 points in area X, but only 6 points in area Y. Attempting to determine any relationships of this nature by clerical methods could well cause long delays for any large volumes of transactions, whereas the effect on computer time would be negligible.

From the foregoing, it can be seen that a computer can in no way substitute for credit management when it comes to the final decision for approval, but can rapidly gather a mass of collated information for the credit function as an aid to that final approval. When faced with a large volume of business, this speed of search and cross-check can represent a dramatic saving in the amount of time taken in the approval process. This is to the advantage of both customer and finance company, especially where the computer is able to identify the straightforward decisions thereby leaving credit management to concentrate on the borderline cases.

Finally, information should be presented to credit management in such a way as to follow logically through the approval process to the decision point. The most important criteria should be reported first, if that is not satisfied then approval is unlikely to be given and this fact should not emerge half-way through the report on that proposal. For their part, credit management should remember that computer decisions are built on yes and no situations therefore very great care should be exercised when establishing the required checks and limits, and any relationships between these.

## COLLECTION LETTERS BY COMPUTER

When instalments are not received regularly, the default situation must be recognised, the amount of arrears accurately calculated, and the required notice of default or 'collection letter' produced. A computer provides a much greater flexibility and speed to this process than other methods and keeps the administrative cost of handling the account to the minimum.

### Accuracy

Because the collection letter process is in the area of customer relations it is very important for it to be under efficient control and, primarily, this control will depend on the accuracy of customer details held on the computer file. It is when dealing with an arrears situation that accuracy during the initial setting-up of the account is of prime importance, for example, if the agreement date is incorrect the account may be assessed for arrears at the wrong time—the result is an unnecessary letter; equally, if the address is inaccurate the letter may not reach its true destination—the result being no response and more letters wastefully required. These are just two examples where collection letters will not perform their proper function because of inaccurate information and both may result in a loss of good customer relations.

Having stressed the need for accuracy at setting-up it is inevitable that information will become out of date because of changing circumstances. Then it becomes necessary to ensure that any proven error or inaccuracy pointed out by the customer results in a physical amendment being quickly made to the customer's details to avoid any further irritation.

**367**

## General form of letters

It would be inappropriate to suggest how individual finance companies should draft the text of their various collection letters, but those concerned with the design of letters should keep some general criteria in mind; do not threaten what will not be performed; be firm, informative, courteous; seek to recover the arrears position whilst retaining goodwill. The chosen text may be preprinted at the time of manufacture of the various types of letter, this causes several items of stationery to be held, or, variable text can be built into and printed by the computer program. This latter method has the advantage of reduced cost from holding only one stock of 'plain letters' but great care must be exercised when establishing the criteria which triggers a given text to be printed. Whichever form of text presentation is chosen, the stationery must be organised so as to allow for all appropriate parties to receive information relating to the default; for example, guarantors.

It would be beneficial for the letters to include the account reference number and the name of the department within the finance company who the customer can contact to discuss the subject matter of the letter. This will avoid the irritation to the customer of being given a grand tour of the switchboard.

It is a feature of the consumer credit industry that a minority of letters will not be delivered; for example, inaccurate or even fraudulent addresses, therefore, the letters must be enclosed in an envelope which clearly states a return address. This enables the postal services to return (unopened) all letters not delivered, and this is important as it may be the first indication of a bad debt situation. A stop should be put on such accounts to prevent any further letters from being produced unnecessarily for that address.

## The million-pound letter

Safety checks should be incorporated into the calculation of arrears process to avoid the 'stupid' letter from being produced, for example, a letter suggesting to a customer that he is in arrears for an amount greater than the original balance outstanding. The built-in checks must prevent the possibility of such a letter being produced by a computer, for example, the checks might provide for the suppression of any letter where the arrears were less than one instalment or greater than three instalments.

Certainly no stereotyped letter should be produced by a computer where a legal situation has been reached. The details of all letters not produced because of failure to conform to safety checks should be printed on plain paper to enable a detailed examination of why an apparent incorrect arrears situation was assessed. Should a letter be produced for an account in arrears where it is subsequently proven not to be the fault of the customer, ensure that a procedure exists for clearing off any misleading performance information from the customers file which could prove detrimental at a later date.

## Timing

Whatever schedule is established for producing letters, for example, daily, weekly, etc., it should be based on a 'due date' that is, the day on which the finance company is entitled to receive the instalment. There are two important aspects which must be related to the schedule:

1 The receipt and application of cash to customers' accounts. Payments, even prompt ones, do become delayed and this may not be the fault of the customer. Therefore, before an arrears assessment takes place for a given due date, time should be allowed for any instalments arriving late to be applied to the account. A similar situation can arise from payments which, although arriving on time, do not have a correct account reference number allowing it to be posted. Such payments may well be directed to an 'unidentified cash account' and a day or so elapse before application to the correct customer account.

2 The amendment of customer details. The need for accuracy to prevent unnecessary letters from being produced has been mentioned earlier and it is obviously important that, before any assessment of arrears takes place, all the known changes are made to customer detail which may affect that assessment.

The time cycles for collection letters must be established in relation to the calendar schedule. These may differ dependent on whether the instalments are weekly, monthly, quarterly, etc., and whether these are due to be paid in advance or in arrears. The following examples of assessment timings for three main types of collection letter are typical of a monthly in-arrear instalment cycle related to fixed sum credit.

1  A first reminder at due date plus 10 days, thereby allowing a reasonable time for any postal delay, bank error, or mis-posting.
2  If there is no response to the first reminder and the account remains in arrears, a second reminder at due date plus 20 days.
3  Again, if there is no response, a third and probably final reminder at due date plus 35 days. By now, the customer's payment is a month overdue, a second instalment has fallen into arrears, and this account should be appearing on overdue reports to collection management. At this time, all further letters should be suppressed automatically until such time as the account is brought up-to-date, whereupon the cycle is reset.

Although not a notice of default it is worth mentioning congratulatory type letters, more popularly known as 'good boy' letters, because it is likely that these will also depend on a time cycle for their production. These might be produced at set times during the life of those agreements where there is an acceptable record of payment, possibly reminding the customer of other forms of credit available and attempting to cover the situation where the account may be settled without warning. A large proportion of agreements do not run their full term and it would be beneficial to have 'average running times' available for all types and periods of credit agreement; these can be used to produce a good boy letter at the time when there is statistical evidence which suggests early settlement for that type of agreement. For those agreements which appear to be running their full term nothing is lost by producing a letter at say the final due date less 35 or 70 days in anticipation of the final payment. The aim of these letters is to retain the good customers by offering further credit facilities, in order to achieve this the timing must equate to the most likely points when the customer can be lost.

## Running account credit

In the matter of arrears assessment the management may wish to take a different viewpoint in relation to defaults on running account credit. By the terms of the agreement the customer has agreed to pay regular instalments and when these are not forthcoming, the customer is without doubt in default of that agreement. Nevertheless, the finance company may wish to take a different attitude in its stereotyped letters than for fixed sum credit, especially where the customer's account has a credit balance. For example, where a small credit balance exists, the finance company is paying interest on the balance and incurring the cost of producing collection letters without much hope of redressing the situation; the account may be producing little or no profit.

Congratulatory letters are also slightly different on running account credit. Here, while the finance company will certainly wish to mail-shot their good customers at frequent intervals, reminding them of further advances which become available when the balance on the account drops below the credit limit by a specific amount— say four instalments of £50—it should be done before the account reaches a natural nil balance; the customer may close and be lost to the finance company.

## Types of stationery

When considering the production of collection letters by computer there are two basic types of continuous preprinted stationery available:

1 The conventional type which utilises one-time carbon or no carbon required papers. This type has complete freedom of choice in design, size, number of copies (up to the maximum that a computer printer can reasonably handle), but the individual letters are subject to all the normal mailing operations before posting.

2 The letter in a self-sealed envelope type which is gaining popularity for applications of this nature. The printing of arrears information takes place on a blacked-out portion of the envelope and is selectively carried through on to the letter by a carbon patch on the inside of the envelope. A return envelope and other material can also be sealed inside the envelope during

manufacture if desired. With this type of stationery all pre-mailing operations are eliminated but there are some restrictions on design and size.

Both types can utilise the Post Office prepaid impression mailing system and this should be negotiated with the local head postmaster. The postmaster will also negotiate a discount if the volume of regular mailings is sufficient to warrant this, and providing that the organisation is prepared to pre-sort and bundle to Post Office requirements. If postal codes have been included on the customer address file the computer is an ideal instrument for producing letters in the required order for this discount to be gained.

Self-sealed letters will increase the costs of stationery but, by eliminating the clerical processes of folding and enveloping, dramatically reduces both time cycle and costs; these savings can be significant when dealing with large volumes. If the prepaid facility is incorporated, the self-sealed type of letter is ready for almost instant dispatch from production by the computer. The self-sealed type also obviates the need for critical folding and inserting operations associated with window envelopes, if these operations are not carefully carried out information other than name and address may be disclosed, thereby incurring the problems associated with privacy and confidentiality.


## MANAGEMENT INFORMATION AND REPORTS

The value of information is determined by the improvement in results of the activities it is used to support. This value depends on what use the members of the organisation are able to make of it and the way in which it is presented may strongly affect that use, and thus the value of the information.

Management reports fall into two categories, those which aid management decisions, and those which monitor the results of decisions taken. Both should accurately depict the on-going situation and be as current as the organisation requires to control the business, this may be anything from daily upwards. In this respect a conflict may exist between management reporting and routine accounting reports; for example, where a computer system has been designed originally to serve the accounting month, it may not be sufficient as a monitor of the business which requires weekly management figures. A computer system is not effective unless it has reconciled this situation and is serving both requirements for they have equal importance to the management of an organisation.

## Form of management reports

All computer reports should have a standard heading on each page for the purpose of identification. Such headings should include the name of the report, the date on which the report was produced and a page number, all of these being printed in the same position for all reports. Subsidiary headings should also appear on each page and include any criteria which relates to a particular report, for example, 'date of last cash posted 01/01/84' or 'interest calculated at 9.5%'. Column headings must be informative and be in terms that the user of the report will recognise and understand; if the user is vague about the contents he will not make effective use of the information. Each report should contain the required amount of information, be self-explanatory, and set out in such a way which enables the user to instantly recognise the decision areas. Whilst reports should be as brief as possible in giving the desired information there will be occasions when management require the full backing detail and this flexibility can only be achieved where the organisation is based on a comprehensive coding structure which will allow reports to be produced at any level; for example, branch office, representative, geographical area, etc., and for any aspect of the business.

## Accuracy of reporting

Control must be exercised on computer files to ensure the accuracy of information, this is particularly essential when dealing with finance. To achieve this, the state of each computer file used during processing must appear after each run. This control is ideally printed on the last page of each report, it can then be detached easily at the quality control stage before distribution of the report to the user. Not only will this control identify errors in computer processing

|  | Number of accounts | Original balances | Outstanding balances |
|---|---|---|---|
| B/fwd | 21 076 | 15 698 400.00 | 9 434 219.75 |
| Chngs | 0 | 0.00 | 106 087.40− |
| C/fwd | 21 076 | 15 698 400.00 | 9 328 132.35 |

**Figure 21:1 Computer file control.** The 'Chngs' line reflects the amount of instalments applied to customer accounts and this, plus any postings to unidentified cash suspense (a separate control) should equal the amount of cash received by the company for a given period.

such as use of files out of sequence, but will also provide an audit trail. Whilst each organisation must decide for itself which aspects of the computer files it wishes to control, an example of the principle is given in Figure 21:1 showing minimum control of three aspects as a result of applying cash to the customer file.

## Management reporting

This chapter now examines management information in three aspects of the consumer credit industry; namely, new business targets, receipt of cash payments and control of overdues, giving examples of action and monitoring reports under those headings.

### New business targets

At the same time as entering details of new agreements into the customer file, information must be collated for statistical purposes and clearly identified as to type of business, class of merchandise, branch office, representative, dealer, etc. This collated information will enable reports to be produced for branch management showing the results for a current period together with accumulations to date, with both of these being compared against business targets to determine a performance level. Individual organisations must determine the headings under which this is reported, the example

| Type of Business | Target | (This month) Charges earned | % Perf. to target | Target | (This year to date) Charges earned | % Perf. to target |
|---|---|---|---|---|---|---|
| Hire purchase | 500 | 600 | +20.0 | 3 500 | 3 400 | − 2.9 |
| Credit sales | 1 000 | 900 | −10.0 | 6 000 | 7 000 | +16.7 |
| Personal loans | 1 500 | 2 000 | +33.3 | 8 500 | 8 250 | − 2.9 |
| All types | 3 000 | 3 500 | +16.7 | 18 000 | 18 650 | + 3.6 |

**Figure 21:2   New business targets (showing type of business by company, branch, representative and dealer)**

given in Figure 21:2 uses only charges earned to demonstrate the principle.

The same component information is retained and used to provide a simple summary of performance over a business target period; for example, six months, enabling branch management to detect any trends or fluctuations at their location. It is the details of these branch performance summaries for type of business, representatives, etc., which go to form the summary reports for central new business management. The example given in Figure 21:3 uses the 'league table' principle and shows branch performance for all types of business, again using charges earned for this purpose. This type of report could be produced with moving totals, i.e. always showing the current month plus the five previous months, or could be built up to a six-month statistic for each target period as in the example.

| Target | Location | | Jan | Feb | Mar | Apr | May | Jun | % Perf. to target |
|---|---|---|---|---|---|---|---|---|---|
| 125 | Mth | Branch B | 165 | 207 | 149 | 138 | | | |
| 500 | Acc | | 165 | 372 | 521 | 659 | | | +31.8 |
| 165 | Mth | Branch A | 208 | 184 | 127* | 146* | | | |
| 660 | Acc | | 208 | 392 | 519 | 665 | | | + 0.8 |
| 50 | Mth | Branch C | 22* | 46* | 34* | 26* | | | |
| 200 | Acc | | 22* | 68* | 102* | 128* | | | −36.0 |
| 340 | Mth | All | 395 | 437 | 310 | 310 | | | |
| 1360 | Acc | branches | 395 | 832 | 1142 | 1452 | | | + 6.8 |

*Target not achieved

**Figure 21:3   New business performance (type of business by company, branch, representative and dealer)**

In this example it appears that the company target was achieved; but was Branch B set a low target or did it perform excellently? Was Branch A set a realistic target or did it only perform what was required? Was Branch C set too high a target or did it perform badly? Reference to other performance summaries may show that it was only one representative or dealer who caused these situations. These types of report will allow management to monitor the amount of business at any desired level from company down to individual source of that business, and to be aware of which are reaching pre-determined targets.

### Cash-received reports

These reports are concerned with monitoring the receipt of payments against the organisation's entitlement to instalments due. The funding of a consumer credit transaction is based on the cost of money with its highly competitive interest rates, both for the purchase of funds by the finance company and for the sale of credit facilities to the customer. At the point when a credit facility is granted to the customer, a percentage rate of return (or the profit on the transaction) is established. If instalments are received when due the expected profit is achieved, those not paid when due increases the administrative charge thereby reducing this profit; management will want to monitor this situation carefully. Again, this type of report must have the flexibility to report the position at any level of detail desired, for example, top management may only require the overall situation whereas branch and credit management will wish to identify any areas of short-fall in order to take immediate corrective measures. See Figure 21:4.

The second type of report at perhaps monthly intervals would show the performance of a fixed or moving period over which the improvement or deterioration of payments can be clearly seen. This report highlights which sections of the company are not receiving the expected amount of money thereby posing the question of whether those sections are getting too large a proportion of unprofitable business. The example in Figure 21:5 shows a performance for current instalments only, but obviously all of the cash received categories—e.g. one-month arrears—should be reported on as a percentage of entitlement received.

| Category | Entitlement | Received | Short/over | Shortfall percentage |
|---|---|---|---|---|
| Current instalments | 7 800.00 | 6 750.00 | 1 050.00 | 13.5 |
| Court orders | 100.00 | 100.00 | 0.00 | 0.0 |
| Arrears: | | | | |
| 1 month | 3 200.00 | 1 600.00 | 1 600.00 | 50.0 |
| 2 months | 1 100.00 | 500.00 | 600.00 | 54.6 |
| 3+ months | 700.00 | 250.00 | 450.00 | 64.3 |
| Legal cases | 920.00 | 45.00 | 875.00 | 95.1 |
| Total entitlement | 13 820.00 | 9 245.00 | 4 575.00 | 33.1 |
| Add: Early instalments | 0.00 | 18.50 | 18.50+ | 0.0 |
| Settlements | 0.00 | 200.00 | 200.00+ | 0.0 |
| Unidentified | 0.00 | 45.00 | 45.00+ | 0.0 |
| Total position | 13 820.00 | 9 508.50 | 4 311.50 | 31.2 |

**Figure 21:4 Cash received (daily by company and branch with weekly, monthly and period to date accumulations where required)**

Once the short-fall areas have been identified then further information is necessary to show the individual items which have contributed to the problem; it may be only one bad transaction which has caused the overall bad situation in that section. Management will not wish to search for the bad items so for this level of detail the report should use the 'worst first' principle, then in descending degree allowing the user to decide where to draw his decision line for action. The aids to management should not be forgotten here—is it a recurring combination of branch/dealer/representative that is introducing the bad business?

Overdue reports

Overdue reports are concerned with monitoring those accounts on which the instalments are in arrears. Earlier, this chapter discussed

| Category | | Jan | Feb | Mar | Apr | May | Jun |
|---|---|---|---|---|---|---|---|
| Branch A | | % | % | % | % | % | % |
| Current instalments | (Month | 90.0 | 85.1 | 73.1 | 93.7 | | |
| | (Acc. av | 90.0 | 87.6 | 82.7 | 85.5 | | |

**Figure 21:5 Performance of cash entitlement (monthly by company, branch, representative and dealer)**

the procedures connected with the dispatch of collection letters to customers when instalments are not paid; overdue reports are concerned with information on those defaulters who are two instalments in arrear. In other words, an account is reported as overdue at about the time a third reminder is sent. It is for individual companies to decide whether or not these two events coincide in the time cycle.

*Routine reporting.* Two routine reports provide a means whereby collection management can begin measures for bringing the accounts up-to-date. The first will probably be produced weekly and give details of cases for collection staff to follow up the defaults; this report should provide the maximum information of individual overdue accounts, including such items as an indication of whether or not the 'minimum rule' has been satisfied under hire purchase agreements. The purpose of the second routine report is to allow collection management to be aware of the overdue situation on a monthly basis and for this it is usual to 'age' the various periods of default; for example, one month, two months, etc. This monthly ageing may have a secondary purpose in providing financial management with a basis for reserving funds against potential bad debts. If used for this purpose it would be one instance where accounting and management required must be reconciled on the calendar.

### Monitoring reports

These reports are provided to enable management to monitor the performance of the collection function. The first of these reports is provided at weekly intervals and shows the results of the follow-up process. Figure 21:6 gives a simple form of report for this purpose, showing only the number of cases in arrear; it is equally important to show the amount of arrears for all categories. The percentage performance represents successful collections of the previous (brought forward) arrears situation. The position is expressed as an improvement—or otherwise (carried forward)—as compared to the previous situation.

It would be a simple matter to expand these performance and position statistics into monthly or six-monthly reports with fixed or

| Arrears category | Brought forward | Collected | New overdues | Carried forward | % Perf. of collects | Coll. position (Cases) | (%) |
|---|---|---|---|---|---|---|---|
| 1 month | 1000 | 620 | 540 | 920 | 62.0 | − 80 | 8.0 |
| 2 months | 380 | 230 | 380 | 530 | 60.5 | +150 | 39.5 |
| 3+ months | 460 | 420 | 150 | 190 | 91.3 | −270 | 58.7 |
| Total | 1840 | 1270 | 1070 | 1640 | 69.0 | −200 | 10.9 |
| Add: legal | 24 | 11 | 40 | 53 | 45.8 | + 29 | 120.8 |
| Total | 1864 | 1281 | 1110 | 1693 | 68.7 | −171 | 9.2 |

**Figure 21:6 Collection performance (by company, branch, representative and dealer)**

moving periods, and for these to be at any level required by management, for example, type of business, class of merchandise.

Following on from collection performance, management will then wish to see how the overdue situation relates to the overall business. Here it is necessary to show the total amount of business on the computer files in order that the overdue position can be compared against the rise or fall in that total. If the management has set maximum acceptabilities for the various categories of overdue period, these should be shown on this report in order to indicate which sections of the business are exceeding those percentages. This report, an example of which is given in Figure 21:7, must be based on

| Max. % allowed | | | Jan | Feb | Mar |
|---|---|---|---|---|---|
| | Total outstanding. Bals. | | 260 000.00 | 346 000.00 | 487 000.00 |
| | % increase/decrease | | +10.5 | +33.1 | +40.8 |
| | O/Due—1 month | £ | 9 360.00 | 11 764.00 | 18 019.00 |
| 4.0 | | % | 3.6 | 3.4 | 3.7 |
| | O/Due—2 months | £ | 3 640.00 | 6 574.00 | 10.714.00 |
| 2.0 | | % | 1.4 | 1.9 | 2.2* |
| | O/Due—3+ months | £ | 4 160.00 | 4 844.00 | 5 357.00 |
| 1.0 | | % | 1.6* | 1.4* | 1.1* |
| | O/Due—Legal | £ | 1 560.00 | 1 384.00 | 2 435.00 |
| 0.5 | | % | 0.6* | 0.4 | 0.5 |
| | Total overdue | £ | 18 720.00 | 24 566.00 | 36 525.00 |
| 7.5 | | % | 7.2 | 7.1 | 7.5 |
| | *Maximum % exceeded | | | | |

**Figure 21:7 Overdue position (by company, branch, representative and dealer for type of business, class of merchandise, etc., as required)**

the calculations of financial amounts; the use of number of cases which make up the arrears would give a totally misleading picture because of the differing sums outstanding. Therefore, if the number of cases is required on this report, it should be for memorandum purposes and take a secondary role.

Management reporting must not be aimed solely at head office with the management at remote locations being forgotten. It is these members of an organisation that may have the greatest need for action reports and yet have the least influence in obtaining them.

Where it affects them, branch management must be supplied with information at least equal to that for central management, thereby supplying both ends of the business with a common discussion ground on any remedial actions required.

## COMPUTING FOR THE SMALL BUSINESS

Since the first edition was published many changes have taken place in the world of data processing. By far the most significant event in this period has been the development of the silicon chip, and from this came the emergence of the low cost micro-computer on to the commercial market. Today, the micro-computer is capable of providing as much benefit to the business as computers in the past—but at a fraction of the cost.

This revolution in data processing has resulted in bringing the opportunity for using modern-day methods within the reach of a very wide range of smaller companies who, in the past, would have found the financial burden to be prohibitive. Many smaller instalment credit houses may fall into this broad category and the prompt, accurate, management of new business approvals, cash postings, collections and overdues, is an essential part of their business. All of these topics have been discussed in this chapter; all are capable of achievement by the use of micro-computer systems.

Through the medium of a micro-computer, many hundreds of small companies will now be taking advantage of data processing for the first time. They should bear in mind that the basic principles which underwrite the effective use of computers (see p. 363) have not changed and must still be applied.

# 22

# Consumer Credit Law

**P. J. Patrick, Director, Consumer Credit Trade Association**

### INTRODUCTION

When in July 1974 the Consumer Credit Act reached the statute-book it was expected that by mid-1975 most, if not all, the Regulations necessary to implement the far-reaching changes made in law would have been made and that whilst some of these would not yet be in operation the rules themselves would be known.

In the event, the problems involved in implementation were found to be substantially greater than had been expected and it took over nine years before the last of the Regulations were made. The implementation of the Act took place effectively in three stages. The first, involving licensing, extortionate credit bargains, 'connected lender liability' and the rules affecting credit reference agencies was in 1977. The second, the parts of the Act governing seeking business and the regulations on advertising and quotations came into effect in 1980. The effective date for the rest of the Act and the Regulations made under it to govern documents and a number of other matters including rebates for early settlement was set as 19 May 1985— nearly 11 years after the Act received the Royal Assent.

The Consumer Credit Act comprises 193 Sections and 5 Schedules. Over 50 statutory instruments (that is to say Regulations and Orders made by the Department of Trade and Industry) are now in effect, having been made under powers given in the Act. The Office of Fair Trading has issued almost as many General Notices in connection with its duty to license credit granters and related businesses. So detailed a mass of legislation can only be described in outline in this chapter and credit managers operating in the consumer field will find it necessary to refer to some of the specialist works on this subject.

## DEVELOPMENT OF CONSUMER CREDIT LAW

The development of consumer credit law in the UK represents, for the most part, two major themes. The first is to ensure that the customer is made fully aware of what commitment he is undertaking, whilst the second is to provide him with adequate protection against the unscrupulous once the agreement is made. The law grew up, however, in a fragmented fashion, particular forms of credit being regulated as the need arose.

The first really substantial measure was the Moneylenders Act 1927 which provided a form of licensing, forbade circulars and canvassing and severely restricted advertising. It set out requirements as to documents and included a number of other measures to protect the borrower including a power of the court to reopen harsh and unconscionable transactions and amend them.

Legislation to control hire purchase and later conditional sale and credit sale was first introduced in Scotland in 1932 (the Hire Purchase and Small Debt (Scotland) Act 1932) and was followed in England by the Hire Purchase Act 1938, introduced to Parliament by Ellen Wilkinson. The latter Act regulated hire purchase and credit sale agreements where the total price (subject to certain exceptions) was not more than £100. A written agreement form had to contain specified information and the owner under the agreement was made responsible for the quality of the goods supplied. Where an agreement was terminated the hirer's liability was limited to the arrears plus (when applicable) sufficient to bring the amount paid up to half the total price. Where one-third of the total price had been paid the owner could not repossess goods without a court order, the court being given special powers in connection with actions brought under the Act. The '50%' and 'one-third' rules, as they came to be generally referred to, appear with very little change in the Consumer Credit Act.

The Advertisements (Hire Purchase) Act 1957 and its successor in

1967 provided a measure of regulation for advertisements for hire purchase and credit sale.

The next major step was the Hire Purchase Act 1964 which raised the financial limit to £2000 (it had in fact been raised once in the interim) but excluded contracts where the hirer or buyer was a body corporate. It introduced for the first time a 'pause for reflection' where a hirer or buyer signed an agreement at home or away from trade premises and required the owner to serve a 'notice of default' before seeking to recover the goods, giving seven days warning in which the hirer could bring his payments up-to-date. It also provided protection for the 'innocent private purchaser' who bought a motor vehicle not knowing it was on hire purchase.

Almost all of the provisions contained in the Hire Purchase Acts of 1932, 1938 and 1964 were subsequently consolidated in the Hire Purchase Act 1965.

The situation as it stood after passage of the 1965 Act was that hire purchase, credit sale and conditional sale were regulated by one set of Acts while moneylending was regulated by entirely different legislation. Lending by banks and 'near banks', option accounts, budget accounts, check trading and some less common forms of credit were not regulated at all. This patchwork form of regulation was widely felt to be unsatisfactory and in 1968 the Crowther Committee was set up to review the law governing consumer credit.

The report of the Crowther Committee is a wide-ranging study, and can be read with advantage even to this day Its main recommendations were as follows:

1  Since all forms of credit had a common purpose there should be one framework of law governing them all.
2  The law relating to security interests should apply equally to all forms of security.
3  There should be fuller disclosure of information in consumer credit transactions, particularly on rates of charge.
4  There should be a regulatory body charged with licensing of credit businesses and overall supervision of the consumer credit industry. Responsibility for local enforcement of the law should be given to trading standards officers.

The first, third and fourth of these recommendations were embodied in the Consumer Credit Act 1974, the Director-General of

Fair Trading being given the function of overall regulation. The second recommendation was not proceeded with.

## THE CONSUMER CREDIT ACT

As previously noted, the Consumer Credit Act 1974 is in many respects an 'enabling Act' permitting the government department responsible to make Regulations setting out the detail. It will therefore be necessary when ascertaining the law's requirements not only to examine the Act but also to refer in many cases to one (or more) sets of Regulations.

Much of the complexity of the Act is due to the rich diversity of forms of consumer credit to be found in this country.

Part I of the Act is principally devoted to specifying the responsibilities of the Director-General of Fair Trading so far as they affect consumer credit.

### To what agreements does the Act apply?

Part II of the Act defines the contracts to which the Act applies; basically these are contracts for the provision of credit (whether on a loan, hire purchase, credit sale or any other basis) where the customer or borrower is an 'individual' and the amount of the credit (excluding charges or any deposit) is £5000 or less (£15000 or less from May 1985).

'Individual' means anyone *except* a body corporate and thus, in the ordinary way, 'individual' includes not only consumers as such but also partnerships and sole traders. The Act therefore regulates a considerable number of commercial transactions as well as consumer credit in the true sense.

In addition the Act applies to contracts of hire (which includes, of course, lease and rental) where the hirer is an 'individual' in which the amount which has to be paid by the hirer to avoid any breach of the contract is £5000 or less (£15000 or less from May 1985) and the contract can last for more than three months.

Even within its upper financial limit the Act provides that certain agreements may be exempted (e.g. loans at a very low rate of charge and ordinary trade credit where the whole balance owing on one month's account has to be settled with one payment). Any agreement within the limit and not exempted is a 'regulated agreement'.

Part II of the Act also contains a mass of highly technical definitions which cannot be summarised and which, for those likely to be involved in these matters, requires detailed study. The Act distinguishes, for example, between debtor–creditor–supplier agreements which may be regarded as vendor credit agreements such as hire purchase or credit sale and in which, of course, the supplier and the creditor may be the same (but including loan agreements arranged so that a loan and a purchase of goods are effectively part of one transaction) and debtor-creditor agreements which may be regarded as agreements for an outright loan (the debtor being free to use the money how he likes). The Act also distinguishes between fixed sum credit (e.g. a loan for £500) and running account credit (e.g. a budget account) and in this Part of the Act and elsewhere makes special provision for 'linked transactions' (e.g. a maintenance agreement entered into in connection with a TV set on hire purchase). In almost every case the definitions are complex and in some they are abstruse. The various explanations given above thus represent a considerable (and therefore not altogether accurate) simplification.

Finally this part of the Act requires the Secretary of State 'to make regulations... for determining the true cost... of the credit provided'. In short he is to make regulations to provide for 'truth in lending'. The Regulations made for this purpose are described on p. 387.

## Licensing

Virtually anyone who provides consumer credit (or consumer hire) within the meaning of the Act and who provides it more than 'occasionally' will require a licence (issued by the Office of Fair Trading (OFT)) to carry on his business. This is by no means all, however, since not only will such people as credit reference agencies, debt collectors, debt adjusters and the like also require a licence but so will 'credit brokers' and this has a very extended meaning.

In general terms, anyone who introduces individuals to a source of finance (or e.g. leasing facilities) is a 'broker' for the purpose of the Act, so that quite apart from brokers as such (e.g. second mortgage brokers), any retailer whose credit business is financed by a finance house is a 'credit broker', as is, for example, a manufacturer who, having a number of unincorporated customers, is in the habit of introducing at least some of them to a finance house from time to time to obtain hire purchase or leasing. In short, the term credit broker includes many people who would not in the ordinary way regard themselves as 'brokers' at all.

Although very detailed provisions indeed are made in respect of licensing as such (Part III of the Act), only one will be mentioned here. Section 25 of the Act provides that a licensee must be 'fit' to hold a licence and, in deciding whether this is so, the Director-General can take into account whether the applicant *or any 'associate' of his* has committed any offence 'involving fraud ... or violence', has contravened the Consumer Credit legislation, has practised 'discrimination' (sex, colour, race) or has 'engaged in business practices appearing to the Director-General to be deceitful, oppressive or otherwise unfair or improper (whether unlawful or not)'.

In practice the Director-General has used his power sparingly and whilst over 100 000 licences have been issued, less than 1000 had been refused or revoked by the end of 1982. An appreciably greater number of persons have only obtained or retained their licences after giving assurances as to their future conduct and it cannot be doubted that the possibility of licensing action by the OFT is a considerable deterrent against adopting unlawful or even questionable methods of trading.

Failure to get a licence is potentially disastrous as not only is trading without a licence a criminal offence but it can also result in the trader's credit agreements being unenforceable at law.

Finance houses who take business from dealers or brokers have an additional responsibility put on them by the Act since agreements made on an introduction by an unlicensed credit broker are unenforceable at law. A finance house therefore needs to check that any dealer from whom it accepts business has a valid licence as a credit broker.

Information on the licensing system and application forms for licences can be obtained from the Office of Fair Trading, Government Buildings, Bromyard Avenue, Acton, London W3 7BB.

### True rates of charge

The Consumer Credit (Total Charge for Credit) Regulations 1980 made or required by Part II of the Act perform two functions. Firstly they prescribe what ancillary and related charges have to be regarded as forming part of the total charge for credit, for example 'option fees' in hire purchase agreements, compulsory maintenance charges, some types of insurance premiums and charges in respect of providing security for a loan.

The second function of the Regulations is to prescribe the basis for calculating the annual percentage rate of the total charge for credit, now universally known simply as the APR. This rate must take into account the amount and timing of all charges forming part of the total charge for credit and must be calculated as an 'effective rate' based on compound interest principles, a rather more complex method than the 'nominal rate' used in the 'truth in lending' legislation in the USA. The effect is that a rate of 2% per month as in a store budget account gives an APR rather more than 12 times this amount (in fact 26.8%). For hire purchase or similar transactions the APR is approximately twice the 'flat rate' commonly used in the calculation of the charges, sometimes more and sometimes less depending on the rate and period of repayment.

The Regulations also prescribe assumptions to be made in calculating the APR when not all the facts are known and require it to be shown to one place of decimals, further places being disregarded (an exact rate of 21.765% is to be shown as 21.7%). The circumstances where the APR has to be given are prescribed in the Regulations described in the next two parts of this chapter. It is always required to be included in a credit agreement document.

Tables giving values of APR for the more common forms of credit transaction are published by HM Stationery Office (the 'Consumer Credit Tables', Parts 1 to 15).

## Advertising and seeking business

Regulations governing advertising took effect in 1980. They apply to spoken as well as visual advertising of all types and provide for APR disclosure in many but by no means all credit advertisements. They divide credit advertisements (and those for hire) into three varieties—simple, intermediate and full.

A simple credit advertisement must give no indication of willingness to extend credit other than the advertiser's name and occupation. Any mention of the price of goods, etc. is forbidden. In other words it is prestige advertising only.

The intermediate credit advertisement must only show certain permitted information. If prices are shown an APR must be shown and if an APR is shown rather more information can be included than if it is not. In all cases an intermediate advertisement must indicate that the customer can obtain further written information on request.

A full credit advertisement must include a fairly extensive minimum amount of information including always the APR but can include further information if desired. For some types of credit the amount of information is not great but for hire purchase the requirements become rather cumbersome.

The Regulations require important information to be shown 'together as a whole' and prominence must be given to the APR where this must be shown. In some cases, however, information can be split up between price tickets on goods and a more general notice in the same part of the shop about the credit terms.

Section 46 of the Act prohibits 'false or misleading' advertisements whilst the Advertisements Regulations themselves ban the use of certain phrases in a misleading way.

Other Regulations establish the right of a consumer to obtain a written quotation for a credit transaction, the information to be shown being broadly similar to that required in a full credit advertisement.

The Act itself restricts 'canvassing off trade premises', in other words visits to homes by salesmen offering credit facilities (although the definition embraces a wider range of activities). Canvassing debtor–creditor agreements (i.e. the selling of cash loans door-to-door) is forbidden whilst the selling of goods or services on credit door-to-door is only permitted where a trader's licence covers him for this.

The Act forbids sending documents, circulars, etc. offering credit facilities to minors.

Finally there is a prohibition on sending 'unsolicited credit tokens'. Intended to prevent the mass mailing of credit cards without request, it also affects check trading and can impose constraints on some types of credit advertising.

## Entry into agreements

The rules governing the making of credit agreements are set out in Part V of the Consumer Credit Act and in Regulations made under it. Between them they prescribe the form and content of agreements, the giving of copies to the customer and the consumer's right to cancel some types of agreement where he signs otherwise than at trade premises.

The Act itself prescribes that an agreement will not be properly executed (and hence will usually be unenforceable against the debtor) unless a document complying with the Regulations and containing all the prescribed information is signed by the customer and by or on behalf of the creditor or owner. The document must embody all the terms of the contract (in some cases reference to another document given to the debtor is sufficient) and it must be easily legible.

The Regulations specify in considerable detail the information to be contained in agreement documents, much of which has to be set out 'together as a whole'. They prescribe the statutory statements or 'forms' setting out shortly and simply the more important rights given to the customer by the Act. They also require that the customer sign in a 'signature box' with prescribed wording drawing his attention to the nature of the contract he is signing. Separate schedules set out the information to be included in credit agreements, hire agreements and 'modifying agreements' for credit and hire. For all forms of credit agreement this includes the APR. The detail of the Regulations is not appropriate for a work of this nature. Suffice it to say that drafting of regulated agreement forms is a matter for the specialist and that care must be taken to ensure that such forms are fully and correctly completed before the customer signs. Failure to do so can lead to contracts that cannot be enforced against debtors.

The Act specifies the right of the debtor or hirer to receive copies of the agreement which he signs. Where both parties sign on the same occasion the debtor receives one copy, there and then, and the agreement becomes a binding contract right away. When, as is more common, the agreement is signed by the debtor but then has to go to head office or to the finance house for acceptance, the debtor must receive two copies, one when he signs and one following acceptance by the creditor. The agreement does not become binding on the debtor in this situation until dispatch of the second copy. Failure to observe the rules on copies can also lead to agreements being unenforceable.

## Rights of cancellation

There are two situations in which the Act allows a customer a 'pause for reflection'. The more commonly found of these applies where the customer signs an agreement at home or otherwise away from trade premises and where there have been face-to-face 'negotiations' before the agreement is made (but not where the agreement is made entirely through the post). In this situation the customer has a right to cancel the agreement which extends until five days after he receives his second copy of it as described above. Both copies of the agreement have to contain a prominent notice giving details of this right and in the (relatively uncommon) situation where a debtor gets one copy only, this must be followed by a separate 'right of cancellation notice'. Any failure to observe the rules about copies of a cancellable agreement will mean that an agreement will not only be improperly executed but will be totally unenforceable against the debtor. This right of cancellation sounds forbidding when set down on paper but in practice problems occur very rarely since a customer who genuinely wants what he has been sold will not want to cancel. The true benefit to the customer is that it discourages undesirable practices by door-to-door salesmen offering credit.

The second situation where the Act provides a pause for reflection is in respect of land mortgages or, as the Act calls them, agreements secured on land. Not all such transactions are regulated since there are wide exemptions for building societies. Many other transactions will be outside the upper financial limit of the Act. Where, however, they are regulated agreements, as is usually the case with 'second mortgages', the borrower must be given a statutory pause for reflection *before* the agreement is signed, and this will apply no matter where the agreement is signed. The reason for providing a pause before rather than after signature is because of problems if a mortgage were to be cancelled after it had been registered.

**Protection during the life of an agreement**

The nature of hire purchase contracts, together with provisions originally contained in the Hire Purchase Acts means that, where such facilities are arranged through a finance house, the hirer has the right to sue the finance house if the goods are not delivered or are faulty. This was formerly not the case with finance house loans arranged by the supplier of goods or payment by a bank credit card. The Consumer Credit Act now allows the debtor to seek redress from the creditor in two ways. Firstly, it provides that in all kinds of 'debtor–creditor–supplier' agreements the supplier is to be treated as the agent of the creditor when he makes representations about the quality of the goods or services to be financed. Secondly, in the case of point of sale loans, credit cards or similar transactions, Section 75 of the Act provides that if there is a misrepresentation or breach of contract by the supplier, the creditor shall be jointly and severally liable with the supplier (but will be able to recover from the supplier sums which have had to be paid to the debtor). This Section does not apply to hire purchase or credit sale through a finance house since the finance house takes on the role of supplier by buying the goods from the dealer and thereby incurs liability for their quality.

Part VI of the Act contains a number of other measures to protect the debtor. He has the right to demand information on the state of his account and where credit is in the form of a running account he must be sent statements of account at regular intervals. Protection is also given where, for example, a credit card is stolen or misused through no fault of the debtor. Rules provide for notice to be given to the debtor if an agreement is varied (for example where a creditor alters the rate of charge on a budget account as such agreements normally permit). Finally the Act forbids termination of an agreement solely because of the death of a debtor or hirer.

## Default and termination

A large part of the Act's consumer protection is aimed at preventing the creditor from exercising too harshly his remedies against the debtor where the latter fails to maintain his repayments or otherwise defaults on his agreement.

The first measure of protection afforded the debtor or hirer is the requirement that before the creditor or owner can terminate an agreement, demand early payment, repossess goods or enforce a security he must first serve a default notice on the debtor or hirer and allow him seven days from then in which to put right the default. Only then can he take the specified action against the debtor. Similar rules also apply to terminating an agreement or enforcing the creditor's rights where the contract allows this if no default has occurred. In any of these situations it is however permitted to prevent a debtor obtaining further credit with immediate effect, e.g. by putting a credit card on a 'stop list'.

Reference was made on p. 382 of this chapter to the '50% rule' in the Hire Purchase Acts limiting the liability of a hirer under a hire purchase agreement which was terminated and where the owner recovered the goods. This is re-enacted in the Consumer Credit Act, as is the 'one-third' rule forbidding repossession of goods on hire purchase or conditional sale agreements where one-third has been paid without obtaining a court order or the hirer's express permission given at the time. The Act also provides that a creditor or owner must not enter premises to effect repossession of goods or land without obtaining the debtor's permission or a court order.

Section 93 of the Act provides that where interest is charged on overdue payments the rate of charge shall be no higher than the APR under the agreement. This has awkward implications for those companies which offer 'interest-free" credit.

Section 101 gives a hirer under a consumer hire agreement an absolute right to terminate the agreement once it has run for 18 months. No 'minimum payment clause' requiring payment of more than 18 months rental would be given effect by the courts. Few problems exist with genuine consumer transactions where the most usual minimum hire period is 12 months but this Section could have made it commercially impossible to offer leasing facilities for goods to sole traders or partnerships. The '18 months rule' does not therefore apply in the following situations:

(a) where the rentals in any year exceed £900; or
(b) where the goods are hired for use in a business and are acquired by the owner from the supplier at the hirer's request, the supplier not being an 'associate' of the owner; or
(c) the goods are hired for the purpose of sub-hire.

## Early settlement

The Act allows a debtor under a regulated consumer credit agreement to pay off his indebtedness at any time before the end of the agreement. Regulations provide for the debtor to be given a rebate of the charges where he exercises this right. This rebate must be given not only for a voluntary early settlement but also if a balance is carried forward to a new agreement and where a debtor has to pay off the whole or part of a balance owing ahead of time. In no case, however, will a right to rebate arise until payment is made, although of course the debtor can be informed in advance of the rebate to which he will be entitled if he settles on a particular day and he has a right to demand this information.

The rebate rules do not affect hire agreements or running accounts or other transactions where no charges are to be made in respect of any period after the 'settlement date'.

The rebate to be given on an instalment transaction is calculated by the 'rule of 78', a relatively simple formula which will be familiar to many. An extended version of the formula must be used where the payments provided for under the agreement are unequal or are to be made at unequal intervals. Interpolation is not needed where settlement occurs between instalment dates except where the interval between instalments exceeds one month. Where settlement of transactions payable by weekly or monthly instalments is made between instalment dates the next instalment date becomes the 'settlement date'.

To allow the creditor to recover his 'setting up costs' he or she may calculate the rebate by reference to a date two months after the settlement date. For agreements running for more than five years only one month's deferment is allowed.

## Security

The Act controls all forms of taking security in respect of regulated agreements, whether given by the debtor, for example a charge, mortgage or pledge, or by a third party as in the case of a guarantee or indemnity. It only applies to a security given by a third party where it is given at the request of the debtor. It does not therefore affect 'recourse agreements' or other forms of indemnity given by the supplier of goods financed.

The Act and Regulations made under it impose requirements as to the form and content of guarantees and indemnities which are generally similar to those governing agreement forms (and the statutory statement of guarantor's rights is one of the longest required in any document by the Act). The guarantor must receive a copy of the guarantee when he signs and a copy of the credit or hire agreement to which it refers within 7 days of it taking effect. If these requirements are not met the guarantee will be 'ineffective' except where the creditor can obtain a court order to enforce it.

The Act gives guarantors similar rights to information as are possessed by debtors and provides that a guarantor must receive a copy of any default notice served on the debtor or hirer.

Section 113 prevents the Act being evaded by the use of security by providing that a security may not be enforced to provide a benefit greater than could be recovered direct from the debtor or hirer. There is, however, a specific exception so that an indemnity given in respect of a contract by a minor can be enforced as though the minor were of full age and capacity to contract.

The Act forbids the use of negotiable instruments (bills of exchange, cheques and promissory notes) as ways of taking security for a regulated agreement but allows cheques to be used as a means of payment only.

## Judicial control

For all practical purposes it is the county court, or in Scotland the sheriff court, which has jurisdiction in respect of contracts regulated by the Consumer Credit Act.

The Act specifies various types of order which the court can make. The first listed is the 'enforcement order' which a creditor will have to obtain if he wishes to enforce a contract despite some breach of the strict requirements of the Act. Some more serious breaches of the Act's requirements cannot however be remedied by an enforcement order, particularly where a right of cancellation exists as was mentioned earlier.

A debtor or hirer can ask the court for a Time Order allowing him time to bring his payments up to date or remedy any breaches of an agreement. In the case of a hire purchase or conditional sale agreement the order can deal with sums not yet due. For other transactions it can only deal with arrears.

In relation to hire purchase and hire agreements the court can make a 'protection order' in respect of the goods pending the actual hearing of the case. The court can also grant financial relief to a hirer under a consumer hire agreement relieving him from financial liablity where the owner recovers the goods.

The court has the power to make orders in respect of hire purchase agreements for return of the goods or (more rarely) for the hirer to keep some goods and return the rest.

The court can suspend any of these orders or make any terms of the order conditional on the doing of specified acts by one or other party.

In addition the court has a general power to deal with any personal credit agreement (even in excess of the top financial limit of the Act) which it holds to be 'extortionate'. For a credit bargain to be extortionate the charges must be grossly exorbitant or it must otherwise grossly contravene ordinary principles of fair dealing. The Act sets out guidelines for determining whether a bargain is extortionate and gives the court very wide powers to amend or strike down an extortionate transaction.

The court's power to reopen extortionate credit bargains has been available since 1977 but there have so far been few cases which have come to court and fewer still which have ended in victory for the debtor.

## Credit reference agencies

The Act provides a procedure whereby an individual (but not a limited company) can find out what information a credit reference agency has on file about him. This procedure comprises two parts.

Firstly, where there have been negotiations for credit (and whether or not these have resulted in credit being advanced) the customer can within 28 days make a written demand for the name and address of any credit reference agency consulted during those negotiations. The creditor must furnish this information in writing in response to the request but is not obliged to give other information. He does not have to give reasons for refusing credit or disclose any information about trade or bank references taken up since the sources of such references do not come within the Act's definition of a credit reference agency. Where a creditor takes business through a credit broker and he turns down a request for credit he must inform the credit broker of the name and address of any credit reference agency consulted so that the latter can give this information if the customer enquires of him, as the law obliges him to do.

The second part of the procedure is embodied in Sections 158 to 160 of the Act which give any individual the right to obtain a copy of the information held about him by a credit reference agency. He must give sufficient particulars to identify himself and forward a fee of £1. The credit reference agency must then give him a copy in plain English of the information held about him in full (subject to some limitation if a sole trader or partnership seeks this information).

The Regulations set out a procedure for the correction of wrong information held on file and provide that, if the individual and the credit reference agency cannot agree on a correction, either of them can approach the Office of Fair Trading for a final ruling on the matter.

## Enforcement

Some of the previous legislation on credit has failed to achieve its object because no authority had been given the task of enforcing it, an example of this being the Advertisements (Hire Purchase) Acts which were more honoured in the breach than the observance.

Under the Consumer Credit Act both the Director-General of Fair Trading and local Trading Standards Officers have responsibility for enforcement of the Act, the main day-to-day burden falling on Trading Standards Officers although the Director-General may sometimes originate prosecutions and may revoke or threaten to revoke the licence of a trader who does not abide by the Act's requirements.

The Act gives powers to Trading Standards Officers generally similar to those under other legislation such as the Trade Descriptions Acts. They can inspect and if necessary seize goods or books or records, enter premises, make test purchases and take copies of books and records. In some cases a warrant may be needed to enter premises.

The criminal offences specified in the Act do not require the prosecution to prove intent to commit them but the Act does provide that it is a valid defence to show that what took place was an accident or the fault of another person and that the defendant took all reasonable steps to prevent the breach of the law.

## OTHER LAWS

Although most of the law's requirements affecting consumer credit are contained within the Consumer Credit Act there are a number of other Acts which remain in force and which must be mentioned if this chapter is to be complete.

The Bills of Sale Acts 1878–83 regulate the taking of security on personal property and provide strict rules for the documentation and regulation of such security. If not observed such security will be void. It was indeed the existence of these Acts which led to hire purchase developing in its present form.

The one remaining part of the Hire Purchase Acts which remains in force is Part III of the Hire Purchase Act 1964. The general rule where a person buys goods from the hirer under a hire purchase agreement before the agreement is completed is that such a buyer does not obtain good title to the goods and the owner under the hire purchase agreement can recover the goods or sue for sums still owing under the agreement (or the value of the goods, whichever is less). The 1964 Act makes an exception to this rule by providing that a 'private purchaser' who buys a motor vehicle in good faith and without notice of the existence of the agreement will obtain a good title to the vehicle. The owner under the agreement cannot take action against him or against any person who buys the vehicle from him. 'Private purchaser' is defined to mean anyone other than a motor trader or a finance house active in the motor field.

The Sex Discrimination Act applies to the granting of credit as to the supply of other forms of services. It prohibits two kinds of discrimination—direct and indirect. Direct discrimination is where credit is not made available to a woman in circumstances where it would be made available to a man or where additional requirements are imposed on a woman which would not be required of a man in similar financial circumstances, for example if the customer was a woman who earned her own living and a male guarantor was required. Indirect discrimination is where the creditor sets his requirements for the granting of credit in such a way that sub-stantially fewer women can obtain credit and where there is no valid reason for setting the requirements in that way. Breach of the Act can lead to a claim for damages whilst the Equal Opportunities Commission has considerable powers to deal with any creditor whose company procedures offend against the Act's requirements.

The Race Relations Act sets out similar rules in respect to dis-crimination on grounds of race.

There is a very considerable body of case law affecting hire purchase agreements which are not regulated by the Consumer Credit Act, particularly concerning the rights of the parties following breach of an agreement.

Hire purchase agreements, both regulated and otherwise, are also affected by the law governing such matters as distress for rent and repairer's lien. The Unfair Contract Terms Act and the Consumer Transactions (Restrictions on Statements) Order 1976 apply in respect of clauses excluding (or attempting to exclude) liability where goods are defective and in many cases prevent the use of such clauses.

The VAT legislation affects credit transactions since although credit is an 'exempt supply' the supply of goods on hire purchase or credit sale is normally a taxable supply, so that such an agreement represents two supplies, a taxable supply of the goods and an exempt supply of the credit. Much complication arises from this.

From time to time 'Control Orders' are made setting minimum deposits and maximum repayment periods for hire purchase and credit sale transactions and minimum advance rentals for hiring agreements. No such orders were in force at the time of writing.

## CONCLUSION

This chapter contains no more than a brief outline of the law affecting consumer credit. Anyone regularly involved in this kind of business will need to study it in greater detail and should refer to more detailed works, a variety of which are available.

# PART IX
# COMMERCIAL CREDIT LAW

# 23

# Legal Enforcement of Contractual Rights

**M. A. Barry, Principal Lecturer, Credit Management Training**

## THE DECISION TO SUE

This usually stems from the debtor's failure to respond to normal collection techniques.

At that stage the account will have had considerable attention. Nevertheless, certain basic matters must be considered before passing an account for legal action.

### Are we dealing with a debtor?

Is the non-paying customer a debtor—a person who will not, or cannot pay—or a dissatisfied customer?

If the latter, have his complaints been investigated and resolved? Is it quite certain that the complaints are unjustified?

Remember—it may cost more to sue than to rectify the complaint.

### What is the legal status of the debtor?

It is vital to know whether the debtor is an individual, a firm or a limited company.

On this depends the way proceedings are (i) issued, (ii) served and (iii) enforced.

The necessary information should be readily available—but check it!

An over-conscientious employee may have written 'John Smith & Co. Ltd' when in fact your debtor is 'John Smith & Co.'

*(a)  Individuals.*  It is necessary to know the full name—or at least the correct surname and initials.

If the debtor is a male he can be named in proceedings by his initials, his surname and the word 'male' in brackets thereafter.

If the debtor is a female then, even if her full names are known, she must be described in any proceedings as:

(i)   married woman, or

(ii)  widow, or

(iii) spinster, or

(iv)  if a divorcee, 'femme sole'.

*(b)  Partnership.*  A partnership may be sued in the firm's name— 'John Smith & Co. (a firm)', or in the names of the partners, i.e. 'John Smith and Frederick Brown trading as John Smith & Co. (a firm)'.

*(c)  The 'one-man firm'.*  In law one person running a business under a firm name is called the 'sole proprietor'. Such a person may be sued either in his own name or in the name of the firm. The most satisfactory way is to sue as 'John Smith trading as John Smith & Co.'

*(d)  The limited company.*  A limited company must be sued in its name exactly as registered with the Registrar of Companies.

### Is the debtor worth suing?

Before credit was granted some enquiry was no doubt made as to the credit wothiness of the debtor. Check again. Any legal action will involve court fees and legal costs.

Before incurring this expense make enquiries to ascertain whether the debtor is likely to have assets to satisfy any judgment obtained.

Remember, to obtain judgment for a debt is comparatively simple. Obtaining payment under a judgment is sometimes a very different matter.

**The decision to sue—checklist**

When making the decision to sue, check the following:

1  Are we really dealing with a debtor?
2  Who is the debtor?
3  Is the debtor worth suing?

**Instructions to sue**

Having made the decision to sue, then instructions must be given to your solicitors or your legal department.

It is important that you provide them with the relevant information.

The 'herewith file—please take appropriate action' approach is not recommended. In a busy practice such instructions will go to the bottom of the pile!

A long and detailed history of your dealings with the debtor is unnecessary. All that is needed is a form letter setting out:

*1  What the claim is for.*   Claims of the nature dealt with here are almost invariably for goods sold, services rendered or work done and materials provided.

The instructions given must specify into which of these categories the claim falls. Copy invoices should be attached to the instructions.

*2  The dates on which liability arose.*   Details of the dates on which the goods were sold or the work done should be provided. The dates of invoices rendered should also be given.

*3  The amount of the claim.*   Specify exactly how much is due and ensure that the invoices submitted with the instructions agree with the total sum claimed.

*4  The legal status of the debtor.*   This will have been ascertained as part of the process of deciding to sue.

*5  General relevant detail.*   Pass on any information that will assist in recovery procedures. For example—deal with any complaints raised by the debtor that have been resolved—or proved unjustified.

6 *Copy invoices.* Submit copy invoices or statements to support the claim. Make certain they total to the amount you are claiming— and that none are missing!

### Instructions to sue—checklist

Use standard form letter of instruction (see Figure 23:1) and provide:

1 Details of what the claim is for.
2 The dates on which liability arose.
3 The amount of the claim.
4 The correct name, current address and legal status of the debtor.
5 Any other *relevant* detail.
6 Copies of invoices or statements which should show a total liability as set out under 3.

### HIGH COURT OR COUNTY COURT

The county court has jurisdiction to deal with claims up to and including £5000. Claims over that sum must be made in the High Court.

---

To:

Dear Sirs,
   Re: (Debtor's full name)
   Address/Registered office:
Please issue proceedings against the above person/firm/company.
The amount due to us is £   in respect of
Copy invoices to support the claim are herewith.
The following facts may assist in processing this matter:

Yours faithfully

---

Figure 23:1 Form letter of instructions to sue

The creditor may, if he wishes, bring a claim for a sum below £5000 in the High Court, but, in that event:

(a)   if the claim is for £650 or less, no costs will be awarded;
(b)   if the claim is below £5000 and the debtor defends, the claim may be transferred to the county court for trial;
(c)   if the claim proceeds in the High Court the creditor may be awarded only those costs he would have recovered if the action had been taken in the county court.

With the exception of certain claims under the provisions of the Hire Purchase Act 1965, the jurisdiction of the county court is limited to £1000. This means that claims for sums up to and including £1000 may be dealt with in the county court, whilst claims over that sum *must* be brought in the High Court.

Claims under £1000 may—at the wish of the creditor—be brought in the High Court. However, if the amount recovered in the High Court is less than £100 no costs will be awarded.

**Proceedings in the county court**

*(a)   Venue.*   Each county court covers a fixed area. Actions to recover debt may be commenced either:

1   in the county court in whose area the debtor resides or carries on business; *or*
2   in the county court in whose area the contract was made.

The contract will normally be made at the plaintiff's offices—and payment under the contract will normally be due at those offices.

Thus in most cases proceedings can be commenced in the court nearest the plaintiff's offices. This makes attendance at court more convenient to the plaintiff's representative. Note, however, that on application by the defendant, the court may transfer the action to the defendant's district court.

*(b)   Default summons.*   A claim for a debt or liquidated sum must be dealt with by the issue of a default summons.

*(c) Issuing the summons.* If the plaintiff (the creditor) can certify that by posting the summons to the debtor's address the court can bring it to his notice, the county court provide a form numbered N202 which is entitled Combined Request and Particulars of Claim. A specimen is shown in Figure 23:2. This form has, on the reverse, 'Notes for Guidance' which detail the information the plaintiff must provide on the form (see Figure 23:2).

In the space on the right hand side of the face of the form there is a space in which the plaintiff inserts particulars of his claim.

When using this form the plaintiff must sign a Certificate for Postal Service (see Figure 23:3).

In cases where the plaintiff cannot certify that postal service will be effective a Default Summons for Personal Service must be issued.

To issue this Summons the plaintiff completes Form N201 (see Figure 23:4) and must lodge, on a separate sheet of paper, his particulars of claim. Under this procedure he must lodge one copy of the particulars for the court, and one copy for each defendant to be served.

*(d) Particulars of claim.* This is a statement, in precise and simple terms, of how much the plaintiff is claiming, and what the claim is for. A specimen form is included in Figure 23:5.

*(e) Court fees.* These are on a sliding scale based on the value of the claim. The fees are:

> 10p for every £1 or part thereof with a minimum fee of £6 for claims up to £300.

| | |
|---|---:|
| Over £300 but less than £500 | £35 |
| Over £500 but less than £2000 | £38 |
| Over £2000 | £40 |

In addition, if the plaintiff cannot certify for service by post, a sum of £5 must be added to the court fees to cover service by the court bailiff.

### Preparing the summons

On receipt of the papers the court will issue the summons. They will allocate a reference number to the case (called a Plaint Number).

IMPORTANT BEFORE COMPLETING THIS FORM SEE INSTRUCTIONS OVERLEAF

Case Number

## COUNTY COURT

PARTICULARS OF CLAIM

Plaintiff

Plaintiff's Solicitor

Ref. No.

Defendant

Signed                    Date

What the claim is for

I apply for this action, if defended to be referred to arbitration (Mark box if appropriate)

1. Any claim for £500 or less which is defended will be referred to arbitration automatically, but the reference may be rescinded on application.
2. When a defended claim is arbitrated the right of appeal against the arbitrator's award is very limited.

JURISDICTION (DEFENDANT OUT OF DISTRICT)

The facts relied upon as showing that the cause of action arose within the district of this court are:–

If the claim is founded on a hire-purchase agreement you must state above the address where the defendant (or one of them) resided or carried on business when the contract was made.

N202 Combined request and particulars of claim for default summons (postal service only).
Order 3 Rule 3(1)

Amount claimed

Issue fee

Solicitor's costs

TOTAL

Date of issue

Date of service

By posting on the

Officer

The summons in this case has not been served having been returned by the Post Office marked "Gone away" or

Officer          Date

## Figure 23:2   Combined request and particulars of claim form

NOTES FOR GUIDANCE

Please read these notes carefully before completing the request.
IMPORTANT NOTE:
This form can only be used for issue of a default summons for postal service. It will not be accepted unless the requirements for issue are met. The form should be completed by typewriter or computer and the entries must not extend outside the boxes provided. At the discretion of the court handwritten forms may be accepted provided the information is clearly legible and otherwise complies with the requirements.

1. *Postal Service:*
   When using this form it is necessary to sign a certificate for postal service. When several summonses are to be issued at one time only one such certificate need be prepared, suitably adapted.

2. *Plaintiff:*
   Enter the plaintiff's name in full and residence or place of business.
   If the plaintiff is:
   a) Suing in a representative capacity, state in what capacity.
   b) A minor required to sue by a next friend, state the fact, and names in full, residence or place of business, and occupation of next friend.
   c) An assignee, state that fact, and name, address and occupation of assignor.
   d) Two or more co-partners suing in the name of their firm, add "A Firm".
   e) An individual trading in a name other than his own, give his own name followed by the words "trading as" and the name under which he trades.
   f) A company registered under the Companies Act, 1948, state the address of the registered office, and describe it as such.

3. *Plaintiff's Solicitor:*
   If the summons is entered by a solicitor his name, address and reference number should be entered in this box.

4. *Defendant:*
   Enter the defendant's surname, and (where known) his or her initials or names in full; defendant's residence or place of business (if a proprietor of the business). State whether male or female. State occupation (where known).
   If the defendant is:
   a) Sued in a representative capacity, state in what capacity.
   b) Two or more co-partners sued in the name of their firm, add "A Firm" or if a person carrying on business in a name other than his own name who is sued in such name add "A Trading Name".
   c) A company registered under the Companies Act, 1948, the address given must be the registered office of the company, and must be so described.

5. *What the claim is for:*
   Make a brief statement of the nature of your dispute: (e.g. goods sold and delivered, work done, money due under an agreement).

6. *Particulars of claim:*
   Give the relevant dates and sufficient other details to inform the defendant of the nature of the claim made against him. He is entitled to ask for further particulars but there should be sufficient information in the particulars given overleaf for the court and the defendant to be properly aware of the basic cause of action.

7. *Signature:*
   The person completing the form should sign and date it.

8. *Arbitration:*
   If you wish you may apply for the summons, if defended, to be dealt with by arbitration by marking the box.

9. *Jurisdiction:*
   Unless the defendant or one of the defendants resides or carries on business within the district of the court you must show that the cause of the action (i.e. the circumstances or transaction giving rise to the claim) arose wholly or partly within the district of the court. The court has jurisdiction to entertain the action pursuant to Order 4 Rule 2 of the County Court Rules 1981, if, for instance:
   a) The claim is founded on a contract made at an address within the district (the address must be stated).
   b) The claim is founded on a contract under which payment is to be made at an address within the district (the address must be stated).

10. *Amount claimed:*
    Enter the total amount you are claiming. The issue fee is based on this amount.

2602009 D 8309768 500m 6/82 P.A.D.S. Ltd.

Case Number

**Figure 23:2** *concluded*

I request that the defendants whose names and addresses are shown overleaf be served with the summons by post. I certify that I have reason to believe that the summons, if sent to the defendant(s) at the address(es) stated overleaf will come to his/their knowledge in time for him/them to comply with the requirements of it.

I/The plaintiff understand(s) that if judgment is obtained as a result of postal service and is afterwards set aside on the ground that the service did not give the defendant(s) adequate notice of the proceedings, I/the plaintiff may be ordered to pay the costs of setting aside the judgment.

DATED

Signed
Plaintiff('s solicitor)

N.219 Certificate for postal service Order 7 Rule 10(2)

**Figure 23:3   Certificate for postal service**

| IN THE | COUNTY COURT |
|---|---|

CASE No.

THIS SECTION TO BE COMPLETED BY THE COURT

Summons in form:    N.1 Fixed Amount ☐      N.2 Unliquidated ☐

Service by: Bailiff ☐   Plaintiff('s solicitors) ☐   Post (Certificate overleaf) ☐   Post (At defendant company's R.O.) ☐   Date issued ☐

Please use block capitals

**Statement of Parties**

1. PLAINTIFF'S names in full, and residence or place of business.
2. If suing in a representative capacity, state in what capacity.
3. If a minor required to sue by a next friend, state that fact, and names in full, residence or place of business, and occupation of next friend.
4. If an assignee, state that fact, and name, address and occupation of assignor.
5. If co-partners suing in the name of their firm, add "(A Firm)".
6. If a company registered under the Companies Act, 1948, state the address of registered office and describe it as such.

Plaintiff's solicitors name and address for service

Solicitor's reference

7. DEFENDANT'S surname, and (where known) his or her initials or forenames in full, defendant's residence or place of business (if a proprietor of the business).
8. Whether male or female.
9. Whether a minor (where known).
10. Occupation (where known).
11. If sued in a representative capacity, state in what capacity.
12. If co-partners are sued in the name of their firm, add "(A Firm)" or if a person carrying on business in a name other than his own name is sued in such name add "(A trading name)".
13. If a company registered under the Companies Act, 1948 is sued the address given must be the registered office of the company, and must be so described.

WHAT THE CLAIM IS FOR

AMOUNT CLAIMED.................

ISSUE FEE .........................

SOLICITOR'S COSTS ...............

TOTAL ............

[Strike out if inappropriate: I apply for this action, if defended to be referred to arbitration].

NOTES:

1. Two copies of the plaintiff's particulars of claim are required before a summons can be issued, and if there are two or more defendants to be served, an additional copy for each additional defendant.

2. Any claim for £500 or less which is defended will be referred to arbitration automatically, but the reference may be rescinded on application.

3. When a defended claim is arbitrated the right of appeal against the arbitrator's award is very limited.

4. If the defendant's address is outside the district of the court you must complete Section A overleaf.

5. The certificate in Section B overleaf should be completed and signed if service by post is required.

N.201 Request for default summons (single case) Order 3 Rule 3(1)

## Figure 23:4   Default summons for personal service form

SECTION A

This section must be completed by the plaintiff to show that the court has jurisdiction under Order 4 Rule 2 of the County Court Rules, 1981.

NOTES:–

(i) Where the claim is for the amount of any instalment or instalments due and unpaid under a hire-purchase agreement Question 3 must be answered.

(ii) Where the claim is founded on a contract for the sale or hire of goods Question 2 must be answered and if the answer is "No" Question 3 must be answered.

(iii) Where the claim is founded on contract but neither of the foregoing descriptions applies such of Questions 1, 4 and 5 as are applicable should be answered, or, if none of these are applicable Question 6 must be answered.

(iv) Where the claim is not founded on contract, Question 6 only, is applicable and must be answered.

| | |
|---|---|
| 1. Was the contract made in the district of the court, and, if so where? ... ... ...<br>(If the address given is within the district of the court no further questions need be answered) | |
| 2. Was the purchase price or rental payable in one sum? ... ... ... ... | |
| 3. Did the defendant reside or carry on business in the district of the court at the time when the contract was made and, if so, where? ... ... ... ... ... | |
| 4. Where, and how, was the order for the goods [or ] given by the defendant to the plaintiff [or assignor]? ... ... ... ... ... | |
| 5. Where was payment to be made by the defendant under the contract? ... ... | |

6. What are the facts upon which the plaintiff relies as showing that the cause of action arose wholly, or in part, in the district of the court?

SIGNED ...................................................... PLAINTIFF   DATED .................................

NOTE:–If the action is wrongly issued in this court because this section has been wrongly answered the court may transfer the action or order it to be struck out, and may order the plaintiff to pay the defendant's costs.

SECTION B    I request that the defendant(s) (1)

(1) State surname and where known initial(s) or fore-names

be served with the summons by post. I certify that I have reason to believe that the summons, if sent to the defendant(s) at the address(es) stated overleaf will come to his/their knowledge in time for him/them to comply with the requirements of it.

I/The plaintiff understand(s) that if judgment is obtained as a result of postal service and is afterwards set aside on the ground that the service did not give the defendant(s) adequate notice of the proceedings, I/the plaintiff may be ordered to pay the cost of setting aside the judgment.

DATED

Signed
Plaintiff('s solicitor)

N.219 Certificate for postal service Order 7 Rule 10(2)          8309767   1000M   6/82 UPS(A)

**Figure 23:4**  *concluded*

| | | |
|---|---|---|
| In the | County Court | Plaint No. |
| Between: | | |
| | A Creditor Ltd | Plaintiffs |
| | and | |
| | Albert William Debtor | Defendant |

Particulars of claim

The plaintiffs claim is £300 the price of goods sold and delivered.

Particulars

| | | |
|---|---|---|
| 1983 | To goods sold and delivered | |
| May | by the plaintiffs to the | |
| to | defendant on and between | |
| July | these dates. | £300 |

The plaintiffs therefore claim:

   i) £300
   ii) Costs

Dated the     day of      19

......................................
X, Y and Co.
of A.B. Buildings,
Stone Court, WC2
To: The Registrar      *Solicitors for the plaintiffs*
     The Defendant

**Figure 23:5 Specimen particulars of claim form**

The court will attach to the particulars of claim a front sheet, showing the names and address of the parties. To the back of the particulars will be attached a form on which the debtor may admit the claim, or write his defence.

Once the summons is issued the court will send to the creditors a plaint note showing the account number allocated to the claim, the date on which it was issued and details of fees paid.

**Difficulties in service**

If the bailiff cannot effect service he will advise the creditor. In that event the creditor may attempt service. It may be that process servers will be employed to trace and serve the debtor. It should be noted that process server's fees are not, as a rule, recoverable against the debtor.

In cases where the debtor is avoiding service, application can be made to the court for leave to post the summons or to advertise it.

## Steps the debtor can take

Once the summons has been served the onus is on the debtor, who may:

(i)    ignore the summons;
(ii)   admit the claim;
(iii)  defend the action;
(iv)   deliver a defence—or defence and counterclaim.

*(i) Debtor ignores summons.* If the debtor does nothing, then 14 days after service the creditor may sign judgment in default.

*(ii) Debtor files an admission.* If the debtor admits the claim, judgment can be entered. The debtor may pay the debt and scale costs into court. The court will then advise and pay the creditor.

The debtor may admit the claim and offer to pay by instalments. In doing so he will give particulars of his income and his expenses.

The creditor may write to the court accepting the offer—and judgment will be entered on that basis.

If the offer is not acceptable then the creditor writes to the court rejecting the offer and asking for a date for 'disposal'.

The court will then fix a date for the disposal of the action. This will be dealt with by the registrar. No evidence will be required—as the claim is admitted. The creditor's solicitors will attend and the debtor may be cross-examined as to his means. The registrar will then make such order for payment as he thinks appropriate.

*(iii) Defended actions.* If the claim is for £500 or less and the defendant delivers a 'defence' the action will be referred, automatically to 'informal arbitration'.

The court will fix a date for this hearing which will be held in the registrar's office and will be as informal as possible, without strict rules of evidence being applied.

The plaintiff may, on issuing a summons for any sum over £500, complete the appropriate section of the form to request that, if defended, the action be dealt with under this informal arbitration procedure.

*(iv) Debtor delivers a defence.* If the claim is for more than £500 and the plaintiff has not requested automatic arbitration, the court will, on receipt of the defence, fix a date for the pre-trial review.

The court will take the same step if the defendant, as well as denying the claim, makes some counterclaim on his own behalf. He may, for example, allege that he has not paid for the goods supplied because they were defective, and the defect caused him to suffer loss or damage. This constitutes a 'defence and counterclaim'.

### Pre-trial reviews

A pre-trial review is heard in the registrar's chambers and is, as its name suggests, a preliminary review of the case.

The registrar may order the parties to file more detailed particulars of their case and direct what documents should be made available at the trial.

The purpose is to ensure that all necessary steps to prepare the case have been taken by the parties so that on the date fixed for the hearing of the case the court's time will not be wasted.

On the pre-trial review the registrar has power to enter judgment for either party. He may also direct that the defendant pays part of the claim—if he appears to admit any part of it.

The pre-trial review also gives an opportunity for the parties to meet—and perhaps to explore terms of settlement.

If the matter is not resolved and when the registrar is satisfied that the matter is ready for trial, he will fix a date.

### Trial of the action

On the day fixed for hearing the creditors will be required to bring evidence to prove the claim—and to deal with any counterclaim.

The person giving evidence for the creditor *must* have knowledge of the claim. He or she must be competent to deal with any questions raised by the debtor, or the court.

Having incurred the expense of bringing a case to trial, do not put all this at risk on the trial. Executive's time is valuable—but someone of executive level must attend on behalf of the creditor. The office junior or junior secretary will not do!

Apart from giving evidence the representative of the creditor should be in a position to give instructions to the solicitor or barrister conducting the case.

If—at the court door—the debtor makes an offer, then the creditor's representative should have authority to reject it or accept it on behalf of the creditors.

Remember that the calibre of your witness may effect the outcome of the claim. Your witness is projecting the image of your organisation to the court—and perhaps to the press!

### Summary judgment procedure

The 'automatic arbitration' procedure is designed to speed the hearing of defended cases where less than £500 is involved.

In cases involving sums over £500 the defendant can, by delivering, or indicating an intention to deliver, a defence delay payment.

The summary judgment procedure is designed to deal with this situation, and applies to cases where the claim exceeds £500.

The plaintiff sues, and the defendant delivers a 'defence', perhaps saying: 'I did not order any goods from the plaintiffs'.

On receiving a copy of this sort of defence the court would normally fix a date for a pre-trial review.

The plaintiff may however seek to obtain judgment immediately. To do so he prepares and swears a short affidavit setting out the facts and asserting his belief that there is, in fact, no defence to the claim.

A copy is sent to the defendant and the original lodged with the court, asking for a hearing date.

This date will be fixed very quickly or, if the court have already fixed a date for the pre-trial review that date will be used to determine whether or not the defendant has a valid defence. He will be required to satisfy the court that he has, by swearing an affidavit which he must produce at the hearing, setting out the facts he relies on.

The court will consider the affidavits and, if the defendant cannot convince the court that he has a genuine defence, they will enter judgment for the plaintiffs.

A form of affidavit for use by the plaintiff in this situation is shown in Figure 23:6 and can be adapted to meet the circumstances of the particular case.

### Enforcement procedure county court

Having obtained a judgment it may be necessary to take steps to enforce it.

*(i) Execution.* For a further fee the court bailiff will seize and sell goods belonging to a judgment debtor. Sometimes the threat of a forced sale will produce payment. It must be remembered that the 'habitual debtor' is unlikely to have any goods worth selling.

Again the debtor's wife may claim that all the furniture in the house belongs to her—difficult to disprove!

Execution may be successful against partnerships or limited companies. Before incurring the costs of execution it may be worth making some local enquiries to ascertain what, if any, goods might be available to the bailiff.

*(ii) Attachment of earnings.* Under an attachment of earnings order the debtor's employer is ordered to deduct a specific weekly or monthly sum from the debtor's salary and pay it to the court.

The court will first fix a minimum figure which it is felt the debtor needs having regard to his commitments.

This sum is the debtor's 'protected earnings'. The employer is ordered to deduct from earnings in excess of the 'protected earnings' such sum as the court thinks proper.

Application for an attachment of earnings order must be made to the court for the district in which the debtor resides.

The application is made on a prescribed form and the debtor is then served with a detailed questionnaire asking details of his employment, income and outgoings.

The court may require the debtor's employers to give particulars of his earnings. On the day fixed for the hearing of the application

**Suggested wording – Affidavit supporting
a request for summary judgment**

IN THE                COUNTY COURT

BETWEEN:

A. B. Ltd.
    Plaintiffs
and
C. D. Ltd.
    Defendants

I (Full Names) of (Home address) make Oath and say as follows:

1.    I am the Credit Manager to the above named Plaintiffs, duly authorised by them to make this Affidavit on their behalf. The facts herein deposed to are within my own knowledge.

2.    I have read what purports to be a copy of the defence delivered by the above named Defendants.

3.    In that purported defence the Defendants deny placing any order with my company. Now produced and shown to me marked 'A' is a copy of a letter from the Defendants addressed to my company and dated 3rd April 1982 ordering the goods which are the subject of the Invoices set out in the particulars of claim herein.

4.    Prior to the issue of these proceedings written and telephone requests for payment were made by the Plaintiffs to the Defendants and at no time did the Defendants deny placing an order.

5.    I verily believe that there is no defence to this action, notwithstanding the delivery of the purported defence, and I respectfully ask that Judgment be entered for the Plaintiffs for the total claim and costs herein pursuant to the provisions of Order 9 Rule 14 of the County Court Rules 1981.

Sworn etc.

**Figure 23:6    Affidavit supporting a request for summary judgment**

the registrar may make an order. The creditor need not attend but may write to the court asking for such order as may seem appropriate.

If the registrar does not have sufficient detail as to the debtor's finances he may order the debtor to attend. Failure to attend may lead to the debtor's committal to prison.

The order will be directed to the employer. If the employee changes his employment the order lapses until the court serves it on the new employer.

The employer must inform the court when the debtor leaves his employment and any employer engaging an employee who has an order against him must advise the court.

There is no obligation on an employer to enquire if there is an order in force against a new employee!

As the attachment procedure applies to the debtor's earnings, it is of no effect against the self-employed. Nor will it be of any effect against a partnership or a limited company.

*(iii) Garnishee procedure.* By this procedure anyone owing money to the debtor may be ordered to pay that money to the judgment creditor.

A current bank account or a deposit account in the debtor's name may be 'garnisheed'; a Post Office savings account may *not.*

To proceed, the creditor swears an affidavit alleging that the party to be 'garnisheed' is indebted to the creditor. A summons will then be issued—and must be served on the prospective 'garnishee'.

The 'garnishee' may pay the sum due into court; in default of payment the matter will come before the court for hearing and determination.

*(iv) Bankruptcy.* If the debtor is in business or is a company director, bankruptcy procedure may be effective.

If the amount due under the judgment is £750 or more, the debtor may be adjudicated bankrupt.

The creditor may issue a bankruptcy notice. The notice is issued either in the county court having bankruptcy jurisdiction for the debtor's area or, if the debtor resides in the London bankruptcy area, in the High Court.

The creditor prepares the bankruptcy notice, and a form of request. These documents are lodged with the court, and the bankruptcy notice will be sealed and signed by the registrar.

The notice must be served on the debtor, in person.

Thereafter the debtor has seven days in which to pay the debt or to satisfy the court that the debt is disputed.

In default he will have committed an act of bankruptcy. Any creditor may then present a petition, asking the court to declare the debtor bankrupt.

If, on the hearing of the petition, the court are satisfied that the debtor is insolvent a receiving order will be made.

The debtor's affairs will then be administered by the official receiver in bankruptcy. Usually forms will be sent to all creditors asking them to file proofs of their debt.

The official receiver will manage the financial affairs of the debtor with a view to providing payment for the benefit of all creditors.

*(v) Charging orders.* If the debtor has any interest in property or land a creditor may apply for an order imposing a charge on it.

Application is made to the court, supported by an affidavit alleging that the debtor is the owner of the asset to be charged.

If the court are satisfied that the debtor has a chargeable interest an 'Order Nisi' will be made. This directs that unless, within a specified time, the debtor shows cause to the contrary, a final order, an 'Order Absolute' be made.

This order is served on the debtor with notice of the date on which the Order Absolute will be determined.

After further consideration the court will either discharge the order—or make it absolute.

If the order is made absolute it must, to be effective, be registered as a Land Charge at the Land Charges Registry.

The charge may then remain on file until such time as the debtor attempts to dispose of the land or it may be enforced.

Enforcement will entail an application to the court for an order for the sale of the property.

A charging order may also be obtained over stocks and shares held by the debtor. The procedure for obtaining such an order is as described in respect of property or land.

*(vi) Appointing a receiver.* If the debtor is receiving rents, or

income from trust funds, the court may, on application of the creditor, appoint a receiver.

The receiver will 'receive' the income normally 'received' by the debtor. The receiver is allowed a proper salary or fee for his services and the balance is payable to the creditor.


## HIGH COURT PROCEDURE

Proceedings to recover debts in the High Court are commenced by the issue of a writ. This is a pre-printed form with space for the names of the parties and particulars of the claim (see Figure 23:7). When issuing a writ the Plaintiff must also prepare a form of Acknowledgement of Service for the use of the debtor.

This form (see Figure 23:8) consists of three pages: Directions for Acknowledgement of Service; Notes for Guidance; and a tear-off section, Acknowledgement of Service.

Two top copies of the writ, and copies of the acknowledgement forms for each defendant are taken to the High Court, or the District Registry Office and the court fee of £55 is paid.

The court seal and date the writ, and give it a number. The writ is now 'issued' but must next be 'served' on the defendant.

### Service

The plaintiff is responsible for serving the writ. Service on a limited company is effected by sending a copy of the writ and a set of acknowledgement forms by first class post, addressed to the company at its registered office address.

An individual may be served by handing the documents to him personally, by post, or by putting them in an envelope addressed to the debtor, and putting it through the letter-box at his address.

If service is effected by post the court 'allow' seven days for it to come to the defendant's notice.

### Procedures after service

After service the defendant has 14 days to complete and return the Acknowledgement of Service. In doing so he can:

**Legal Enforcement of Contractual Rights**

COURT FEES ONLY

Writ indorsed
with Statement
of Claim
[Liquidated
Demand]
(O.6, r. 1)

# IN THE HIGH COURT OF JUSTICE

19   .— .—No.

## Queen's Bench Division

[             **District Registry**]

**Between**

Plaintiff

AND

Defendant

(1) Insert name.   **To the Defendant(¹)**

(2) Insert address.   of (²)

**This Writ of Summons** has been issued against you by the above-named Plaintiff in respect of the claim set out on the back.

Within 14 days after the service of the Writ on you, counting the day of service, you must either satisfy the claim or return to the Court Office mentioned below the accompanying **Acknowledgment of Service** stating therein whether you intend to contest these proceedings.

If you fail to satisfy the claim or to return the Acknowledgment within the time stated, or if you return the Acknowledgment without stating therein an intention to contest the proceedings the Plaintiff may proceed with the action and judgment may be entered against you forthwith without further notice.

(3) Complete and delete as necessary.

Issued from the (³) [Central Office] [       District Registry] of the High Court this      day of             19

NOTE:—This Writ may not be served later than 12 calendar months beginning with that date unless renewed by order of the Court.

## IMPORTANT

Directions for Acknowledgment of Service are given with the accompanying form.

# Figure 23:7 Example of a writ

**Commercial Credit Law**

## Statement of Claim

The Plaintiffs claim is for

(Signed)

---

If within the time for returning the Acknowledgment of Service, the Defendant
pay     the amount claimed and £                    for costs and, if the Plaintiff
obtain     an order for substituted service, the additional sum of £
further proceedings will be stayed. The money must be paid to the Plaintiff   ,   h
Solicitor   or Agent

(1) If this Writ was
issued out of a
District Registry.
this indorsement
as to place where
the cause of action
arose should be
completed

(2) Delete as
necessary

(3) Insert name of
place.

(4) For
phraseology of this
indorsement where
the Plaintiff sues in
person, see
*Supreme Court
Practice*, vol 2,
para 3

($^1$) [($^2$) [The cause] [One of the causes] of action in respect of which the Plaintiff
claim     relief in this action arose wholly or in part at ($^3$)
in the district of the District Registry named overleaf.]

---

($^4$) **This Writ** was issued by

of
[Agent for
of                                                                                    ]
Solicitor     for the said Plaintiff   whose address     ($^2$) [is] [are]

---

High Court A2A

## Figure 23:7 *concluded*

Acknowledgment
of Service
of Writ
of Summons
(Queen's Bench)

# IN THE HIGH COURT OF JUSTICE    19   .—   .—No.

Queen's Bench Division

[                                          District Registry]

*The adjacent heading should be completed by the Plaintiff*

**Between**

                                                                    Plaintiff

                              AND

                                                                    Defendant

**If you intend to instruct a Solicitor to act for you, give him this form IMMEDIATELY. Please complete in black ink.**

**IMPORTANT.** Read the accompanying directions and notes for guidance carefully before completing this form. If any information required is omitted or given wrongly, THIS FORM MAY HAVE TO BE RETURNED. Delay may result in judgment being entered against a Defendant whereby he or his solicitor may have to pay the costs of applying to set it aside.

---

*See Notes 1, 3, 4 and 5*   1    State the full name of the Defendant by whom or on whose behalf the service of the Writ is being acknowledged.

---

2    State whether the Defendant intends to contest the proceedings (*tick appropriate box*) ☐  yes                                              ☐  no

---

*See Direction 3*   3    If the claim against the Defendant is for a debt or liquidated demand, AND he does not intend to contest the proceedings, state if the Defendant intends to apply for a stay of execution against any judgment entered by the Plaintiff (*tick box*)                          ☐  yes

---

*See Direction 4*   4    If the Writ of Summons was issued out of a District Registry and

    (*a*)   the Defendant's residence, place of business or registered office (if a limited company) is NOT within the district of that District Registry

            AND

    (*b*)   there is no indorsement on the Writ that the Plaintiff's cause of action arose wholly or in part within that district,

    state if the Defendant applies for the transfer of the action (*tick box*)  ☐  yes

*State which Registry*   If YES, state—                    ☐  to the Royal Courts of Justice, London :
(*tick appropriate box*)                   OR
                                           ☐  to the*                              District Registry

---

*† Where words appear between square brackets, delete if inapplicable. Insert "Defendant in Person" if appropriate*

**Service of the Writ is acknowledged accordingly**

(*Signed*)

†[Solicitor] [Agent for

Address for service *(See notes overleaf)*

---

*Please complete overleaf*

## Figure 23:8   Acknowledgement of service form

**425**

# Notes for Guidance

1. Each Defendant (if there are more than one) is required to complete an Acknowledgment of Service and return it to the appropriate Court Office.

*Not applicable if the Defendant is a Company served at its Registered Office.

*[2. For the purpose of calculating the period of 14 days for acknowledging service, a writ served on the Defendant personally is treated as having been served on the day it was delivered to him and a writ served by post or by insertion through the Defendant's letter box is treated as having been served on the seventh day after the date of posting or insertion.]

3. Where the Defendant is sued in a name different from his own, the form must be completed by him with the addition in paragraph 1 of the words "sued as (*the name stated on the Writ of Summons*)".

4. Where the Defendant is a **FIRM** and a Solicitor is not instructed, the form must be completed by a **PARTNER** by name, with the addition in paragraph 1 of the description "partner in the firm of (                    )" after his name.

5. Where the Defendant is sued as an individual **TRADING IN A NAME OTHER THAN HIS OWN**, the form must be completed by him with the addition in paragraph 1 of the description "trading as (                    )" after his name.

6. Where the Defendant is a **LIMITED COMPANY** the form must be completed by a Solicitor or by someone authorised to act on behalf of the Company, but the Company can take no further step in the proceedings without a Solicitor acting on its behalf.

7. Where the Defendant is a **MINOR** or a **MENTAL** Patient, the form must be completed by a Solicitor acting for a guardian *ad litem*.

8. A Defendant acting in person may obtain help in completing the form either at the Central Office of the Royal Courts of Justice or at any District Registry of the High Court or at any Citizens' Advice Bureau.

9. A Defendant who is NOT a Limited Company or a Corporation may be entitled to Legal Aid. Information about the Legal Aid Scheme may be obtained from any Citizens' Advice Bureau and from most firms of Solicitors.

10. These notes deal only with the more usual cases. In case of difficulty a Defendant in person should refer to paragraphs 8 and 9 above.

**Figure 23:8** *continued*

Acknowledgment
of Service
of Writ
of Summons
(Queen's Bench)
(O.12,r.3)

## Directions for Acknowledgment of Service

1. The accompanying form of **ACKNOWLEDGMENT OF SERVICE** should be detached and completed by a Solicitor acting on behalf of the Defendant or by the Defendant if acting in person. After completion it must be delivered or sent by post to the District Registrar(*)

(*) *Insert address*

2. A Defendant who states in his Acknowledgment of Service that he intends to contest the proceedings **MUST ALSO SERVE A DEFENCE** on the Solicitor for the Plaintiff (or on the Plaintiff if acting in person).

If a Statement of Claim is indorsed on the Writ (i.e. the words "Statement of Claim" appear at the top of the back of the first page), the Defence must be served within 14 days after the time for acknowledging service of the Writ, unless in the meantime a summons for judgment is served on the Defendant.

If a Statement of Claim is not indorsed on the Writ, the Defence need not be served until 14 days after a Statement of Claim has been served on the Defendant. If the Defendant fails to serve his defence within the appropriate time, the Plaintiff may enter judgment against him without further notice.

3. **A STAY OF EXECUTION** against the Defendant's goods may be applied for where the Defendant is unable to pay the money for which any judgment is entered. If a Defendant to an action for a debt or liquidated demand (i.e. a fixed sum) who does not intend to contest the proceedings states, in answer to Question 3 in the Acknowledgment of Service, that he intends to apply for a stay, execution will be stayed for 14 days after his Acknowledgment, but he must, within that time, **ISSUE A SUMMONS** for a stay of execution, supported by an affidavit of his means. The affidavit should state any offer which the Defendant desires to make for payment of the money by instalments or otherwise.

4. **IF THE WRIT IS ISSUED OUT OF A DISTRICT REGISTRY** but the Defendant does not reside or carry on business within the district of the registry and the writ is not indorsed with a statement that the Plaintiff's cause of action arose in that district, the Defendant may, in answer to Question 4 in the Acknowledgment of Service, apply for the transfer of the action to some other District Registry or to the Royal Courts of Justice.

**Figure 23:8** *concluded*

(a)    admit the debt;
(b)    admit the debt but ask for a 'stay of execution';
(c)    indicate his intention to defend.

If the defendant admits the debt the plaintiff may apply for judgment. If, in admitting the debt the defendant asks for a 'stay of execution' the plaintiff may apply for judgment but cannot take any steps to enforce it.

Within that 14 days the defendant must file an affidavit giving particulars of his assets, expenditure and income and make an offer for payment by instalments. If the plaintiff accepts the offer, payments will be ordered on that basis. If he rejects the offer the court will make such order as they think appropriate.

If the defendant fails to file his affidavit within the 14 days the plaintiff at the expiration of that period, may seek to enforce the judgment.

If the defendant, in his Acknowledgement of Service, indicates that he intends to defend he has 14 days in which to deliver it. The 14 days runs from the date the court receive the completed Acknowledgement of Service.

If he fails to deliver it within that time the plaintiff may apply for 'judgment in default of defence'.

If the defendant simply ignores the writ and does not return the Acknowledgement of Service then, 14 days after service (21 days if service effected by post) the plaintiff may apply for judgment. In doing so he must prove that the writ has been served. He does this by means of an affidavit showing the date and method of service which he files at the court office.

### Summary judgment procedure

The defendant, by indicating his intention to defend, gains time.

The summary judgment procedure in the High Court operates in the same way as in the county court.

Because this procedure is governed by Order 14 of the Rules of the Supreme Court it is generally referred to as 'Order 14 procedure'.

It is a very useful means of:

(a)    preventing a debtor from gaining time;
(b)    obtaining judgment quickly.

## Defended actions

If the defendant delivers a defence or a defence and counterclaim, the action will proceed to trial.

Once the creditor's solicitors are satisfied that the matter is ready for trial they issue a 'Summons for Directions'.

They must, in that summons specify any particular directions they require. Such things as documents that should be agreed, expert witnesses to be called, and the probable length of the hearing must be set out.

The debtor may ask for any directions he requires.

The summons is heard by a master and is similar to the pre-trial review procedure in the county court.

## Preparation for trial

In matters which proceed to trial in the High Court it is usual to brief counsel to attend to argue the case.

The creditor's solicitors, when they have concluded the preliminary preparations for trial, will send all the papers to counsel to enable him to 'Advise on Evidence'.

Counsel will then advise as to the witnesses that should be called and the documents that should be made available to the court.

The creditors will have to arrange for the appropriate witnesses to attend court on their behalf to prove the claim.

## Enforcement procedures

The procedures for enforcing judgments through the High Court are similar to the county court procedures.

However, the High Court has no procedure for collecting money by instalments and passing it to the creditor. Nor will the High Court order payment by instalments. Any arrangement for instalment payments must be made between the parties—and paid direct.

The High Court has no bailiffs to enforce execution. A writ of execution is enforced by the Sheriff of the county in which the defendant resides.

As has been noted, attachment of earnings procedure must be taken in the county court for the district in which the debtor resides. Proceedings may be transferred to the appropriate county court to enable the creditor to take attachment procedure.

## BILLS OF EXCHANGE

The law relating to bills of exchange is set out in the Bills of Exchange Act 1882. The Act deals with bills, cheques and promissory notes only.

A bill of exchange is defined by Section 3 of the Act as 'an unconditional order in writing addressed by one person to another, signed by the person giving it, requiring the person to whom it is addressed to pay on demand, or at a fixed or determinable future time, a sum certain in money to, or to the order of, a specified person, or to bearer'.

A bill of exchange may be either a cheque, or a promissory note, or bank notes.

### Cheques

A cheque is a bill of exchange drawn on a banker, payable on demand. It must be payable to, or to the order of a specified person, or to the bearer.

Anyone endorsing a cheque is, usually, liable with the drawer.

A cheque must be presented for payment. If it is dishonoured then notice to that effect should be given to the drawer. There is no statutory form of notice but a draft is at Figure 23:9.

If a debtor pays his debt by cheque and the cheque is dishonoured, the creditor may sue for the debt—or in respect of the dishonour.

Whereas a debtor may be able to raise defences as to the quality of goods sold or services rendered, there is—prima facie—no defence to a claim on a dishonoured cheque.

### Promissory notes

As defined in Section 83 of the Act, a promissory note is an

---

Notice of dishonour

To: The Debtor

Dear Sir,
We write to give you notice that your cheque in the sum of £    drawn in our favour on XY Bank Ltd, KP Branch and dated    has been dishonoured on presentation.
Unless the sum of £   is in our hands in cash within seven days of today's date, we shall immediately thereafter, and without further notice, take such steps against you as are available to us.
Yours faithfully

---

**Figure 23:9   Notification of a dishonoured cheque**

unconditional promise in writing made by one person to another signed by the maker, engaging to pay, on demand or at a fixed or determinable future time, a sum certain in money to—or to the order of a specified person or to bearer.

The consideration is usually expressed as 'for value received' but consideration need not—in fact—be specified.

The promissory note may stipulate payment by instalments, with a proviso that in default of payment of one instalment the total balance due becomes payable forthwith.

As a 'negotiable instrument' the note may be endorsed—and the endorsee will become liable.

The signature to a promissory note is often witnessed. In fact this is not a legal requirement.

Bank notes

Bank notes are a variety of promissory note. They are, in England, issued only by the Bank of England for fixed sums as approved by the Treasury. Bank notes are always expressed as payable to bearer on demand.

## SALE OF GOODS

A contract of sale of goods is governed by the Sale of Goods Acts 1893 and 1979 which define a contract of sale as 'a contract whereby the seller transfers or agrees to transfer the property in goods to the buyer for a money consideration called the price'.

## Delivery

The place of delivery is, unless the contract expressly varies it, the place of business of the seller.

If the seller agrees to send the goods by carrier then delivery to the carrier is prima facie delivery to the buyer.

## Passing title

Title passes when the parties intend it to pass. In the absence of any express or implied terms in the contract, the Sale of Goods Act specifies the following:

*(a) Unconditional contracts.* Where the goods are ready for delivery property passes immediately, even if delivery or payment is delayed.

*(b) Goods sold on approval or 'sale or return'.* The title passes when the buyer approves of the goods or does something to show that he accepts them. He will be deemed to have approved of the goods if he retains them without giving notice that he rejects them within a reasonable time.

*(c) Where goods are to be measured or weighed.* In these cases title will pass only when the goods are so weighed or measured—and when notice is then given to the buyer.

*(d) Goods to be manufactured and sold by description.* Title passes when goods of that description, fit for delivery, are unconditionally allocated to the contract by one party with the express or implied assent of the other.

If the seller allocates goods—and gives notice to the buyer then, unless the buyer objects within a reasonable time it will be assumed that he agrees, and title will pass.

*(e)   Where the seller clearly imposes conditions.*   Title will not pass until the conditions are met.

Rules (a) to (e) apply only in the absence of a different intention, express or implied in the contract. In the event of any dispute a court will look at the whole contract.

## Form of contract

Contracts for sale may be made in writing or orally, or partly in writing and part orally. A written contract may be varied orally.

## Rights of the unpaid seller

A seller who has not been paid the whole of the agreed price has certain remedies.

*(i)   Stoppage 'in transit'.*   In the event of the insolvency of the buyer, the unpaid seller has the right to stop delivery of goods in the hands of the carrier. This remedy cannot be used if delivery has been completed.

*(ii)   Lien.*   This is the right of the unpaid seller who still has possession of the goods to retain them until the sum due to him is paid. The remedy is lost if the goods have been delivered to a carrier for transmission to the buyer, or if the buyer or his agent has lawfully gained possession of the goods.

If goods are stopped in transit or retained by the seller claiming a lien the contract of sale is still in effect. The seller may resell only:

(a)   if the goods are perishable; *or*
(b)   when the seller gives notice of his intention to resell and such notice is ignored; *or*
(c)   where the seller has, by his contract, reserved the right to resell.

The general remedy of the unpaid seller is to sue for the price.

In recent years sellers have taken advantage of their right to 'retain' title in goods delivered to the buyer, but not paid for. They have inserted a clause in their Conditions of Sale to this effect and, where it can be shown that the buyer was made aware of this condition, and when the seller can identify his goods, the clause, by allowing the unpaid seller to take back his goods has enabled him to reduce his loss.

'Retention clauses' as they are called need to be very carefully drafted to be of effect.

# 24

# Receiverships and Liquidations

**M. A. Barry, Principal Lecturer, Credit Management Training**

## LIMITED COMPANIES

The formation, management and winding-up of limited companies is governed by the Companies Act 1948.

The Act is a complete statement of the law relating to limited companies, and was subject to amendment by the Act of 1967.

The 1967 Act abolished the status of the 'Exempt Private Company'. All companies are now required to file balance sheets and accounts with their annual returns.

Another important provision of the 1967 Act is the power given to the Board of Trade to investigate the affairs of a company.

The Companies Act of 1981 made further significant changes, particularly by specifying the form and content of balance sheets and accounts filed at Companies House and requiring clearer public identification as to whether a company was a private or public limited company.

### Kinds of limited company

There are four kinds of limited company: (i) statutory; (ii) chartered; (iii) unincorporated; (iv) registered. Today the most common form of trading company is the registered company.

*(i) A statutory company.* This is a company created by Act of Parliament, such as a public utility, e.g. The Water Board.

*(ii)   A chartered company.*   This is the name given to a company created by the grant of a Royal Charter, e.g. the Bank of England.

*(iii)   An unincorporated company.*   This is a company created by registration with the Registrar of Friendly Societies, e.g. building societies and housing associations.

*(iv)   A registered company.*   A registered company is created by the registration of the documents prescribed by the Companies Act with the Registrar of Companies.

A registered company may be limited by shares, or by guarantee. There is also an 'unlimited company'. In such a company every member is personally liable to meet the debts of the company. This liability continues for 12 months after determination of membership.

## Private and public companies

*(i)   A private limited company.*   A private limited company is one which cannot offer shares for sale to the public. Nor must it invite the public to subscribe to a debenture.

The transfer of shares is restricted and the number of members must not exceed 50.

A private limited company may be formed by as few as two members.

*(ii)   A public limited company.*   A public limited company is one which offers shares to the public and may invite the public to subscribe to a debenture.

A minimum of seven members are required to subscribe to shares to form the company.

The company is subject to strict rules as to the disclosure of information relating to shares and finances to all members and the holding of 'statutory' meetings to report to members.

The 1981 legislation requires a public limited company to display the letters 'plc' in its name, e.g. National Westminster Bank plc, and thus to identify itself as a public limited company.

## Company formation

The limited company is formed—'incorporated'—by the persons concerned called the 'promoters', preparing and lodging the requisite documents with the Registrar of Companies. The objects of the company are set out in the Memorandum of Association.

The Memorandum of Association will define:

1 The company name.
2 The objects, and powers of the company.
3 The situation of the registered office.
4 Details of the share capital.
5 The fact that the liability of members is limited.

The Articles of Association will define:

1 The rules for the conduct and management of the company.
2 The powers of the directors.
3 The way in which assets are dealt with if the company is wound up.

## The officers of the company

The 'officers' are the directors and the secretary. Every public company must have at least two directors. A private company may trade with only one.

Every company must have a secretary. Although a private company may have only one director, such sole director cannot also be the secretary.

## What is a company?

A limited company is an association of people incorporated under one of the four heads mentioned on p. 435.

A company is a legal entity existing quite apart from its members. It is created by law, its functioning is governed by law and it can be brought to an end only by due process of law.

## The company seal

Every company must have a seal with its name engraved on it. The seal is used to authenticate legal documents requiring to be executed by the company.

## The registered office

Section 107 of the 1948 Act directs that, from the 14th day after its incorporation, a company must have a registered office to which all notices and communications may be sent.

Notice of the situation of that office must be filed with the Registrar of Companies.

## The share capital of the company

The issued share capital consists of the shares taken up by members. The authorised capital is the total amount of shares the company is authorised to issue.

For example, the authorised capital may be £100, divided into 100 shares of £1 each. The issued share capital may be £10—each of two officers of the company taking up 5 × £1 shares.

The liability of a shareholder is limited to any sums they owe the company for shares sold to them.

A company may increase its capital. To do so will require a resolution of a general meeting of the company.

## Debentures

A debenture is a document, usually under seal, which is evidence of a charge created by the company. There are two classes of charge:

(a) A fixed charge, which is a charge on specified assets of the company.
(b) A floating charge, or charge on the assets, stock, uncalled capital and book debts of the company.

A debenture holder may, if he is unpaid:

(a) sue for repayment;
(b) foreclose;
(c) present a petition to wind up the company;
(d) appoint a receiver.

## The company in operation

The directors of the company have, subject to the limitations laid down in the articles of association, full power to manage the company and conduct its day-to-day business.

*(i) Contracts.* A limited company may, by Section 32 of the Companies Act, contract in exactly the same way as an individual.

*(ii) Resolutions.* A company acts either as a result of a resolution passed in general meeting or by resolution of the directors at a board meeting.

There are three classes of resolution that the members of a limited company may pass at a general meeting:

| | | |
|---|---|---|
| (a) | *Ordinary:* | an ordinary resolution requires only a simple majority of members voting. All business of the company may be dealt with by ordinary resolution. |
| (b) | *Extraordinary:* | an extraordinary resolution requires a three-quarters majority of members who vote. It is required for special purposes only such as winding up. |
| (c) | *Special:* | a special resolution can only be passed at a meeting after 21 days' notice of such a meeting has been given. A special resolution is required to alter the name of the company or its objects. |

*(iii) Accounts.* Section 147 of the Companies Act 1948 directs that every company keeps proper books of account with respect to:

(a) All sums of money received and expended by the company and the matters in respect of which the receipt and expenditure takes place.

(b)   All sales and purchases of goods by the company.

(c)   The assets and liabilities of the company.

Section 149 of the Act directs that 'Every balance sheet of the company shall give a true and fair view of the state of the company at the end of its financial year and every profit and loss account of a company shall give a true and fair view of the profit or loss of the company for the financial year'.

The eighth schedule to the Act sets out the detailed information to be disclosed in the accounts.

Sections 155, 156 and 157 of the Act stipulate the requirements as to the signature of balance sheets by the directors of the company and the requirement of an auditor's report and a director's report.

### Meeting of the company

Every company must hold an annual general meeting to consider the annual accounts, reports and other relevant matters. Each member is entitled to receive 21 days' notice of the meeting with copies of the balance sheet and accounts.

An extraordinary general meeting may be held at any time to conduct business which cannot wait until the next annual general meeting.

The company may call such a meeting but members, provided they hold one-tenth of the paid-up capital, may demand that the directors call such a meeting.

### The annual return

Section 124 of the 1948 Act requires every company to file an annual return with the Registrar of Companies. The return must be filed within 42 days of the annual general meeting, and must be signed by a director and the secretary.

The annual return must contain the information required by the sixth schedule of the Act and must show, among other things:

(a) the address of the registered office;
(b) particulars of share capital;
(c) details of mortgages and charges;
(d) particulars of the directors and the secretary.

A copy of the audited accounts must also be attached to the return for filing.

## WINDING-UP PROCEDURES

Just as a company may only be created by operation of law, so its existing may only be terminated by process of law. This termination is known as winding-up.

Section 211 of the 1948 Act directs that the winding-up of a company may be either:

(a) by the court; *or*
(b) voluntary; *or*
(c) subject to the supervision of the court.

### Winding-up by the court

A company may be wound up by the court when:

(i) The company has by special resolution resolved that the company be wound up by the court.
(ii) Default is made in holding any statutory meeting or delivering any statutory report.
(iii) The company does not commence trading within a year of incorporation—or suspends business for one year.
(iv) The number of members falls below the statutory minimum.
(v) The company is unable to pay its debts.
(vi) The court considers it just and equitable that the company should be wound up.

### Voluntary winding-up

Section 278 of the 1948 Act determines the circumstances in which a company may be voluntarily wound up. These are:

(a)  When the period, if any, fixed for the duration of the company by the articles expires, or the event, if any, occurs on the occurrence of which the articles provide that the company is to be dissolved, and the company in general meeting has passed a resolution requiring the company to be wound up voluntarily.

(b)  If the company so resolves by special resolution.

(c)  If the company resolves by special resolution that it cannot by reason of its liabilities continue in business and that it is advisable to wind up.

If the company passes a resolution for voluntary winding-up, notice of that resolution must be published in the *London Gazette.*

A voluntary winding-up commences at the time of the passing of the necessary resolution. The company shall thereupon cease to carry on business except as may be required for the beneficial winding-up thereof.

*(i) Declaration of solvency.* In a voluntary winding-up the directors may make a statutory declaration to the effect that, having investigated the affairs of the company, they have the opinion that it will be able to pay its debts within 12 months.

If such a declaration is made the winding-up proceeds as a 'members' voluntary winding-up'.

In the absence of that declaration the winding-up proceeds as a 'creditors' voluntary winding-up'.

**Members' voluntary winding-up**

This is governed by Sections 284–291 of the 1948 Companies Act.

*(i) Appointment of liquidator.* The company in general meeting must appoint a liquidator. His appointment is often made at the same general meeting at which the resolution to wind-up is passed.

A body corporate may not be appointed as liquidator.

*(ii) Duties and powers of the liquidator.* A liquidator must pay the debts and adjust the rights of the contributories. He must realise and distribute the assets of the company in the following order:

(a)  in payment of all the costs of liquidation including his own remuneration;

(b)  in satisfaction of the company's liabilities *pari passu;*

(c)  in distribution among the members as provided by the articles of association.

The liquidator is an officer of the company and may summon meetings of the company to obtain approval of special or extra-ordinary resolutions.

If the winding-up continued for more than one year he must call a general meeting at the end of the first year to present an account of his conduct of the affairs of the company during the year.

The liquidator may, with the authority of an extraordinary resolution of the company, take and use all the powers given to a liquidator in a winding-up by the court of:

(a)  paying any class of creditors in full; and

(b)  compromising claims by and against the company.

The liquidator may, without any other authority than his appointment, exercise any *other* power given to a liquidator in a winding-up by the court to:

(a)  take and defend actions in court in the name of the company;

(b)  carry on the business of the company and sell the property of the company.

*(iii) Liquidator's remuneration.*   This is fixed by the company in general meeting.

*(iv) Books and accounts.*   The liquidator is required to keep accounts of his conduct of the company's business. He is required to make up a final account when the affairs of the company are fully wound up.

In addition the liquidator must submit certain specified information to the Registrar of Companies, reporting the stages of the liquidation.

If the liquidator has received nothing and made no payments by the time his report is required, this information must be submitted to the Registrar.

## Creditors' voluntary winding-up

If the directors are of the opinion that the company, by reason of its liabilities should be wound up and, on the basis that they are unable to complete a Declaration of Solvency, the winding-up proceeds as a 'creditors' voluntary winding-up'.

The procedure is governed by Sections 292–300 of the Companies Act 1948.

*(i)  Meeting of creditors.*  The company must convene and advertise a meeting of creditors. At that meeting the directors must present a full statement of the financial position of the company, with a list of creditors and the estimated amount of their claims.

The creditor or the members may nominate a liquidator. If the creditors nominate a person other than the person nominated by the members then the *creditor's nominee* shall be the liquidator. The creditors may, if they think fit, appoint, in addition, a committee of inspection.

*(ii)  Committee of inspection.*  The committee of inspection consists of creditors and contributories or persons holding their power of attorney.

The committee has powers to supervise the liquidation and the administration and distribution of the assets.

The liquidator must in general follow the directions given to him by the committee. The committee may also control the liquidator's remuneration.

*(iii)  Duties and powers of the liquidator.*  Subject to the committee of inspection, the liquidator may exercise all the powers set out above, including those available to a liquidator in a winding-up by the court.

However to exercise the power to (a) pay any class of creditor in full, and, (b) compromise claims by and against the company, he must obtain either the sanction of the committee of inspection or of the court.

The duties of the liquidator are the same as those set out above.

*(iv)  Books and accounts.*  The liquidator must keep such books of

account as the committee of inspection direct. If there is no committee he must keep such as the creditors direct.

All such books are to be open to the inspection of the committee or any creditor.

## The creditors

Any creditor who could prove in a winding-up by the court is entitled to prove in a voluntary winding-up.

Certain debts of the company must be paid in priority to all others. These are detailed at length in Section 319 of the Companies Act 1948.

## The court

The liquidator or any creditor or contributory may apply to the court to determine any matters arising in the liquidation that cannot be otherwise determined. The court has power to stay actions against the company. The court will as a rule order a stay in executing a judgment against the company so as to ensure a distribution of the assets *pari passu.*

## *Pari passu*

The liquidator applies the assets of the company in satisfaction of:

(a) Costs charges and expenses of the liquidation.
(b) Preferential debts.
(c) The liabilities of the company *pari passu;*
(d) the rights and interests of members of the company.

Thus, after discharging the matters set out in (a) and (b), a certain sum of money will be available for distribution. There may not be enough to pay those claims in full. Then each will be required to accept the same proportion of his total claim. They are then said to take the money *pari passu.*

If the liabilities total £20 000 and the only money available is

£10 000, the liquidator will pay 50p in the pound to each creditor. Each, no matter how large or small his claim, receives the same dividend of 50p for every pound of his claim.

### Winding-up under supervision of the court

The fact that a company has commenced voluntary winding-up does not prevent any creditor or contributory applying to the court for a compulsory winding-up order.

If a contributory applies he must satisfy the court that the voluntary winding-up would prejudice the rights of the contributories.

The court may, as opposed to granting a compulsory order, continue the voluntary winding-up order under the supervision of the court.

After the making of a supervision order the liquidator may, subject to any directions the court wish to give, exercise all his usual powers.

He may not, however, pay any class of creditors in full, or compromise claims without court approval.

The court may, if it thinks fit, appoint an additional liquidator or remove a liquidator and appoint another.

## WINDING UP BY THE COURT

The High Court has power to wind-up any company registered in England.

A company that is unable to pay its debts may be wound up by the courts.

A company will be deemed to be unable to pay its debts if:

(a) A creditor serves on the company a demand for payment and the company has for three weeks thereafter failed to make payment, or agreed terms of payment.

(b) Execution on a judgment is abortive.

(c) The court are satisfied that the company cannot pay its debts.

(i) 'Unable to pay its debts'. The company's inability to pay its debts may be proved in other ways than those listed in (a) and (b) above.

The dishonour of a bill of exchange or the failure to pay a judgment debt may show the insolvency of the company.

The creditor should remember that if the debtor company ignores a statutory demand for payment, *any* creditor may petition for winding-up.

It should also be noted that a winding-up order will not be made on a debt which is *bona fide* disputed. The debtor company's failure to reply to a statutory demand for payment of a disputed debt will not support a petition.

A company may be 'commercially insolvent', i.e. unable to pay its debts as they fall due even though its assets, when realised, will exceed its liabilities.

A company in that position may be wound-up.

In deciding whether a company is unable to pay its debts, the court must take into account the current and contingent liabilities of the company.

*(ii)  Statutory demand for payment.*  The statutory demand for payment is defined by Section 223 of the Companies Act 1948 and must be:

(a)   made in writing under the hand of the creditor; and
(b)   a demand for payment of the sum due within three weeks.

Proof of the insolvency of the company is its failure to pay within the three-week period. Thus a petitioner relying on this procedure cannot present a petition before the expiration of the three-week period.

## The petition

A winding-up order is made as the result of a petition to the court. The petition must be in the prescribed form.

In it the petitioning creditor must set out the following detail:

(a)   The full name and address of the petitioning creditor.
(b)   The full name and registered office of the debtor company.

(c)   The date of the debtor company's incorporation, particulars of its capital and shares and its principal objects.

(d)   The facts on which the creditor relies to support the allegation that the debtor company is insolvent.

A draft petition based on a statutory demand for payment is shown in Figure 24.1.

*(i)   Presenting the petition.*   The petition is 'presented' at the companies court and thereupon a date and time for the hearing will be fixed.

The date and time will be endorsed on the petition. The court will allocate a number to the petition and seal a copy for service on the debtor company. The appropriate court fee must be paid.

*(ii)   Serving the petition.*   The petition must be served on the debtor company at its registered office. Service is effected by leaving a copy with any member, officer or servant of the company at the registered office. An affidavit of service will be required.

*(iii)   Verifying the petition.*   Within four days of the presentation of the petition the creditor must file a formal affidavit verifying the debt. If the creditor is a limited company, the affidavit must be sworn by the secretary or a director who is authorised by the company to swear it.

Unless the debtor company files an affidavit in answer no further evidence need be filed.

*(iv)   Advertising the petition.*   The petition must be advertised in the *London Gazette.* A material mistake in the advertisement may invalidate it and prevent the petition being effective.

*(v)   Lodging papers.*   On a day fixed by the court the petitioner must attend the registrar to satisfy him that the matter is in order for hearing.

The petitioner must:

(a)   show that the petition has been properly advertised;

(b)   satisfy the registrar that the required affidavits of verification and service have been filed and are in order.

---

In the High Court of Justice          No.          of 198
Chancery Division
Companies Court

in the matter of A Debtor Ltd
                and
in the matter of The Companies Act 1948

to Her Majesty's High Court of Justice:

The Humble Petition of Creditors Ltd
whose registered office is at Credit House, Wright
Way, Conkley, Creditors of the above named
Company

Sheweth as follows:

1   A Debtor Ltd (hereinafter called 'the Company') was incorporated on 1 April
    1949 under the Companies Act 1948.

2   The Registered office of the Company is situate at
    ...........................................................................................................................

3   The nominal capital of the Company is £100 divided into 100 shares of £1
    each all of which have been issued and are fully paid up.

4   The objects for which the Company was established were (here set out main
    objects) ...... and other sums more particularly set forth in the Memorandum
    of Association.

5   The Company is justly and truly indebted to your Petitioner in the sum of
    £      for ...................................................................................................
    ...........................................................................................................................

6   Your Petitioner has made application to the Company for the payment of the
    said sum but the Company has failed and neglected to pay the said sum or any
    part thereof.

7   The sum of £      is still justly due and owing to the Petitioner.

8   The Company is insolvent and unable to pay its debts.

9   In the circumstances it is just and equitable that the Company should be
    wound up.

Your Petitioner therefore humbly prays as follows:

1   That A Debtor Ltd may be wound up by the Court under the provisions of the
    Companies Act 1948.

2   That such other order may be made in the premises as to the Court shall seem
    just.

And Your Petitioner will ever pray, etc.

Note:  It is intended to serve this Petition on
       A Debtor Ltd

---

**Figure 24:1   Draft petition for statutory demand for payment**

*(vi)  Persons appearing.*  Any person who intends to appear on the hearing of the petition must serve on the petitioner a notice to that effect. The notice must show whether the person giving it intends to support or oppose the petition.

The petitioner must prepare, on a prescribed form, a list of the names and addresses of persons giving notice of their intention to appear. This list must be lodged with the court immediately prior to the hearing.

*(vii)  Hearing the petition.*  The petition is heard in open court. In the case of unopposed petitions no evidence is required to be called. The court have power to make an order for winding-up, to adjourn the petition for further evidence or for a compromise or scheme of arrangement to be put into effect.

*(viii)  The winding-up order*  When a winding-up order is made the registrar must on the same day give notice of the order to the Official Receiver. Thereupon he takes possession of the assets of the company.

The order discharges all the employees of the company and dismisses its directors.

## THE OFFICIAL RECEIVER

The Official Receiver is an officer of the Department of Trade and Industry. When a winding-up order is made, the Official Receiver takes over the company assets as provisional liquidator. The Official Receiver then has the duty to compile:

(a)  a statement of affairs of the company;
(b)  a preliminary report for the court.

The secretary or director of the debtor company must submit to the Official Receiver a statement, verified by affidavit, listing the assets or liabilities of the company and giving the information required by Section 235 of the Companies Act.

The Official Receiver may require the directors to come before him and answer any points he puts to them.

As soon as possible a statement must be prepared by the Official Receiver for the court detailing the following:

(a)  particulars of the share capital;
(b)  an estimate of assets and liabilities;
(c)  the causes of the failure of the company.

He may also specify whether further investigations into the affairs of the company should be carried out.

### Calling a meeting of creditors

The Official Receiver must call a 'first meeting of creditors and contributories'. This is to determine whether or not an application should be made to appoint a liquidator or whether he should continue to conduct the winding-up of the company. Officers of the company may be directed by the Official Receiver to attend the first meeting of creditors. If no liquidator is appointed then the Official Receiver will act as liquidator.

### Further reports to creditors

The Official Receiver may, if he thinks fit, place a further report before the creditors. He may, if he feels it right, express an opinion as to any fraud committed by any person or officers of the company. In that event the court has power to order the public examination of the person or officers concerned.

### The liquidation

The liquidation will continue, either under the control of the Official Receiver or the liquidator appointed, in much the same way as described under 'creditors voluntary winding-up' and subject to the provisions of the Companies (Winding-up) Rules 1949.

## COMPOSITIONS AND ARRANGEMENTS

### A composition

This is an arrangement by which all or some of the creditors agree to accept so much in the pound in full settlement of their claims against a debtor. This may be proposed by the debtor at the first meeting of creditors.

The creditors usually agree to defer taking legal action against the debtor so long as he honours the terms of the composition.

### Deed of arrangement

A debtor may, as part of an arrangement with creditors, assign some property to a trustee for division among his creditors. Any creditor who wishes to participate in the division must assent. Only creditors who do so are bound by the deed.

### Act of bankruptcy

An assignment by means of a deed of arrangement is an act of bankruptcy if executed for the benefit of all creditors. A composition may, in certain circumstances, be an act of bankruptcy or it may involve notice by the debtor that he is unable to pay his debts.

### Registration

A deed of arrangement must be registered under the Deeds of Arrangement Act 1914.

### Consent

Where a deed is for the benefit of creditors generally it must, to be effective, have the consent of the majority of creditors in value and number.

If the deed is void and the debtor goes bankrupt no creditor will be bound by it and all may prove their debts.

## RECEIVERS AND MANAGERS

### A receiver

Is a person appointed to protect property or to realise assets? His appointment enables a creditor to recover money due to him out of his assets or property which cannot be taken in execution.

If there is a dispute as to the entitlement to property the court may appoint a receiver until the question is determined.

### Receiver for the debentureholder

A debenture will normally give the lender power to appoint a receiver if sums due under it are not paid or if the security is at risk.

### Appointing a receiver

A receiver may be appointed under the creditors powers in a mortgage or debenture. In those cases there is no need to apply to the court for the appointment.

A receiver may be appointed by the court. The general ground of appointment is the preservation of property for persons claiming to have an interest in it.

Before making an appointment the court will have to be satisfied as to the suitability of the proposed receiver and will usually require him to give security. This may be by guarantee bond or undertaking.

On appointment by the court the receiver takes control of the property in question and acts as an officer of the court.

### Powers and duties of a receiver

The receiver appointed by the court has a duty to collect the property of which he is appointed and to pay all money received into court.

A receiver for the debentureholder has a duty to realise the assets of the company for the benefit of the debentureholder.

A receiver, however appointed, may insure the premises over which he is appointed, and may pay the taxes, rates and other outgoings thereon.

A receiver appointed to collect debts may give debtors time to pay.

## Managers

As a receiver is often appointed to preserve property it is equally often necessary for a receiver appointed by the court to act as manager of the business concerned.

### Appointing a manager

Because of the powers a manager will have the court will sanction his appointment for only a fixed short period. This period may be extended in appropriate cases.

The right of appointing a manager will only arise if the business itself is included in the security.

The appointment will not, of course, dissolve the company or terminate the business. It will simply vest the running and the general conduct of the business in the manager.

### Powers of a manager

The manager has power to carry on the business and so to:

(a) pay the running expenses;
(b) employ staff;
(c) to buy and sell and, unless expressly ordered not to, to enter into new contracts.

He must preserve the assets and goodwill of the business.

# PART X

# EXTERNAL CREDIT AND FINANCE

# 25

# Factoring

Roger Pilcher, former Managing Director, Credit Factoring
International Ltd

## DEFINITIONS

Since the word factoring was introduced in Britain in a financial services context, in the early 1960s, it has been applied in such a number of ways that any treatise on the subject must inevitably start by defining variations. In a non-financial context 'factor' has been used for centuries in Scotland to describe the profession of estate management, and in the remainder of the UK is commonly used in several industries as an alternative to 'wholesaler'.

The following definitions will help the reader who is interested either in the use or the effect of factoring in a financial sense.

### Non-recourse factoring

This is the form of factoring providing the most comprehensive range of services to manufacturers, wholesalers or service companies. It embraces maintenance of the sales ledger, credit control, 100% protection against bad debts arising from approved transactions and collection from customers. The combination of these services constitutes 'maturity' factoring; the factor is usually willing to provide up to 80% finance against the value of indebtedness in the sales ledger and the addition of this facility converts maturity to 'financed' factoring, thus arriving at the full package of non-recourse factoring.

Non-recourse factoring may be 'disclosed' or 'undisclosed'. The former, which is by far the more common arrangement, involves notification by the supplier to his customers that payment must be made to the factor; the latter involves some form of arrangement that disguises the factor in order that customers believe they are still paying direct to their supplier.

### Recourse factoring

Superficially, recourse factoring is similar to non-recourse factoring with the important exception that credit protection is not afforded to the supplier by the factor. All indebtedness is handled by the factor with full recourse to the supplier in the event of customer insolvency, though recourse factors usually provide an advisory service to assist their clients in assessing the creditworthiness of customers.

Recourse factoring can be either disclosed or undisclosed.

### Invoice discounting

Whilst invoice discounting, the provision of advances against receivables without any of the service elements of factoring, has been available in various forms for many years, it has tended in recent years to become embraced by the term factoring, being advertised either as 'invoice discounting' or 'confidential invoice factoring'. It is more generally known in the USA and most other countries outside Britain as 'receivables financing'.

### Bulk factoring

Effectively a disclosed invoice-discounting arrangement with customers being instructed to make all payments to the factor as opposed to the supplier.

### Agency factoring

Similar to bulk factoring but provides a measure of credit protection.

Sales to selected customers, credit approved by the factor, are discounted with customers being instructed to send payment to the client's office made out in favour of a special account maintained in the name of the factoring company.

## HISTORY OF FACTORING

During the Industrial Revolution the textile mills in the North of England appointed representatives on the eastern seaboard of North America, primarily to sell their merchandise but also, due to slow transatlantic communications, to look after customer relationships generally. These representatives were responsible for importing in bulk, for selling and collecting and remitting the proceeds of sales back to Britain. Not surprisingly, being similar in many respects to traditional wholesalers in this country, they became known as 'factors'. However, they soon found that more profit could be made by concentration on the administration of their clients' businesses in America than from simple commission on sales and it was not long before they dropped the latter function in favour of collection and credit insurance services. Their increasing prosperity soon put them also into a position to bridge the long collection period involved in the American trade by offering immediate payment at the time of export to British suppliers and thus the full package of administrative and financial factoring was born. It was from this beginning that the term 'old-line' factoring has been derived, meaning the whole range of services developed by the original American factors.

As the US developed its own industry the factors concentrated increasingly on domestic as opposed to import business with the result that there are today some 20 major factoring companies in the United States, with an annual volume of business amounting to $29 000m (1982). A number of present-day factoring companies are descended from the original factors so, until quite recently, there has been a natural tendency for the service to be concentrated in the textile industry. Since the last war there has, however, been an increasing diversification of industries served by factoring and the intervention·of a number of major banks, either by acquisition of existing factoring companies or the establishment of their own, has greatly increased the knowledge and hence use of factoring by distributing and manufacturing businesses of many kinds. The emphasis continues to be very much on old-line services, though most factoring companies have accounts receivables divisions under separate management which provide advances against collateral of debtors and inventory.

Inevitably an effective service with a pattern of profitable growth had to come eventually to Europe and it was in 1960 that the first factoring company opened its doors in Britain. This was followed in rapid succession through the sixties by ten or more other companies, some of which provided full old-line services and others a continuation of existing invoice discounting facilities but under the newly-introduced title of factoring. As is often the case, particularly when a new form of financial service is introduced, the first ten years saw a full crop of the problems of mushroom growth; companies using factors for all the wrong reasons; factors taking on business for which their service was not suitable simply to build volume in a race one against the other; poorly developed and totally inadequate supporting services.

This could well have spelt disaster for the whole concept of factoring in Britain. Relief and respectability arrived as a result of the major clearing banks taking an interest and since 1970 most of the principal banks have become involved either through their own subsidiaries, or associated companies. Services based on what are probably the most advanced and sophisticated computer systems yet developed for sales accounting and credit control have now been in use for several years with the result that many well known companies are making use of factoring, both for their home and export sales, either on a financed or maturity basis.

In Western Europe the pattern of development has been similar to that in Britain with most countries now having several factoring companies, many of which are related to major banks. So far there tends to be more emphasis on receivables financing and recourse factoring within continental Europe, though old-line factoring is steadily gaining popularity and is the system most usually followed in handling international business.

There is little doubt that, despite the unsteady start during the 1960s, factoring is now here to stay in Britain as a solid administrative and financial support for growing companies. The better understanding that now prevails of its value in strengthening and better securing the businesses of user companies entitles such companies to greater respect both from their suppliers, whom they can meet on better terms, and their customers, who can depend upon adequate credit for their requirements coupled with efficient sales accounts administration.

## THE USE OF FACTORING

It is intended to concentrate here on the application of non-recourse factoring, as opposed to the other alternatives that have been defined, in order to demonstrate the operation and effectiveness of the service in the broadest sense. Variations on this will be discussed later.

First let us look more closely at what non-recourse factoring comprises. Underlying all other parts of the service is the maintenance by the factor of the supplier's sales ledger. Performance of this function, with the very valuable live experience that it gives of payment patterns, enables the factor to take a fully informed and up-to-date view in assessing customer creditworthiness and to operate effectively in the collection field. By providing this service to a multiplicity of companies, many of which are in the same industries, a considerable insight is gained into the credit standing of customers throughout the length and breadth of the land, since many will have a simultaneous open-ledger relationship with the factor in respect of a number of their suppliers.

### The sales ledger

It is not the task of the factor to make sales or even to raise invoices at the time of delivery of goods. These functions are performed by the supplier in the normal way, against the background of the factor's credit approval of the customers, with copy invoices being sent in regular batches to the factor for entry in the sales ledger. With the recent, much-increased sophistication of computer systems, this transfer of information can be effected by magnetic tape output from the supplier's computer being input direct to that of the factor;

in either case the factoring company will normally update its records, including allocation of cash received from customers, every night with the result that an absolutely up-to-date open-item record is carried forward from day to day.

Whilst, as already mentioned, the factor will often be working for a number of suppliers selling to the same customer, each customer's accounts in relation to its individual suppliers are maintained separately with regular statements and collection letters being sent by the factor making due reference to supplier in each case. The most advanced systems provide for automated production of dunning letters direct from computer records, these being presented in such a way that they are completely personalised so far as individual customers are concerned. Whilst at first glance it may appear that such a system could, by virtue of the very scale of operation, achieve precisely the opposite result to that intended, the combination of absolutely up-to-date information on the customer payment position, together with efficient mechanisation of letter writing, has been proved beyond doubt to have a significant effect not only on collection performance but also upon strengthening good customer relations.

Credit control

The processing of the customer's account provides the factor with much of the basis for effective credit control. Constant input of information regarding disputes, changes in terms, credit information from other sources, etc., added to an established track record of payment patterns, all stored within the computer but immediately available both on hard copy and video display, enables the most realistic possible evaluation to be carried out.

Figure 25:1 illustrates a display on a video terminal showing the daily updated position of a buyer's account within the factor's computer file. This photograph was taken on 25 April 1984 and shows in the top section the position between the buyer, Amalgamated Superstores, and the factored client (no. 04410) on that morning. It will be noted that it shows that the last cash received from the buyer arrived on 13 April; the initials on the left-hand side F, C and T stand for factor's risk, client's risk and total outstanding, respectively. The heading of the second column, UAC's, stands for

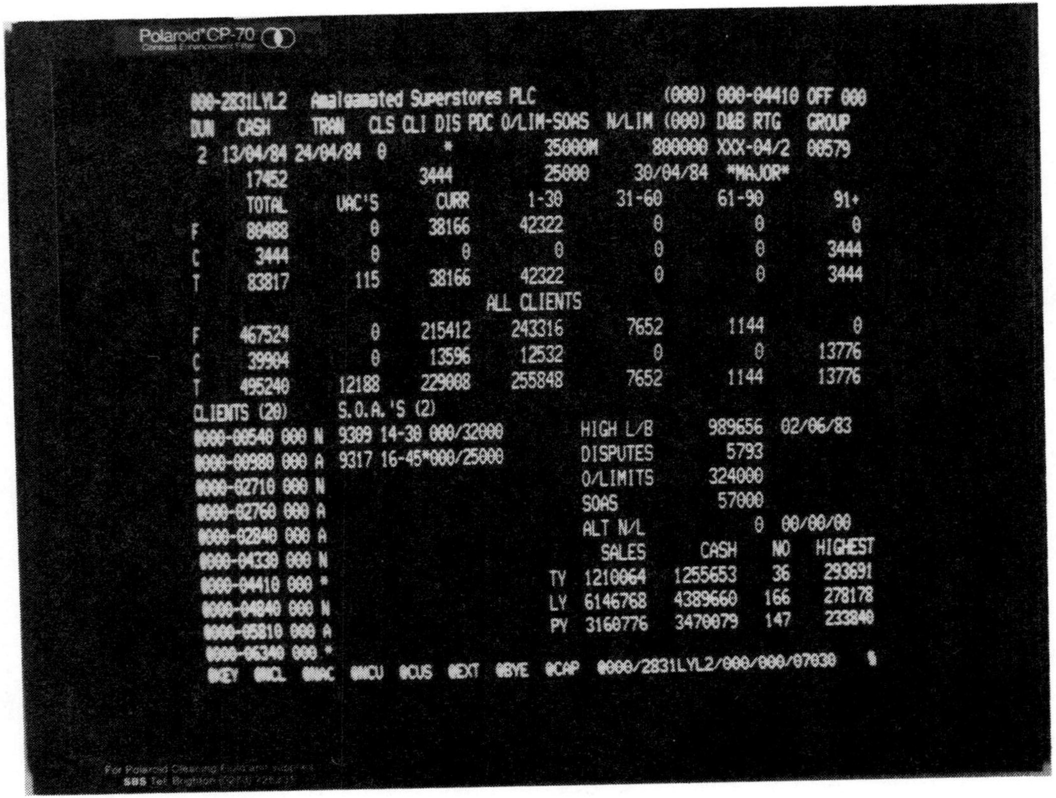

Figure 25:1 Video display as an aid to credit control

unapplied credits, the number being cash received credited to the buyer's account but as yet unallocated to specific invoices. The information on the lower half of the picture relates to the aggregate position between this buyer and all its suppliers serviced by the factor whose numbers are shown at the bottom of the screen. On the right lower side of the picture is shown the highest ledger balance (L/B) as yet seen by the factoring company together with a range of other historic statistics. An individual credit controller can thus see at a glance the position between any one customer and supplier, or equally take a view on the factoring company's total exposure in relation to the customer and all its factored suppliers.

Consolidation within the factor's credit department of the current position and previous experience of an individual customer's activity in relation to a number of different suppliers further enhances this capability. Recent technological advances have also provided the opportunity for data links to be established between factors and their clients with the result that the latter can enjoy direct on-line access to their customer ledgers and up-to-date credit information.

It will thus be readily understood that a factoring company is in a very different position from a credit insurer when it comes to making a quick decision with regard to fresh credit. Unlike the credit insurer, the factor does not have to depend upon information that is either 'hearsay' or somewhat out-of-date; in most cases there is a wealth of live information and at worst at least some current practical experience upon which to base a decision. For this reason, whilst some factors do still follow the pattern set by credit insurers of establishing credit limits, most of the factors with the type of facilities referred to above usually prefer to allow their clients to deliver goods up to a certain value each month at their (the factor's) risk, thus at the same time obviating the necessity for constant applications for credit approval and also overcoming aggregation problems that flow from too many unused lines of credit on the same customer being outstanding at the same time. Whilst this is the more usual procedure for regular business, factors do require new customers (though sometimes only those with initial orders in excess of an agreed discretionary limit) and orders from existing customers buying outside the monthly discretionary arrangement, to be put forward for specific approval. Thanks to their considerable library of information the greater part of decisions are given on the day of request though, inevitably, in some cases responses are held up due to the necessity for deeper investigation before large sums are approved.

## Customer claims and disputes

As the factor undertakes full responsibility for both the sales ledger and credit functions it is inevitable that customer claims and disputes become a part of the daily processing operation. Whilst it might be expected that a third party interposed between supplier and buyer might have difficulty in providing effective service in this area, in practice the factor is both a useful catalyst and a necessary discipline if the supplier's cash flow is not to be impeded by frivolous arguments or problems arising from his own delivery procedures. Upon being notified by a customer that some problem has occurred that (in the customer's view) prevents payment according to terms, the factor will usually provide details of the claim to the supplier on an automated 'dispute notice', allowing a set period of say, 30 days, for its resolution. This enables the supplier to investigate the problem and, if the customer's claim is justified, to raise a credit note or, if it is seen simply to be a means of deferring payment, to instruct the factor to proceed with collection. Most factors tell their supplier clients that, if they follow neither of these courses nor ask for an extension of time to complete investigations, the disputed items will be automatically charged back to them at the end of the 30-day period—thus providing a long stop deadline that ensures good relations between supplier and customer.

Customers are obliged to make their payments to the factor as the latter obtains security in its credit control and when making advances by taking an assignment of debts from the supplier; however, by doing this they can be sure that their accounts are immediately brought up-to-date thus allowing the most liberal view to be taken in assessing future credit requirements. Customers who from time to time find themselves in difficulties in meeting their bills can of course talk freely to the skilled credit staff in the factoring companies when they will receive the same sympathetic consideration that would be accorded to them by a supplier looking for their future support.

## The client's cash flow

Factors are generally looking after hundreds if not thousands of customer accounts on behalf of any one supplier and therefore usually make payment to the supplier in respect of these collections on an 'average maturity' date, as opposed to passing on each collection, large or small, as it is received. By working on a fixed revolving average maturity, the supplier is easily able to calculate cash flow and to plan ahead in the certain knowledge that predetermined amounts are due so many days forward from the factor (subject of course to any offsets in the way of credit notes issued by the supplier, which have the effect of reducing the total indebtedness at any point in time). Maturity periods tend to grow shorter following the introduction of factoring, due to the more precise sales accounting and collection procedures of the factor, with the result that after a while the supplier will experience an additional benefit as the maturity period is adjusted downwards with a consequent improvement in cash flow. The improved debt turn also means interest savings in funding debtors or alternatively the release of working capital for other purposes within the business.

These comments do of course apply to businesses where the sales pattern, terms, etc. continue on an equal basis. Following the introduction of factoring should terms be varied in such a way as to provide additional credit to customers this is automatically taken into account in the factor's calculations with a resultant lengthening of the maturity period.

## Advances in anticipation of customer payments

The final part of the non-recourse factoring package is the advance that is available from the factor to the supplier in anticipation of collection of outstanding receivables. The facility that is available tends to vary somewhat from factor to factor, and from industry to industry, but is normally in the region of 70% of outstanding debtors in the supplier's ledger, though in some industries factors are prepared to advance up to 80%. This advance can be taken either immediately on passing copies of invoices to the factor or at any time and in any amount up to the agreed ceiling against revolving debtors. This is clearly a very flexible facility as it increases automatically as sales grow but can be drawn off and paid for precisely when it is required. Whereas some companies take immediate advantage of the maximum drawings that they can make from the factor, others tend to use the facility to meet their seasonal or monthly buying peaks, knowing that funds are always available at the end of a telephone.

### The cost of factoring

As there is a distinct division between the administrative and credit protection services of factoring and the financial facility, the factor's charges are calculated and applied quite separately in the two areas. First of all, there is a service charge which reflects the cost of sales accounting, collection, credit control and credit protection, which is normally in the region of 0.75% to 2.5% of the gross sales volume serviced by the factor (it is usual for factors to provide their services on an all turnover basis as they would otherwise be in danger of being unevenly exposed in providing credit protection). This charge is normally measured against the workload in handling each individual client's business and should be more than balanced by direct cost savings and intangible benefits such as saving in management time, better customer relationships, improved debt turn (with consequent savings in the cost of borrowing), etc. If a client takes advances from a factor these are usually provided at a rate geared to the clearing banks' base rates or the finance houses' base rate; in general the cost is likely to be slightly above that which a company would be charged for bank overdraft facilities.

### EXPORT FACTORING

An area of recent rapid growth, export factoring undoubtedly provides the most comprehensive package of export services available today to British short-term exporters.

In addition to the basic services available in the home market that have already been described, the exporters are able to invoice their customers in their own currencies without any of the attendant book-keeping problems, are relieved of forward currency risks and suffer none of the problems normally associated with collecting money from foreign buyers, whose knowledge of English tends to evaporate very rapidly immediately their accounts pass due date.

It is the factor's responsibility to maintain the supplier's sales ledger, regardless of currencies invoiced, in eactly the same way as in the home market. The factor makes an immediate conversion to sterling for the exporter's account of the total value of invoices submitted for factoring and is then responsible for collection from the customers overseas in their own currencies and on the terms most appropriate for their own industries and markets. Not only does the immediate conversion of the value of the export sales to sterling obviate the exchange risk, it also removes the accounting problems otherwise experienced in having to deal with fluctuations that arise between the time of invoicing and customer payment.

Credit cover is usually 100% on approved customers and there is no necessity for the exporter to submit reports and claims in respect of slow and defaulting customers as is the procedure under a credit insurance policy. Customer collections are handled in most of the principal export markets either by the British factors' own offices, staffed by locally employed specialists or through correspondent factors—this means that customers are in most cases dealt with in their own languages with the effect that delayed payments and disputes are cleared up in the shortest possible time. Similarly, funds collected overseas find their way more quickly to the country than is usually the case when an exporter has to make his own individual collection arrangements in each market.

A variation on straightforward export factoring is the arrangement whereby a British company arranges for factoring services to be provided locally to its sales subsidiaries by the overseas offices or associates of a British factor. The implications of this, particularly in the Common Market, are evident; by nature an overseas sales operation is usually motivated and controlled by sales-orientated management and the administrative efficiency and credit and collection security afforded by the factor play an important part in achieving a balanced growth for the sales company.

The full range of services provided does vary somewhat from one factoring company to another. There are at present four inter-national factoring organisations with British members; three of these operate on a 'correspondent' basis between members and the fourth has its own network of regional offices, covering Europe and North America, tied to a central processing and clearing system in the UK.

## VARIATIONS IN FACTORING

In the opening section, the various forms of factoring were defined. Whilst disclosed non-recourse factoring is undoubtedly the service that is commonly understood from the simple description 'factoring', it would be helpful to show how the other forms vary from this standard.

### Undisclosed factoring

This form of factoring, having been tried in Britain during the 1960s, is now extremely rare if not entirely obsolete. Its purpose was to enable the supplier to make use of the full range of services and finance offered by the non-recourse factor without any awareness on the part of his customers that this was the case. This was effected by the supplier, let us say the Acme Abrasive Co. Ltd forming a second company, Acme Abrasive (Sales) Ltd, which entirely controlled by the factor, would be used as a cover for the factoring relationship with customers.

The need for such arrangement stemmed from the fear, not always unjustified in the early days, that factoring might be harmful to the reputation of the supplier. The involvement of the major banks in factoring has beyond doubt by now removed all sign of this stigma and there are many companies today that openly attribute a great deal of their successful growth to the support they have received from their factors.

### Recourse factoring

It will be remembered that recourse factoring comprises very much the same service as non-recourse factoring other than protection against bad debts. The factor is responsible for maintenance of the supplier's sales ledger and this service is particularly useful when dealing with a relatively complicated book-keeping situation where the customers are of undoubted risk.

As the supplier carries the credit risk it is clearly necessary for him to have very up-to-date information as to every customer situation within the ledger, unless he is content to rely upon periodic copies of statements or computer print-outs from the factor.

Recourse factoring is usually provided on a financed as opposed to maturity basis.

## Invoice discounting

Whilst invoice discounting is not strictly speaking a form of factoring service it is often described as such.

The purpose of invoice discounting is to enable a supplier to raise funds against the security of debtors, or more precisely against the indebtedness of selected well-rated customers buying on a regular basis. An invoice discounting arrangement does not provide any form of sales ledger or credit control and protection services and interest rates can be above those normal in factoring. However, this service offers particular advantages to some companies in that they are able to obtain short-term relief from liquidity problems by taking advances without having to commit themselves to full factoring services. In some cases, particularly where one or two well-rated customers make up the bulk of a supplier's business, this is a very practical way of releasing cash to take advantage of better terms for raw materials, etc. As an 'off balance sheet' arrangement, invoice discounting is proving increasingly popular to large companies wishing to make better use of their debtor asset without disturbing their normal banking arrangements.

Invoice discounting is undisclosed, the supplier's customers knowing nothing of the arrangement. It should be borne in mind that most forms of agreement between invoice discounters and their clients give the former the right to notify and collect direct from customers should anything prevent a supplier from repaying the discounting facility.

## EVALUATION OF COMPANIES USING FACTORING

Now that there are many companies making use of the different forms of factoring service, it is most important that anyone involved in granting credit to such companies should be able to make a fair assessment of the implications of factoring in any particular case. Clearly there is a large difference between a company that is using only the service elements of factoring to improve its sales accounts administration and to gain credit protection and at the other extreme a company that may simply be borrowing on rather expensive terms to alleviate liquidity problems.

The company that is using the full range of services regularises and usually speeds up its cash flow and in place of a wide range of assorted customers has one undoubted debtor, the factor. Its senior executives are freed from the chores and problems of customer collections and bad debts and are better able to concentrate on buying and selling relationships with their suppliers and customers.

A company known to be taking advances from a factor, in addition to making use of the services, may well be doing this under a banking-factoring arrangement where the bank has agreed improved facilities against the background of the presence of the factor. Such a situation is likely to enable the supplier to buy more and on better terms and present a stronger position as a result of the factoring relationship. The same applies to a company using invoice discounting facilities wisely as a means of maximising profitability by taking advantage of better prices and off-season buying.

In making an assessment it is therefore important to try to ascertain how far the company is using factoring as a genuine means of improving efficiency, security and its own buying powers as opposed simply to raising funds in order to tide itself through difficult times or even to stave off possible disaster. A great deal obviously depends on the information that the company itself is willing to provide with regard to a factoring relationship (most will be very happy to talk about this) and also a clear understanding on the part of the assessor of credit of the form of services provided by the factoring company concerned.

Many names have appeared in the field of factoring over the past 20 years or so and those interested in credit assessment of factoring users may find it useful to consult the Association of British Factors for advice. The Association, established in 1976, embraces most of the principal factoring companies. It has, as one of its major aims, the promotion of the highest possible standards of professionalism within the industry. Members of the Association in March 1984 were:

| *Company* | *Principal shareholders* |
| --- | --- |
| Alex. Lawrie Factors Ltd | Lloyds & Scottish Group |
| Anglo Factoring Services Ltd | J. Rothschild & Co. Ltd |
| Arbuthnot Factors Ltd | Arbuthnot Latham Bank Ltd Yorkshire Bank plc |
| Century Factors Ltd | Close Brothers Ltd |
| Credit Factoring International Ltd | Wholly owned by National Westminster Bank |
| Griffin Factors Ltd | Forward Trust Group Ltd, a member of Midland Bank Group |
| H. & H. Factors Ltd | Walter E. Heller Overseas Corporation Hambros Bank plc |
| International Factors Ltd | Lloyds & Scottish Group |

# 26

# Credit Cards

A. F. Cook, Manager (Training), Barclaycard

The plastic credit card is a familiar object. There are over 24 million cards of varying sorts in use in the UK, providing perhaps £3000 millions credit. Clearly they play an important part in the provision of credit, but they also arouse a wide range of responses. They are popular with a large number of users, but it is surprising the amount of antagonism they generate from individuals who see them as immoral invitations to obtain goods without saving, to consumer watchdogs who are concerned with too easy provision of credit, subsequent overspending, and over-commitment, to finally the government itself, which has sometimes imperfectly understood the industry with some fiscal and legal requirements, and this not been entirely corrected by the searching Monopolies Commission Enquiry.

The plastic credit card is, of course, a means to an end—a means of identification and a delivery mechanism to permit use of credit accounts operated by a wide range of financial, retail, and service organisations. The credit accounts may allow monthly or much longer credit facilities and settlements; they can provide personal or business credit.

However, the popular conception of credit cards concerns the dominant Visa, Access, American Express, and Diners Club cards; here money transmission plays a very important part, since card-holders use their accounts in a very large number of third party outlets, and many take no real credit. For them, a card is merely a convenient substitute for cheques. Although most plastic card transactions now result in paper vouchers for later processing, the large card organisations are vigorously developing electronic transfer systems using special features of the modern card so reducing the paper-flow and the costs of money transfer. Retail card issuers are facing the same problem with their individual stores and central processing systems.

The two aspects of credit cards, money transfer and short-term credit, allow us to see the credit card market itself in perspective, and to look more clearly at the true competition it provides in personal finance, some business finance, and in money transmission.

## BACKGROUND AND TYPES OF CARD

The modern credit card was created in the United States after the Second World War. The basic retail credit facility, monthly settlement or slightly longer term credit, was long established both in Great Britain and elsewhere. There was also a system of a third party, a credit organisation, providing finance both for a purchaser and indirectly for a shopkeeper, sometimes with paper vouchers; the trading checks issued by Provident Check Trading in the Midlands and the North illustrate this well. However, it was in the United States after 1945 that the development of the sales draft (the creation of a voucher at the point of purchase which would be honoured by a credit organisation, reimbursing the shopkeeper, and charging the purchaser, calling on him for repayment at regular intervals) allowed the expansion of the two dominant parts of the newer credit card business. The first was that provided by banks which places more emphasis on short-term credit, and the second that provided by the travel and entertainment cards, whose normal terms of business require full monthly settlement.

Diners Club, and later American Express and Carte Blanche, led the way in the United States; they clearly met a need in a country where the unit banking system can cause problems for personal purchases outside the immediate local environment. The travel and entertainment card appealed to those who required travel services, hotels and meals. Their first customer base was the fairly affluent traveller, often incurring expenses for business purposes, with assured repayment. Diners Club, American Express and Carte

Blanche still depend heavily on this market. They had made a limited entry into the British market by the mid 1960s.

Yet private individuals with their more local and certainly more particular credit purchases for consumer durables were a proper market, and American banks recognised this. There were a number of false starts; mistakes were made in a too fragmented approach and in over-generous provision of credit, with no clear understanding of interest rates to be charged.

By the early 1960s many banks had left the field, but the elements for success were present in a number of ventures. The Bank of America in California had determined where success could lie, principally in economies of scale and a proper monthly interest charge to the cardholder, with a contribution from the shopkeeper or merchant, a discount on the value of the paper transaction honoured. This successful system was licensed successively to other banks in the United States, and in 1966 to Barclays Bank in Great Britain, establishing in time the international bank card system now known as Visa International. Other competing banks in the United States, and later internationally, established a rather looser organisation first called Mastercharge, and now Mastercard.

Retail organisations, particularly department stores in the United States and Great Britain, have always offered a variety of local credit; they have not only accepted the travel and entertainment and bank credit cards direct, but they have often remodelled their in-house systems on the lines of the main cards. Most department stores' credit accounts are now operated by plastic cards, creating paper sales vouchers later billed to customers at regular intervals, and the overall terms of credit are very similar.

Plastic cards are also used for identification or preferred customer purposes rather than as a form of credit; these cards are occasionally referred to as courtesy cards.

The boundaries between the three main types of cards, the travel and entertainment, the bank cards, and the store cards are becoming more blurred. Travel and entertainment cards have stayed relatively static in purpose, introducing privileged customer facilities like Gold Cards but not changing their *raison d'être* substantially; bank cards can be both credit cards and charge cards like the travel and entertainment cards, and often in direct competition with them for the upper end of the market. Store cards are not only similar to other cards in operation, but are often not administered by the retail stores themselves, sometimes not even directly funded by them, and the stores may merely be a source of introduction to credit facilities. The finance and administration are handled by other organisations perhaps even banks.

## THE BRITISH MARKET

The ownership of credit card companies in Great Britain is very diverse. Diners Club Limited in Farnborough is partly owned by Diners Club Incorporated, the American parent company, itself part of Citicorp, and partly by National Westminster Bank. The British operation of American Express is based in Brighton, and it is only a part of the large American finance, insurance, travellers cheque, and banking organisation.

In Britain, banks belong to either the Access group or the Visa International group. Access, the Joint Credit Card Company Ltd (JCCC) based at Southend, is owned by and provides the credit card operations for National Westminster, Lloyds and Midland Banks and the recently merged Williams & Glyn and The Royal Bank of Scotland. The first three banks each provide 30% of the operating funds of the JCCC; the JCCC is responsible for marketing, sales and advertising, for processing purchases and repayments, and for general accounting. The individual banks maintain special credit card departments which service the credit and general needs of over 7 million cardholders.

Barclays Bank was the pioneer of bank credit cards in Great Britain, a considerable act of faith in 1966, but one which it has not regretted, having seen its competitors respond by launching Access in 1972, and welcoming other banks like Yorkshire Bank, Co-operative Bank, Bank of Scotland, and the Trustee Savings Bank into what is now the Visa network (other banking institutions will follow in the future). Barclays originally processed card operations directly for these banks and now sees the emergence of their separate processing systems. In early 1984, Barclaycard had 6.8 million, Trustcard 2.0 million and Co-op Bank over 80 000 cardholders.

Barclaycard is an autonomous division of Barclays Bank, though is not a separate company like Trustcard. Barclaycard and other Visa issuers incorporate their parent banks' cheque guarantee facility in the same plastic card as the credit card itself. This combination offers considerable economies of issuing costs. With the information contained in the magnetic stripes in the cards themselves, they can be used in automatic teller machines (ATM) and point-of-sale terminals (POST). ATMs are now familiar sights in the 'high streets' providing automatic banking services, and POSTs will have some part to play in future money transfer—a machine similar to a cash register which can capture data for non-cash transactions and allow transmission to a central processing facility for the debit of purchasers and credit of the seller.

Store cards are an important part of the total credit card and retail market; there are certainly well over 5 million in Great Britain. The two largest card organisations in the world are Sears Roebuck and J. W. Penney in the United States, both multi-purpose retail and catalogue companies, with widening financial interests. In this country, the administration of cards is very varied; some store groups service their own operations, and some use finance houses' and banks' systems. Unicredit, the card operation of Provident Mutual Finance, Citibank, and Welbeck Finance are important in this field.

An increasing number of petrol companies, garage chains, and travel systems like British Rail provide credit facilities, through plastic cards, to improve their market share, encourage trading-up, ensure customer loyalty and repeat business, responding to the general demand for both personal credit and business credit. Businesses often seek to streamline their internal accounting for employees who incur frequent expenses and they provide an attractive market for some credit card systems. In the United States, cards issued by the gasoline companies are a very large part of the overall market; in Britain, petrol company cards are less important, and petrol sales are a significant part of British bank cards' operations, perhaps as much as 25% of Barclaycard's turnover.

The most noticeable feature of the British market is the dominance of the bank credit card systems with over 15 million cards issued and with modest personal duplication of ownership of the competing cards—perhaps 7 million cards are issued by other organisations. There are over 1 million travel and entertainment cards and this is in sharp contrast to the US experience where travel and entertainment cards are very significant, although outnumbered by bank cards and heavily outnumbered by retail and gas cards. An important feature in the United States is the duality of issue and ownership of bank cards—banks are members of both the Visa and Mastercard schemes and promote both cards vigorously. This feature is noticeably absent from the British Market.

The basic distinction between the travel and entertainment cards, bank cards and retail cards allows us to consider both the similarities and the differences in the markets which they service, and the customers they attract. The travel and entertainment cards and the special charge cards issued by the banks, like the Barclaycard Premier Card and Visa Company Cards, are clearly intended for executive travel and accommodation needs. The travel and entertainment cards' coverage is markedly in travel, hotel, and superior tourist facilities. The bank cards are intended for a more universal audience and for use in any form of retail purchase. The purchasing facilities are those characterised by 'high street' shops with hotel, restaurant, and garage trade, but the range extends further, and now includes public utility bills, subscriptions, mail order facilities, and ultimately anything that is wanted by cardholders and which can provide profitable trade for the card companies.

Profit of course is important—has the purchase any potential for creating interest bearing extended credit income, as with consumer durables, whose purchase is to be repaid over a period? Is the purchase of sufficient value that the merchant service charge, the discount, is capable of making a good contribution to processing the sales voucher and billing costs? There is no enthusiasm in any credit card company for low value purchases, say less than £20, which are likely to be repaid quickly, and which produce little direct income.

Store cards have a more clearly defined market, the customers of a particular store, a garage chain, or those using a special facility. Perhaps credit cards are a defence mechanism here in order to maintain customer loyalty or provide credit facilities to match opportunities available in other shops. In-house credit in retail stores is surprisingly large, perhaps 25% of Debenhams turnover is accounted for by credit cards.

The banks themselves provide the customer base for their own credit card operations; their customer profile is noticeably ABC1, salary earning, and invariably satisfactory current-account holders.

Retail cards have a much wider spread; some of the specialist travel and hotel groups may have customers no different from the travel and entertainment cards or the company cards of the banks, while some store cards reflect the ordinary customers of the establishment. Each card organisation will adopt a promotion strategy for new customers most suitable for its future profit, and will adjust its card issuing policy, often based on credit scoring techniques, to achieve the best penetration of its perceived market.

There is a sharp contrast between the banks' and the retail stores' card issuing techniques. In order to maintain the customers' purchasing interest, stores often provide immediate credit facilities. They may pay for providing this purchasing power with a high bad debt ratio, although this can be covered by higher interest rates and by higher retailer mark-ups. Banks are cautious card issuers, using detailed credit vetting techniques and initiating reference enquiries and credit searches.

There is overall a clear distinction between the personal lending and consumer credit of the retail store cards and much of the banks' card business, and the more dominant money transfer, monthly settlement facilities of the travel and entertainment and the accounting system, executive cards.

**COMPETITION**

The cards are obviously in competition with each other—there are two primary travel and entertainment cards (and bank systems provide additional direct competition), there are two main groups of bank cards, and there is the huge variety of retail cards. They compete with each other directly, and perhaps some retail organisations rather reluctantly accept the more universal cards, but overall, external competition must be recognised.

The money transfer characteristics of the travel and entertainment and bank cards must in some ways compete with cheque books and direct drawings on bank accounts. In the United States debit cards (cards debiting checking accounts direct) and special ATM cards also illustrate plastic use of bank accounts.

The extended credit, personal lending facility of either bank cards or retail cards is comparable to traditional hire purchase. A number of retail stores have rationalised their personal credit facilities of the hire purchase sort into a plastic card system, with budget accounts or fixed term repayment facilities.

Although the overall plastic card market may be dominated by a limited number of organisations in any of its individual fields, in fact these organisations are surrounded by competitors dealing with the same customers, offering similar facilities, but not actually activating them with plastic cards.

The bank cards in particular, whether credit cards or charge cards, are increasing automated features for use in cash dispensing machines or point of sale terminals, and are very conscious of the developing competition from other financial organisations, like building societies, in the use of automatic cash dispensers and electronic funds transfer; there are already some important, perhaps defensive links being made between credit card organisations, banks and building societies to ensure a rational approach to the future and competition.

Some part of the future will involve expensive and sophisticated automated systems, and the costs will be particularly severe for companies who provide universal cards, and central data collection. The provision of auto-reading and electronic transfer systems at all retail establishments with some linking to card companies' processing facilities has frightening implications for costs. After extensive study, the banks with their ordinary payment systems, the credit cards with their specialist ones, and retailers at large, are unable to be sure what the future entails, except the substantial cost, an inability to agree who pays for it, and who gets the greatest benefit. These costs are additional to the significant costs which have to be borne already.

## COSTS

Costs are appropriate for the dual purpose of plastic cards—the operational cost of money transfer, of crediting the seller, debiting the purchaser, advising the latter of amounts outstanding, and processing repayments; the costs of creating the account, servicing it and obtaining repayments, the costs of marketing and promotion, and of all operations in general are significant. They are containable with operational efficiency and high levels of automation, but it is surprising the special pressures which must be controlled. All the card companies are basically centralised, and depend for customer contact on telephone and post; with the volumes they handle, 1p on postage rates or 10% increase in telephone charges, can represent many millions of extra operating expense. These expenses are not immediately covered except by profitable expansion and increased business, since only the travel and entertainment and charge cards like company cards actually charge cardholders a specific fee for issue, and by implication, for processing.

Operational costs can be partly borne by card holder subscriptions where they exist and rather more substantially by the merchant service charge paid by the merchant for the facilities provided by accepting cards. The service charge varys from 1% to 5%, the main determinants being the average transaction value and volume of business. There are significant advantages for merchants to accept travel and entertainment and bank cards—casual trade increases since cardholders frequently look for card acceptance when making certain purchases, there is a pronounced tendency to trade up, buy more expensive items, because credit is involved. Certainly twice the amount of petrol is bought than when cash is used. Local credit may be eliminated, credit which is very expensive to administer and is fraught with problems; there is a noticeable diminution in problems of security and theft. The cost of providing customers with credit facilities can be rationalised at the agreed merchant service charge.

The major card companies would prefer the costs of processing purchases to be covered by merchant service charges and they pay much attention to increasing the average value of sales vouchers in order to maximise the income from this source, and to minimise the actual flow of paper. Store cards, particularly when organised totally in-house, have no service charge income, and the larger retail organisations must have substantial operating costs turning branch paper into centrally processed bills.

However, the most outstanding cost problem associated with credit cards is that implied in the word credit. If consumer or business credit is to be created, then funds have to be provided to service lending. In the case of bank cards, merchants are reimbursed when the vouchers are paid into bank branches, but cardholders are allowed considerable variation in their repayment periods. The travel and entertainment systems reimburse their merchants after receiving the vouchers through the post. Both bank card systems advise cardholders monthly of the outstanding balance and call for some level of repayment within 25 days. The travel and entertainment cards call for full repayment at the end of such a period. They will all need to fund the reimbursements made to merchants pending the income receiveable from cardholders. Between 25% and 30% of the bank cards' cardholders in fact pay back their accounts in full each month, and neither the bank cards nor the travel and entertainment cards charge interest to the full repayers. There was some criticism in the Monopolies Commission Report on credit cards about these 'free riders' in the bank card systems, and a concern about inability to cost or eliminate cross-subsidisation of activity between merchant and cardholder, between turnover and interest charges. The travel and entertainment cards and the bank charge cards levy an annual fee which should cover these interest losses. The remaining bank cardholders take credit, either short-term, perhaps 3 months, or long-term, say a 2-year period (minimum monthly repayments are 5% of the outstanding balance). The store cards are deliberately designed for similar purchasing and repayment levels; both charge interest at variable amounts, typically in 1984 at 1¾/2% per month, an annual percentage rate of charge at 23.1/26.8%. The success of this lending operation lies in maintaining a proper margin between the costs of the money employed and the income received from the cardholders.

Unlike some bank card operations in the rest of the world, no British card system raises money directly from the public for its card needs. The bank systems would normally employ additional money to their retail banking needs raised on the wholesale market, and some of the financial institution servicing retail card systems will no doubt do the same. Other retail systems providing their own facilities may be able to borrow advantageously or to use accumulated funds, and American Express has substantial financial resources derived from its banking and travellers cheques' activities. Overall, successful card operations will be dependent on operational efficiency and good money management, particularly the maintenance of correct interest margins. There are however two other serious cost constraints. The early 1980s saw a considerable escalation for all cards of two large problems, fraud and bad debt.

## Fraud and bad debt

Fraud is the misuse of plastic cards by those to whom they were not issued. A number of cardholders are surprisingly careless in controlling and keeping something with such a specific value. Unfortunately, a number finish up in wrong hands and are heavily misused. Until 1980 the bank credit cards in particular could show that fraud represented less than 0.2% of turnover, and that this was a containable cost. 1981 and 1982 saw a serious rise in fraud, both nationally and internationally. In 1982 over £20 million was lost through fraudulent activities for all forms of plastic cards, bank cards, cheque guarantee cards, travel and entertainment cards and retail cards. The development of new fraud prevention and control systems was accelerated; with greater merchant and cardholder awareness, some significant, cost effective, auto-dial telephone terminal equipment and improved security characteristics of the cards themselves, the problem is now being contained. The auto-dial terminals use the magnetic stripe information on the cards to establish the telephone link with the card companies' cardholder files for more automatic and faster authorisation of a larger number of purchases. The card companies, of course, not only have a commercial need to control fraud, but they must also recognise the moral and social obligation to check this abuse.

The economic recession has affected credit card companies as much as any other sector of commerce and industry. Yet bank cards have observed a very high level of cardholder responsibility for debts now proving difficult to repay because of personal circumstances. The lending policies of the card organisations are varied— the travel and entertainment cards technically have no upper limit to the amount of monthly credit, but they monitor keenly ability to repay each month's purchases. Bank cards deal mostly with established bank customers, and have good knowledge of credit and repayment abilities. The retail cards must be cautious in balancing increased turnover and profitable sales with irrecoverable, profitless debt.

The bank cards and retail cards, looking to interest earnings as a significant part of their income stream, are very aware of the inroads which bad debt can make into overall profit; many adopt sophisticated credit scoring systems to identify the poorer risks amongst card applications. They are also aware of the clear differences between cardholders who are faced with problems of unemployment or temporary difficulties, but who are essentially reliable repayers, and the almost professional bad debtors who are much closer to deliberate fraud. Controlling this problem is dependent upon early identification of delays in repayment, of early contact with the cardholder to establish the reasons for failure to keep the original repayment programme, and in re-establishing a modified, acceptable, and successful programme. Overall the card companies have a good reputation for sympathy, but they are determined to overcome any beliefs that they are too soft with some recoveries, and to eliminate the now less common prejudices about encouraging debt which were frequent when cases came before courts.

## THE FUTURE

The card companies' success in controlling operational costs, managing funds, and overcoming the problems of fraud and bad debt will give them a successful entry to opportunities of the future. The future is less an entry into new types of credit or into new types of purchasing needs. The characteristic revolving, renewable, credit facility with a variable repayment programme of the bank cards, and similar or budget systems of the retail cards clearly meet a need, are popular with cardholders and are profitable for card companies. The range of purchasing opportunities is wide, and expansion is mostly detailed infill rather than provision of purchasing in areas not associated with cards, which may be more the province of longer-term credit.

What the future is more likely to involve is the provision of electronic funds transfer with reasonable cost terminals at points of sale, allowing a continuing control over operational costs, and a wider range of auto-dispensing systems. Cash is already available in machines which are activated by plastic cards, and which allow direct drawings on credit card accounts; petrol can be purchased with plastic cards from pumps and debited direct to card accounts. More auto-dispensing, some in travel facilities, and later a very wide range of goods, is likely in the near future. Mail order purchasing and home banking with telephone and television screen links can easily be serviced by plastic cards. Perhaps rather than an increasing proliferation of plastic cards, each servicing a segment of financial needs, there may be a consolidation into more general purpose plastics. However, increased facilities will attract new competitors. The competitors may only provide credit facilities particularly suitable to their background, since one thing is clear, the costs of setting up a separate universal card are extremely high. Local cards are more suitable for the pure retail establishments. In any case, there are a number of severe restrictions imposed by the Consumer Credit Act, both on creation of cards and on detailed operations. Retail cards will continue to emerge, travel and entertainment cards will probably continue with the familiar market leaders; bank cards may be subject to greater change. The Visa system is particularly suitable for new banks to enter, although it is mostly appropriate for those with fairly large customer bases. The British clearing banks do not seem to have exhausted their own customer bases for their card issues; yet credit cards mostly came from the United States, and many developments first emerge there. It is possible that the banks may adopt the American dual card systems, and not be totally devoted to just one of the main systems—they may consider being members of both and offer their customers both.

# 27

# Finance Houses

Owen G. Mayo, Advisor, BESO

## HOW FINANCE HOUSES BEGAN

As the world recovered from the calamity of the First World War the 1920s saw a growing demand by the working people of this and other industrial nations for consumer goods which hitherto had only been available to the very rich, who mostly paid cash for the newfangled motor car or sewing machine.

The credit finance industry began with a few small hire purchase companies enabling purchase of motor cars and household goods (chiefly furniture) then radio, then domestic appliances such as vacuum cleaners.

However, growing up at the same time as consumer credit was a significant industry providing credit to increase the growing railroads in the UK. Manufacturers changed from using canals to move goods by the railways. Railway wagons would have required vast capital resources, so there emerged credit for wagons to carry goods and many of the wagon hiring companies are still in the credit granting business today, although wagon hiring is not nearly so important as in the early years of this century. Some of the 'wagon' companies became major finance companies and retain the word wagon in their title.

Private coalfield owners also preferred credit for wagons, as did the industrialists. It was a very happy and profitable business for both the mine owner/industrialist on the one hand and the finance/wagon company on the other.

It is interesting to note that buying of consumer goods on credit was certainly in existence at the turn of the century. Before the First World War, credit terms were available either direct from the manufacturer, as in the case of Singer Sewing Machines (one of the earliest manufacturers to introduce credit terms), or from the shop or large store. Such credit also existed in Europe and the USA, as this extract from *An Idler in France* by the Countess of Blessington, 1841, shows:

> To my surprise and pleasure I find that a usage exists at Paris which I have nowhere else met with, namely that of letting out rich and fine furniture by the quarter, half or whole year in any quantity required for even the largest establishment and on the shortest notice.
>
> I feared that we should be compelled to buy furniture or else put up with an inferior sort, little imagining that the most costly can be procured on hire and even a large residence made ready for the reception of a family in forty-eight hours. This is really like Aladdin's lamp and is a usage that merits being adopted in all capitals.
>
> We have made an arrangement that if we decide on remaining in Paris more than a year and wish to purchase the furniture, the sum agreed to be paid for the year's hire is to be allowed in the purchase money which is to be named when the inventory is made out.

As credit business was not on a very great scale, the problem of the shop or manufacturer waiting for his money over a period of time did not arise until the 1920s, when more and more of the general public demanded goods on credit.

It was this demand that gave birth to the 'finance company'. Shopkeepers and manufacturers needed funds immediately for the goods being sold and could not wait 24 months or so for the price to be paid so they looked for an extra source of money to pay them on behalf of their customers. Thus those with money, not necessarily bankers or discount houses, but often industrialists with money to spare, formed companies and agreed to lend their money by way of what has always been considered a 'device' for money lending and which we still call 'hire purchase'.

Hire purchase companies as they were then known, did not

always enjoy a good reputation in their methods of operation and were certainly fragmented and non-standard in organisation for many years.

## THE USE OF FINANCE HOUSES IN CREDIT

The need had arisen and the use and method became clear and simple. The car, sewing machine, furniture, etc. owned by the shop was sold not to the customer but to the 'hire purchase company', the name that finance houses had in the beginning. As such, their documents consisted of an offer to sell by the shop, garage etc. and an agreement whereby the customer hired (or rented) the goods, agreeing to pay a fixed number of rentals to the hire purchase company. In the agreement was an option whereby after completing the number of rentals the customer could for a nominal sum, perhaps 5p in the early days, buy the goods outright from the hire purchase company and become the owner.

This system put the shopkeeper or garage in the position of a cash sale transaction every time he sold goods, thus making cash available to him to replace stocks. Most of all, he was able to expand his business by the availability of funds and the equally important fact of having customers who were only possible because credit was available to them. This basic fact has not changed even though the hire purchase company has.

As mentioned earlier, the hire purchase companies did not always enjoy a good reputation and the first Act to protect credit customers came into force in 1938. Some of the less reputable companies were engaging, for example, in 'snatch-back' tactics, which were to retake possession of the goods on trivial default, often towards the end of the hiring period, sell the goods and make a profit out of the hirer's misfortune. As the hire purchase companies always had a hire purchase charge in their agreement they could thus make a fat profit and the government stepped in with the Act to protect against this insidious practice and many other areas of dubious activity.

After the Second World War the 1950s saw a big acceleration in demand for credit facilities. The hire purchase companies which arose out of a need to serve mostly ordinary working people now saw a growing demand from industrial companies who wished to buy similar items on a much larger scale—perhaps not one motor car but a fleet—not one sewing machine but 20 to equip a factory. Industry thus required better-organised, large-scale credit and there began the change from hire purchase companies to finance companies. New ways and means were found other than the basic hire purchase agreement for lending money to the bigger borrowers. Quite often the major banks were not prepared to make loans to certain customers, or for certain purposes, whereas the finance companies were willing to do so. Many of our leading industries today only became possible because of support and lending from finance companies who were prepared to take a wider view and possibly a greater risk in lending money than the traditional lenders.

Unlike the banks, who had plenty of cheap money in their vaults (i.e. current accounts on which they paid no interest), the finance companies had to borrow from institutions and discount houses and re lend at a rate sufficient to make a profit yet guard against the possible loss inherent in the greater risk they sometimes underwrote.

The name of 'finance company' came into general use as the finance facilities expanded far beyond the hire purchase transaction.

## WHEN CAN CREDIT BUSINESS PROFIT BY USING A FINANCE HOUSE?

Almost any business wishing to realise more quickly on its products or to expand its activity can consider the use of a finance company.

Before using a finance house it is essential that the company or shop or business thinks out very carefully indeed the pros and cons.

Let there be no illusions on this score. Borrowing money is always costly and many a business has failed by borrowing money and not counting the costs.

A shop owner, for example, should never work on an assumption that by buying more stock he will necessarily make more profit. Put more simply, if a shop owner is offered the chance of 100 washing machines at a special extra discount of 10% for cash and turns to his finance company for the cash, he needs to do his sums carefully as to the cost of borrowing this sum related to that extra discount.

Miscalculation may make his bargain buy from the manufacturer into a regrettable loss. However, provided the cost/benefit comparison is done, here is an excellent example of using a finance company wisely and profitably.

## WHAT OTHER SERVICES ARE AVAILABLE IN THE CREDIT FIELD?

In addition to lending for consumer products and to industry for capital goods, finance houses are actively involved in a number of related activities.

### Block discounting

Many stores and larger groups of shops made their own agreements with customers but sometimes found they were financing too much debt on credit. It became possible to discount the agreements held between themselves and customers, with the finance company advancing as much as 80% of the value of agreements. Thus the store would be in possession of liquid funds, paying back the finance companies monthly as it received its instalments from the customers.

### Credit sale

This is a simple form of the original hire purchase agreement with the main difference that ownership is passed immediately to the purchaser on signing the contract. The customer pays the finance company agreed instalments until the price of the goods, plus interest, has been met.

### Contract hire or renting

A simple form of hiring motor vehicles or mobile agricultural equipment and sometimes office equipment and furniture. The user cannot at any time purchase the goods and they are returned at the end of the hire period. There are distinct advantages in this form of credit, e.g. car renting is indeed a very useful facility for the larger user of vehicle fleets. He knows his costs, does not suffer depreciation and usually has none of the problems of maintenance.

## Leasing

Mainly a service for industry for expensive machinery but, as with renting or contract hire, the ownership remains with the leasing/ finance company.

The advantages, as with all credit, is in obtaining immediate use of the goods with payment over a long period. Often there is an option to continue to lease at a nominal payment after the expiry of the original lease period.

As all equipment depreciates, the use of leasing facilities needs careful study. It is best to discuss fully your needs and the working life of the equipment being bought with the leasing company. As experts in leasing they will not want to lease goods to you which could be better supplied by other forms of credit.

## Loans

As many finance companies now have a banking status, they are able to offer loans for a variety of purposes. Usually they will want security and will probably charge a higher interest rate than a major bank. Against this, there is the advantage that the finance house may lend where the major bank may not be willing to take the risk that the finance company through commercial experience has learned to evaluate.

## THE FINANCE HOUSES ASSOCIATION

In the UK it is difficult to estimate the number of companies providing finance for credit—perhaps 2000 or more, who simply have money as their stock in trade. Of these probably 50% provide money direct on credit to their customers.

Of the mass of finance companies there are 42 making up the

Finance Houses Association and it is these 42 who provide perhaps 90% of all money for credit. However, there is also a number of smaller finance companies who belong to the Consumer Credit Trade Association. The two organisations together provide an excellent base for the sound conduct of credit finance.

The Finance Houses Association was formed in 1945 and is incorporated as a company limited by guarantee, with its offices at 18 Upper Grosvenor Street, London W1X 9PB. The policy of the Association is determined by the management committee, which is composed of the senior executives elected from 16 member companies. One member of the management committee is elected chairman of the Association for a two-year period.

The object of the Association is to encourage, promote and protect the interests of its members in the exercise of their business. Thus the main work of the Association is in establishing contacts with government departments, the Bank of England and the EEC Commission in Brussels in order that the interests of finance companies should be taken into account whenever legislation, regulations or directives are prepared.

The Association operates through a series of sub-committees composed of specialist staff of member companies, such as accountants, lawyers or computer specialists. These sub-committees give detailed study to such matters as taxation or legislation, emanating either from the UK Parliament or from Brussels. For example, during the last few years a sub-committee has given detailed consideration to the consumer credit legislation, starting with the *Crowther Report on Consumer Credit,* followed by the Consumer Credit Bill and subsequently by the regulations issued under the Consumer Credit Act. As a result of the work of these sub-committees, it has in many instances been possible to effect changes in draft legislation or regulations which would otherwise unwittingly have caused many problems for finance houses.

The Association is a member of the European Federation of Finance Houses Associations, Eurofinas, which has its headquarters in Brussels. Eurofinas has 13 European members and two non-European correspondent members. Although the membership of Eurofinas is wider than the EEC membership, it is nevertheless a useful vehicle for negotiating with the EEC authorities, and provides a forum for the discussion of problems common to all finance houses.

Both the Finance Houses Association and the Consumer Credit Trade Association are always being called upon for advice to their members, but they also stand ready to receive from the general public any query concerning the conduct of any particular member in its day-to-day trading. Thus the public also know that they can rely on the best possible service in arranging their financing needs with a registered member of these associations.

The following is a list of members of the Finance Houses Association. A full list containing addresses is available on request to the Association's Offices.

Allied Irish Finance Co. Ltd
Associates Capital Corporation Ltd
AVCO Trust Ltd
Bank America Finance Ltd
Beneficial Trust Ltd
Boston Trust & Savings Ltd
British Credit Trust Ltd
Cattle's Holdings Finance Ltd
Chartered Trust plc
Charterhouse Japhet Finance Ltd
Citibank Trust Ltd
Commercial Credit Services Ltd
Copleys Ltd
First Co-operative Finance Ltd
First National Securities Ltd
Ford Motor Credit Co. Ltd
Forthright Finance Ltd
Forward Trust Group Ltd
HFC Trust Ltd
ICFC Leasing Ltd
Industrial Funding Trust Ltd
JCB Credit Ltd
KDB Finance Ltd
Lloyds and Scottish plc
Lombard North Central plc
London Scottish Finance Corporation plc
Lynn Regis Finance Ltd
Medens Ltd

Mercantile Credit Co. Ltd
M.H. Credit Corporation Ltd
Moorgate Mercantile Holdings plc
North British Finance Group Ltd
North West Securities Ltd
St. Margaret's Trust Ltd
Security Pacific Trust Ltd
Shawlands Securities Ltd
United Dominions Trust Ltd
Vernons Finance Corporation
The Wagon Finance Corporation plc
Welbeck Finance Ltd
Wrenwood Leasing Ltd
Yorkshire Bank Finance Ltd

# 28

# Leasing Finance

Peter Austin, former Leasing Manager, ICFC, and Jason Cross,
Director, ICFC Leasing Ltd

## THE LEASING OF INDUSTRIAL EQUIPMENT

For the purposes of this chapter it is assumed that credit managers
are concerned solely with items of capital equipment (i.e. plant)
which will attract capital allowances in an owner's hands. The
concern will be to ensure that a prospective purchaser can meet
standard conditions of sale by paying in a timely way; they may
need to advise on how payment terms may be agreed or modified for
a product or project having regard to a customer's needs and credit
rating. The point of time at which they join the dialogue between
'sales' and 'production' will presumably be determined by the
product. For items sold off the shelf their entry point will be
comparatively late in the day; for tailormade products they should
join the dialogue at a very early stage in the planning.

Leasing as a sales (and a payments) aid is a recognised and
established technique which manufacturers should have in mind
when marketing their wares. Equally, more and more users of
equipment are finding it a convenient addition to their financial
armoury. It is certainly a simple transaction but, none the less, it is
prudent to see that negotiations for the lease are set in hand
reasonably in advance of a payment date so that the three parties,
that is to say the supplier, the user and the leasing company (who
will become the owner), can each make their own essential arrangements. When the lease agreement is set up, and assuming that both

the supplier and the user have complied with the sales contract, then the credit manager's burden disappears—his contribution was to steer a worthwhile customer with a cash flow problem towards an acceptable financial solution.

## LEASING DEFINED

Leasing is not easily defined—in the context of this chapter it excludes contracts for rental, and hiring, but it does have a common denominator with these techniques in that they all separate use from ownership. This concept is basic to any consideration of leasing in the UK and distinguishes it from, say, a term loan or hire purchase where the user either has ownership of the equipment from the outset (a loan) or the option to acquire ownership at the end of the hire purchase agreement. Putting it another way, a loan contract, or its equivalent is a means of enabling a company to purchase an asset. A lease is a means of financing the use of the asset, and under a lease the title remains with the lessor but a lessee has the full use of that asset during the period of the lease. Furthermore, it is fundamental to leasing, as described here, that the lessee has the use of the equipment of his choice. Leasing can, therefore, be defined as:

> A contract between lessor and lessee for hire of a specific asset selected from the manufacturer or vendor of such an asset by the lessee. The lessor retains ownership of the asset. The lessee has possession and the use of the asset for an agreed period on payment of specified rentals.

Within this broad definition there are two sub-divisions—the finance lease (also known as a full pay-out lease) and an operating lease.

A finance lease is a contract involving payment over a certain period of specified sums which in total liquidate the lessor's capital outlay and provides him with profit. The agreed period will be dependant on two principal factors—the lessor's estimate of the useful life of the asset and the lessee's requirements.

An operating lease is a different animal in that the asset is not wholly amortised during the opening period of the lease and the lessor is relying on a renewal of the agreement at the end of the opening period, leasing the same equipment to a second lessee, or selling the equipment at or above an estimated residual value. Operating leases are found, for example, with computers, where it is normal practice for the agreement to include a maintenance contract which will be performed by the lessor or his agent. Because of the rather specialised nature of operating leases they are not further discussed in this chapter.

The basic definition of a lease is 'use without ownership'. The lessor as owner of the equipment has the benefit of the capital allowances. This (taxation) benefit is passed on to the lessee within the rental calculation. Any suggestion that the lessee might have a right to purchase the equipment would destroy a significant ingredient within the rental calculation. This mischief would arise because the Inland Revenue might take the view that the nature of the transaction had changed through an option—whether entered into at the outset, or late on in the agreement—and that it had become in effect an option to buy; that is to say, a hire purchase contract. Thus with leased equipment there are two tax points which are essential:

1  the lessor obtains the benefit of the capital allowances and passes them on within the rental calculations; and
2  the lessee can charge all the rentals against his taxable liability.

With a hire purchase transaction there is a significant difference— the finance house has no right to the allowances whatsoever. They flow to the user when the agreement is signed. Thus a change in the nature of a leasing transaction, when set up, can affect the taxable position of both lessor and lessee to neither's advantage.

## THE LEASING AGREEMENT

A finance leasing agreement will be broken down into two parts: the primary period and the secondary period. The primary period is, normally, calculated as up to 80% of the useful life of the equipment. The secondary period is often of indefinite length and can take the agreement through to the end of the actual useful life. The principal rental burden falls within the primary period, during which the lessor will seek to recover his capital outlay and his profit. When calculating his rental the lessor will not only take into account the capital allowances mentioned above, but will also have regard to the cost of money, and to the timing of the receipts of the rental, as well as to the period over which the agreement is to be performed. The secondary period is normally written at a nominal annual rental— say 1% of original cost.

Within the conditions of a leasing agreement the following normally apply:

1   The lessee enjoys the unfettered use of the equipment so long as he observes the terms of the agreement.
2   The lessee is responsible for the maintenance of the equipment in good working order and for its insurance.
3   Sub-letting is usually prohibited.
4   The lessee undertakes not to move the plant from a site without the lessor's permission.
5   The lessor will have the right of repossession if there is a significant breach of the agreement.
6   The lessee is required at the outset to confirm that he has chosen and accepted the equipment. The lessor will not, and cannot, give a warranty as to fitness, but will, as far as he is able, pass on the suppliers' warranties to the lessee. In many cases it is advisable for the lessee to obtain the suppliers' agreement that the lessee will receive the benefit of the suppliers' warranties.
7   The lessee is generally required to settle rental payments (which normally attract VAT) by way of a standing order on the lessee's bank or through a direct debit. In the majority of transactions rentals are fixed from the outset though for some large transactions adjustments may be made to reflect the changing cost of money during the lease period.

## WHAT ARE THE ADVANTAGES OF LEASING?

Essentially these can be broken down into two main headings: namely financial and operational.

### Financial

A lease rental reflects the benefits of capital allowance in the lessor's hands and thus provides a comparatively inexpensive vehicle for a lessee whose own taxable allowances are fully utilised through, for example, commitment to other capital expenditure. This is essentially a cash flow feature in which timing plays an important part. Lease rentals are charged wholly against taxable profit in the hands of the lessee.

A regional development grant is available if the lessee qualifies for a grant: the grant, however, is paid to the lessor as owner of the equipment and its value is normally reflected in lower rentals. Alternatively, some lease agreements require the lessor, when he receives the grant, to make a refund of rentals to the lessee so as to pass on the benefit of the grant to the lessee.

Leasing is a method of obtaining 100% finance for equipment whereas an hire purchase contract for similar plant may require a deposit equal to 10% of the cost or more.

### Operational

A lease rental provides for a fixed regular payment, and this fixed element in the contract makes for easy cost control and is readily available for pricing policies. It can also aid budgeting, forward planning, and cash flow control. It renders the delegation of divisional authority more easy within a capital budget.

### WHAT CAN BE LEASED?

The short answer to this is that any equipment which will qualify for capital allowances. Obvious examples spring to mind—machine tools, mechanical handling equipment, computers, process plants, heavy goods vehicles, ships, containers, aircraft, office equipment, textile machinery, printing machinery, etc. More unusual items include demountable partitions and films. The nature of the equipment will determine the length of the primary period; and the underlying residual value of the equipment will colour the lessor's approach to any particular proposition.

## WHO PROVIDES FINANCE LEASING?

There are about 60 members of the Equipment Leasing Association, and between them they are responsible for a substantial part of the leased equipment in the UK. As at a recent count, members of the Association had some £12 000 million worth of assets on their books at original cost, leased to companies up and down the country, and transacted nearly £3000 million of new business in 1983. A recent estimate is that the leasing industry financed over 25% of capital investment in equipment in the UK in 1983. The clearing banks' subsidiaries dominate this field, but there are a number of large independent and specialist (e.g. for ships, computers, etc.) operations as well. Anyone requiring more knowledge of the industry can readily obtain the names of the members of the Equipment Leasing Association from the Secretariat at 18 Upper Grosvenor Street, London W1X 9PB, telephone (01) 491 2783.

## MARKETING WITH LEASING

The selling technique in any organisation will be determined by its product. Some equipment by its very nature must be available for immediate delivery. It is with items such as this that 'sales aid leasing' can play a significant role. Under this system the manufacturer's sales force will have with it standard leasing documents (including rental charges). These can be completed on the spot—then sent to the leasing company for formal approval. The leasing company has the right to say 'No' on receipt of the formal application and it is therefore far better marketing if the manufacturer has assessed the credit risk himself thus avoiding complications. With sales aid leasing, close contact between the supplier and the leasing company is essential if the joint operation is to prosper. By and large, sales aid leasing lends itself to comparatively small items which are readily identifiable. This marketing technique accounts for a significant part of the leasing business transacted. Typewriters, office equipment, computers (large and small), commercial vehicles, agricultural equipment and many other items are 'sold' in this way.

Outside sales aid leasing is direct leasing, and this almost certainly still accounts for the greater part of all investment via leasing in value terms. Here the lessor and the lessee discuss the proposal together—often before an order is placed. Many purchasers will have established relationships with leasing companies which have matured over a number of years. Equipment suppliers, though, need to be alert to detect a good sales prospect who very properly may require outside support. In these circumstances the credit manager has a part to play simply by having some knowledge of and contact with leasing companies. This knowledge should be readily available to the sales force. The plain hard fact is that any selling organisation which can make an intelligent and timely suggestion on whom to contact for leasing is one step ahead of competitors with a less enlightened approach.

## APPRAISAL CRITERIA USED BY LESSORS

It will be of help if the credit manager is conscious of the yardsticks employed by those banks and companies operating in the leasing field. The degree of the appraisal by a leasing company will, to an extent, be determined by the cash value involved. Clearly a supply of a few typewriters will not command the same strict approach by a lessor as would an expensive piece of workshop equipment or process plant. In both cases however the aim of the appraisal will be to seek to confirm that the user of the equipment will be able to meet the rentals.

Amongst the main areas to be explored by the lessor during the course of this investigation will be the quality of the company's management; here he will be keen to see that those responsible for the running of the company are properly qualified, have themselves a good record in management, and that there is a reasonable degree of management succession within the organisation. He will look at the company's record as shown by the audited balance sheets and accounts, together with information on the manner in which a company has traded since its latest audited figures, which may well include a survey of an order-book position. Balance sheets and trading accounts are not just of historical interest, inflation has eroded some of the value to be gleaned from these documents, but in the final analysis they are a record of the quality of the management and of the product.

Other factors to be gleaned from the figures, of which the lessor will take heed, include the debt ratio. By this is meant that a company is not overstretched through having too much borrowing on too small a capital base. Frequently heavy borrowing produces an unacceptable burden (in terms of interest and in capital redemption) on the cash flow of a business. An over-structured edifice of any description finds it difficult to withstand stormy conditions.

Alongside this, the appraiser should satisfy himself that a prospective lessee has sufficient working capital to support extra sales generated by the new investment.

Another factor the lessor will have in mind will be the nature of the industry in which the customer is engaged. Industries with a cyclical record will have one rating, industries where future prospects can clearly be seen to be excellent will have another.

Also to be taken into account will be the anticipated residual value of the equipment to be leased. With certain equipment the lessor will be concerned to see that the manufacturer himself has sufficient standing to continue maintenance contracts where these are essential to the well-being of the equipment.

Investment appraisal in its widest sense is a very subjective operation. The appraiser will knit together all the various threads of information that he needs, and from this will build up a composite picture which will allow him to determine, first, whether or not he is prepared to undertake business. Assuming he is, then this composite picture will enable him to determine for what length of primary period the lease can be written and the rental required to equate to the risk involved. He will have taken account of the cash flow situation. Thus, where a start-up business is involved and its cash flow is perhaps limited in the early days then the lease payments can be phased to run in parallel with a projected cash flow. In other words, the prospective lessor having taken a positive view of the proposal, may prove flexible to the needs of the proposed lessee.

However, essentially leasing is a comparatively simple operation where payments are made on a regular basis and where the lessor confidently expects the primary period to continue without let or hindrance. Except in the case of larger transactions any major departure from this simple situation may indicate that leasing is not the ideal vehicle for the proposal. Indeed the company might be better advised to seek its finance on a long/medium-term basis and there may perchance be within the proposal a risk capital situation where the manufacturer's customer would be better advised to seek some form of additional equity. It is also true to say that an intelligent appraiser of a capital investment programme may produce a hybrid mixture—that is to say, a balanced financing structure, perhaps including leasing, which will allow the company the better to realise the greater value from its venture. This approach applies mainly to comparatively substantial schemes.

## SUMMARY

The virtues of leasing include the fact that it is speedily negotiated, and the transaction generally conducted on a firm basis at a fixed price. From the supplier's point of view it allows for a sale which might not otherwise have taken place at the time. It gives the user immediate benefit from the installation of new equipment and thus allows him to generate improved profitability and to extend his business; this extension could lead to repeat orders for further equipment to accommodate even more expansion.

# Appendix: Sources of Credit Data

Herbert Edwards, Managing Director, Jardine Financial Risk
Management Ltd

This appendix provides details of some information sources in the following areas:

1   Company information sources.
2   Credit reference bureaux.
3   Textbooks, journals and articles.
4   Training courses.
5   Credit organisations.

## COMPANY INFORMATION SOURCES

Information required by credit staff on customers and potential outlets is often akin to that used by marketing and research departments and may already be held somewhere in the company.

Many organisations provide data reports on companies, either free, for a fee, or as part of a membership service.

The details given here can by no means include every source, and as the information 'market' is a fluctuating one, some of those quoted may be already out-of-date. We do stress that readers should check for current status where appropriate.

## Company data

### General

*Registrar of Companies.*
Companies House, 55–71 City Road, London EC1. Tel: (01)
253 9393. Main office at: Company Registration Office, Crown
Way, Maindy, Cardiff CF4 3UZ. Tel: 0222 388588.
Gives the following data on all England and Wales registered
limited liability companies:
(a)  Formation details, articles of association.
(b)  Mortgages.
(c)  Annual return (directors, shareholders, capital).
(d)  Accounts (sales, exports, employees, P & L balance sheet).
  Files are searchable at £1 per file per search. Three-day
photocopying sevice available at 10p per page. Fundamental
source on all UK companies (excluding divisions of a major
company). Smaller companies reluctant to publish financial
data may avoid filing returns up to two years.
  Scottish companies are filed in Edinburgh, Northern Ireland
companies in Belfast and Eire companies in Dublin.
*Dun & Bradstreet Ltd.*
26–32 Clifton Street, London EC2P 2LY.
Tel: (01) 377 4377.
  Gives credit-rating reports on any UK and most overseas
companies. Special in-depth reports also undertaken.
  Prospect Identification Service, based on computerised
credit-rating data on 200 000 enterprises, can select firms by
size, area, etc., as required.
  Three useful directories summarise data on most British
companies:
1  *Key British Enterprises* covers 20 000 companies.
2  *Who Owns Whom* gives details of the ownership of major
   UK and overseas companies.
3  *Stubbs Directory* is classified by trade to give instant market
   identification.
*Directories*
There are many useful directories on companies, most being
somewhat specialised and beyond the scope of this chapter.

*Current British Directories,* published by CBD Research, 154 High Street, Beckenham, Kent, is a good 'directory of directories'. In addition to the Dun & Bradstreet directories mentioned, there is also the Kompass service available from most libraries (City Business Library have a complete set on all countries).

## Public companies

*Annual reports and accounts.*
Copies obtained for any public company by ringing up (or writing to) the company secretary. He will be reluctant to refuse you. He cannot know you are not a potential investor.
*Exchange Telegraph Cards* ('Extel'). These are summaries of accounts and business on most public companies, updated as often as necessary. Extel also have European and Australian services, and a UK service for private companies.
*Stockbrokers' reviews.* These are excellent background material; the difficulty is to get hold of them, as they are done for private circulation to clients. Reviews may cover one company, or an industry; all are from an investment point-of-view.

## Private companies

*Financial information.* Can be obtained from Companies House or from Extel's Private Company Service.
*'Extract Service'.* Provides financial data on private companies.
*Inter Company Comparisons Ltd. (ICC).* At 81 City Road, London EC1. Tel: (01) 253 0063. Publish surveys by comparing companies in the field.

## Overseas companies

*Embassies.* Most have commercial sections with directories and generally help with translations. Usually a photocopying service is available.
*Chambers of Commerce.* (E.g. American Chamber of Commerce.) Organisations to help businessmen, so use them for problems.
*Banks.* All banks are helpful with economic intelligence sections. Look especially for London offices of banks from the

country you are interested in. Most big banks issue periodic reviews on countries.

*Department of Trade and Industry.* Statistics and Market Intelligence Library at Hillgate House, 26 Old Bailey, EC4. Tel: (01) 248 5757, contains a mass of foreign directories. The Export Intelligence section can be useful, but is product-orientated.

## General business data

### Libraries

Libraries contain a wealth of information, and often have commercial sections. If a book is not immediately available it may be obtained via the National Lending Library Scheme.

*Westminster Public Reference Library.* One of the best London libraries, with a full set of all HMSO publications, e.g. *Hansard.*

*City Business Library.* At Basinghall Street, London EC2, Tel: (01) 638 8215. Contains a full set of *Economist* Intelligence Unit Publications (normally available only by subscription).

A separate management section contains numerous directories and reference books. Most newspapers and magazines are kept, including foreign ones. Has complete Extract Company Files.

*Department of Trade and Industry Library.* Hillgate House, Old Bailey, London EC4. Contains a mass of UK and foreign statistics, directories, buyers guides, and telephone directories. Tel: (01) 248 5757. Excellent for import and export data.

*United Nations Library.* At 14 Stratford Place, London W1. Contains a useful collection of UN and allied statistics and publications.

*Other libraries.* Can be found in embassies, chambers of commerce, and various institutes, e.g. BIM, Gas Council, Institute of Petroleum, IEE, BSI, etc.

### Government bodies

*Department of Trade and Industry.* 'Export Intelligence' can be helpful, and the Hillgate House Library has a mass of data.

*NEDO.* 'Little Neddies' for most industries, with various

publications on statistics and problems in their industries. NEDO, Millbank Tower, London SW1, Tel: (01) 211 3000. 'Neddy' summarises all publications quarterly.

*The Monopolies Commission.* Publishes detailed reports on monopoly situations. These are excellent sources of information; obtained from HMSO.

*Customs and Excise.* At 27 Victoria Avenue, Southend-on-Sea, Tel: Southend 49421. Their monthly 'Overseas Trading Accounts' are a useful summary of export/import figures.

*Hansard.* The official daily minutes of Parliament containing statistics not available elsewhere.

*HMSO.* As the official Government publisher it is a prolific source of data. Annual reports of all state-controlled organisations, all official statistics, white papers, handbooks, special reports, *Hansard,* etc. Is also official UK agent for UN and OECD publications.

## Statistics

*Central Statistical Office.* At Great George Street, London SW1, Tel: (01) 233 3000. Is the best centre for finding out about available official statistics. *Statistical News* is published quarterly. The CSO produces a concise guide list of 'Principal Statistical Series and Publications'—what statistics are available and where to find them—HMSO.

*Business Statistics Office (DTI).* At Lime Grove, Ruislip, Middlesex, Tel: (01) 866 8771. Publishes the *Census of Production and Census of Distribution* at five-yearly intervals. Although rather out-of-date when published, they are excellent baseline material.

*British Business* magazine. Carries regular statistical series, and news of statistical developments.

*DTI Statistics Library.* Hillgate House contains most statistical series.

*Trade associations.* Invariably collect statistics from and for their members. Quite often these are available to non-members (a diplomatic approach to the secretary is wise). There are trade associations for most trades—thoughtful browsing in a phone book can often turn up obscure ones.

## Other UK sources

*Newspapers and journals.* All have some form of research department, and are generally helpful in tracking down articles on particular subjects. *The Times, Financial Times* and *Economist,* are perhaps, the most useful.

*Economist Intelligence Unit (EIU).* At 27 St. James Place, London SW1, Tel: (01) 493 6711. Is an international market research organisation with a number of regular reports on markets, normally only available on subscription. A full set is at the City Business Library. Although associated with the *Economist* it operates quite independently.

*Market research organisations.* Sell surveys at varying prices.

*The Consumers' Association.* At 14 Buckingham Street, London WC2, Tel: (01) 839 1222, acts for consumers, testing many products and services. Publisher of *Which.*

*The National Institute of Economics and Social Research.* Publishes quarterly reviews.

## International

*General.* Embassies, chambers of commerce, banks, the Department of Trade and Industry are the most useful. British banks do regular general reviews on the economy of many countries. Embassies and chambers of commerce often have useful libraries.

*The United Nations and its various sub-organisations (e.g. UNESCO).* The UN library at the London Information Office, 14 Stratford Place, London W1 (off Oxford Street), Tel: (01) 629 6411, is the best starting point. Publications via HMSO.

*OECD.* The Organisation for Economic Co-operation and Development—produces many useful studies on countries, markets and industries, 2 Rue André-Pascal, 75 Paris 16e. Publications through HMSO.

*The International Monetary Fund (IMF).* Produces regular financial/economic statistics on countries; available through HMSO. Extremely useful is the monthly Summary of External Debt, indicating transfer delays of hard currency from many countries.

## CREDIT REFERENCE BUREAUX

There are dozens of companies providing credit reports and only a selection can be listed here:

ATP International, Sutherland House, 70/78 Edgware Road, London NW9 7BT. Tel: (01) 202 8212.

British Mercantile Agency Ltd, Sidcup House, 12/18 Station Road, Sidcup, Kent. Tel: (01) 300 6815.

Commercial Credit Consultants, Unicredit House, 2 Cotton Street, Liverpool L3 7DY. Tel: (051) 207 5777.

Dun & Bradstreet Ltd, 26–32 Clifton Street, London EC2P 2LY. Tel: (01) 377 4377.

F.R.S. Reporting Services, 168 Whitchurch Road, Cardiff CF4 3NA. Tel: 0222 619905.

Infocheck, 16–18 New Bridge Street, London EC4V 6AU. Tel: (01) 353 7722.

Inter-Credit International Ltd, Inter-Credit House, 205/207 Crescent Road, New Barnet, Herts. Tel: (01) 440 8532.

Irish Trade Protection Association Ltd, Park House, North Circular Road, Dublin 7. Tel: 0001 309522.

Manchester Guardian Society for Protection of Trade, 47/51 Mosley Street, Manchester M60 8AA. Tel: (061) 236 2635.

United Association for Protection of Trade (UAPT), Zodiac House, 163 London Road, Croydon CR9 2RP. Tel: (01) 686 5644.

In addition, there are many trade protection companies serving industries and regional areas.

## TEXTBOOKS, JOURNALS AND ARTICLES

*Accounts Receivable—Is Now the Time to Tighten up,* Research Institute of America, New York, 1969.

*Awareness and Flexibility.* D. E. Miller, NACM, New York, 1974.
*B.I.M.—Guidelines for the Smaller Business No. 5 Credit Control and Debt Collection,* BIM, London.
*Bad Debt Reserve Ratios,* Credit Research Foundation, New York.
*Bankers References,* A. W. Wright, Macdonald and Evans.
*Bank of England Quarterly Bulletin,* Bank of England.
*Better Way to Monitor Accounts Receivable,* W. G. Lewellen and R. W. Johnson, Harvard Business Review, June 1972.
*Cash Flow Projections,* CRF Inc., New York.
*The Changing Nature of Export Credit Finance and its Implications for Developing Countries.* World Bank Working Paper 409.
*Consumer Credit Act—Students Guide,* R. M. Goode, Butterworth.
*Consumer Credit Control,* O. Mayo (ed) Gower, 1971.
*Control of Working Capital,* M. Grass (ed) Gower, 1972.
*Credit and Collection Letters,* NACM, New York.
*Credit Control and Administration,* CRF Inc., New York.
*Credit Control and Debt Collection,* BIM, London, 1974.
*Credit Department Operations—A Guide to Profits,* CRF Inc., New York.
*Credit Department Reports to Top Management,* CRF Inc., New York.
*The Credit Executive—Creator of Profit,* NACM, New York.
*Credit and Financial Analysis,* Dun & Bradstreet, London.
*Credit and Financial Management,* NACM, New York, monthly.
*Credit Management,* official journal of ICM, Easton, Lincs.
*Credit Management,* R. M. V. Bass, Business Books.
*Credit Management Handbook,* CRF Inc., Irwin, USA.
*Creditnews,* Dun & Bradstreet, London, monthly.
*Digest of Commercial Laws of the World,* NACM Service Corp., New York.
*Economist,* London. Weekly business magazine.
*E.D.P. Systems for Credit Management,* Conan D. Whiteside, John Wiley and Sons, 1971.
*Electronic Funds Transfer System for Business Payments,* CRF Inc., New York, 1973.
*Export,* monthly journal of the Institute of Export, London.
*Export Credit,* H. Edwards, Gower, 1980.
*Export Credit Financing Systems in OECD Countries,* OECD, Paris.
*The Export Trade,* Clive Schmitthoff, Stevens.
*Finance of International Trade,* A. Watson, Institute of Bankers.

*The Finance of Overseas Trade,* W. W. Syrett, Pitman.

*Financial Times,* London. The world's best business newspaper.

*Handling Deductions and Disputes in Accounts Receivable,* CRF Inc., New York.

*How to Read a Balance Sheet,* ILO Geneva.

*How to Supervise Credit Accounts,* L. Bernstein, Gower, 1972.

*Improving Credit Practice,* D. E. Miller and D. E. Relkin, AMA, New York, 1971.

*Incoterms,* ICC, Paris.

*Instalment Credit,* A. L. Diamond (ed), Steven and Sons.

*International Trade Credit Management,* G. V. Benz, Gower, 1975.

*Law and Practice of Credit Factoring,* P. M. Briscoe, Butterworth, 1975.

*The Law Relating to Bankruptcy, Liquidation and Receivership,* J. A. Thompson, Macdonald and Evans.

*Leasing in Perspective,* E. R. Gillett from 'Accountancy', pp 24–28, April 1972.

*Management of Trade Credit,* T. G. Hutson and J. Butterworth, Gower 1983.

*Managing Money and Finance,* G. P. E. Clarkson and B. J. Elliott, third edition by Alan Johnson, Gower, 1983.

*Managing Trade Receivables No. 540,* BIM, 1972.

*Microfilm Systems for Credit Departments,* CRF Inc., New York.

*Money for Exports,* Bank of England.

*Order Entry and Billing Systems,* CRF Inc., New York.

*Psychology in Letters,* H. N. Sommers, NACM, New York.

*Retail Credit Fundamentals,* Phelps, HPTA.

*Sales and Credit—Teamwork for Profit,* NACM, New York.

*Service Charges, Help or Hindrance?,* Credit and Financial Management, New York, 1970.

*Services for Exporters,* Midland Bank International, London.

*Short Guide to the Consumer Credit Act,* C. McNeil Greig, CCTA, London.

*Sources and Management of Export Finance,* W. W. Syrett and R. F. Pither, Gower, 1971.

*Standard Forms for the Opening of Documentary Credits,* ICC, Paris.

*Survey of Training Programmes for Credit Department Personnel,* CRF Inc., New York.

*Systematic Export Documentation,* SITPRO, London.

*Trade Finance Report,* monthly from Euromoney Publications.

*Trends in Cash Application and Control of Accounts Receivable,* CRF Inc., New York.

*Uniform Custom and Practice for Documentary Credits,* ICC, Paris.

*Uniform Rules for Collection of Commercial Paper,* ICC, Paris.

## TRAINING COURSES

### Dun & Bradstreet

'Financial and Credit Analysis' is a correspondence course of 16 chapters with 14 question papers, marked constructively at weekly intervals for about 5–6 months. The subject matter is quite detailed and involves a few hours private study each week. Details from: Dun & Bradstreet, London. Tel: (01) 377 4377.

### Institute of Credit Management

Operate one and two day credit seminars in London and regional centres for all grades of credit staff plus workshops for experienced creditmen. A series of evening lectures is held each winter in London for students and interested members. The examination course leads to professional qualification (MICM). Details from: Secretary, Easton House, Easton on the Hill, Stamford, Lincs. Tel: 0780 56777.

### Rapid Results College

Provides correspondence course tuition for all ICM examinations. Details from: Tuition House, London SW19 4DS. Tel: (01) 947 2211.

### Graduate School of Credit and Financial Management

Nearly 40 years old, the school provides qualified credit and financial executives with a programme to develop corporate responsibility. The curriculum divides into (a) finance, (b) money and credit, (c) policy and procedures and (d) human resources. The course consists of three annual resident summer sessions of two weeks each at a choice of Dartmouth College, Stanford University, Williams College (all USA) and the London Graduate School of Business Studies. Details from: 3000 Marcus Avenue, Lake Success, NY 11040, USA.

Several other organisations arrange credit training courses in addition to the above list.


## CREDIT ORGANISATIONS

The official body promoting the interests of credit staff in the UK is the Institute of Credit Management, which has regional branches and also encourages and aids several industry credit groups. There is an Irish Credit Managers Association, in Dublin, relatively in its infancy but growing fast. Mention must also be made of the vast, long-established, USA organisation, the National Association of Credit Management (NACM) which has influence in the UK and Europe, both directly and also through its European arm Finance, Credit and International Business known usually as FCIB due to the support of European subsidiaries of North American corporations. In addition to the above national bodies, there are several regional and industry credit groups which exchange information on common customers for mutual benefit but strictly without any degree of collaboration to restrict the interests of customers.

### Institute of Credit Management

'A corporation limited by guarantee and devoted to the interests of the credit controller' is the description of the UK's professional institute in its magazine *Credit Management.*

Founded in 1939 as the Institute of Creditmen, it changed to the present style in 1947 and is now nationally recognised as the representative voice of the professional credit executive in addition to being consulted by governments and official bodies on national credit matters.

Entrance to the Institute is normally by examination, held in various UK cities and overseas in May and November each year but experienced credit managers may be admitted directly if the Council are satisfied as to credit knowledge and seniority. There are four classes of membership: Student, Affiliate, Associate (MICM) and Fellowship (FICM).

The Institute is controlled by a Council which has active subcommittees dealing with its detailed work. Branches have been set up in 13 areas of the country where local members can meet to exchange views and news and listen to experienced speakers.

Regular courses of evening lectures are provided for students and members who wish to further their knowledge. The Institute also organises one and two day credit seminars around the country with credit workshops at intervals for the more experienced practitioners.

The Institute maintains an appointment bureau to provide a job-finding service to members and to encourage companies to employ qualified credit staff.

Highlights of the year are the national conference in London which has top credit executives, bankers, politicians and national figures as speakers and the glittering ceremonial occasion of the annual banquet at the Guildhall.

Further details: Easton House, Easton on the Hill, Stamford, Lincs. Tel: 0780 56777.

## Finance, Credit and International Business (FCIB)/National Association of Credit Management (NACM)

The FCIB, an international association of executives in finance, credit and international business, has an international membership in over 20 countries and is the international arm of the NACM in the United States with a membership exceeding 45 000 companies. The NACM was formed in 1896 in Toledo/Ohio, and the FCIB in 1919 in New York City as non-profit making professional organisations.

The FCIB has a European chapter, and a representative in Brussels, Belgium. Three times a year, the FCIB conducts International Round Table Conferences in Europe on credit, collection, documentation, finance, and exchange problems in major European financial centres. This enables members to exchange credit experience on customers, countries, government actions or laws, and to 'facilitate the free flow of goods from one country to another' (quoted from FCIB booklet).

Over 45 000 members worldwide can benefit from international round table conferences in the US, Canada, Europe and Asia, bulletins (published bi-monthly), reciprocal credit reports, industry credit groups, an association newsletter, a worldwide collection service, credit consultancy, international workshops in the US and Europe, country credit reports, special credit reports, and educational and research programmes (through Credit Research Foundation and the National Institute of Credit) and various publications, led by the monthly magazine *Credit and Financial Management.*

Further details: 475 Park Avenue South, New York, NY 10016, USA. Tel: (212) 578 4417 20, Telex: 649191.

# Index

# Index